D1109720

Francine du Plessix Gray

ADAM
&
EVE
and the
CITY

Selected Nonfiction

SIMON AND SCHUSTER
NEW YORK · LONDON · TORONTO · SYDNEY · TOKYO

Published by Simon and Schuster
A Division of Simon & Schuster, Inc.
Simon & Schuster Building
Rockefeller Center
1230 Avenue of the Americas
New York, New York 10020
SIMON AND SCHUSTER is a registered trademark
of Simon & Schuster, Inc.
Designed by Edith Fowler
Manufactured in the United States of America

10 9 8 7 6 5 4 3 2 1

Library of Congress Cataloging in Publication Data

Gray, Francine du Plessix.
   Adam & Eve and the city.

   I. Title.   II. Title: Adam & Eve and the city.
PS3557.R294A6   1987   814'.54   87-9677
ISBN 0-671-64497-1

*To Robert Silvers
with devotion*

Contents

TO A WOOD THRUSH

Singing across the orchard
before night, answered
from the depths
of the wood, inversely
and in a lower key—

First I tried to write
conventionally praising you
but found it no more
than my own thoughts
that I was giving. No

What can I say?
          Vistas
of delight waking suddenly
before a cheated world.

from "Adam and Eve and the City"
          William Carlos Williams

POLITICS AND SALVATION

The Ultra-Resistance

ONE of the many myths which distort our views of literature is the notion that the writing of factual prose is a process more calculated and objective, less intimately personal than the writing of fiction. In fact, the practice of journalism or the essay form can be inspired by sources quite as Orphic, subconscious, intense as those that fuel the writing of novels or short stories; the choice of a subject to report on feeds just as much on our childhood hang-ups and their resulting fixations, on our most secret lusts, our most unadmitted faults and griefs. Few literary projects I've undertaken have been kindled by sources more subjective and emotional than the articles which I began to write in the 1960s on various aspects of the resistance to the Vietnam War, and particularly on those citizens who were risking years of prison to express their conscience concerning it.

On an October day in 1967, I opened my copy of *The New York Times* and saw, on the front page, the photograph of a powerfully built man in clerical clothing standing in the offices of a Baltimore draft board, pouring blood on draft files in protest against the war. His name was Father Philip Berrigan. I was overwhelmed by that image. Beyond its courage, Philip Berrigan's action immediately struck me as very Biblical, as both archaic and totally relevant. The vision of this man risking years of his freedom to protest an illegal war also conjured much guilt. Although I'd been steeped in the antiwar movement since the mid-1960s, and would engage in the one-night jail stays then fashionable among my bolder peers, I'd sensed the feebleness and inefficacy of our gestures. The highly charged emotions evoked by the sight of Philip Berrigan's action may have been heightened by the events of my childhood during World War II: by my father's death in the French Resistance, by my guilt, perhaps, at having survived him, by my lifelong admiration for gestures of radical dissent against any government's injustice.

Beyond these personal factors, I was impelled to write about Philip Berrigan and his accomplices by the following historical irony: For the first time in American history, a sector of the Catholic community was suddenly becoming a challenge and a menace to the secular establishment; the radical wing of the antiwar Movement—the most extensive crusade of protest to have affected the United States since the issue of slavery—was beginning to be led by Catholic priests, most of them of Irish-American stock. As a Catholic and an immigrant striving to become "American" in the late 1940s, I had always been fascinated by the extent of American Catholics' conservatism. They had entered a predominantly Protestant culture whose origins were tinged with Calvinist intransigence. And for the past centuries they'd tried to be superpatriots, their classical prototype the law enforcement officer, their ethos most succinctly symbolized by Francis Cardinal Spellman's motto "My country right or wrong."

Yet in 1967 it was becoming clear that a band of Catholics were protesting our government's conduct in Vietnam more militantly than any other group in the country; that the moral absolutism of the Catholic tradition could satanize the Vietnam War as fervently as it had satanized Communism in the 1950s. Like political intrigues of seventeenth-century Europe, many of the draft board raids staged by these dissenters were being plotted in abbeys, monasteries, the convent next door. With the help, perhaps, of John Kennedy's presidency, Catholics were beginning to lose their immigrant jitters, were finally becoming a potentially radical, dissenting force in American society. Yet this community of protest within the Church was still a very small minority, made all the more fanatic by the memory of its previous docility. The very theatrical gestures of Father Philip Berrigan and his Catholic colleagues were aimed not only at the government's war-making structure but at that most reactionary structure of all, their own Church.

Civil disobedience is grounded on the notion that the breaking of small laws—defying bus segregation laws, antistrike laws, laws forbidding us to shelter runaway slaves or destroy draft files—can point to the existence of higher laws such as the brotherhood of man or the atrocity of war. It often entails attacks on property symbolic of the unjust rulers: Jesus Christ overturning the tables of the money changers in the Temple; William Lloyd Garrison burning a copy of the American Constitution in protest against the inhumanity of slavery; Martin Luther burning a copy of canon Law; Jeremiah smashing clay pots in the hall of the Temple (in protest, by the way, against his king's war policy). Whether practiced by Christ, Tolstoy, Gandhi, or Martin Luther King, Jr., non-violent civil disobedience has been based on hope and faith: on the often arrogant faith that allegiance to our moral conscience must always precede our allegiance to the state; on the hope that the system is reformable by attacks on minute items of material property without the need for physical violence toward people. Challenging minority terrorism, Richard Nixon's cynical escalation of the war and national passivity, Philip Berrigan and his fellow protesters would continue to create bold, brutal metaphors for the distorted moral priorities of our society: We were giving medals to men who dropped napalm on civilians in Southeast Asia; we were meting out four, five, six years of prison to men who poured blood on pieces of government-owned paper in the United States.

So I went on to attend many of these felons' trials. I listened hard and sang "Amazing Grace" with them and generally educated myself about the necessities of conscience and sacrifice in a tragic time. My first essay on this theme—"The Ultra-Resistance"—is concerned with a group of resisters called the Milwaukee Fourteen, and begins with a brief history of some earlier acts of civil disobedience, all too readily forgotten, that had protested our history's most unjust war.

O N a warm spring day in 1966, a nineteen-year-old Minnesotan by the name of Barry Bondhus broke into his local draft board and dumped two large bucketfuls of human feces into a filing cabinet, mutilating several hundred 1-A draft records in protest against the Vietnam War. The offender and his eleven brothers, sons of a mechanic who had threatened to shoot anyone who attempted to induct his boys into the American army, had fastidiously collected their organic wastes for two weeks in preparation for the raid.

This primordial deed became known in the annals of the anti-war protest as the Big Lake One action, in honor of Barry Bondhus's hometown, Big Lake, Minnesota. Barry Bondhus, who had

calmly awaited arrest after his performance, served an eighteen-
month sentence at Sandstone Correctional Institution and came
home in March of 1968 to run his father's machine shop. Big Lake
One was hardly mentioned in the press, but Bondhus's was "the
movement that started the Movement."

Since Bondhus, many hundreds of Americans have awaited
arrest after destroying government draft records with the less rustic
media of blood, paint, and fire. A partial list of the protest actions
that followed the Big Lake One:

The Baltimore Four (600 draft records defiled with blood by
Father Philip Berrigan and three accomplices, October 1967).

The Catonsville Nine (Father Philip Berrigan strikes again in
the company of his brother Father Daniel Berrigan and seven other
Catholic priests and laymen, destroying draft files with homemade
napalm, May 1968).

The Boston Two (several hundred draft records mutilated
with black paint, June 1968).

The Milwaukee Fourteen (some 10,000 draft records napalmed,
September 1968).

The Pasadena Three (some 500 records burned, May 20, 1969).
The following day, the Silver Springs Three (several hundred records of a Maryland draft board mutilated with black paint and
blood). And four days later, the Chicago Fifteen (some 40,000
draft records burned).

Women Against Daddy Warbucks (several thousand records
mutilated in a Manhattan draft board by the first all-women band
of draft board raiders, July 1969).

The New York Eight (some 75,000 records mutilated in a
Bronx draft board on August 1, and several thousand more in a
Queens draft board on August 15, by a group of four women and
four men, three of them Catholic priests).

There was no particular name for this radical core of the Peace
Movement. The only noun given to its forays was the word "action"; the participants were called "actors"; the only verb assigned
to their gestures was "act." "When is so-and-so going to act?" Men
and women who believed they had exhausted every other means of
protesting the Vietnam War raided a draft board, hauled out rec-

ords and burned them, stood around singing liberation songs while awaiting arrest. The draft board actions had elements of both terrorist strike and liturgical drama. They aimed to destruct and to instruct; to impede in some small way the war machine; to communicate its evil, at a time when verbal and political methods had failed, by a morality play which would startle, embarrass the community; to shame the Movement to heightened militancy, perhaps to imitation. The word "witness" was used by members of this Ultra-Resistance, with its historical implications of sacrifice and penance, of moral primitivism, romantic egoism, psychological violence.

The draft board actions in which the raiders demanded arrest were called "stand around" to differentiate them from acts of "hit-and-run" sabotage; they were grounded in the hope that a man's witness in jail can move the conscience of a nation; that it can abate the violence of its rulers, and, like a monk's years of passive prayer, aid to purify society. According to this mystique, the presence of the man awaiting arrest, sacrificing his freedom to witness to his moral indignation, is the ingredient that transforms sabotage into a religious and constructive act. As in most tragedy and liturgy, sacrifice is seen as the most powerful means of communication.

The monastic stand-arounders, Barry Bondhus included, usually came from highly authoritarian and conservative backgrounds, which perhaps explains some of their differences from the permissively reared young people in the Movement at large. Many of them had had a more immediate exposure to the poor than the average college rebel, and felt drawn to the evangelic principle of sharing, in jail, the powerlessness of the dispossessed. There was another important difference between the guerrillas of the campuses and the jail-bound draft board raiders: the latter were distrustful of imported jargon. Their ideological heroes were likely to be Thoreau and A. J. Muste rather than Mao or Che; they wanted to do something "typically American." And although they rebelled as fiercely as the rest of the Movement against the familiar demons of capitalism, racism, colonialism, and militarism, they had chosen to channel their protests against that uniquely American form of oppression, the Selective Service System.

The draft board raids thus created a curious form of nonviolent guerrilla activity. For beyond their symbolic, theatrical aspects these forays did produce some tangible results. The files took some months to recompose, the boards remained closed for a few weeks or months, inductions temporarily ceased. The protesters felt that they had liberated an area for a short while, that their acts would incite others to further and larger acts of liberation. A member of the Milwaukee Fourteen, at their trial, described his inner feelings as he carried sackloads of draft files toward a bonfire ignited by his accomplices outside of the Milwaukee Draft Board.

> I really felt within myself that I was performing a small and simple act of liberation that day, taking pieces of paper that would free a great majority of my neighbors and brothers, people I love. So I took a bag or two, dragged them down the stairs and across the street into the center of the green, and I stood and waited for arrest, I stood with my brothers quite joyfully, sang and listened to the Gospel, joining with my brothers in singing and rejoicing.

Another important function of the draft board raids was to turn American courtrooms into political forums on the illegality and the immorality of the Vietnam War. And the Milwaukee Fourteen, which comprised twelve Catholics, five of them priests, brought an important innovation to the Peace Movement: Twelve of the accused, a few days before they came to court, grandly dismissed a prestigious team of civil liberties lawyers headed by William Kunstler, and claimed their constitutional rights to defend themselves. The decision made by the Milwaukee Twelve, as they were henceforth called, was an intended blow at the state of Wisconsin, which had posted the preposterous bail of $400,000 each, and through considerable political maneuvering had managed to schedule its trial before the federal trial.

It was certainly the first time in legal history that gum-chewing seminarians cross-examined each other while walking barefoot to the water fountain. There was a bizarre contact between the genteel provincial decorum of the Milwaukee County District Court and the impertinent informality of these self-styled lawyers and of their frazzled supporters. One of the two district attorneys who carried on the prosecution was black, the other white and Jewish.

They were both twenty-nine years old, both noted doves who had supported Eugene McCarthy's Wisconsin campaign. "If I were boss I'd have our boys home by tomorrow noon," Deputy District Attorney Allen Samson would say during a court recess. "But *I* don't burn draft records, it's bad for the Peace Movement." "I'm as violently antiwar as anyone in the courtroom," his assistant, Harold Jackson, Jr., would say. He was from East Harlem and had gone through Groton and Colgate on scholarships. "Our draft laws are obscene. But these draft-file burners are the worst thing that could happen to us liberals." The two DAs, looking lonely and uncomfortable at the prosecution bench, would glance frequently, apologetically at the Milwaukee Twelve's supporters behind them.

Confronting the shiny hardware of the court, jamming its seats to capacity, sat the spectators from the Movement—priests, students, and defendants' relatives decorated as thickly as Bolivian generals with Resistance buttons. Among them were several Movement celebrities: George McVey, a Movement dentist from Rochester who, out of devotion to his former Holy Cross classmate Philip Berrigan, drilled resisters' teeth at no charge late into the night; Father Bernard Meyer of the D.C. Nine, a group comprising four other priests and two nuns which had ransacked the offices of the Dow Chemical Company the preceding March in what was called "the first witness attack upon the military-industrial complex." ("It's very easy for us priests to go to jail after all those years of seminary," observed Father Meyer, who faced a maximum sentence of thirty-five years, "three square meals and no women anyway.") In the front row of the courtroom, chewing on raw carrots, pawing at each other like puppies in a litter, lounged a large contingent of pink-cheeked teenagers from a Summerhill-type school in Canada. Their year's study consisted of a course in "Crime and Punishment," and they had been taken to the Milwaukee trial as their school outing of the year.

The defendants sat at a long book-laden table at the left of the courtroom well, reading from law volumes, taking notes, raising their hands to address the court, looking like a graduate seminar at a respectable university. Their ages ranged from twenty-two to forty-seven. At the right of the table, by the prosecutor's bench, sat the eldest and most scholarly of this brain trust, Christian Brother Basil O'Leary, Ph.D. in economics from Notre Dame, head of the Economics Department at St. Mary's College in Minnesota; Father Anthony Mullaney, a tall, imposing Benedictine monk with a Ph.D. in clinical psychology, formerly a professor at Boston University. Brother O'Leary, a wry and spectacled scholastic in an impeccable pinstriped suit, was a contributor to *Commonweal* and an associate editor of *Continuum,* in which he had recently published an article entitled "The Role of Moral Theology in the Universe of the Person." Father Mullaney's diction was equally formidable: "Picketing and burning draft files are not discrete variables, they are a continuum of action."

Others sitting around the defendants' table: four Catholic parish priests, one from St. Paul, Minnesota, three from Boston, Massachusetts; a mathematician and Yale graduate, only Jewish member of the group, who was the author of several manuals for grade school mathematics classes; a minister of the Church of Scientology; four Catholic laymen, one of whom, James Forest, was a prominent pacifist to whom Thomas Merton had dedicated his last book. Forest, whose bushy mustache and steel-rimmed glasses gave him the air of a Victorian intellectual, was the son of a Communist party organizer and a convert to Catholicism. He had been editor of *The Catholic Worker,* and was a founder and cochairman, along with Philip Berrigan, of the Catholic Peace Fellowship.

The defendants, on good days, referred to their judge as "Grandpa," a kinder name than the Movement had yet given to any other man on the bench. A benign, gauche man in his sixties, his official title was "Ozaukee County Judge Charles Larson." Tall and mournful-faced, heavy-lidded, cauliflower-eared, his manner evoked some folksy early morning TV show like "Captain Kangaroo," on which a fumbling jurist presides over a court of rebellious puppets. Commander of the Wisconsin chapter of the American Legion, father of several Vietnam veterans, barely acquainted with the facts of the Vietnam War, Judge Larson was an ardent amateur poet who was fond of quoting couplets he had written in honor of young women's weddings: "She is blessed with qualities rare, / Statuesque, impeccably attired, / Always knowing what to wear / That which makes her most admired."

Judge Larson was also a devout Roman Catholic. And the presence at the defendants' table of five priests, to all appearances the safest kind—jovial, handball-playing bingo-organizing Irish cu-rates—must have added much to the grief and confusion of his small blue eyes. One could not help pitying this pious provincial for whom priests were replete with an authority and sacredness un-distinguishable from that of policemen and National Guardsmen, and whose allegiances to God and Country were suddenly sun-dered by having to judge the saviors of his soul. Yet he looked more grieved than annoyed, and one felt that he was not so much a war lover as a man who devoutly followed any dictate of his state or church.

"These defendants are very intelligent, honest men," Judge Larson once said to a group of us in his chambers, "but look, this morning at five A.M. I was reading *Newsweek*, and it said in *Newsweek* that Ho Chi Minh . . . what's his post up there in North Vietnam?" "President of the Republic," someone suggested. "Thank you," he continued, "it says in *Newsweek* that their presi-dent Ho Chi Minh has executed fifty thousand people and jailed another one hundred thousand for not agreeing with his way of doing things, and if we pull out of there it will be wholesale slaugh-ter. Why don't we hear a bit about that too at this trial?"

And upon that he had walked into the courtroom to preside over the trial of twelve men who were pleading that they were in-nocent in committing burglary, arson, and theft upon property which they "reasonably believed to be illegal and unconstitutional," that they had committed these acts "with the intent of saving lives," at the biddance of a "moral law higher than that of any nation"; and that they had been bound to act by their religious consciences, which they defined as "the contact point between an individual and God."

As the defendants' testimonies began to unfold on the sixth day of the trial, it became clear that their central tactic would be to plead that they had tried every legal course they could to stop the war. Their act of civil disobedience, they would argue, "had the purpose not of disobeying the law, but of demonstrating its unconstitutional character." Crucial in the defense's argument, because it involved the admissibility of evidence, was its contention that in order to prove "reasonable belief" the defendants were entitled to offer as exhibits scholarly opinions contained in books, documents, and legal journals testifying to the illegality of the Vietnam War. The offered exhibits—some three dozen in number and all rejected by the court—ranged from the *Congressional Record*'s list of the war dead and Pope John XXIII's encyclical "Pacem in Terris" to the New Testament. Judge Larson overruled the prosecution, which had agreed to admit the New Testament as an exhibit, on the grounds that "to admit [the New Testament] into evidence may create substantial danger of undue prejudice or of misleading the jury."

To sustain their argument of "apparent threat," and of the "reasonableness" of their views on the war and on civil disobedience, the defendants had also used their defense funds to fly three expert witnesses from the East Coast. The three—Boston University historian Howard Zinn, legal experts John Fried and Marvin Gettleman—seemed to make Judge Larson highly uncomfortable. During Howard Zinn's hour and a half on the witness stand, the prosecution objected at every few words that his opinions were irrelevant; the judge sustained the objections, pounding the gavel like a Grand Guignol policeman batting down the hobo when he tries to rise. The pandemonium was heightened by the audience, which kept bursting into delirious applause at Zinn's truncated testimony.

HOWARD ZINN: The tradition of civil disobedience goes as far back as Thomas Jefferson and it comes right up to today . . . people distinguished in the field of law and philosophy recognize that there's a vast difference between a person who commits an ordinary crime and a person who commits an act which technically is a crime, but which in essence is a social act designed to make a statement. . . .

[*Great clapping from the audience, a few shouts.*]

COURT: I must stop you. There was an objection to that . . . did someone cry out back there?

FATHER MULLANEY: The whole American people are crying out, Your Honor.

Judge Larson eventually threatened Howard Zinn ("I'm going to have you arrested and have you put in the place where persons are placed for contempt of court"). Professor Zinn was dismissed from the stand and took the next plane back to New York. "This is like being stoned to death with marshmallows," cracked Father Cunnane, who spent idle moments in court reading *The Gospel According to Peanuts.* "It's very soft, and it takes very long."

The second star witness, John Fried, a Viennese-born scholar, had been chief consultant to the American judges at the Nuremberg trials, and adviser on international law at the Pentagon. The defendants stated that they had called Fried to testify on "a hierarchy of law in the international world order." The prosecution and the court objected that testimony drawn from such documents as the UN Charter and the Nuremberg Principles concerning the United States' violation of international law would be irrelevant to charges of burglary, arson, and theft. Fred Ojile, a wiry, tousled Catholic graduate student whose feline stride gave him a startling resemblance to Nureyev, replied that the defense's purposes in calling expert witnesses was to show it had "reasonable belief" in the war's illegality.

"That has been said over and over again, Mr. Ojile," Judge Larson said in a tired voice.

"Well it will continue to be said until it's understood by the court," Ojile answered grandly, stalking, pantherlike and barefoot, from the defendants' table to the water fountain. "I consider my state of mind, at the time of the action, very much related to Nuremberg Principles, and I would like the witness to have the opportunity to explain that, and it's not being allowed. At this rate, you know, it's a travesty of justice."

For once the defendants' gambit worked. Whatever the reasons—their unpredictable and agile tactics of self-defense, some growing anguish that seemed to gnaw at the prosecutors—Professor Fried's testimony, under Brother O'Leary's cross-examination, plunged more deeply into a discussion of the morality of the war than any yet tolerated at a resistance trial.

FRIED: I say with a very, very grave heart and after very, very careful study that the U.S. military intervention in Viet-

nam does violate essential and basic provisions of the United
Nations charter, and this is not an isolated opinion of myself.

BROTHER O'LEARY: What recourse does a citizen have . . .
when his country pursues war in violation of international
treaties which the citizen holds have been violated?

("No objection," said District Attorney Harold Jackson;
"if he can answer that, God bless him.")

FRIED: The International Tribunal at Nuremberg, at which
the United States was represented, stated that it is the moral
choice of the individual if he feels that for him obedience to
the higher order—to the world order—is more important, . . .
then he has to take the moral choice and do the things which
he considers morally proper. That is the great ethical and moral
method of Nuremberg.

BROTHER O'LEARY: No more questions.

The defendants and the spectators were very still. James Forest, whose conversion to Catholicism had been aided by seeing a
shaft of sunlight filtering into the east window of a church at evening, looked as if he were repeating that experience. Fried's testimony on the illegality of the war was something quite new in the
brief history of war protesters' trials. This delicate legal surgery
had been performed by Brother Basil O'Leary, the most traditional of the defendants, a conservative economist, a strong be-
liever in market economy. There was an amiable pedantry about
this wry, slight man who wrote on natural law for arcane theological
journals. Earlier the prosecution had asked him, "Did you just say
to yourself, 'Okay, Basil, you can go in there today?' " "Well Basil
doesn't operate that way," Brother O'Leary had answered. "Basil
operates more in a reflective way in which he likes to know all the
relevant factors to a situation. Basil weighs all the consequences of
an act and then decides."

The tensest moment of the trial occurred during the testimony of Father Rosenbaugh, a priest who had worked as a long-
shoreman on the Milwaukee docks and often said that he looked
forward to prison life as being "just like seminary, with more time
and freedom to read." Rosenbaugh elaborated on how the Vietnam War was crippling the nation's war on poverty. The court

interrupted the testimony as irrelevant. District Attorney Samson, in an increasingly frequent moment of leniency, asked the court to take notice of that testimony, even though it was immaterial, because "everyone knows that the war is taking money away from urban planning." Judge Larson replied that the court should shut off such testimony because it "would be giving dignity to their position, which I don't think should be done."

Shortly thereafter, Father Mullaney took the stand with the following words:

> There were three states of mind in particular which I think were important on September 24th. The first of these is a really felt need to be responsible. And there are three things I think that define a monk that are connected to responsibility:
>
> The first of these is being a Benedictine with 1400 years of tradition, the motto of the order having always been peace. The second is that the vows of the monk can be summed up as a single vow to set up the conditions whereby man can be fully human. . . .
>
> The third characteristic of the monastic life that has defined it down through the ages is that the monk is supposed to be a sign of hope, he is supposed to be a sign that history can be moved in the direction laid down in the Gospels, and therefore a sign that we are responsible for history and the direction that history takes.

The Mullaney testimony went on some three hours and was composed in strict Thomist style, I-a, I-b, I-c. It was delivered in a luminous, booming voice into an utterly still courtroom.

> The second frame of mind that was very important that day was the anger that stems from a correct assessment of a present moment in history. My anger comes out of two places, one is the college scene, and the second is the urban scene. My anger on September 24th was very definitely based on first-hand evidence that I had that the draft was doing violence to the consciences of young men, that it was doing real psychological damage to young men.
>
> The third state of mind that I think was very important in my own case was what can only be described as fear . . . of a very deep and very pervasive polarization that is going on in

the United States; by polarization I mean that we are a nation that's very, very seriously divided . . . black-white, rich-poor, young-old, a pervasive and very, very deep polarization.

Now there are four reasons which give rise to this particular fear that grew out of polarization: Number one, the ineffectiveness of speech in American life. Secondly, the growing gap between the powerful and the powerless. Also, the growing priority of things over people. And finally, the distorted priorities—the Vietnam War versus the poor of the cities . . .

The court conducted a half-hour dispute about the "irrelevance" of poverty in Roxbury, Massachusetts. The clinical psychologist resumed his oration.

And so, on September 24th, I participated in the burning of draft records as my attempt to say something about the polarization, which, if it is not checked, is going to lead to great disaster in this nation. I participated in what I considered a very beautiful liturgy, and this is the work of the monk. . . .

The tall, grave priest continued, I-a-1, I-a-2 . . .

Now through my participation, I intended the following: Firstly, I intended to show in a society where speech is in such danger of being stifled, that man as public speaker is still alive.

Secondly, I intended to show in a society where the inadequacy of legal channels for redressing injustices is apparent, that civil disobedience is part of due process in that society. I acted to affirm that law in a free society compels obedience only when it furthers the justice that enables men to lead a more fully human life.

"Father," Judge Larson interrupted very gently. Mullaney was the defendant whose decorous manner had most endeared him to the court and the prosecution. "Father, are you still giving reasons why you participated on the 24th of September?"

"That's the end of my statement," Father Mullaney said modestly after three hours on the stand.

At the beginning of the trial, Harold Jackson, Jr., the assistant district attorney, had described his emotions toward the defendants as "one of intense anger and hatred, because I'm Catholic and violently against the war, and black, and their actions seem to polarize all the sentiments against us liberals." But the defendants' testimonies, however often he interrupted them, seemed to affect him even more deeply than they seemed to affect Samson. "I'm more torn by this case than I was at the beginning," he admitted to me at midtrial; "I see nothing but honesty and intelligence here, depth of perception and integrity, an atmosphere that I can only describe as very loving."

Later, toward the end of the trial, after Father Mullaney had been speaking with particular moral passion, Jackson, obviously upset, asked that the jury be dismissed from the room.

"The State is very much opposed to the position it finds itself in," he said, "because both counsels for the State do not think that the war in Vietnam is irrelevant in and of itself. We find it to be irrelevant in terms of the act for which we are prosecuting. And we request that this Court instruct the jury as to the legal reasons why certain evidence is not admissible. We request that it not be done in terms of the customary lawyer's nomenclature . . . it is impossible for the State represented by human beings to sit here any longer having it said that they believe in and of themselves that poverty and the war are irrelevant."

His voice broke. "I just can't take it," he said. And he walked out of the courtroom.

Two weeks later, after the state trial was over, Harold Jackson left his district attorney's job to work exclusively with black civil rights cases. "Negroes in this country are being sent to jail like Jews to Auschwitz," he said to me in his office on his last day there. "There's not enough legal talent around to help them. . . ."

"That trial tore me up," he added; "I'm still not sure what they accomplished politically. But whatever religion is, they're where it's at. . . . I suppose the essence of religiousness is to break rules at the proper time. . . . What the hell do you expect when a great priest like Mullaney leaves the monastery after nineteen years and sees what life is like in Roxbury, Massachusetts?"

On May 26, 1969, the eleventh and last day of the trial, Judge Larson charged the jury, a dour, impassive, perplexed bunch—eight men, four women, one of them black, eight of them Catholics. Larson used almost the same words with which the judge of a federal court in Baltimore, seven months previously, had charged the jurors of the Catonsville Nine. "The law does not recognize political, religious or moral convictions, or some higher law, as justification for the commission of a crime, no matter how good the motive may be . . . people who believe that the Vietnam War is illegal or unconstitutional or morally wrong have the right to protest in various ways. . . ."

The defendants went out for beer. There was a glimmer of hope for a hung jury in a sideburned computer analyst, and in two women jurors who had wept during James Forest's and Father Mullaney's closing statements. But the twelve were soon recalled. The jury had deliberated for only seventy minutes before returning its verdict, charge by charge, defendant by defendant, thirty-six times in a row, as guilty of arson, burglary, and theft.

There was a half-minute of silence in the courtroom. Judge Larson began to sum up the jury's findings. Then, as if ignited by a slow fuse, pandemonium erupted. It was set off by a young spectator in the back row who called out, "If they are guilty I am too; from this day forward I am a draft resister!"

Rhythmical applause by the two hundred people wedged into the courtroom, a chorus of sobbing and weeping, a melee of clenched fists and V signs. Dozens of spectators rose, linked arms throughout the courtroom, started singing "We Shall Overcome." The jurors tried to pick their way through the milling, swaying throng. "Clear the court, I've got to have more sheriffs," Judge Larson shouted, helplessly standing behind the bench. Eight frantic bailiffs started to drag limp spectators out of the courtroom. "Good God," the judge cried again, "I've got to have more policemen!" In the hall outside the courtroom one hundred persons still milled about. Three young men burned their draft cards, and the supporters of the Milwaukee Twelve made the sign of the cross on their foreheads with the remaining ashes. The trial ended, as it had proceeded, in a bizarre mixture of burlesque and religious fervor.

The Milwaukee Twelve were free on bail until June 6, when they returned to Judge Larson's court for sentencing. Judge Larson gave the men two years—a benign sentence compared to the six years given Philip Berrigan the previous spring for burning draft files in Baltimore, the three years given to most members of the Catonsville Nine, the four and five years still being given to men refusing induction. As the judge began to sentence Father Mullaney, he choked on that good Irish name and fumbled among his black robes for a handkerchief. He wept for a few seconds, and then in a timorous voice resumed sentencing the monk, who stood before him triumphantly, dressed in clerical black, his arms folded as if he were the executioner.

This first attempt at legal self-defense had raised political issues as no previous resistance trial had done. It had tortured the consciences of a few in power. The defendants had been let off lightly. The twelve could be paroled in fourteen months. Movement lawyers began to write manuals for lay advocacy.

During the second week of the Milwaukee trial, three more acts of destruction took place. On May 20, in Los Angeles, three young men removed and burned several hundred 1-A draft files from a downtown induction center. At seven the following morning, three young men entered the Selective Service office at Silver Spring, Maryland, and mutilated part of its records with a mixed medium of black paint and blood.

Five days later thirteen men and two women entered a draft board in Chicago's South Side, grabbed an estimated forty thousand draft records out of the filing cabinets, and celebrated Pentecost by burning them in a nearby alley. The group included two priests— a Carmelite monk and a curate from Father James Groppi's Milwaukee parish; a twenty-three-year-old woman truck driver; and two men, Charles Muse and John Phillips, who became the seasonal heroes of the Ultra-Resistance for their sheer persistence in choosing to live in jail.

Twenty-year-old Charles Muse had left Allenwood prison in Pennsylvania the previous December after serving a jail term for burning his draft card, and had been discharged from parole supervision only eighteen hours before he took part in the Chicago Fifteen's draft board raid in May. As for twenty-two-year-old draft-card burner John Phillips, he had refused to leave jail when his term was up. He had been rolled out of Allenwood in a wheelchair, and had gone home to Boston to found an organization named the Prisoners' Information and Support Service, called PISS for short. Its mottoes were "Void Where Prohibited," and "Words Are Shit." In John Phillips's style, the draft board witnesses had recaptured some of the scatological splendor of their origins.

The insouciance of Phillips and Muse were characteristic of the recent communities of witness. The Chicago Fifteen's loot— forty thousand draft files—was the biggest to date. Yet the group had only two briefing sessions before their foray. "We brought them out in pillowcases, in potato sacks," a member of the Fifteen describes it, "in shopping bags, in duffel bags, oh it was gorgeous." "We had drunk and celebrated the night before most joyfully," another member of the Fifteen reported. "We all slept in a pad a few floors below the draft board. Everyone was so relaxed, I got up to go to the john a few hours before the action was scheduled to go and I heard most of the guys snoring, fast asleep."

The attitudes of this new vintage of raiders were more cynical than those of the witness movement's pioneers. As the Ultra-Resistance grew younger and more secular, it expressed increasing frustrations with the narrowness of its audience. However brilliant the trials of the Catonsville Nine and the Milwaukee Twelve, they failed to produce the forum which the protesters had hoped to obtain. The trials seemed like chamber music played to the intimate audience of the peace community. The acts themselves were beginning to appear too symbolic, not political enough. There was a growing anguish among the young about the obscurity of the witness they were offering.

The leaders of the Movement, the older, more established men like the Berrigans, O'Leary, James Forest, would continue to expound their mystique of protest in the religious and Left press. But the jail terms of the Chicago Fifteen, the Pasadena Three, the Silver Spring Three, would have little educational impact. The Ultra-Resistance was starting to question its basic premise of witnessing in jail. It was debating whether the "stand-around" actions for which they would surely be arrested were really preferable to the more destructive possibilities of anonymous hit-and-run sabotage. "Is it going to be a stand-around or a hit-and-run?" was becoming the new stock question in the last half of 1969.

Some young purists were still holding out for the original pristine stand-around. "There is no point to running," John Phillips wrote in his PISS newsletter. "We are demythologizers, in running we maintain the myths. . . . Do your thing but run means not doing your thing, unless your thing is running. . . ."

If, as others predicted, the hard core of the Movement moved away from the moral violence of witness actions to the physical violence of sabotage, it could retard the violence of the government but would not expose it so well. Actions such as those of the Milwaukee group's were a witness to hope. The hit-and-run actions would be a witness to despair. And whatever token moves would be taken by the Nixon administration to de-escalate the Vietnam fighting, the most terrible toll taken on this country by that insane war was precisely the loss of hope, the sense that not only legal means but also the process of nonviolent civil disobedience had been tried and left wanting in reforming various areas of injustice.

The federal trial of the Milwaukee Twelve which began on June 9, three days after the state sentencing, was brief, abortive, and totally unexpected in its results. The charges were destroying government property and interfering with the working of the Selective Service System. After a tedious voir dire of two and a half days in which he cross-examined 141 prospective jurors—mostly hostile to the defendants—Federal District Judge Myron Gordon dismissed the government charges against the twelve on grounds that "prejudicial pretrial publicity" caused by modern press media had made a fair trial impossible. The decision was said to have no precedent. Other court rulings involving news coverage of criminal cases, such as the Sam Sheppard case, had never resulted in dismissal of charges but in reversal of conviction followed by retrial. But, however favorable the federal court's decision, the Milwaukee defendants were scheduled to start the jail sentences meted out by the state of Wisconsin.

A few days after the Milwaukee Twelve had begun their prison term, the wives of James Forest and two other defendants drove to Waupun State Penitentiary, an hour north of Milwaukee, to make their first visits to their husbands. "We drove through miles of farmland," Linda Forest told me, "and arrived at a place which looked very much like Thomas Merton's Gethsemane, very monastic—a wall some fifteen feet high, four blocks long, broken up by wrought-iron arches. When they see you coming there's a large humming and snapping sound coming from a watchtower, which issues a loud report when the gate swings open. You walk to the guardhouse across a large stretch of grass—there's a lot of grass everywhere. We were cordially received by the guards, who took us to the sergeant. Everybody was polite to us, they kept saying 'Ma'am, ma'am.'

"The sergeant accompanied us through what looked like a series of cloisters, one building enclosed inside the other, past the chapel enclosure, the gymnasium enclosure, past a first set of dorms, you're always walking on very soft grass. Prisoners were hanging out of windows, some windows had boxes of geraniums on them. We made the V sign at them and they flashed it back. The sergeant ushered us into a very neat building, the architecture was very clean, very modern. The guard on duty there was a Robert Young type with a pipe in his hand, extra friendly. 'Linda,' he said, 'you have two hours of visiting time a month; you can have them both at once if you want.' Finally he ushered us into the reception room; it was like a seminary, or a university. There were lots of century plants around, smart brown curtains, Danish-type modern chairs scattered around modern coffee tables. On each coffee table there was a plastic-coated slip of paper which said the following:

> We have made a conscientious effort to create as much of a living room atmosphere as possible for you and your relatives. We hope that you won't embarrass us by extreme displays of any sort. Visitors are allowed to embrace and kiss prisoners before and after each visit.

"Jim looked very well. He looked about nineteen years old with his head clean-shaven, and without his mustache. He says the food is very good, cafeteria-style; they are forced to eat everything on their plate. For the first few days he's not allowed any books except his Bible and his breviary. He's been saying his breviary every hour, he's been saying his hours. We sat and talked about how we would grow through this, how it might be the best thing for our marriage. When I hugged Jim he smelled so good, a smell of clean plain soap, and of fresh clean linen, he smelled like a nun, or like a child when you put him to bed."

Harrisburg:
The Politics of Salvation

In October of 1969, a few weeks after the Milwaukee Twelve began to serve their prison terms, Father Daniel Berrigan, Father Philip Berrigan, and seven other Catholic priests and laymen were found guilty in a Baltimore courtroom of destroying some 370 draft files in protest against the Vietnam War.

The Catonsville Nine, as the group was called, were sentenced to jail terms that ranged from two to three and a half years in federal prison, and were declared free pending appeal. The case went to the Supreme Court, where it was refused a hearing. In April of 1970, the night before he was to surrender to federal authorities, Daniel Berrigan went underground, seeking refuge with a nationwide network of citizens—doctors, lawyers, housewives, teachers, priests—who had offered him shelter.

Daniel Berrigan, a fine poet and a member of the Society of Jesus, is a slender man of rigorous, almost military posture. His wizened, elfin face and teasing smile have always reminded me of a slightly jaded, mischievous Zen monk. I went to see him a few months after he had taken flight from the FBI, at the home of one of his hosts in the suburbs of a large Eastern city. He came out to greet me dressed in sandals, blue jeans, and a plaid sport shirt, carrying a volume of French Surrealist poetry under his arm. I was struck by his exuberant good health. He had put on several pounds since beginning his flight from authority, even though he had changed domiciles several dozen times. He was very suntanned, and seemed considerably more serene and cheerful than when I'd last met him for lunch, aboveground, the previous winter.

It was a very hot summer day. We talked in the living room of a spacious, sunny house. Dan spent much of our meeting sitting cross-legged, in the lotus position, on a straight-backed chair. He told me that whenever he was "living in the country" he gardened a great deal, weeding, planting, cutting grass; and that he was working on an essay on Saint John of the Cross in the light of the Resistance—Saint John, in his opinion, had written his best poetry in jail. In the evenings there was always some kind of meeting with whatever community was supporting him: organizing moves to the next city, planning the sending out of tapes and magazine articles, scheduling talks with reporters. Heated discussions always occurred, he said, whenever a decision had to be made to approve or veto a press interview; there was a delicate balance to preserve, he felt, between "educating the public" and keeping security measures. He had already held underground conferences with several members of the press, including *The New York Times* and NBC News.

This last detail amused and interested me. I found that my friend Daniel, like many other Catholic radicals, was continuing to behave toward authority in a startlingly flirtatious manner: showing a curious ambivalence toward openness and secrecy, condemning the media and yet enjoying its uses whenever the media could serve his needs.

Daniel and I had met three years before and had struck up a tenuous friendship: I had made him uneasy by citing that very reservation (and a few others) about his tactics. He had implied that persons making sacrifices equal to his and those of his Catholic peers should be considered beyond reproach, and that anyone not ready to spend many months in jail for the cause of peace was a liberal cop-out. Hence our relationship had stumbled along somewhat warily, but the fact that he had beckoned me for a summer lunch underground indicated that a measure of healing trust had been restored.

So I needled Dan about his being something of a tease, and that day he gave his radiant, fey smile. "One of the reasons I do it this way," he said, "is to prove the powerlessness of power. The FBI are overtechnologized and dehumanized, that's why they can't find me. It's like the U.S. Army, which, with all its matériel, can't win against the North Vietnamese people." The cloak-and-dagger aspects of this "precarious and interesting existence," as he termed it, also seemed to amuse him immensely. "The FBI are the politest bloodhounds I've ever had on my tail. A disproportionate number of them are Catholic, and they never lose their Catholic manners. I hear that they're still doing the rounds of the convents, peeking under the nuns' beds and saying 'Are you there, Father Dan, are you there?' "

On that note we broke for a lunch of tuna-fish salad prepared by our hostess, and Dan, who like most Catholic radicals likes to emphasize his conservatism, elaborated on the underground tradition in the history of the Jesuit order, which he had joined at the age of eighteen. Out of the twenty-seven Jesuits canonized as saints, thirteen had been martyrs, men who had in some way defied secular authority—a higher ratio of martyrs, perhaps, than in any other order of the Church. "Edmund Campion!" Dan called out to me over our iced tea. "Lived underground in disguise under Queen Elizabeth, when Catholicism was outlawed, until he was captured and hanged for treason. And look at Robert Southwell, also put to death after a long stint in the Maquis . . . you must reread his poem 'The Burning Babe': 'The Metal in this furnace wrought / Are men's defiled souls . . .' "

There was one particular question which I needed to ask Daniel Berrigan more than any other, and I saved it for the end of our visit because it was rather severe. It went this way: The classic theory of civil disobedience, as it had been advocated by Gandhi, Martin Luther King, and the Berrigans themselves, stated that when men break a small law to prove the immorality of a larger law they must take due punishment: you do your thing and you take the rap. Why had he forsworn that principle? Was he improvising a new blend of the stand-around and the hit-and-run? What did an underground interview with *The New Yorker* (in whose "Talk of the Town" section I would publish the substance of our conversation) have to do with his years of preaching on nonviolence and on our need to do "witness" in American jails?

Dan Berrigan looked elusive but composed, and as he answered I kept thinking, Well this is a great Jesuit. "I'm trying to separate the essentials of nonviolence from its accidentals," he said. "The essentials involve retaining nonviolent means; the chain of crime and punishment is an accidental. I decided that in view of the illegitimate way in which the war was being escalated, the 1960s tactical details have become questionable . . .

"We have to face the fact that the war has gravely worsened," he continued with great weariness, "that the courts are worse than useless, that they're being used to break up the peace movement. So I decided to up the ante in an imaginative way. . . ."

It is with a memory of the disillusionment and fatigue expressed by Dan Berrigan on that summer day that I went to attend the trial of the Harrisburg Seven held a year and a half later, in February of 1972. By then Daniel Berrigan had been caught and arrested by the FBI, had finished serving a sixteen-month sentence in a federal penitentiary, and was free to sit in on the trial in the visitors' gallery. (He had been appre-hended by the authorities at a friend's home in Block Island, Rhode Island, some three weeks after our meeting. "You see, I had to get caught," he had written from jail, "otherwise it would mean that I was hiding too much.")

I

IN 1849 a maverick priest in the town of Béziers, France, founded an order of nuns which he called Les Religieuses du Sacré Coeur de Marie, whose aim would be to educate young girls to work among the poor. Father Jean Pierre Gailhac was an eccentric and a social activist. He had chosen to be chaplain at the local *hôtel-Dieu* rather than preach or teach, and had also set up a rehabilitation center for prostitutes. Like the order he founded, Gailhac seemed destined for occasional trouble, and was even accused, midway in his career, of poisoning some nuns. Notwithstanding his personal tribulations, his order flour-ished, and a small mission was sent to the United States in the 1880s to establish a convent on these shores.

Its arrival was forlorn. The American sponsor of the mission, a rich Cincinnati widow, had died while the nuns were en route from France, and they were left stranded at the docks. A priest took pity on the sisters and offered them his house in Sag Harbor, Long Island. But their troubles were not over. The priest fell in love with the youngest of the nuns, who had not yet taken her vows, and the group's mother superior had to return to France for further counsel. This episode is documented in the archives of the Religious of the Sacred Heart of Mary (RSHM) under the title "Les Tristes et Douloureuses Epreuves de la Maison de Sag Har-bor." Such afflictions did not prevent the order from opening many distinguished schools and colleges throughout America, one of the most noted of which is Marymount College in Tarrytown, New York. It is at Marymount that Sister Elizabeth McAlister, a nun of the Religious of the Sacred Heart of Mary, indicted in 1971

on charges of conspiring to kidnap Henry Kissinger and blow up
heating ducts in Washington, D.C., attended college and later
taught.

Elizabeth McAlister is one of seven children of Irish immigrants who had come to the United States in the 1920s, and had
set up a successful construction business in Montclair, New Jersey.
Her childhood was peaceful, uneventful, and fairly prosperous.
She had always loved to draw, and early in her college life she
designed holy name day cards and place cards for the nuns' religious holidays—the Feast of Saint Joseph, the Feast of the Immaculate Conception. The only seed of nonconformism to be
found in those years is that she loved contemporary art and made
abstract designs on these greetings which her order found "highly
unacceptable" because of their avant-garde tenor.

The call for a religious vocation had come to Elizabeth in
the most traditional way. Sometime in her freshman year, while
in prayer, she received what she believed to be a call from God.
It had come as a surprise to her and as a discomfiture to her liberal-
minded parents, who looked upon the rules of the Religious of
the Sacred Heart of Mary as harshly restrictive. Until 1962 or so
the regulations of this semicloistered order forbade the nuns from
ever entering their parents' house again after they had taken their
vows, short of a death in the family. They were also prohibited
from seeing any films, or reading any newspapers or any books
beyond the slim collection of saints' lives on the convent's shelves.
There was a single radio set in the convent on which the sisters
were allowed to listen to only one program: Fulton Sheen's. Older
members of the RSHM vividly recall the great excitement with
which they greeted a showing of *Snow White and the Seven
Dwarfs*, which Joseph Kennedy, whose ailing daughter Rosemary
was at the college, once brought to Marymount on a Tuesday of
Holy Week as a special dispensation for the community.

Elizabeth McAlister, a tall, long-limbed girl with blue eyes
and thick dark brown hair, was an exemplary, compulsively disci-
plinary nun who spent her early twenties perfecting herself in her
vocation. She did not even chafe against such rigid convent cus-

toms as the *amende honorable*, a penance which she had to recite publicly, kneeling on the floor of the refectory at breakfast time to confess any small instances of misdemeanor; turning a light out too late, breaking a teacup. The order having shrewdly perceived Elizabeth's talent, she was sent to Hunter College in New York City in 1962 to acquire a master's degree in art history. The head of the department, Eugene Goossen, remembers her as "a person with fringes of great firmness and stubbornness, full of preconceived ideas but with very radical tastes in art for a nun." Religious orders are noted for overworking the few specialists they have. Returning to Marymount in 1963, Elizabeth taught medieval, Renaissance, Oriental, and American art within the same semester. Her greatest pleasure was to lecture on her favorite twentieth-century masters— Jackson Pollock, Joan Miró, Barnett Newman, David Smith.

Into the mid-1960s Elizabeth was still dressed in the vestments that had been traditional to her order since the nineteenth century: a floor-length habit of blue serge, over which hung a highly starched white linen wimple which reached halfway down to her waist. On her head she wore a cap of white muslin to which she pinned the enormous coif of starched white linen that framed her face. Over the coif she wore a third layer of white veiling reaching to the waist, and a fourth layer of black veiling would be added when she attended chapel. She rose at 5:30, and until 1968 her daily schedule would include the following: a period of meditation at 6:00 A.M., Mass at 6:45, and three more hours of meditation and prayers interspersed throughout the day.

During the political turbulence of the 1960s, persons like Elizabeth McAlister underwent transformations that were unnatural in their intensity. The revolution in the Church, the maelstrom of the sixties' dissent induced in her changes of terrifying rapidity. Elizabeth had had strong feelings against the Vietnam War since 1965, and in May of 1968 she was on the verge of joining Philip Berrigan and the Catonsville Nine in their foray on draft board files in Maryland. She desisted from so acting only the night before, with characteristic dutifulness toward her order. But the compulsive rigor and dedication that she had brought to her nun's vocation were now put fully to the uses of the Movement.

A characteristic image of the 1970 Elizabeth McAlister: She drives with a friend down the highway toward a Movement meeting, high beyond the speed limit, the window open. She is now clothed in a brief-skirted sport dress; on her lap is an open copy of the New Testament which she looks at frequently during her voyage. It was during such a trip, on January 12, 1971, as she was getting into a car in a parking lot in Newark, New Jersey, that seven FBI men walked up to her and said, "You're under arrest, Sister Liz." "Please," she replied, her Irish temper rising, "my name is Elizabeth—my friends call me Liz." They read her the charges: conspiring to kidnap Henry Kissinger and blow up heating ducts in Washington, D.C. "Over, over," the agents radioed when she had entered the car, "we've got the package, over."

That same evening a posse of FBI men came to arrest Eqbal Ahmad, a Pakistani scholar living in Chicago. In Baltimore, the FBI went to the apartment of Anthony and Mary Scoblick, and to the apartment shared by Fathers Joseph Wenderoth and Neil McLaughlin. The best known of the Harrisburg Seven, Father Philip Berrigan, was told of his indictment at the Federal Penitentiary at Danbury, Connecticut, where he was already serving a six-year sentence for the destruction of draft files in 1967 (Baltimore) and 1968 (Catonsville).

The indictment brought against these seven persons in January 1970 relied solely on conversations reported by an FBI informer, Boyd Douglas, a convict with a long record of lying and of violence, and on letters exchanged at Lewisburg Prison between Elizabeth McAlister and Philip Berrigan. The charges against this predominantly Catholic group were ironically Catholic in nature. The charges implied, as does the old Church teaching, that one can be as guilty for thinking sinful thoughts as for committing thoughtful sins. The indictment blurred all distinction between discussion and agreement, between conversation and action, and invaded that most private and sacred part of humankind which is our fantasy life. And the indictment had been triggered, in turn, by the fantasies of the angry spymaster, the late J. Edgar Hoover, who was seeking to reestablish his prestige at the wane of a long career.

When Hoover appeared before the Senate Subcommittee on Appropriations in November 1970 to make the allegations that led to the Harrisburg indictment, it was his first visit to any Senate group in fifteen years. He had come under the pretext of asking for additional funds for the FBI which had already been voted to him by the House. Hoover announced, that day, "an incipient plot on the part of an anarchist group" which, led by the imprisoned Berrigan brothers, was planning to blow up government heating systems and kidnap a high government official.

One must sense the full measure of Hoover's desperation. He had made several previous attempts to force an indictment of the group, but neither the White House, the Republican Policy Committee, nor the Internal Security Division had wanted to make his charges public. Hoover's stubborn determination to obtain an indictment seems to reflect his frustration at the Justice Department's failure to indict Daniel Berrigan under the fugitive law. Berrigan had evaded the FBI for nearly four months, had mocked and derided it. But the attorney general had wisely decided not to enlarge this priest's well-publicized martyrdom.

The Justice Department is reported to have been appalled by Hoover's public revelations, and dead set against an indictment at the time because of insufficient evidence. The group was simply one of several that were continually being watched and followed by the FBI. But Hoover's Senate appearance forced Justice to take very swift face-saving action. And the indictment on charges of conspiracy to raid draft boards, blow up heating tunnels, and kidnap Henry Kissinger was drawn up in a mere six weeks.

The Harrisburg Seven went to trial the following year, on January 24, 1972. The man who had triggered Hoover's ire and indiscretions—the quixotic Daniel Berrigan—had been dropped from his status of coconspirator in the new indictment and would come to court only as an infrequent visitor to the spectators' gallery.

II

The courtroom of the Harrisburg Federal Building is like an ultramodern mortuary. Its carpeting is slime green; the benches have the thinness of imitation hickory coffins; the ceiling is an expanse of fifty-four squares of floodlit panels that give off a garish light; the sole adornment is an enormous American flag. It is the fifth time in recent years that I sit in the press section of a courtroom seeing a group of Catholics—all of them acquaintances, some of them good friends—prosecuted for their activities against the Vietnam War. In this bleak courtroom I am filled with a despair that I never experienced at the trials of the Catonsville Nine or the Milwaukee Twelve.

In 1968 and 1969 the defendants at such trials were clearly the moral aggressors, having deliberately brought punishment upon themselves by the sacrificial gestures of draft board raids. Four years later, at Harrisburg, the government is the aggressor, and the rulers' violence has increased. The government is the inquisitor, prosecuting not disobedience but absurd fantasies of disobedience. Sitting in this cavernous, heavily guarded courtroom, I am haunted by the fact that this could be the trial of any antiwar citizens merely discussing possibilities for action: If the government came for them in the morning, it may come for us at night.

The thought that Fathers Joseph Wenderoth and Neil McLaughlin may be convicted fills me with particular dejection. They sit next to each other alongside the left wall of the courtroom, wearing their white collars throughout the trial. They remind me of Bernanos's country priest, conventional, devout, dedicated curates, the kind who used to get the longest line at the confessional. Neil McLaughlin is a frail, cerebral young man given to rigorous theologizing. Joseph Wenderoth is an athletically built Boys Town type with a scrubbed, ingenuous face. He tells me that when he kneels down by his bed every night he includes the prosecuting attorneys in his prayers.

Joe raided a draft board in Philadelphia a few months after Neil had raided one in New York. They spent their priesthood years in Baltimore's black ghetto, and the dilemma of integrity and identity that has pervaded the more radical clergy since the sixties recurs often in the analysis of their actions. "What was I supposed to do, sit around the parish and be a parasite on the black community?" "I was sick and tired of leeching off the poor."

Anthony and Mary Scoblick fell in love on the way to raiding a Boston draft board. They are a clean-cut, ebullient, savvy pair. They have been radicalized by their years of work in the black ghetto, and argue emotionally about links between the race problem and the war. Tony is the son of a former Pennsylvania congressman. He is the wit of the group, and regales me out of court with Robin Hood tales of his years as a parish priest in the inner city, when he used to raffle off his parish's furniture on bingo nights and distribute the earnings to his black parishioners. Mary is a slight, pretty, red-haired former nun who is a doctoral candidate in French literature. Her specialty is contemporary French drama and the theater of the absurd—Ionesco, Beckett. She softly hums Gregorian chants to herself throughout the trial, requiems she remembers from convent days.

Cast in Harrisburg as the sinister alien, the foreigner brought in to foster American paranoia about outside agitators, Eqbal Ahmad of Pakistan has been given a role familiar to conspiracy trials. One of the marshals refers to Eqbal as "that spooky Asian" and "that camel driver." Riding in the elevators of the Federal Building one day, a Harrisburg citizen tells me "that Pakistani should be shish-kebabed for bringing the country more trouble than it already has."

Eqbal is an extremely polite man with dazzling white teeth and large dark divergent eyes which give him an abstracted look. The inclusion of this sophisticated, agnostic Third World radical in the unschooled Catholic melee is another oddity of the Harrisburg trial. Eqbal traveled for a year with Mahatma Gandhi, writes and speaks fluent English, French, Arabic, and Urdu, received his doctorate from Princeton with highest honors, and was offered a diplomatic position in the government of the Pakistani president, Zulfiqar Ali Bhutto. I have come to admire his sense of honor. When I ask him why he does not skip to Pakistan rather than suffer through the absurdities of this trial he puts out his hand in a severe, categoric gesture and answers: "That is not done."

For recurring periods since his first draft board raid of 1967, Philip Berrigan has been shuttled between prison cells and courtrooms, hands and feet shackled, surrounded by a posse of federal marshals. In Harrisburg his temporary residence is the Dauphin

County Jail, which looks out upon gigantic branches of Gimbel's and Wanamaker's. He is thinner than I have ever seen him. There is the pent-up rage of the caged lion in the hulking movements of his body. We have been friends for almost four years. During this time he has often needled my conscience by the absoluteness of his commitment and his fortitude.

In 1972, with the war still expanding, I am further haunted by the possible futility of any sacrificed freedom. On my last visit with Philip Berrigan, before the Harrisburg trial began, he talked with a new sense of disenchantment and isolation. "I used to have a hopeful view of resources in church or in student coalitions, or in minority group militants. This hope was unfounded. We found that these alliances had no roots, that they bloomed and died overnight like desert flowers. I have absolutely no regrets about what I have done. But would I do it again? Probably not." He became silent, and I sensed some loss of that hopefulness which had shaped the savage courage of his past five years.

In the Harrisburg jail Philip Berrigan can receive visits only from codefendants and relatives. We occasionally look at each other across the courtroom, and I flash him a peace sign as old and as worn as the decade.

Elizabeth McAlister and Philip Berrigan had met in 1966, when she was still wearing her habit, and he had come to her convent to celebrate a funeral Mass for a mutual friend. Now they sit next to each other every day in the Harrisburg courtroom, taking notes on the trial with academic punctiliousness. There is wit and great stubbornness in Elizabeth's blue eyes. Her hair has grayed much since her indictment. Throughout the trial I remain tortured by a dilemma facing many writers in this time of crisis: whether I can remain critical of this defendant while remaining her friend, whether I can see her actions in both their nobility and their rashness.

A day in court, at midtrial, in early March. Boyd Douglas is about to take the stand. Judge R. Dixon Herman sits at the bench. He is a sixty-one-year-old Nixon appointee with a grim and skull-like face, who is an American Legionnaire, a Veteran of Foreign Wars, a Moose, a Lion, and a Mason, has a license to make elderberry wine, and goes swimming in the nude at the YMCA every day, vigorously spanning forty laps.

To the left of the courtroom sits the most prestigious team of lawyers yet assembled in a resistance trial, headed by Leonard Boudin, New York City activist Paul O'Dwyer (who later became the president of the City Council), and former U.S. Attorney General Ramsey Clark. To the right of the courtroom sits the jury, three men and nine women who look amazingly cheerful notwithstanding the fact that they have been sequestered and given the longest list of forbidden television programs in legal history. Lodged at a nearby motel, they are prohibited by the judge from watching "Hawaii Five-O," "Dragnet," "Ironside," "Perry Mason," "Mod Squad," "The D.A.," "Cade's County," "Sarge," "Mannix," "Cannon," "O'Hara, U.S. Treasury," "Adam 12," the lawyer segment of "The Bold Ones," and any news shows or talk shows, including "Meet the Press," David Frost, Dick Cavett, Merv Griffin, and even Johnny Carson.

The prosecutor of the Harrisburg case, William Sebastian Lynch, is a short, fleshy, high-strung man with straw-colored hair, a rose-hued complexion, and an exceedingly curt handshake. A graduate of a Brooklyn parochial school, Fordham University, and Harvard Law School, he exudes pugnaciousness and craftsmanship. His only private practice consisted of brief stints in stock market and admiralty law. He favors fastidiously traditional clothes. One of his favorite costumes is a very pale gray suit, a white shirt, and a checkered tie of two alternating hues of light silver, in which he presents a spectral image of shimmering, flaxen roundness.

Although guarded at first, now, toward the end of the trial, Lynch banters occasionally with the press. One learns that he is a lector at his parish. That he sees Pope John XXIII as the destroyer of his Roman Catholic Church. That his favorite reading is naval history. Also, he and Mrs. Lynch are dedicated cyclists, and Mrs. Lynch is totally preoccupied, down in Virginia, with her own movement—the movement to build a continuous bicycle path from Alexandria to Washington.

Lynch seems a man straight out of the fifties, totally untouched by the events of the past decade. When he occasionally bumps into a reporter at one of the modest diners he frequents to avoid the press, he raises the index and pinky of his hand in that old fraternity sign that used to communicate "up yours." Prosecuting Catholics transformed by the turbulence of the sixties, he appears determined to remain untainted by their contact, refusing throughout the trial even to acknowledge the defendants' greetings. In this encounter with nuns and priests freeing themselves from traditional molds of Church authority, Lynch remains an entrenched example of the autocratic, disciplinarian Catholic ethos. Anthony Scoblick has an interesting view of this prosecutor: "He hates us for not behaving like priests," Tony says. "He hates us because he can't look up to us and be dominated by us." Lynch, Scoblick tells me, exemplifies a new variation on the Grand Inquisitor theme: he is the oppressed who hates the oppressor for ceasing to fulfill his need for authority.

When I first watched Boyd Douglas walk into court, he gave the impression of great confidence and surliness. His chest was thrust rigorously forward, his mouth twisted into a defiant pout. He is about five feet nine and solidly built, has a strong rectangular face, medium-cut, neatly parted, glossy dark brown hair, the beginning of sideburns. He has a slightly jutting chin, heavy-lidded chestnut brown eyes, an unusually handsome nose, sharp and fine. He emanates a powerful all-American boy sexuality. He favors flamboyant clothes, and my most vivid recollection of him is in a Chagall-blue hunting-style jacket, an orange shirt, a purple-lozenged tie. His expression remains predominantly arrogant and scowling throughout the trial, although it occasionally becomes coquettish: When he is not being questioned, when the lawyers read some other document and his eyes are free to roam the room, he scrutinizes the jurors with a sly, flirtatious look.

As the facts of this informer's astonishing record of crime, fraud, and impersonation were revealed in the Harrisburg courtroom, Prosecuting Attorney William Lynch's description of the trial's protagonists became particularly memorable. He had recently stated that the defendants were "more dangerous than the Mafia." He had described his chief government witness, Boyd Douglas, as a man of "sterling character." Boyd Douglas, he had added, was "a man of compassion and growth."

Boyd Douglas is a high-school dropout whose mother committed suicide by drowning when he was eight years old. He enlisted in the U.S. Army in 1959, at the age of eighteen. His father, an itinerant pipeline worker with whom Boyd traveled until he joined the army, and whom he never saw again after that time, once commented that his son had never told the truth in his life.

Boyd Douglas had already stolen money while still in his teens; his first serious conviction occurred while he was stationed in Korea. Charged with committing larceny in Hong Kong, he was sent to the Presidio Stockade in California for inquiry, and escaped six days later. Within the following two years he escaped from another military stockade, was charged with being AWOL, defrauded hotels, and, under a variety of aliases, passed sixty thousand dollars' worth of bad checks before skipping to the Acapulco Hilton, where he was caught in 1962. Throughout the sixties Douglas impersonated others and lived out numerous dreams of power. He posed as an army officer. He used forged checks and stolen money to go bear hunting in the Northwest, to charter private planes to fly from Mexico to Canada, to live it up at hotels in Acapulco, Reno, the Caribbean islands, and Miami. In the space of eight years he lived his brief periods of freedom under sixteen different aliases, including William Cook, Meredith Dickinson, Bob C. Hill, Jr., David Summerfield, Donald Rogers, Dr. James Link Shipley.

Having received an unsuitable discharge from the army, Douglas first arrived at the federal penitentiary at Lewisburg, Pennsylvania, in 1963. While in Lewisburg he volunteered as guinea pig for a National Institutes of Health experiment to study genetic properties of human proteins, which called for several injections of emulsions into his muscles. His reactions were severe, and he was left with long deep scars on his legs and arms. Having sued the government for two million dollars in damages, he absconded from the institute illegally a few months before he could have had his freedom. He was again arrested for interstate transportation of some twenty thousand dollars' worth of forged checks in two states and for pulling a Beretta gun on the FBI agent who apprehended him in Milwaukee.

Douglas received sentences of five years, to run concurrently, on each of three charges. After another attempted escape from the Federal Reformatory in Reno, Nevada, he returned to Lewisburg Federal Penitentiary—known as the Wall—in 1968.

The career of this shrewd, handsome swindler who had spent the sixties shuttling between the American Dream places and prison is a curious mixture of successes and defeats. It seemed easy for Douglas to persuade hotel cashiers or bank clerks that he was a rich playboy, but impossible for him to continue to play the role convincingly for more than a few months. Always living in the fantasy of a still future role, Douglas would overstep his bounds, become too greedy, get arrested and unmasked. One could see Boyd Douglas as a man driven by fantasies of power and self-indulgence which had been tragically lacking in his lonely, motherless childhood; also as someone who perpetually needs to return to jail as if prison offers him the only protection he knows, the sheltering security he never experienced as a child.

But in 1970 Boyd Douglas's life underwent a mysterious change: the prison system suddenly began to offer him extraordinary privileges. The previous fall, while still in medium security at Lewisburg, he had applied for the student release program at Bucknell University, a small liberal arts college by the bank of the Susquehanna River, two miles from the prison. He was admitted there as a "special student." The freedom offered him was totally bizarre for a man with his criminal record: he was allowed out of prison six days a week from 7:00 A.M. to 6:00 P.M., and often given dispensation to stay at the college until later hours. He was even allowed to rent an apartment off campus for which he paid with money earned from his suit against the National Institutes of Health.

Immediately upon his arrival at Bucknell, three months before Philip Berrigan started serving his prison term at Lewisburg, Douglas went out of his way to frequent antiwar students and teachers. In his métier of impostor, Douglas had always been most skillful at the first stages of conning—charming and seducing his victims. Introducing himself to Philip Berrigan after chapel the first Sunday after the priest's arrival at Lewisburg Prison, Douglas posed as a fervent new convert to the Peace Movement. And he became the courier for the unauthorized and incautious correspondence between Elizabeth McAlister and Philip Berrigan within a week of the priest's arrival at prison. Berrigan had been placed in maximum security, and denied the right to any correspondence beyond his immediate family. Boyd Douglas, who bicycled between prison and campus, carried the letters out in his college notebook, had them copied by two of his Bucknell girlfriends, and made photocopies which he later gave to the FBI.

"Quite a witness you have there," someone said to Prosecuting Attorney Lynch at a court recess during Boyd Douglas's testimony. "We didn't choose him," the prosecutor snapped. He pointed to the defendants. "They did."

The government at the Harrisburg trial, and Boyd Douglas himself, argued that he had befriended antiwar persons at Bucknell because he wanted "freedom of movement." He pleaded that he had copied the Berrigan-McAlister letters for a while out of patriotic duty, because he was alarmed by their implications, with the eventual prospect of turning them over to the FBI when there was enough evidence; and that he was forced to turn informer to avoid prosecution for contraband, after one of the letters he had smuggled was found inside a copy of *Time* magazine during a routine shakedown of Philip Berrigan's cell.

I believe that the government's story was a total lie, that Boyd Douglas was a plant from many months back: not necessarily a plant to keep watch on the Berrigans, but to infiltrate the general campus and prison complex in a small university town with a small but fairly vigorous antiwar community. There are simply too many unanswered questions, which would remain all the more obscure because of the defense's decision not to call any witnesses.

How could a high-school dropout with a criminal record of violence and three evasions, who was serving *three* concurrent sentences for forgery and armed assault, and who had not been released from maximum to medium security until the spring of 1969, be the *only* one of Lewisburg's fourteen hundred inmates admitted to the student release program that same year? (The only prisoners admitted to the program in preceding years were two disbarred lawyers in minimum security.)

Without an intimate connection with FBI and prison authorities, how could Douglas get access as he did to highly classified

prison records, such as the special processing orders for Philip and
Daniel Berrigan?

One of the most likely explanations is that the government
offered Douglas the privileges of being an informer in order to
silence his suit against the National Institutes of Health, which had
ended in a $15,000 settlement too measly for Douglas. (The de-
fense would suggest in court that he had scratched his scars to ini-
tiate the suit.)

In the first political impersonation of his life—that of the convict eager to work in the antiwar movement—Douglas was quickly
and remarkably successful in making his way into the Berrigan
milieu. Within a week of the priest's arrival at Lewisburg on April
20, 1970, he had not only talked with Berrigan but had become a
trusted member of Berrigan's inner circle. Meeting daily with Berrigan in prison, Douglas also met at Bucknell with Elizabeth Mc-
Alister, Neil McLaughlin, Anthony and Mary Scoblick—all of whom
visited the campus from time to time. He talked even more frequently with Joseph Wenderoth, who had decided to serve as liaison between the Bucknell community and the Catholic Left at
large. Wenderoth made the hour and a half drive from his Baltimore parish to Lewisburg every fortnight or so during that spring
and summer to meet with Douglas, and evolved what he thought
was a deep friendship with the convict.

The cunning of government and of informer were aided by
a historical coincidence: Boyd Douglas had infiltrated the Catholic Left at its moment of greatest disarray, and was able to exploit
its turmoil. In May and June 1970, after the invasion of Cambodia
and the Kent State killings, the Peace Movement in general was in
a mood of desperation. The Catholic Left in particular had been
anguished when one Berrigan went underground and the other was
finally imprisoned, held incommunicado in a maximum security
cell. It is in this setting of great confusion that Boyd Douglas, only
months after he arrived at Bucknell, was able to participate in the
rambling colloquies that Philip Berrigan and his friends had held
about bizarre new methods of action; he was even able to instigate
many such conversations. Amiably meddlesome, perpetually offering his services, constantly producing more than he was asked for, a

true Movement busybody, Douglas became a desperately needed link between the imprisoned Philip Berrigan and his friends. Inside the Wall, this convict who bicycled out of jail every morning seems to have become the priest's alter ego, a substitute for his lost freedom.

However tortured the year 1970 may have been for the Berrigans' friends and the Catholic Left, it was the cushiest year of Boyd Douglas's life. After a decade of impersonating at great risk, he could, for the first time, impersonate with no risk at all under the government's protection, and even be paid for it. Besides, Douglas must have liked the campus's Movement life, with its easy access to pot, liquor, and women—three important ingredients in his periods of freedom.

In Bucknell's small antiwar community Douglas, a quiet, mild-mannered though occasionally moody man who always wore dark glasses, shrewdly used his girls to build himself up as a Movement hero. He told them that he was serving a sentence for conspiring to blow up an army convoy in the California desert, and that he had been given away by a girlfriend turned informer. He explained that he had received his scars in a jeep in Vietnam from an explosion which had killed his best buddy. He gave one of his girls Willard Gaylin's book *In the Service of Their Country*, and told her that part of it was about him. ("I felt that this was a good thing to tell the Movement," he would testify in court, "that I was involved in political crime rather than in criminal crime.") His political lies were mixed with many others. He had been a football hero at Ohio State, he had cancer and six months to live and wished his sweetheart to marry him and give him six months of happiness.

Living an 8:00 A.M. to 6:00 P.M. life at Bucknell, where he ate his meals at the Phi Lambda Theta fraternity, Douglas also became a big man on campus by talking profusely about his antiwar activism and his friendship with Philip Berrigan. He had taken easily to Movement sloganeering. He wrote a letter to a Rochester activist, in which he described himself as "a committed nonviolent revolutionary who believes in strategic sabotage" (signing the letter, "Take care—right on—peace—Boyd. P.S. Please destroy this"). In his notes to Movement persons he also copied slogans from Elizabeth McAlister and Philip Berrigan which he had acquired from studying their letters, such as the phrase "Z lives," inspired by the Costa-Gavras film. When asked in court what it stood for, he ventured: "Zorro."

Throughout the months of 1970 when he was informing on the Berrigan milieu, Boyd Douglas would report his findings to a trio of Lewisburg FBI agents headed by Delmar (Molly) Mayfield. Mayfield, a tall, mournful, beaten-faced man of thirty-seven who looked fifty, was Boyd's "handling agent." Boyd and Molly—who referred to FBI headquarters as "SOG" ("seat of government")— were each other's meal ticket. Boyd would pressure Molly to get him as much money as possible from the FBI headquarters (the funds were paid for "information on crimes against the United States"). Molly would pass on Boyd's requests. The FBI would then wheedle them down by a large percent, as in its payment for the disclosure of the Rochester draft board action, for which Boyd had asked two thousand dollars and received fifteen hundred. In this sleazy market where they bargained over the price of others' freedom, Boyd knew that he was getting the raw deal, and kept a few cards hidden up his sleeve. In October 1970, Boyd wrote Molly a letter asking for fifty thousand dollars tax free and an honorable discharge from the army in exchange for his services.

The government's niggardliness in this sordid bartering was amazing. This came out most clearly when court testimony revealed that Boyd Douglas had been awarded only two hundred dollars for enabling the FBI to capture Daniel Berrigan through a hint dropped in one of Elizabeth McAlister's apprehended letters. A paltry pittance, since the capture of Daniel Berrigan had been the principal target of the FBI's surveillance system at Lewisburg throughout the spring and summer of 1970 and since all information compiled by Douglas had been placed in a Daniel Berrigan file at FBI headquarters.

"This is the first time officially I had any knowledge that I led to his capture," Douglas announced on the witness stand when he learned of this fact. And his voice had that ambivalence of pride and petulance which seemed characteristic of him, the fantasy of self-importance mingled with anger toward the authorities who had duped him once again. For one of the most interesting and least revealed stories of the Harrisburg case is the way the government and Boyd Douglas deceived each other.

To what extent was the government aware that Boyd Douglas was not only an informer but a provocateur? This remains another one of the mysteries of the Harrisburg trial. Molly Mayfield mournfully claimed under oath that the FBI did not know the following facts:

Boyd offered a gun to Elizabeth McAlister when he heard of the alleged kidnapping project.

In an attempt to resurrect his Catholic friends' dormant or rejected plans, Boyd initiated most of the telephone conversations he had with the defendants from the Lewisburg Laundromat where he conducted much of his business.

He wrote a Bucknell professor a letter suggesting that he stage a destruction of Bucknell's ROTC building, and verbally incited many other members of the Bucknell community to civil disobedience. The defense implied in cross-examination that Boyd had even suggested to a Bucknell coed that she blow up the state capitol in Harrisburg, Pennsylvania.

Boyd's most serious act as a provocateur was handing two ROTC manuals on explosives to Joseph Wenderoth, whose few fingerprints on these volumes became the principal material evidence for the alleged tunnel plot. In accordance with Douglas's wish to pose to the Berrigan milieu as an expert on explosives, Molly Mayfield had nonchalantly acquired the manuals for the informer from the Bucknell ROTC office, an interesting instance of the government's many uses of university facilities. According to Molly, Douglas did not confess this act to the FBI until 1971, when in preparation for the indictment, Molly and Boyd talked for five weeks in Phoenix, Arizona, to "straighten out discrepancies" in Boyd's testimony.

The FBI's indifference, its lack of control over Douglas's acts, is appalling even if it had not been aware that he was also a provocateur. This use of a man with a pathological record of lying and violence let loose upon a sheltered campus, offering guns, explosives manuals, and advice for the destruction of buildings to students, teachers, and visiting priests continues to strike me as one of the shoddiest chapters to date in the annals of government infiltration.

As for Boyd's conduct, a remark of his quoted by the defense at the trial, that he "wanted to get even with the United States," is one of the clearest windows into his soul. For as his record of the decade shows, he was a man who needed to beat the system every minute of the day, and in the most menial of ways. According to one of the Lewisburg residents who saw him frequently at Bucknell, he poured himself a tumbler of neat Scotch every day a few hours before returning to the Wall, a flagrant violation of prisoners' student release privileges. "You're mad," she once said, "they'll smell it on your breath." "Never mind," Boyd replied, "I chew Sen-Sen."

Boyd Douglas disappeared from Bucknell overnight in early January of 1971, a week before the Justice Department brought down its indictment of the Harrisburg Seven. Upon leaving Lewisburg and the college, he bought a four-thousand-dollar light blue Javelin motorcar, and was carried out blind drunk from the "coming-out party" he had given himself at the apartment of a Bucknell librarian. A few days after the party he went to Washington, D.C., to attend a demonstration at the Justice Department protesting Hoover's charges against the Berrigans—charges overwhelmingly based on his own work. Shortly after that event, unbeknown to his acquaintances, he entered FBI custody and began to testify before the Harrisburg grand jury.

Four weeks later—after a brief FBI-managed stay in Omaha, where he was discovered by the press—Boyd Douglas was married and living in Phoenix, Arizona, where the FBI had provided him with a job at Motorola and a Master Charge credit card. Joseph Wenderoth, who knew Boyd as intimately as any of the defendants, believes that the FBI had arranged the marriage to improve his image. Boyd's new alias was Robert Dunne, and he had grown a mustache. The FBI took him next to Des Moines, where it got him a job as a men's wear salesman in a department store. In December 1971 the government started paying him a witness fee of thirty-six dollars a day in preparation for the trial. In his new role, that of government witness, Boyd Douglas seemed to enjoy impersonating the conservative, law-and-order young American for the benefit of the stolid Harrisburg jury. "What do you mean by the Movement?" he was once asked in court. "Panthers, SDS, . . . all the nuts in this country," he answered.

In his opening statement, Prosecuting Attorney William Lynch argued, with gestures curiously reminiscent of a priest at the pulpit—his hands first clasped, then opened out in *orate Fratres* gestures—that there was a "unitarian" character to the three objects of his indictment's first count. The old draft board raids, he claimed, were "training grounds" for the escalation of tactics to the tunnel and kidnapping plots. He then brought witnesses to testify that the draft board raids had indeed existed, that the Berrigan-McAlister correspondence had in fact been apprehended at Lewisburg, and other witnesses who testified that they remembered hearing Joseph Wenderoth discuss something about tunnels.

William Lynch struck me throughout as a remarkably skillful technician stuck with an obvious lack of hard-core evidence. His principal technique in the trial—one that could have been brilliantly effective if Douglas had been more believable—was to try to back up the Berrigan-McAllister letters with Boyd's testimony. Lynch would read the letters in a clear, flat monotone, during which time Philip and Elizabeth would look glumly at the floor. Then Douglas, in an equally flat, bored voice, would elaborate on the conversations and activities of the Catholic Left that had been mentioned in the letters. Having met with Lynch for some thirty hours previous to the trial, he would deliver in direct examination long, extraordinarily glib and detailed answers, such as the following testimony concerning the alleged tunnel plot:

> I asked Joseph Wenderoth if he knew the number of the generator plants in the tunnels. He told me he did not know, but that he thought there were between three and five. I asked Joseph Wenderoth about the entrances to the tunnel system. He told me that there was no problem in going into the tunnel during the daytime. I told Joseph Wenderoth that if it was all right, that we would use primer cord. . . . I asked Joseph Wenderoth whether ten feet wide and eight feet tall was the

correct dimension of the tunnel. Joseph Wenderoth told me that he had no problem in walking down in the tunnel, or walking around in the tunnel.

If the defense had decided to present a case, and Joseph Wenderoth had taken the stand, this admirable young priest told me that his testimony in rebuttal would have been somewhat as follows: "Boyd would return and return to the tunnel theme we had discussed and scrapped by midsummer. I'd tell him, 'We've scrapped the idea, Boyd, forget about it.' But there was no telling Boyd no. He'd bring it up again and again and after months of persistence when we finally got it into his head that it was scrapped, he said, 'I'll do it myself.'"

In cross-examination Douglas's style was vastly different. He was questioned, in turn, by defense lawyers Ramsey Clark, Terry Lenzner, Thomas Menaker, William Cunningham, S.J., Paul O'Dwyer, and Leonard Boudin. He would cock his head toward the ceiling, and offer interminable pauses before answering—understandably, for he often contradicted himself. Douglas had told the grand jury that he himself offered to carry letters from Berrigan out of the penitentiary; he told the court that it had been Berrigan's idea. One day he testified that he had expressed approval for Philip Berrigan's antiwar position and his philosophy of draft board raids upon first meeting him. A few days later he vehemently denied he had ever talked to the priest about the war in the first month of their acquaintanceship, and said that although they met daily, they mostly "played handball and went to movies." He remained cool when faced with his contradictions. "There's a lot of testimony I'm giving in this courtroom," he once explained, "that refreshed my memory when I testify."

After almost two weeks of cross-examination by some of the country's most gifted lawyers Douglas grew impertinent and restless, but remained as controlled as ever. One was dazzled by his resilience. I understood at the end of the trial why some former Lewisburg convicts have admired him as a cool, accomplished artist. A man, they added, who could no longer remain alive for one hour in any of the nation's jails.

III

How did Philip Berrigan, Elizabeth McAlister, and other learned, intelligent persons like Fathers Joseph Wenderoth and Neil McLaughlin, Mary and Anthony Scoblick, and many others outside Lewisburg come to trust Boyd Douglas so blindly? Was this trust a phenomenon of the 1960s, rising from that sympathy for the dispossessed that has marked the conscience of American liberals since the nascence of the civil rights movement?

The compassion of liberals for the oppressed, like other emotions that flow out of guilt, can easily degenerate into sentimentalism. In the past decades, with a denial of free will that is ironically Calvinistic, Catholic leftists as well as others have tended to see all criminals as helpless victims whose actions are irreversibly conditioned by the nature of the American environment, and therefore beyond moral judgment. The apotheosis of the dispossessed that characterized the 1960s—and the concurrent fatalism that puts all blame on the society—has taken a particularly irrational turn when prisoners are in question. One hears the slogan "all prisoners are political prisoners," accompanied by the axiom that Charles Manson, Sirhan B. Sirhan, Lee Harvey Oswald or Jack Henry Abbott have the same moral and political status as Philip Berrigan because they are equally "oppressed."

This peculiarly American state of mind helps to explain why a student-convict like Boyd Douglas, a prisoner given a suspicious degree of freedom, a man recollected as having no particular intelligence or wit, and frequently compared to "an Appalachian trying to be hip," could have been taken into confidence by a motley group of students, professors, activists, and priests. To them Douglas readily impersonated the fervent Movement convert with the same panache with which he had previously conned and defrauded authorities in Reno, Acapulco, and Miami's Fontainebleau Hotel.

Planting its informer among radical activists and tenderhearted liberals who tended to commiserate with all convicts, the government, in effect, proffered to Boyd Douglas an unlimited bank account of compassion to draw upon. "I distrusted Boyd Douglas from the first," a Bucknell faculty wife said, "but I checked myself and said to myself, 'Don't do the elitist bit, you're being like the white police.' " "As soon as I distrusted him," said a librarian at Bucknell, "I felt like a Hoover, paranoid." "It was more sympathy than attraction," admitted a coed who was Boyd's girl for six months, and who received peace symbol earrings from him as a 1970 Christmas present. "I figured that all prisoners are political prisoners." Elizabeth McAlister also admitted that she had feared Boyd Douglas from the start: "He was always too much there, his English was so atrocious; but I repressed my instincts because I was afraid I was being bourgeois and elitist."

One of the most moving accounts of trusting Boyd Douglas was given by the plucky Bucknell librarian, who chose to go to jail rather than testify as a government witness in a trial she called "a black charade." "Whenever I had misgivings about Boyd I'd say to myself, 'He's a prisoner, he's powerless, his dignity is constantly being undermined . . . he must be given maximum attention,' and I'd say to myself, 'Don't be a lousy stinking doubter.' " The last time she saw Douglas was in early January of 1971, a week before the first indictment was issued, the evening before he disappeared from Bucknell to testify against his friends and enter the FBI's long custody. Douglas came to call on her with no apparent motive. And on the eve of his disappearance, for the first time in the year they had known each other, Boyd Douglas gave the Bucknell librarian a kiss.

The problem of Philip Berrigan's trust is more complex. His perceptions seemed distorted by the fantasies of freedom and of unimpaired power common to many political prisoners. His belief in Douglas was further compounded by a utopian mystique of trust and openness central to most forms of pacifism. He refused the offers of highly skilled convicts to carry mail for him, because they were "organized," or rich. He instinctively gravitated to the orphaned Boyd Douglas because he saw him as a quintessential victim of the American government. "You asked for a few words about our friend Douglas," Philip Berrigan wrote. "We now know him as a vastly complex and resourceful con man, with deep neuroticism, to be sure, but nonetheless one who had made a life-style of beating the system."

Even after Douglas's damning trial testimony, Philip would retain the belief that he had never been duped by the informer. He maintained that Boyd Douglas had been undergoing a genuine process of transformation during their early friendship, which was violently interrupted by the FBI and the prison authorities when they forced him to turn informer. He was not the only defendant whose attitude toward Douglas was shaped by a religious belief in the transforming power of trust. Anthony Scoblick said he distrusted and avoided Douglas because he talked of violence, but then added, with total earnestness, "But perhaps by trusting an informer enough you might convert him."

Of all the defendants, Joseph Wenderoth had been the one closest to Boyd, closer even than Philip Berrigan, whose mind remained obsessed by the politics outside the Wall. Boyd, who was a Roman Catholic, had shrewdly exploited Joe's priestliness, often coming to him to confess his private problems and using this counseling relationship as a means of inciting the priest to violence. The most selfless love offered to Boyd had been rewarded with the greatest vindictiveness. Boyd then went to the witness stand to implicate Joseph Wenderoth more vengefully than any other defendant, even constantly mispronouncing his name as "Wendorf" or "Wendrod." Yet even after Douglas's testimony, Joe seemed interested only in Boyd's future. This scrubbed, shining-faced priest who knelt down by his bed every night to pray for William Lynch and his other prosecutors could only talk about the possibilities of Boyd's rehabilitation, how it would be too late if Boyd didn't meet the right person within the next years. "You mean you're only concerned with his salvation?" I once asked him: "What else is there on earth?" the priest said.

It is in this context of trust, conversion, and swift transformation that one must see the imprudences that led to the defendants' indictment. For these Catholics' radical fantasies and radical rhetoric—which are so recklessly and profusely verbalized—were admixed with a profoundly liberal view of the American system. They accuse the government of being fascist, while behaving as if it were permissive enough to acquit them of civil disobedience. ("Civil disobedience," a young priest once told me, "should be like breathing in and breathing out.") In the turmoil of their sudden turning

away from the Church's traditional structures, they seemed strikingly like adolescents—deeply dependent on their parents yet constantly critical of them. It is, in part, their ambivalent attitude
toward authority, openness, and secrecy (well exemplified by Daniel
Berrigan's flirtatious hiding) that led to the guileless indiscretions
of the correspondence between Elizabeth McAlister and Philip Berrigan.

The letters are curious literary documents. Philip's prose al-
ternates between fine Victorian constraint, the street slang of
the ghetto priest, and an adolescent populism that is reminiscent
of Holden Caulfield. Traditional expressions of devoutness—"In
Him," "The Lord's Peace"—are laced with gangland code words
given to friends and places: "Little Shane" for Neil McLaughlin,
"Big Joe German" for Joseph Wenderoth, "bruv" for Daniel Berrigan, "Minnesota Fats" for still another activist, "Golden Fleece"
for Washington, D.C.

An eighteenth-century touch is further added by the letters'
mysterious titles, which had been shrewdly suggested by Boyd
Douglas, who carried the letters in and out of jail in his school
notebook. These academic titles were intended to convince any
prison guard who might glance at the convict's notebook that they
were the themes of Boyd's college essays: "Some Reflections on
the Presence of Political Prisoners," "On the Elimination of Smog
from the Industrial Environment." (One of them is also titled
"One Flew Over the Cuckoo's Nest," after Ken Kesey's book,
which the fastidious William Lynch is said to have read meticu-
lously, and with some distaste, in a vain attempt to glean some clue
that would lead to new evidence.)

Elizabeth's and Philip's letters were written in strikingly similar hands, tight, cramped, monastic calligraphies with flourished
capitals. The repressed emotions they conveyed reminded me of
troubadour verse, of literature inspired by the hopeless unavail-
ability of the person loved. The reality of the separating wall was
constantly present. (Having first posed as Philip's cousin to visit
him, Elizabeth had been struck off his visitors' list four weeks after
he had arrived at Lewisburg, when one of their clandestine letters
was discovered in his cell.)

The letters are full of diatribes against liberals, and occasionally indicate an interesting rift between Philip and his brother Daniel, whose security measures while underground Philip found too restrictive and liberal in character. "Can't fully understand the reference to bruv [Daniel] and the irrational security surrounding him . . . but it strikes me that the overcaution might stem from inexperienced people . . . who have never done anything for principle before. . . ."

Elizabeth McAlister, throughout the summer of 1970, was occupied with the planning of the Delaware draft board action. Notwithstanding its initial complications (one of the participants insisted on bringing along his mother, his girlfriend, his boyfriend, and his dog), it was one of the most effective sorties to date, destroying every draft board in the state except the one in Wilmington, which was heavily guarded. Elizabeth McAlister was one of the principal choreographers of the raid, and some of the most telling passages in Philip's letters express his admiration for her work.

"I hear you practically killed yourself during the circus, and that you were about 50 percent of every act. I said upon hearing it—nacherly! But why not get away for a couple of days sleep and some fresh air and decent chow. . . . Sweet Jesus Lord! Magnificent show—more hectic and demanding than anything yet accomplished . . . kudos to every one. I'm speechless! And especially to you, because I honestly think it would have broken up without you! No substitute for class, friend—brains, guts, discipline, all the badges of quality. . . . The Lord thanks you, so does mankind, so does America, so do I."

Philip Berrigan was asked during the Harrisburg trial what he found to be the worst temptation of prison life. He tersely answered: "Self-pity." His letters to Elizabeth express the same fortitude. If anything, they express his gnawing guilt that he is in a privileged and sheltered position, while those on the outside are taking all the risk: "All of you, yourself esp., should grow in caution, even as your urgency grows. Imagine what it would mean if you were hurt, killed or unnecessarily arrested. What a contrast to this where I'm protected against those who would like to see us all buried. So the first protection is a resolute reliance on the Lord, and the second, a fine intelligent caution. So take care, huh Irish? Love and peace."

He takes great pride, as he always has, in being a prisoner. "I wouldn't have it different for all our overseas investments—in fact, the thought horrifies me, for if it were so, this present vegetable would be much less a man. The great adventure would be missing, and an incomparably precious possession lost. So I'll take my little cup of gall every day, and thank God for it. What I've already had is sufficient to enrich a dozen better lives, and it ain't ended yet. So does the Lord pay up for tiny acts of service."

Elizabeth McAlister is a complex woman, as deeply secretive by nature as she is indiscreet on occasion. It was incredible to learn that none of the defendants knew of her correspondence with Philip Berrigan—the major material evidence of the Harrisburg trial—until several weeks after the indictment, eight months after the correspondence had occurred. The letters, and the use of Douglas as courier, were the plot within the plot of the Harrisburg case. The nun's and priest's need to be secretive about their communications may be a mark of their conventionalism, part of their attempt to reconcile their growing affection to the very rigorous attitude they had held toward their religious vows. This tension of secrecy may also be responsible for the vast distortions and overstatements contained in Elizabeth's letters. Their exaggerations seem motivated by her need to buttress Philip's sense of retaining power in the Movement, and to reassure him about the Movement's vigor at a time when it was actually in failing health.

Elizabeth's most flagrant and incriminating exaggeration, of course, was her description of a colloquy concerning the possibility of making a citizen's arrest of Henry Kissinger. This bizarre conversation seems to have been hatched in the Third World fantasies of the radical Pakistani scholar Eqbal Ahmad. But, according to Ahmad, it was "one of a dozen alternatives discussed and rejected during the course of a long evening, a preposterous idea which would have been totally counterproductive because it had no political context in American history."

The discussion was held during a long session of wining and dining in Westport, Connecticut, in mid-August, a few days after

Daniel Berrigan's arrest by the FBI, and must be seen against the background of renewed passion and anguish caused by the capture of the priest, who had been Ahmad's closest friend at Cornell. Writing to Philip the next day in this aura of urgency and grief, and needing somehow to assure him that novel tactics of escalation were being aired, Elizabeth put a magnifying glass on a twenty-minute discussion of a citizen's arrest. She devoted an entire letter to this grotesque colloquy, which was to lead to the most sensational charge of the Harrisburg indictment.

In her mention of the idea of kidnapping Kissinger, as in the rest of her letters, Elizabeth's style is musing, as if she were talking out loud. In this case already gorged with fantasies, her letters feed on still another fantasy: She is pretending not to write, she believes she is talking to him, she does not face the reality of the letter as a physical document.

She signs some of her letters, as he does, "In His love." Another time, she commemorates the day of their first meeting: "Hey, buddy, the 15th is coming fast. First met a real great guy on August 15th."

William Lynch read some forty-five pages of the letters in such a flat, dreary monotone that some jurors slept through many passages, waking up to hear Boyd Douglas's cool interspersed testimony. But when Lynch came to the following letter his voice became in turn modulated, dramatic, booming. Everyone sat up and listened. It was like a parish priest reading the Epistle after having finished his financial report:

From Elizabeth McAlister: ". . . Which leads me to No. 3 and this is in utter confidence and should not be committed to paper and I would want you not even to say a word of it to Dan until we have a fuller grasp of it . . . Eq called up to Conn. last night . . . Eq outlined a plan for action which would say—escalated seriousness—and we discussed the pros and cons for several hours. It needs much more thought and careful selection of personnel. To kidnap—in our terminology make a citizen's arrest—someone like Henry Kissinger. . . ."

In the same hortatory voice, Lynch read Philip's reply:

"About the plan—the first time opens the door to murder—the

Tupamaros are finding that out in Uruguay. . . . When I refer to murder it is not to prohibit it absolutely (violence versus nonviolence bag) it is merely to observe that one has set the precedent, and that later on, when gov't resistance to this sort of thing stiffens, men will be killed. More to the point, the project as you outlined it is brilliant, but grandiose. . . ."

"The first motto you are taught when you join a guerrilla cadre in Algeria," Eqbal Ahmad laconically commented about the Berrigan-McAlister letters, "is the following: 'When you are in prison, do not ask for more than oranges.' For every guerrilla knows that no system of unauthorized prison communication is safe. You are at the mercy of blackmail. You are like a Moslem wife caught in bed with another man."

"It takes much revolutionary discipline," Eqbal added with a polite ironical smile, "to resist the temptation of asking for more than oranges. "

IV

Government prosecutor William Lynch had been looking forward with trepidation to cross-examining the defendants. He once described Philip Berrigan and Elizabeth McAlister as people who were "constitutionally incapable of not taking the stand." "You just wait until Liz and Phil take the stand!" he muttered, off the cuff, to a reporter he had met in a Harrisburg diner.

But in the sixth week of the trial Ramsey Clark, starting with the words "These defendants will always seek peace," rose to announce that the defense would rest without calling any witnesses. Lynch jumped to his feet, arms flailing in James Cagney style, to make an objection to what he thought was going to be a political statement. "Your Honor, the defense rests," Clark repeated quietly. Lynch fell back into his seat with an air of amazement.

The defense's astonishing announcement to rest the case without further testimony, without calling one defendant to the witness stand, was a highly unusual legal maneuver which, according to the lawyers, has no precedent in political cases. The main purpose of resting the defense was to stress the preposterous, phantasmagoric nature of the government's charges. Ramsey Clark's soft voice carried, calmly and dramatically, the message of "not guilty." For unlike the Catonsville Nine, the Harrisburg Seven were not concerned with symbols, but with acquittal. There were many concrete legal motives for resting their case—a decision arrived at only in the last four days of the government's prosecution. The defense sensed that it was at the peak of its strength after the government presented its last witness. This flimsy case forced upon the Justice Department by the vindictive fantasies of the late J. Edgar Hoover was extraordinarily lacking in evidence. It had already been greatly weakened when over twenty antiwar activists—whose information the government relied upon to build its case—had followed the courageous example of Sister Jogues Egan, Elizabeth McAlister's superior, and refused to testify to the grand jury.

The only hard-core evidence of the ephemeral kidnapping charge, a tape on which the informer Boyd Douglas identified Eqbal Ahmad's voice, had been disqualified by the court. As for Boyd Douglas, the defense lawyers felt that their powerful cross-examination of the informer had destroyed his credibility, and they wished to leave their demolition work freshly imprinted on the jury's mind.

V

During the summations a curiously sexual struggle emerged between the government and the defense over the person of Boyd Douglas. The defense contended that the informer was "a streetwise and accomplished con man" who had duped innocent persons long isolated in religious institutions. The government rebutted that Douglas was an innocent orphan who had been led astray by men and women blessed with the opportunities of high education. It was like a rape case. How aggressive was the seducer, how willing was the seduced? It is ironic that the conservative Justice Department lawyers assume the same fatalistic view of Douglas as was held by many extreme radicals: that he was a helpless victim of American society.

Hovering over the trial, throughout, was the lanky, contrite figure of former Attorney General Ramsey Clark. Hawk-nosed, sad-eyed, laconic, dressed in extremely ill-fitting, rumpled suits, the former attorney general remained the most reserved of the defense counsels. One would have expected that this gangling Middle American, with his southwestern twang and his winsome Jimmy Stewart manner, with his great aura of authority, had been made to order for the stolid middle western jury. But Clark, by choice, made few objections during the trial and conducted low-keyed and extremely brief cross-examinations. He shied from all conversations, seldom mingled, as did the other defense counsels, with the crowds in the corridors of the Harrisburg courthouse. His closest relationship seemed to be with Philip Berrigan, with whom he managed to have a private visit every day, frequently sharing a liturgy with the priest in jail. The few comments one could wrench out of Clark were in a terse ranch-hand style. ("I don't know if the skunk is pissing," he once drawled when asked if his phone was tapped, "but it's awful wet around my telephone.")

Yet Clark's opening statement and his summation were the most dramatic moments of the trial. As if waking from a deep sleep, he delivered jingoistic but curiously moving speeches that were in the finest tradition of Fourth of July rhetoric, full of "truth," "love," "justice," "the individuality we so cherish in America." He ended his summation with these words: "These defendants say, 'We are not afraid of peace and freedom.' "

Many months before the trial began, when the defendants were beginning to select lawyers, they had to decide whether Ramsey Clark should be asked to be a defense counsel. The final word came from Philip Berrigan. He thought for a moment and then gravely answered, "Yes, let's have Clark. It would be so good for him."

VI

The Harrisburg jury voted 10–2 for acquittal on all charges except those of contraband against Elizabeth McAlister and Philip Berrigan. Their deliberation lasted seven days, and is said to be the longest deliberation in the history of federal trials. The govern-

ment's choice of Harrisburg—a notoriously conservative town sheltered and removed from twentieth-century events—had been regarded as one of the most punitive aspects of the Harrisburg
indictment. Yet perhaps it was the Harrisburg jurors' almost total
isolation from the protests and turmoil of the 1960s, the fact that
they had never witnessed a picket line or a demonstration, that left
them free of prejudices against antiwar dissenters, free to pierce
through to the truth with the blunt clarity of their consciences.

Lawrence Evans, owner of several large supermarkets, the most
prosperous member of the jury, was the only male juror who voted
for conviction. He was described as a blindly obedient servant of
the state who believed that "if the government has spent all this
money on the case there must be truth to its charges." He was also
described by one of his fellow jurors as "an unbalanced man who
wanted conviction on all counts from the moment deliberation
began, before we had even opened the evidence box." From the
beginning, Evans had shrewdly perceived the malleability of the
only woman to vote for conviction, a Mrs. Schwartz. He sat next
to her daily in the jury box and throughout every meal the twelve
citizens shared during the two months of the trial. If it were not
for Evans the defendants might have had the triumph of total
acquittal on the conspiracy charges.

With the exception of Mrs. Schwartz the women of the jury
were strongly in favor of acquittal because the government witness
Boyd Douglas had lied to his girlfriends and treated them so
badly—they could not, on those grounds, believe his testimony.

The jury's 10–2 vote for acquittal seemed to reflect the reasoning behind Leonard Boudin's brilliant three-hour summation on
conspiracy law. He argued that to be convicted the defendants must
be proved to have made a clear-cut decision to carry out an illegal
objective. Thus even if Joseph Wenderoth had crawled through the
heating tunnels of the Federal Building, such an action was in the
realm of "investigation, not even preparation"; it was not the firm
commitment that constitutes a criminal conspiracy. Boudin ended
with this plea to the jurors: They must bear in mind the crucial difference between expressions of hope—or what Philip Berrigan had
termed "meandering or desultory suggestions"—and concrete criminal plans. Leonard Boudin was the jurors' favorite lawyer. One of

the twelve, an instructor at a state school for fire fighters, said of him: "He was a ham but he was fascinating. . . . I could listen to him go on forever."

The fire-fighting instructor, the jurors' most active in arguing for acquittal, was a round-faced, frequently smiling, benign man who seemed to be the most attentive of the twelve. In the voir dire, preceding the trial, upon being asked whether he had read of the alleged plot in the papers, he had slapped his thigh and said, "You mean that story about zipping off with Kissinger? I always thought that was a big joke." "I wouldn't mind trying it myself," he quipped after the end of the trial.

A few days before the verdict came in, I had a drink with Anthony Scoblick in a restaurant across from the courthouse. It was a little past six, the height of the dinner hour in Harrisburg, and the restaurant was packed.

"Hey, Tony, what are you going to do after you're acquitted?" I asked.

"I'm going to kidnap Henry Kissinger and blow up the heating tunnels!" he yelled out at the top of his voice.

Nobody even turned around.

Nixonland

UPON being asked by *The New York Review of Books* to cover the second inaugural of the thirty-seventh President of the United States, I sent the following report.

WHEN Richard Nixon walked onto the inaugural stand—it was the first time I had seen him in the flesh and I was only twenty yards away from him, in the second row of the press section—I began to weep. I don't know precisely why. Anger for the lives he had wasted? Fear of the enormity of his power? During my brief outburst a women's page reporter near me was talking into her tape recorder: "Pat in green coat with imperial Russian sable collar, Julie in apricot melton wool with sable collar, Mamie Eisenhower in crimson with matching hat, black gloves, no fur." Below the inaugural stand the U.S. Marine Band's mammoth silver-plated tubas brilliantly reflected the white, red, and gold costumes of the players. Members of the Marine Chorus stood farther down, their bodies pressed angularly against each other's, their young faces turned toward the audience with smiles of cherubic innocence, as in a high-school class picture. Above, in the Corinthian-columned portico erected for the inaugural, stood the President and, at his right, Pat, Mamie, Julie.

"Tricia Cox in pink tweed, blue fox collar and matching muff," the women's page reporter continued, "standing behind her sister and a marine banner."

I followed her observations and, as the wind lifted the purple and yellow tassels of the flag, I observed one of the most curious human beings I had ever seen. A creature so pink and white and vaporous, so serene of pose and tranquil of expression, her fixed smile so sweet and yet so abstract, her bundle of blond ringlets so immobile in the wind, that even metaphors about Meissen porcelain or plastic doll are too hard and real. Standing there in her very pale pink coat, her little hands stuffed into her large silvery muff, Tricia Nixon Cox seemed made of marzipan, her veins flowing with peach milk shake. She brought to mind George Eliot's cornflower-eyed Rosamond Vincy, "a lovely little face set on a fair long neck . . . turning about under the most perfect management of self-contented grace."

Yet Tricia lacked any of the reality of Eliot's heroine, for she seemed to belong to that realm of fantasy which does not allow for any pain or suffering, one in which society will be preserved in a state of impeccable prosperity and repose. And watching this inauguration I realized that Richard Nixon had few weapons more powerful in his arsenal than this rose-hued girl and the two other women at his side: that this pristine family was a central triad in that mythology of well-being which it had been Nixon's genius to create in the midst of national crises, and in the illusion of personal irreproachability which he fashioned through more than six crises of his own.

A mirage of the placid society emanated more powerfully from Tricia than from the other two. Julie's round, swift-eyed face is more mercurial. Pat Nixon's fixed features expressed some ecstasy of decorum rather than the solace of prosperity, and her mirthless smile, set in concrete, resembled not so much her daughter's docility as the grimace of a mortuary mask. Tricia, the most conservative member of the Nixon clan, the one said to resemble her father so strikingly in character, had greeted her parents, when they first came to the newlywed Coxes for dinner, with a table decorated with giant lollipops.

Trivial thoughts often come to mind when politicians mouth their platitudes: How do they make love, what do they drink, what cassettes do they listen to? Since the Nixons' aseptic sexlessness seemed part of their sedative effect upon the nation, I glossed swiftly over the first question. But even blander facts were increasingly unavailable, for rigorous privacy was essential to preserve the magic of Nixon's secret politics and surprise tactics, and his palace guard had grown increasingly guarded. ("Does the President wear reading glasses?" "Now and then, but don't quote *me*." "Does the President ever catnap?" "Yes, but *get it from somebody else*.") He had recently boasted, however, that he was the first president in our history who had never missed one day of work through illness, and that he had not even had one headache *in his life*. It had also been revealed that his weight has not changed in twenty years; that he had recently rendered his austere lunch of RyKrisp and cottage cheese even more Spartan by giving up ketchup; and that his sole sport, since he had given up bowling and golf, consisted of the solitary exercise of running two hundred paces in his bedroom in the same spot.

In his inaugural address, as he pronounced his solipsistic question, "What can you do for yourself?" I reflected upon the newly grandiose nature of his metaphors. He saw himself as having spent "those eight years in the wilderness, the way de Gaulle and Churchill were," before returning to power. In his growing isolation he was identifying himself increasingly with the State, through Walter Mitty metaphors of sports and leadership. "The team goes just as fast as the leader, as the quarterback, and coach, and I am both." "*L'Equipe, c'est Moi.*"

He ended his address, of course, by asking us for our prayers, rather than our ideas. As he exited after the benedictions, I saw only one mark of aging upon that changeless, perpetually suntanned sixty-year-old face: the deepening of the nose-to-cheek lines have emphasized those traits of self-denial and discipline that both shaped his ascent to power and enabled him, when young, to drive Pat home after her dates with other men. Self-denial. Is it possible that reality is one of the substances which this elusive man, curled over his sense of destiny, has been until now denying himself? That once the great triumph of his reelection was achieved he would open the door a crack? Trying to maintain certain Quaker princi-

ples, I don't want to believe in the irreversibility of evil, therefore
in the irreversibility of his monstrous isolation.

Later that day as he watched from a glass booth this most expensive of inauguration pageantries—part of his campaign to free
us from dread—he brusquely leaned forward, fascinated by a pa-
pier-mâché float of the Spirit of '76, and briefly pressed his strangely
shaped nose to the glass, looking upon the outside world as a penniless child looks into a pastry shop. The parade he was observing
was pigeon-proofed, Pennsylvania Avenue having been sprayed with
a special chemical for the occasion.

Among a choice of six sites, I picked the Middle Western
States Inaugural Ball at the Pension Building because Guy Lombardo was playing there. Like all the other balls it was an utterly
disorderly affair. Running the four-million-dollar inaugural "like a
corporate enterprise," Inaugural Committee Chairman and Hot
Shoppes tycoon J. Willard Marriott did not produce much joy;
nor did the daily visits of analysts from a management consultant
firm attempting to coordinate the work of four thousand inaugural
employees divided into thirty-four committees. Instead of dancing,
some five thousand persons stood about in disconsolate clusters
waiting for a room to pee in, to check their coats, get their free sou-
venirs (charms and cuff links emblazoned with the presidential
seal), to see the President arrive.

There was a surprisingly large number of black people, of young
people, of Democrats for Nixon, and droves of men who claimed
that they worked for "the biggest company" of this or that kind in
the United States. It was a hard-drinking crowd, who drowned
their gripes rather than expressed them; and the bars seemed to
have been set up accordingly, with drinks available only in coupon
sets of six for nine dollars. This was the first time in ten years that I
had been in a crowd of over a thousand people that was not a demonstration or a reform-Democrat fund-raising event, with everyone
wearing buttons. I recollected with nostalgia the slogans of an era
past: Republicans for McCarthy, Free the New York Times 21,
Stop the War on November 15, Vacuum Hoover, Free the Berrigans, Save Our Constitution. There was only one motto-wearer in
sight: a short-haired collegiate who wore on his lapel, as if in echo

of Nixon's inaugural address, the words POWER TO THE INDIVIDUAL.

Wayne and Jerry Martin of Bloomington, Illinois, had come to the inaugural with Bert and Katie Butler and their daughter, Bonnie. Old friends from neighboring towns, the Martins were Republicans, the Butlers lifelong Democrats until the 1972 elections. ("We want a negotiated peace, not a surrender, and McGovern was asking for a surrender.") They were fiftyish, effusive, offering to buy me drinks by the six-coupon set, and insisted that their names be printed.

"We've been to Europe an awful lot in the past few years," said Mrs. Martin, in brandy-hued Lurex, "and it's obvious that Americans are so hated over there because we've *given* them so much, too much. It's the same with welfare. When you give people too much they can't possibly respect you. I loved that part of the President's speech."

"Sure," Mr. Martin said. "If you're a man, you work."

"Of course FDR," former Democrat Mrs. Butler said, "I was a hundred percent behind his policies, his measures were needed because that was a time of crisis, but now we're living in such a stable, prosperous time."

"And what about China?" demanded Mr. Butler, a towering man who said he worked for the largest flat-rate construction industry in the world. "You've got to be a genius to pull that off the way Nixon did."

"Marvelous," said Mrs. Butler, rolling her eyes.

"Wizardly," said Mrs. Martin, holding her glass up in a toast.

"That's why I'm against those friends of mine who're still demonstrating," said Bonnie Butler, a graduate of the University of Illinois who verged on Movement style, no makeup, very long straight hair. "Back in sixty-eight, though I never demonstrated myself, I approved of those of my friends who did; but how can you do it now, Nixon has done too many good things."

"And here they are again demonstrating against the bombing when it brought the enemy back to the table," her father rumbled. "They should be ashamed of themselves."

"You haven't asked us what *I* like *most* about Nixon," Mrs. Butler reproached me. "What I like the most is the dignity and beauty of his family. So much poise. Have you ever seen anyone with so much poise as Pat and those gorgeous girls? They're just . . ."

"I think that's what every president should have," Mrs. Martin interrupted. "A beautiful family like Nixon."

"That's one thing the Kennedys don't have," Mrs. Butler said, waving her finger at me. "A beautiful family. Or poise."

Guy Lombardo was playing "It seems like old times / Doing the things we used to do / Making the dream come true." I talked to a long-haired student from the University of Michigan who had registered Republican for his first vote because "Nixon was a miracle worker." "Look at China," he said. "Look at the trade deal with the Soviet Union. I'm a government major and I know how important these things are. I'm a little disappointed that he didn't find an earlier solution to end the war, but the bombing must have been necessary. Look, it brought them back to the negotiating table."

Guy Lombardo played "Enjoy Yourself, It's Later Than You Think." I found the only persons who objected to the Christmas bombing, two black women from Chicago, sisters, both lifelong Democrats until '72. "We voted for Nixon because of China though he didn't have anything else to offer—and McGovern had nothing to offer." Guy Lombardo played "Boo-Hoo, I'll Tell My Mom on You."

I talked to a red-eyed businessman from Ohio who described Nixon as a "miracle worker" for his China trip, loved the President because "everything he does and says has a dynamic, aggressive aspect," and grew apoplectic at the possibilities of reducing penalties for marijuana. "There are two cultures in this country," he bellowed, "the grass culture and the alcohol culture. I'm from the alcohol culture and I'm proud of it. I'm half-Irish and half-German, two fine strong alcohol cultures, and I have a theory that this grass stuff comes from the ethnic groups very different from mine: the Latin, Jewish, Mediterranean stock you could call them, those people you see sitting around Horn and Hardart's drinking coffee, like Bella Abzug, those are the ones who like pot with their coffee."

The alcohol lobbyist loved all the inaugural proceedings. He hoped they would occur every few months, every few weeks:

"Nixon is good at pageantry, that's what America needs more

of. Pageantry is an affirmation of our American heritage. It stresses the good, positive, old-fashioned American values at a time when everyone is knocking them and being so negative. Look at England, the changing of the guard every day. We need more of that. . . ."

In stentorian loudspeaker tones, a voice booming from everywhere and nowhere: "Ladies and gentlemen, the President of the United States!" Guy Lombardo strikes up "Hail to the Chief." The Family comes in to ecstatic applause, dressed in the colors of the American flag. Pat in beaded blue. Julie in beaded white. Tricia in shimmering red satin with matching boa, behind which she teasingly hides half of her sweetly smiling face. The President's stance of pockets in hand, his swooping nose, his newfound ease with fun and jokes suddenly remind me of Bob Hope. He tries to make this part of the country, the Middle West, feel more special, more dearly loved than any other region. "I have a special affection for the Middle West. . . . It's always been called the heartland of America and it's led the way, because since the last election the *whole* nation is the heartland. . . ." (Cheers and roars.) "And of course as you know my dad came from Ohio. . . ." (More cheers.) "And another reason why this is my favorite ball of all, it's the one where my favorite bandleader, Guy Lombardo, is playing!"

Arms outstretched and fingers in the V sign to express boundless admiration. One arm falls heavily on Lombardo's shoulder.

"You know, I remember way back in the forties when Pat, my wife, and I used to go to New York City. That's before I was a household word. . . ." (Laughter.) "We always used to go and hear Guy Lombardo and his Royal Canadians because even if you were poor he made you feel so *good*. Why, he's the best bandleader ever. Hey, Guy, if you make more money you'll give me a cut, won't you. . . ." (Big laugh, started by Nixon.) "And now, I'd like to show you how much I love Guy's music by dancing to it. . . . Guy, give me a four beat, will you?"

"I'll Be Loving You, Always," the band softly strikes up. Dick and Pat dance limply to the tune, not quite cheek to cheek, their smiles fixed. In the last reel of the movie *Millhouse*, Nixon stands by Guy Lombardo at the 1969 Inaugural Ball recollecting the end of World War II. "When VJ day came . . . I remember Pat and I . . . saved up our money and went to the Roosevelt Hotel and

we danced to the music of Guy Lombardo . . . and I just hope
that we are dancing to his music when we end the next war."

The night before the 1973 Inaugural Ball he had said to a
crowd at the Kennedy Center, "Well, I've got great news for you.
This year, 1973, Bob Hope is going to spend Christmas at home."
The same evening the crowd cheered when the Pat Boone family
sang "a personal pledge of allegiance to Jesus," and when Roger
Williams played "Autumn Leaves," "The Impossible Dream," "I'm
Forever Blowing Bubbles." In the privacy of his own automobile,
so cassette dealers relate, Richard Nixon listens to more Pat Boone,
more Guy Lombardo, and particularly to Lawrence Welk, whose
best known hits include "Ain't She Sweet," "I Want To Be
Happy," "I'm Always Chasing Rainbows," "Nearer, My God, to
Thee," "Bibbidi-Bobbodi-Boo." Nostalgia for old-time religion and
for the quiet Eisenhower fifties. Let's forget the sixties: foreign
songs, hundreds of thousands of draft resisters underground, an
equal number exiled in Canada, fifty-six thousand dead, twenty-five
million living under the poverty level, jailed priests, crumbling ghettos, rising crime, drugged veterans, drugged army, drugged kids,
troubles. Pack up your troubles in your old kit bag and smile,
smile, smile. Bibbidi-Bobbodi-Boo. Is this inaugural a salute to a
vanishing America, or is it the *real* America? Who can say?

Back in my hotel room, I read with fascination the names of the
Inaugural Committee's VIPs who dominate Washington's social
scene throughout the week: Billy Graham cochairs the Symphonic
Concert Committee with heavy campaign contributor W. Clement
Stone, Chicago insurance tycoon and activist of fundamentalist re-
ligion (in 1969, Stone voted to elect Nixon "Churchman of the
Year"). Charlton Heston cochairs the Inaugural Concert Commit-
tee with Pam Powell, daughter of Dick Powell and June Allyson,
Redskins Coach George Allen is a cochairman of the Parade Com-
mittee. Mrs. Vince Lombardi is cochairman of the Inaugural Ball
Committee. Hamburger tycoon Anthony McDonald, Jr., one of
Nixon's largest campaign contributors, is director of Advertising
and Promotion. One is struck by the almost total absence of the
old guard East Coast Republican establishment. Not an Aldrich, a
Dillon, a Lodge in sight at the festivities. These are post–World

War II fortunes, many of them from the South and Southwest, heavy in oil; heavy too on sports, old Hollywood, resort hotels, hamburger stands, the stuff our dreams were made of.

Gathered from the *Washington Post*'s society column: W. Clement Stone, who contributed two million dollars to the campaign, is taking riding lessons in hopes that he will be made ambassador to England. The new D.C. inseparables are Spiro Agnew and Frank Sinatra, who is looking for a house in D.C. to live near Spiro. At their frequent dinners together, Frankie sits down at the piano to croon for Spiro: "This Greek, Unique." Nixon does not have Sinatra on records or cassettes. Evans and Novak have observed that the White House's coolness toward Agnew is based in part on Agnew's friendship with Sinatra, whose life style is clearly too racy for our Spartan President. Witness the grimly abstemious palace guard, led by Haldeman and Ehrlichman, heavily Mormon and Christian Scientist, men who will remain as blameless in their private lives as they grow increasingly ruthless in their hiring and firing.

For Nixon's strength is in part based on that very pristine irreproachability of family style that so reassures Mrs. Martin and Mrs. Butler, that softens the edges of any scandals he may have been associated with. Pat and Julie and Tricia are his continuous Checkers speech, veiling the contradictions and crises of his career. "What can I do for myself?" has been a much maligned phrase, the only honest moment of his inaugural address. Avoiding the "unifying" platitudes or Wilsonian idealisms of 1969, it was the most fitting of mottoes for the shady entrepreneurs and real-estate wheeler-dealers who slinked in and out of Nixon's past and present, the backers of the Cuban refugees who would surface in the Watergate break-in. It was an ideal slogan for the secret slush funds, the Hughes loan of 1960, the ITT dealings, the wheat, milk, corn, and other scandals which lay beneath the veneer of his fairy-tale family life and whose closely concealed tracks history may at some future date reveal.

But beyond its unintended candor, was that phrase any more dangerous than the jingoism of John Kennedy's upon which it so bitterly played? "Ask what you can do for your country" now evoked the horrors of reckless patriotism. "Ask what you can do for yourself" simply stated the loneliness of the huckster, an apolitical, metaphysical solitude. At the end of a decade bloodied by the most misguided patriotism in memory, in the middle of an administration marked by the greatest corruption we have known, which seemed worse?

Some twelve thousand persons attended the first of the inaugural activities, a reception for the Agnews at the Smithsonian Institution. The theme of the party—as of all the inaugural events—was The Spirit of '76. Hostesses dressed like Williamsburg belles, pioneer women, and Indian squaws passed around food meant to emulate ancient American values and Republican symbols: Indian pudding, spoon bread, sugar cookies in the shape of elephants. The patience of the guests, as they waited in line for two or three hours to shake the Vice-President's hand, recalled ancient pilgrimages where crowds stood for hours to kiss some precious relic: a fragment of a sandal, of a toenail. Only once did they swerve from the worshiping line to mob the Nixon women during their brief appearance. I retain from that day an image of Tricia swathed in boa feathers, that mysterious smile of abstract innocence fixed on her face as by a spray gun, her palms spread apart as if about to clap, like one of those dolls that one cranks up with a key, from the back, to dance under a little glass dome.

Shortly thereafter Greyhound buses arrived by the hundreds to load the visitors for the next inaugural event—a Salute to the States at Kennedy Center featuring Bob Hope, Lawrence Welk, and the Pat Boone family. Thousands of Americans burst out of the Smithsonian holding plastic glasses stamped with the blue presidential seal. They had ripped them off by the dozens, relics to carry back to Michigan, Texas, Ohio. Sitting alone on the bus in the middle of the boisterous, roaring crowd, I was joined by a sober and sad-eyed California businessman who told me he had never received his tickets to any of the inaugural events although he had sent his money months earlier. He had to pay for them a second time—a matter of several hundred dollars—yet he accepted this fate with blind submission. "The lady at the inaugural office told me that they wouldn't know until early November who was going to win the election," he explained. "That's why they're so disorganized."

He expressed a similar attitude when we discussed the recent Christmas bombings, whether they had harmed the President's prestige. "Ah, those people have been bombed for twenty-five years," he said, "first by the French and then by us. What do three months more or less matter?"

The week of the inaugural I had lectured at Amherst College, where over one third of the faculty and the student body had been arrested some months before, in protest against the Vietnam War. Sitting with students afterward, I understood that many of them were feeling, with varying degrees of candor, a strong sense of disorientation about the supposed ending of the war. "First of all most of us don't believe it can end," one student said. "It's been with us for ten years, ever since we can remember." Others expressed not so much their disbelief in the reality of the peace as their fear that a ceasefire would deprive them of the one unifying focus of "the Movement," as if the constant dying of Americans were necessary to keep us whole, as if this cancer were necessary to remind us that we were ill. Now more than ever, it was those most opposed to the war who seemed most terrified by the fairyland of well-being, the mirage of peace that Nixon would attempt to conjure up in his second term. "What's going to keep us together when our side of the war ends," one student exclaimed, "when we have lost the majesty and horror of it?"

Blissing Out in Houston

On an October night in 1973, I met with a former leader of the Peace Movement to discuss his newborn self and the salvation of all mankind. Rennie Davis, one of the most dedicated young activists of the Vietnam era, had renounced all political protest some months before to receive the Divine Knowledge being offered by Guru Maharaj Ji, a fifteen-year-old Indian who claimed to be an incarnation of God sent to humanity to bring us a thousand years of peace. Rennie and I sat at a vegetarian restaurant not far from the New York headquarters of the guru's organization—Divine Light Missions—on Park Avenue South. Rennie asked me what I thought the Marharaj Ji was about.

I talked about the proliferation of diverse mysticisms in the United States in reaction to the sixties' failures; about the disarray of shattered marriages, shattered lives lost to the Movement, the arrogance and Millennialism that had undermined it, our loss of hope for any genuine change; about our despair over the technological mess, our disillusionment with the myth of material progress, the failure of secular humanism. Rennie smiled cynically. "I know you have all the right historical dimensions," he said. "But you've left out the only thing that really matters." He stopped smiling and suddenly spoke in a curt, intense voice.

That crucial fact, he said, was that in the next few years the entire world was destined to recognize the Perfect Master Maharaj Ji. Perfect Master would trigger an awakening of our consciousness which would allow us to plug into the Ground of Being—God—Divine Energy—and to realize the full potential of that energy within us. The Perfect Mas-

ter's Knowledge would abolish all greed, hunger, violence, and bring a
thousand years of world peace such as we had never witnessed in recorded history. This Millennium would begin in precisely three weeks,
on November 8, in the Houston Astrodome, where the Perfect Master
would give his practical plan for world peace. . . .

"Peace Now!" "Out Now!" The slogans of the sixties flashed
through my mind, along with a previous memory of Rennie Davis: a
meeting of peace coalitions in a state of mayhem. Rennie standing in
isolation from the disorder, dressed in blue jeans and sneakers, quietly
bouncing a tennis ball against the wall. . . .

"As a matter of fact," Rennie was saying, "I wouldn't be surprised
if a UFO landed in the Astrodome while the Perfect Master is there, all
the astrological conditions point to that possibility . . . beings on other
planets must be equally thirsty for his Knowledge. . . ."

As we talked at the restaurant, Rennie ate his vegetarian meal with
his left hand, Indian fashion, deftly cupping the food with his fingers.
He told me that he had first heard of the Perfect Master from one of
his devotees while flying to Paris the previous January to meet with
Madame Binh, wife of the South Vietnamese leader. Shortly thereafter
he left for India to stay at the guru's ashram. He had received Divine
Knowledge—the Maharaj Ji's equivalent of Zen satori or Buddhist
Nirvana—one week after his arrival and had been in meditation for
several hours a day ever since. I expressed my qualms about the rapidity
of this enlightenment. The difference between the Perfect Master's technique and others, Rennie said, is that it gives you a *practical* way of
meditation which enables you to realize the Godhead within you very
quickly, transforming your consciousness and hence your body.

For a second the former politico returned: "It's like Hegel, rather
than Marx. Spirit over matter."

"And the marvelous thing about it," he continued, "is that *everyone has the same vision. Everyone experiences the same thing.* Oh, after
the infighting of the Movement, the quibbling, the disorder, to have the
unity we talked about in the sixties. . . ."

I asked Rennie how the Maharaj Ji's devotees felt about sex. He
told me that another great thing about this movement was that there
were no strict rules. "You are not *ordered* to give up anything. You just
lose your desire for it—be it grass, meat, or sex. There's no renunciation
whatsoever of the world, as there is among the Hare Krishnas or Jesus
people. As for sex, it's only forbidden in the ashrams; otherwise Mata Ji,
Perfect Master's mother, says it's better to have sex just for procreation."

"Christ, Rennie," I said, "do you think there's any fifteen-year-old masturbating between here and Scarsdale whose mother doesn't tell him that?" I regretted the words, feeling uneasy with this new Puritan, but he didn't seem to have listened. As we walked out of the restaurant, he was staring at the sky, saying, "One of the most beautiful things about Divine Light is its cleanliness, its purity. . . . The ashrams are always kept impeccably clean in case Maharaj Ji drops in. . . . Wow, after the filth of the sixties' communes, the loose living . . ."

This is an account of my inquiry into the nature of the Maharaj Ji's Divine Light movement, as I recorded it in the following weeks.

November 1

THERE are some twenty Divine Light ashrams in New York City. This afternoon I have been asked to one to hear *satsang*—spiritual discourse or truth giving, several hours of which are prerequisite to receiving Knowledge—from one of the Divine Light mahatmas. This particular ashram is in a large, prosperous apartment building on Shrink Row, at the corner of Eighty-fifth Street and Central Park West. A pile of shoes lies heaped on the elevator landing. The scrubbed living room is dominated by a stuffed chair upholstered in white satin, set high on a dais like a throne, and surmounted by a photograph of the chubby, lotus-positioned guru. In front of the throne *premies*—the Indian word for "lovers" or devotees—have deposited offerings: a grapefruit, some chrysanthemums, an enormous stick of cinnamon candy. The ashram is mostly populated by gentle, serenely smiling young women in long flowing robes. Bhole Ji encourages floor-length garments because they are more modest.

The mahatma giving satsang this afternoon on Eighty-fifth Street is one of two thousand mahatmas whom Perfect Master has empowered to spread his Knowledge. He is a frail, impassive former Marxist who had taught languages at a Calcutta university—or so he says.

Throughout his rambling discourse on Eterrrnal Rreality he keeps adjusting the new set of false teeth with which Divine Light has equipped him on the occasion of his first satsang tour of the United States. He wears a white cable-knit sweater on top and the traditional dhoti of white muslin below. He says that he met one of the Maharaj Ji's disciples on the very same day he had planned to commit suicide in the Ganges—Divine Lighters greatly stress coincidence, which is part of the divine play, or *lila*—and had received Knowledge shortly thereafter.

His teaching is not vastly different from that of the Vedantists I listened to when doing comparative religion at Columbia: The rational everyday mind is the obstacle, the great demon that stands in the way of Understanding; suffering is created by the duality which that mind posits; Enlightenment is the resolution of that duality and the merging into the One Consciousness. The mahatma's principal departure from rigorous Vedanta doctrine is that Maharaj Ji does not want his devotees to leave the world. Quite the contrary, we must keep our jobs and enjoy our meals, the only thing we must renounce is *mind*, and much of what we *previously* considered to be "knowledge." As a matter of fact, the new Divine Knowledge of Maharaj Ji will give us increased concentration and will make us *better* businessmen, musicians, writers. We can have our world and eat it too.

"The young, the uneducated, the nonintellectual receive Knowledge very easily because their minds contain less dualities and they are of more guileless heart. It will be very difficult for *you*," he suddenly turns around, pointing at me severely. "But if you desire it enough it is possible . . . remove *maya*, illusions, okay? Very easy."

"Mahatma Ji," I ask, "what about money? What are devotees told to do about money?"

"The 'I'-ness active in you is an illusion," he says in a clipped machinelike voice. "Therefore after dropping the veil of maya and receiving Knowledge whatever 'I' possess is not mine anymore, everything is His. 'I' have nothing to give, since 'I' do not exist, only God gives, since only God exists."

A premie in long, virginal blue robes comes to take the mahatma to a television station to tape a show.

The Divine Light Missions, besides their membership of forty thousand in the United States and the eight million they claim in the world (most of them in India, where such a claim is impossible to verify), also own a formidable lot of subsidiary concerns: Shri Hans Productions (films, records, educational programs); Divine Sales International Thrift Shops; Shri Hans Engineering and Divine Electronics, wholesale marketers of electronic equipment; Shri Hans Aviation, a Divine airline; Divine Travel Services and Divine Travel International, organized to ferry devotees to festivals and special events throughout the world; a palatial vegetarian restaurant on New York's Forty-second Street; and Shri Hans Publications, which produces a weekly newspaper (*Divine Times*) and a full-color, glossy monthly (*And It Is Divine*).

To outline his "practical plan for a thousand years of peace"— the theme of Houston's Millennium festivities—Maharaj Ji has hired the world's largest sports arena, the Astrodome, for $25,000 *a day.* He is staying with the Holy Family—which consists of, besides Himself, His Mother, and His three older Brothers—in the Celestial Suite of the Astroworld Hotel, rentable to anyone at $2,500 a day.

November 7

9:00 A.M.: Flying to Houston the day before the Millennium is to begin, I leaf through the pages of a book called *Who Is Guru Maharaj Ji?* published by Bantam in an initial edition of 125,000 copies. Who is Guru Maharaj Ji? The slogan shouts out at me in many languages, for the plane is half filled with foreign devotees wearing enormous lapel buttons that say WER IST MAHARAJ JI? QUIEN ES MAJARAJ JI? Most of them spend the three hours of flight with their eyes closed, occasionally staring at still another lapel button that presents the guru's chubby face reverently pinned to the seat in front of them.

I talk to a twenty-five-year-old German student whose father owns a supermarket chain. He tells me that the experience of Divine Knowledge is received in the following four ways: a brilliant light of almost blinding power perceived in the middle of the forehead, through that "Third Eye" of ancient Indian tradition; a music of sublime beauty in one's ears; an extraordinary taste of "nectar" in the mouth; and—the most indescribable sensation of all—a vibration sensed in the abdominal area which one can keep meditating upon twenty-four hours a day. "I am meditating right now, as I talk to you," he says cheerfully. "But I cannot describe to you the Divine Knowledge any further than that if you haven't experienced it. Our Knowledge is not a religion, but an experience. Can I describe for you the taste of a mango before you have tasted it?"

He closes his eyes, and returns to his ecstasy. I return to the book, which is mostly a compilation of testimonies from persons who have received Knowledge, and of satsangs by the Perfect Master himself, remarkable for their slangy, machinery-obsessed metaphors: "Special discount; Absolute discount! I am here, ready to offer you this Knowledge without taking a single pence!" "We have to take the airplane and go up, and this ship is inside of us, it has been built within us, it's factory-built. It's not optional, it's standard. It just has to be fueled. And what is this fuel? It is Knowledge."

I proceed to read the numerous testimonies of premies who express their experience of Knowledge as a return to a state of prenatal, uterine bliss. "One day as I was meditating," the secretary to the president of a manufacturing company testifies,

> I got a glimpse of what I had experienced when I was born. . . . I remembered a bright white light in my mother's womb. There was music playing. . . . As I started to come out of the womb that beautiful white light started to fade and become more and more distant. . . . I knew I had found the true path that would eventually lead me back to that state beyond birth I had always been so thirsty for.

It had struck me earlier that the word Divine Lighters use for their devotees, "premie," is nearly the same as the medical slang for a premature baby, "preemie."

12 noon: Rennie Davis is holding a press conference in Houston's Rice Hotel. Premies mill about, the girls not so different from the Movement girls of the sixties, long-haired, wearing sandals and long skirts. The men vastly different: ultrastraight, short-haired, in

business shirts. They greet each other, palms together, with the salutation "Jai Satchitanan," which is the ancient Sanskrit definition of the three aspects of God: Truth, Knowledge, and Bliss. Behind Rennie sit three dour mahatmas with red spots between their eyes.

"And who does the cooking in your ashrams?" a woman reporter is demanding. "Who *does* your goddamn cooking?"

"*En el ashram de Buenos Aires es un hombre que hace la cocina,*" a premie's voice shouts.

"Many men do the cooking in ashrams," Rennie answers gently, "but that's so irrelevant. . . ."

"Whadda you mean it's irrelevant?"

"After you've received Knowledge, attachment to your man or woman role is transcended, we transcend our sex after Knowledge, we really do."

Bal Bhagwan Ji, Perfect Master's oldest brother, and the Missions' mastermind, has indeed prophesied that his baby brother's enlightenment techniques will eventually create a mutation in the human species which will obliterate all sexual differences and make us *totally* alike. And premie doctors have testified to me that plugging into Divine Light meditation has abolished the menstruation of many women devotees. The press release on my lap says that the guru's Millennium spectacle will be "The most holy and significant event in human history." I ask Rennie in what sense Maharaj Ji's arrival in Houston is more significant than the advent of Krishna, Buddha, or Christ to earth.

"Well, it will be known to more men," he fumbles. "I mean we're at a time of history when instead of Christ just having twelve apostles to slowly spread the good news you can spread them more quickly. . . ."

"You mean more media?"

Rennie puts on his mysterious smile, and takes a question from someone else.

2:00 P.M.: The Lord Incarnate is flying into Houston's Hobby Airport from the West Coast sometime this afternoon, and thousands of acolytes are gathering there to greet him. I drive to Hobby with a thirty-four-year-old devotee, a tennis pro who has been national hard court champion of the United States, and was captain of the Harvard Tennis Team in 1960. Tim Galloway is a handsome, thoughtful, gentle man with cornflower blue eyes. He immediately launches into an explanation of how Divine Knowledge has totally transformed his game of tennis. The guru's meditation technique, he says, has given him such powers of concentration that he can receive service from the strongest opponent *one foot behind the service line*, with a half-volley.

"It totally reverses the Big Game," he says modestly. "There I am already in midcourt, so I easily beat the server to net, and the next shot is a put-away. The whole principle of meditation is to slow down inner time. People *think* too much when they play, they're always talking to themselves, the ego is telling the unconscious nervous system what to do. The point is to obliterate the difference between the teller and the doer, make the ego and the unconscious one. I've also devised an underhand serve which bounces off at almost a ninety-degree angle to the flight of the ball. . . ." Tim Galloway's popular book, *Inner Tennis*, was written after receiving Knowledge.

I ask Galloway how he had come to believe Maharaj Ji was God.

"When I first heard him my only approach was to say to myself, 'He's either the real thing or a con artist.' Well, the first times I saw him he just did too bad a job as a con artist. A good con artist wouldn't wear a gold wristwatch or give such stupid answers. When I was staying with him in India I once asked him how much time I should spend on work and how much on meditation and he just said get up an hour earlier and go to bed an hour later, hardly a profound answer. I decided that if he was doing such a bad job of being a holy man he simply had to be genuine."

"Did it ever occur to you that he might be a *bad* con man?"

"Then how could he have six million followers?" the tennis pro replied.

By the hangar of the Hobby airport premies weave garlands of carnations and snapdragons, and complete the festooning of the emerald-green Rolls-Royce which will carry Perfect Master back to the city. Some two thousand persons have congregated on the landing strip, carrying banners from Israel, Chile, Peru, Kenya, Denmark, Argentina, and Colombia, whose devotees are particularly devotional: PREMIES DE COLOMBIA A LOS PIES DE MAHARAJ JI. A dais draped in purple silk is surmounted by the traditional white satin throne and garlanded with still more carnations, gladioli, roses. On either side of the throne stand sumptuous gold velvet chairs for the Holy Family and enormous placards depicting lambs lying down with lions, saying WORLD FAMILY REUNION.

An orchestra is playing a fortyish rendition of "When the Saints Go Marching In." The devotees sit reverently facing the throne, their necks arching toward the sky to watch for his plane. Additional crowds come pouring in; old friends fall into each other's arms with such greetings as, "I haven't seen you since that festival in Delhi!" or, "You haven't changed a bit since that last satsang in Calcutta!" The sun shines down upon the prosperous jet-age pilgrims from a cloudless sky. It is eighty degrees. Every five minutes the premies roar out the Divine Light salute: *"Boliya Shri Satgurudev Maharaj Ki Ji!"* "All Glory to the Perfect Master," a roared crescendo on the last syllable, both arms raised to the sky. Rennie Davis is talking again, this time like a revivalist minister, quoting scripture by the yardful. "Jesus said we must create the kingdom of God on earth by realizing it within us first. . . ."

The scene makes me think of the Great Awakenings, the camp meetings, the revivalism that has always been part of American history. Tocqueville wrote about America's "fanatic spiritualism." In the 1840s the revivalist preacher Charles Grandison Finney received the Holy Spirit in his law offices and passed It on to his friends in a matter of minutes, describing it as "unutterable gushings of the heart," "waves and waves of liquid love." This American Millennium is painless, too, offering presto ecstasy unsullied by any dark night of the soul.

Here in Houston a weird encounter is occurring between the two most religious countries in the world—India and the United States—each poised at the absolute opposite ends of the religious spectrum. India's seething, unstructured spirituality, akin to a lake of cosmic sperm, confronts the despiritualized and pragmatic American religionism that is the backbone of much of our material and political successes. Fifteen-year-old Guru Feelgood is being advised by someone who knows his way around America. He's come to make us feel not only better, but better *off*. Is it the pragmatism of our religion that leads to our sporadic explosions of revivalism and awakenings, millennial sects, faith healers, thundering radio ministers, Oral Roberts, Billy Graham, Marjoe, and now the new Oriental instant mystics?

Marjoe is here, by the way, somewhere in Houston, covering the Millennium for *Oui* magazine.

"The Perfect Master never comes or talks exactly as prophesied," a fat mahatma in a gray business suit is satsanging in front of the white satin throne. "Jesus Christ spoke in parables. Lord Krishna said, 'I am not this body, my real personality is divine light.' Who is Jesus Christ? Jesus Christ is Krishna, Krishna is Christ, and what are Krishna and Christ? They are omnipresent and perfect energy."

A roar from the crowd for energy, arms up: *"Boliya Shri Satgurudev Maharaj Ki Ji!"*

"Christ is love, Christ is knowledge. So what is Maharaj Ji giving? . . . He is giving you knowledge of Christ, knowledge of Buddha, knowledge of Krishna, knowledge of Mahomet. Brothers and sisters, after having received the knowledge of the real Buddha, the real Krishna, the real Christ, the real Mahomet, what is Maharaj Ji giving you? He is giving UNITY. . . ."

Suddenly, from the back of the dais, precisely where he was not expected to come from, the kid appears. He struts up to the podium very briskly, plunks himself down on his throne. The crowd raises its arms in salute, some bend their foreheads to the ground, many weep. A thirty-year-old doctor I have just met, a research scientist at the National Institutes of Health, has collapsed into a friend's arms and is sobbing like a little child: It is the first time he has seen the Maharaj Ji in the flesh.

The photographs have been deceptive. The guru's face, so jowly and custard-bland in pictures, is shrewd, inscrutable, and powerful. The eyes are swiftly roaming and cunning, the chin formidably stubborn. Lei after lei of flowers is placed around his neck. Dressed in businessman seersucker, Rennie Davis kneels at his right, palms together, his aquiline face concentrated on the Master like those of the Magi in Memling's *Adoration*. At his left sits Mata Ji, swathed in a sumptuous white gauze sari, an enormous diamond in her nose.

The kid says a few words, condescendingly and in a very

rushed tone. He talks real American. "The Millennium program will start tomorrow and it'll really be fantastic, it'll be incredible . . . and soon people will get together and finally understand God. . . . There's so much trouble in the world, Watergate is not only in America, it exists everywhere. . . ." And after two minutes he exits briskly, accompanied by roars from the crowd, to enter his flower-garlanded Rolls-Royce.

"Lila, did you see that lila?" A young girl runs out of the landing strip waving her arms excitedly. "He surprised us, he played with us by coming down on the wrong landing strip!"

Lila, Indian for divinely free play, is one of the words most often used by Divine Lighters. Lila is that state of consciousness common to all mystics in which, all contradictions of adulthood abolished, we enjoy that same state of gratuitous pleasure we experienced in earliest infancy: At play in the fields of the Lord, or the divine play of Meister Eckhart. . . . Maharaj Ji's favorite form of lila is to throw devotees into his swimming pool. I also hear that his preferred topics of conversation are tape records, cars, and airplanes, that he freaks out on candy bars, takes Tums for his ulcer, and that his favorite book is *Jonathan Livingston Seagull.*

7:00 P.M.: I have dinner with the young doctor whom I saw collapsed in tears at the airport. He is a graduate of the University of Rochester Medical School, happily married, the father of a newborn son. He is short and solid, with reddish hair and mustache and a very warm, welcoming manner. Like Tim Galloway, the tennis pro, and other adult premies I talk to, he feels he had *everything in life for happiness* and yet was still searching for "meaning." The doctor begins his meal of salad and bread by touching his first forkful to the center of his forehead—the Third Eye—the premies' ritual dedication of food to Maharaj Ji.

"I'm suffering from the paradox of sufficiency and suffering," he says. "You see, I just didn't want temporary states of happiness as I occasionally found with mescaline . . . throughout the sixties all my doctor friends were experimenting with various ways of expanding consciousness. But I wanted *infinite* happiness. I knew there was some cosmic truth that would be totally satisfying forever. I had gotten so *close* to it with some of the other experiences. . . ."

I comment that most traditional schools of meditation—be they Buddhist, Zen, or Vedantist—urge one to remain on the side of brevity, starting at a few minutes a day, gradually working up to an hour over a period of months or years. Since the devotee is a neurologist, does he not see any danger in plunging overnight into two hours of blissing-out sessions? But like most other premies he is uninterested in the traditional East.

"That's where surrender comes in," the doctor answers, his eyes gleaming with adoration. "Our meditation is passive and effortless, we just let Maharaj Ji do it for us . . . you've had this Knowledge inside you right along without recognizing it, so what Maharaj Ji does is to fill in the picture with one fell swoop, one big package. . . . At the time I received Knowledge I still couldn't accept him as God but later when I felt the lasting magnificence of that peace of meditation I accepted him. . . . I had the most beautiful dream about him last night. We were playing together as if we were both children. He kept throwing me into a swimming pool. . . ."

1:30 A.M.: I try to fall asleep in the violent Houston night. The sirens of ambulance and police cars keep screaming down the streets below my hotel room, just as they did one of the last times I was here, the night after John Kennedy's death. Upon hearing the news I had run into a Catholic church for the first time in some years and wept for four hours. The East was in mourning but in Houston that Saturday night restaurants and nightclubs were filled with people dancing. I hear that a seventeen-year-old premie traveling through Dallas's Dealey Plaza on her way to Houston yesterday said, "Gee, some president was shot here, I don't remember his name. . . ."

At 2:00 A.M.—so it is reported the next day—the Maharaj Ji is walking all alone in the world's largest sports arena, playing with his Astrodome.

□

November 8

> *"I want to ask you something, Franny,"*
> *[Zooey] said abruptly. . . . "What do you*
> *think you're doing with the Jesus prayer? . . .*
> *You talk about piling up treasure—money,*
> *property, culture, knowledge, and so on and*
> *so on. In going ahead with the Jesus prayer*
> *. . . aren't you trying to lay up . . . some-*
> *thing that's every goddamn bit as negotiable*
> *as all those other, more material things?"*
> —J. D. SALINGER
> *Franny and Zooey*

Dozens of Hare Krishna disciples are haranguing outside the Astrodome before the festivities begin, claiming that the guru is a fake because he does not know Sanskrit, and because Krishna does not take any bodily form. A few yards away Jesus people hand out leaflets claiming that the guru is Antichrist and carry placards that say, WHAT HAS THE GURU'S RELIGION DONE FOR INDIA? Of the two, the Jesus people are the more aggressive. They are reported to have poured sugar into some of the premies' gas tanks to impair their functioning. Earlier this morning, a bad scuffle broke out between the Hare Krishna and the Jesus crowds as they were trying to monopolize the same sidewalk to protest the guru. Brotherhood, peace, family of man.

Some of the premies—particularly the British ones that make up the bulk of the "World Peace Corps," the Divine Light security outfit which is marshaling the Millennium—are no less aggressive. Dour, didactic, cavernous-faced, they push you roughly back from many sections of the Astrodome barking, "Premies only here, pre-mies only, please obey. . . ." It is through being shoved by them a few times that I receive the first hint of the movement's latent violence, the inevitable violence of any millennial sect hell-bent on infinite happiness.

At one o'clock the Millennium begins. Rennie Davis had pre-dicted that the Astrodome would be filled to capacity, with a hun-dred thousand people weeping to get in; that CBS and NBC would be carrying it live, with Walter Cronkite as anchorman; and that George Harrison and Bob Dylan would receive Knowledge that very weekend. Reality sucks. There are some seven thousand people on the first day, and the only TV coverage of the event is being done by some underground California outfit.

The inside of the Astrodome, however, is a very fascinating sight. Its gigantic field is dominated by a seven-level, thirty-five-foot-high stage made of translucent white plastic that glows fiercely with internal lighting. The top level is surmounted by a throne of blue Plexiglas upon which the guru sits every night to give his satsang. On subsidiary levels, enormous stuffed orange chairs serve as thrones for members of the Holy Family. As devotees start to speak, a screen made of light bulbs alternately flashes programmed electronic images of the guru, his mother, and his father behind the throne.

Illusions of shifting rainbows waft upon a transparent 125-foot-high gauze screen hanging from the ceiling. A gigantic American flag surmounts it all, and at the left is the football scoreboard, with the last game's teams still on it: Seminoles vs. Cougars. Two enormous Texaco billboards complete the picture. Half of the crowd sits cross-legged or lies in a trancelike state on the very floor of the Astrodome, where hundreds of sticks of incense give off a pungent bathroom odor. And in the back of the arena, farthest away from the dais, there are always people practicing numerous esoteric techniques—standing on their heads, doing yoga back bends, moving slowly in T'ai Chi exercises, practicing deep breathing in shoulder stands, or swaying to whatever music punctuates the program.

Joan Apter—a prominent American premie who meditated for several months in a series of caves in India—is the opening speaker. After the customary salutation, "We speak for a tranquillity of peace," etc., she says, "I'd like to tell you about Maharaj Ji's father," but she immediately drops the subject and returns to the ooze of love. To make the old man's early history public might be disastrous. For the devotees most desired by the Mission are the fat cats, and the old man was actually a revolutionary of sorts. After searching for the meaning of life for many years, being rescued from suicide by a guru and receiving Knowledge from him, Shri Hans Ji Maharaj radically challenged India's caste system. He preached to the poorest people in India, the untouchables, the outcastes, and was virulently attacked by the Brahmans for his democratic ways.

In his early years, he led a simple, unmaterialistic life; one of his favorite sayings was "The world is for the wealthy, but God is for the poor." Shri Hans Ji Maharaj shed his mortal coil in 1966. Shortly before his death, he decided to pass on his sainthood to the youngest of his three sons. The Millennium festival in Houston is actually one of the annual birthday celebrations for the Perfect Master's father, which up to now had been near Hardwar, India. But this is history, and the instant mystics of the seventies seem to detest history—particularly their own—even more than did the sixties' New Left.

Rennie Davis's voice drones on about "the future of our golden age of peace." I lie on the floor of the Astrodome munching on a Millennium candy bar, one of the Missions' numerous commercial products. The Perfect Master's dais looks like an Easter Show on the Life of Krishna at Radio City Music Hall, or the Calcutta version of *Jesus Christ Superstar*. Here are the seventies—a procession of consciousness-raising sensitivity-session rock extravaganzas in divine duds. This is a peace rally in Rockette drag.

I feel sick. A pageant on Christ's life is being enacted onstage. Mary keeps screaming, "Jesus, Jesus, where are you, we're going to Jerusalem!" "I haven't been into acid much," a boy lying next to me says, "just about a hundred trips or so." "I'm going to check out this Knowledge," a pre-premie in a crazy cowboy outfit says, "because it's like putting your cock into a new woman; you've got to do it before you know what it's like."

Later that afternoon the kid makes his first satsang on top of his blue Lucite throne. The Astrodome becomes even more eerie. Two enormous color television screens enlarge the Master's image on either side of the throne, and below that another screen presents a parade of 1960s personalities—Marilyn Monroe, Ho Chi Minh, John Kennedy, John Glenn—in obeisance to Rennie's message that this Millennium is continuing the message of the sixties. "I haven't got an MD degree," the kid is whining, obviously nonplussed by the small turnout. "I've got a much greater degree." Still, thousands bowed their foreheads to the floor when he entered and lay prostrate for a few minutes, and Rennie Davis began the evening by kissing the Perfect Master's feet.

After the satsang I have dinner with another doctor, the guru's personal physician. He has an extensive theory concerning the stimulating impact of Divine Light meditation upon the pineal gland, whose increased activity will eliminate all of humanity's aggressive drives. He also explains that the Perfect Master's duodenal ulcer must be understood on three different levels: (1) the habitual physical level—constant jet lag, changes of diet, fatigue, stress; (2) the spiritual level: it is a sign of his compassion for mankind, like the stigmata on Christ's feet; (3) the cosmic level, as a revelation of universal suffering.

The diagnostician of Perfect Master's cosmic ulcer disturbs me more than any other premie I meet because he is the brightest, the most dedicated, the nicest of the lot. He is thirty, and has had a few acid trips, which he describes. I can't understand how they can have screwed up a first-rate mind to that degree. Some pathology of affluence is at work, as it is in Tim Galloway, and all the other intelligent adult premies I talk to. This physician was an all-county football star as a teenager, went to college at Dartmouth and Columbia, has his medical degree from Duke University Medical School, had two years of Freudian analysis as part of his psychiatric training, and always considered *he had everything in life for happiness*. But he wanted more . . . at one point in our conversation, he says, as the neurologist did, "I wanted continual ecstasy!"

Man's most basic drive, he adds, is the transcendence of his ego; the sex drive is nothing more than one form of ego transcendence; and the transcendence offered him by the Master's twenty-four-hour meditation technique is infinitely more blissful than sex.

November 9

Maharaj Ji at his first and only press conference:

"I would be very happy if the press could cooperate with me because if peace is established on earth, you will get the credit! And that would be really fantastic and far out, because this is what we really need today, peace!"

REPORTER: "What about your Rolls-Royce?"

MAHARAJ JI: "If you're going to feed a child this morning he's going to be hungry again this afternoon . . . all a Rolls-Royce is is a piece of tin. If I gave poor people my Rolls-Royce they would need more tomorrow and I don't have any more Rolls-Royce to give them."

He sits a few feet from us in his white satin duds, alternately smiling, pouting, and baiting us. There is a faint mustache on his imperious, round little face. The press has tried to check out a rumor that he's really nineteen going on twenty, and has faked his passport as a *lila*, to get more attention.

REPORTER: "Are you the son of God?"

MAHARAJ JI: "Everyone is the son of God. None of you ain't the uncle or aunt of God."

REPORTER: "Are you God?"

MAHARAJ JI: "I am a humble servant of God."

REPORTER: "Then why do your devotees say you're God?"

MAHARAJ JI: "Why don't you ask them?"

Someone then asks about an incident in Detroit in which a reporter was hit over the head with a blackjack by a man from the Divine Light Mission. The Maharaj Ji's aide says let's pass on to a more relevant question. Mayhem occurs, everyone at the press conference wanting to know more about the incident. The conference is shortly thereafter terminated. A writer covering the events for *Ramparts* reports on a recent astrological prediction: The guru's testicles will descend tomorrow, on the third day of the Millennium.

2:00 P.M.: The best seats in the Astrodome have been reserved for the premies' parents, for Divine Light is big on family solidarity, on healing the sixties' generation gap and getting parents and children together again. However, it is very difficult to talk to parents as most of them have requested not to be disturbed or interviewed. "Some of them are a little embarrassed," a premie explains. In the electric blue-and-gold-walled luxury loges where the parents sit, an elegant woman with a Kenneth hairdo and a Bonwit Teller raincoat is trying to communicate with her teenage son, who sits eyes closed, blissed out by one of the mahatmas's speeches. "It's a charming show, darling, and I love their color schemes, it gives me ideas for my living room."

□

3:00 P.M.: I talk to Gary Girard, who was the very first American to receive Knowledge and has been personal secretary to the guru. He tells me that he first went to India in '68, when he was selling macramé belts on street corners and shooting dope all over Australia and the Far East. His father is a well-to-do California businessman, and Gary started the Asian dope circuit right after high school. Gary has a grandiose vision of the impact Maharaj Ji is already having on the world: "I assure you that the President of the United States is on top of everything the guru is doing. I'm convinced that the President of the United States just loves this because he simply can't deny the humanitarian work Maharaj Ji is doing."

"Do you consider Nixon a humanitarian President?"

"Nixon has served the people well," Gary answers. "He only does what he can do. It's not his fault that he has a mind which doesn't function properly."

"Why are there so few black premies in the United States?"

"Black people are not interested in Maharaj Ji because they're not interested enough in themselves."

"What is your notion of equality?"

"Equality is not how much you have but same-sightedness, unity of vision, which is what *we* have."

The next premie I talk to is a forty-three-year-old architect, once employed by Frank Lloyd Wright, who also sees Nixon as "without fault" because "when people are corrupt they produce a corrupt leader. It's the *people's* fault." The architect had been waiting for Maharaj Ji since 1949, when he read a prophecy by Edgar Cayce which said that in 1969 a boy born in the foothills of the Himalayas would lead the world. He received Knowledge because "my destiny is to be infinite." The architect has designed the Divine City which the Divine Light Missions are planning to start building next year. It will be suspended between the two cliffsides of a great canyon and will have a hall for satsang large enough to seat 144,999 people (a figure from the Book of Revelation). There will be no money or currency of any sort in the Divine City; people will take out whatever they need from the stores . . . and in twelve thousand years, the architect says, there will only be saints on earth; everyone will possess cosmic consciousness.

□

6:00 P.M.: "Sit down on the floor," a California reporter says, "and I'll show you exactly how they give you Knowledge."

We are in a suite at the Shamrock Hilton. The reporter started writing about the Divine Lighters some months ago, and has succeeded in getting a few defecting premies to describe the secret sessions.

"You're taken into a very dark room, there are no more than fifteen of you. The mahatma is sitting against the middle of a wall, with a very bright light shining on him. First he satsangs you for about two hours about the retribution you're going to suffer if you ever reveal the secret of the Knowledge giving. Fire and brimstone stuff, gnashing of teeth, eternal damnation. Then he starts giving Knowledge. First he does your eyes. He presses his knuckles very hard upon your eyeballs and keeps them there until you see the *light*. Then he plugs up your ears with his fingers in a certain way until you hear the *music*. Then he tips your head back in a certain way for the meditative position, and that nectar you taste, that's your snot. Then he tells you the secret word to meditate on, and that's kind of a breath sound that's supposed to represent the divine energy of the world, ah-ha, ah-ha."

As we return to the Astrodome the kid has just finished his second satsang. He is wearing sumptuous red-and-gold vestments and a miter-shaped "crown of crowns" which is the ultimate Indian symbol of sainthood. Below him his mother, Bhole Ji, is leading his Blue Aquarius band, composed of premies who play for nothing and give all the proceeds of their records to Divine Light. Bhole Ji is dressed head to toe in a silver sequin suit and matching silver shoes, and bounces around the podium going "hubba hubba hubba." To the left, a group of sullen mahatmas in pale saffron robes have struck languorous poses. I keep wondering which of them is handiest with a blackjack.

I lie down on the floor and think back to my childhood. I used to get spaced out saying beads, following the Stations of the Cross during Lent, crawling to the Lourdes shrine on my knees. That is precisely what religion has been methodically shedding for the past hundred years: those very techniques of *altering consciousness* which satisfied the unquenchable human need to surrender to something larger than the self. Here we have the results, dear mothers and fathers seated in the luxury loges above, of secular humanism, Unitarianism, bland Reformed Judaism, the postconciliar Church, and permissive education.

There are no taxis at the Astrodome that night, and I hitch a ride back to my hotel with a premie in his thirties who has worked for U.S. Army Intelligence in South America. He is as lovingly secretive about the nature of his work as he is about the arcane techniques of Divine Knowledge. This dude has it twice made. For that's another archetypal need we've been neglecting, another vacuum the Divine Light is filling—our bliss in participating in secret organizations and rites, be they Freemasonry, college fraternities, any exclusive tribe.

November 10

Early on the third day of the Maharaj Ji's thousand years of peace, I go to an ashram in a quiet, wooded back street of Houston where some four hundred young people have come this morning to receive Divine Knowledge. It could be any shrine, at any moment of man's history. Before a ramshackled, colonnaded white mansion the pilgrims stand in droves, waiting for their turn to enter into the presence of fifteen mahatmas officiating inside. A few are reverently prostrated on the ground, a few others advance toward the mansion on their knees. As I elbow my way to the door a man of college age jostles past me. "Sorry," he says, "I figured if I'm going to receive Knowledge this morning, I'd better go to the bathroom first."

I have come to see an Englishman who was instrumental in starting the Master's first European and American campaigns three years ago. That was when the ambitious, precocious, technology-adoring twelve-year-old guru—frustrated by how little attention he was getting in his swami-swarming native country—decided to employ modern public relations methods to spread his message throughout the entire world. The English devotee was one of the first Westerners to help him out. He is a frail man in his thirties, an Oxford graduate in theology. We get into a car to go to the Astrodome. I ask him how long the Knowledge session will last.

"Once they're ready to receive it it goes just like that," he says, snapping his fingers quickly four times, "in just four seconds." He looks at his watch. "I figure they'll be out of there around a quarter of three."

Like an abortion. I ask him how he can compute the session so precisely and he suddenly turns on me quite viciously. "Look," he snaps, "I am very bad at facts. If you want to stay in this car with me please let's not talk about facts, all right? I am only interested in talking about one thing in the world, and that is *love*, divine *love*."

He leans back in the car, petulant.

"Until three years ago when I received Knowledge," the Englishman says, "I used to be able to discuss Gregorian chant, and John Donne, and Cocteau, and André Breton, and Plotinus, and Saint Thomas, and the difference between Mahayana and Hinayana Buddhism, do you understand? I was an intellectual. But once you have received Knowledge you are incapable of having a so-called intellectual discussion. You can only have a discussion *about* Knowledge that *happens* to be intellectual."

We talked at length about that "incidence of coincidence," or lila, or divine play, in which premies have enormous faith. "You can see it in Jungian terms if you wish," he says; "it's what he called 'synchronicity,' bumping into what you need at the moment you need it. That's lila, and it is being brought about by the common consciousness which is creating the universe."

The English devotee is one of the two men whom Rennie Davis met on that plane to Paris, on his way to see Mme Binh, and who convinced him to fly to India to meet the Perfect Master.

3:00 P.M.: Paul Krassner of *The Realist* magazine in California has challenged Rennie Davis to a public debate, and Davis has accepted. I take a few notes.

KRASSNER: Resolved: That Davis has copped out to turn kids away from social responsibility to personal escape.

DAVIS: Ever since I've returned from India I've felt the hope, the incredible joy, which I think can await us all. I have realized that the hopes of the sixties are going to be fulfilled in the seventies, that the sixties' generation of peace is going to finally peak. . . . We grew up at a time in the sixties, with the New

Left, when we were inspired to not start with a blueprint or phi-losophy or doctrine. . . . Only a commitment to process and to learning to control the process. In the same way, Divine Light Mission is an experience that's being offered and you can't draw judgments on it until you've had the experience. The Maharaj Ji gives us an experience of the mystery of life, of the purpose of creation, of God.

KRASSNER: I find that the Maharaj Ji is the spiritual equivalent of Mark Spitz. . . . I'm interested in knowing the status of Ren-nie's love life. I hear that it's okay for mahatmas to have sex but not for the premies.

DAVIS: In the ashrams we practice celibacy to suspend con-fusion. . . . We see that sex is not only for pleasure but for bring-ing another soul into the human body so it can come to realize Knowledge.

KRASSNER: It's natural for the kids to turn to the Second Com-ing of Santa Claus. . . .

DAVIS: He's no Santa Claus. He's the Lord. His trip is our trip. . . . When I decided to receive Knowledge I felt the light technique was questionable . . . but then I saw this incredible light in the center of a circle in the middle of my forehead . . . a diamond was there spinning and spinning and getting larger and larger . . . and then the divine music . . . a heavy roar for a while then dinnnnnnnng, every fiber of my being began to vibrate . . . an incredible wave of bliss shot through me . . . then my mind began to play this incredible rock and roll, Bam boum boum boum boum.

KRASSNER: This is like being with CREEP. . . . Did the Maharaj Ji give Richard Nixon a secret contribution?

DAVIS: Yes—he gave Richard Nixon his life.

Later that evening we hear the Perfect Master's third and last satsang. He compares our consciousness to the gas tank of a car. The car isn't running because our gasoline is clouded by all the dirt clogging up the engine, and he is the filter that will make the engine clean and give our car a perfect functioning. The Blue Aquarius band plays only briefly after the satsang. For the millen-nial accoutrements must be quickly dismantled in order to restore the Astrodome to its original function. Reality returns. The following day at one o'clock the Cleveland Browns are scheduled to play the Houston Oilers in the Houston Astrodome.

November 11

"I had everything in life," a beautiful young English premie says to me as we sit on a plane bound for New York, chatting with Spanish and American devotees: "terrific grades at university, a super boyfriend, a lovely job at a macrobiotic shop. But somehow I was always trying on different egos for size. I came to Maharaj Ji by divine coincidence, of course. I was in Amsterdam, and had just spent a solid night weeping, saying 'help me, help me' to the Universe. I couldn't say it to any *one* because I was an atheist, as my parents are. And that same morning a girl gave me the address of an ashram. I received Knowledge two days later. When I came home, my mother—she's a professor at the University of London, as is my father—kept showing me a picture of myself as a four-year-old saying, 'You've become like this again, so happy and peaceful. . . .' You see we're all really children and we're just *playing* at being grown-ups."

"Knowledge is just like a pair of roller skates," an engineer from New York interjects crisply. "You can use them or not use them. The main thing is that you *have* them."

The British premie spins around toward the New Yorker. "Look, do you mind going back to your seat?" she barks out sharply. "You're disturbing our talk, you're giving out bad vibes."

"The British premies are famous for being tough, authoritarian," she continues as the engineer returns dejectedly to his seat. "That's one of the reasons I left England, in order to give satsang in Spain. Spanish premies are about the loveliest, so gentle. Germans either freak out or make particularly *solid* premies, curiously gentler than the British. Americans are so insecure, America is a bad environment for saints. For instance, Americans are always asking Maharaj Ji to come to the United States to have material reassurance of their faith."

Are all Knowledge sessions equally long? I ask. I describe the line at the ashram which I'd seen the previous morning.

"Oh, they vary a great deal," she says. "I know some people

who got Knowledge in four minutes yesterday because they had a flight to catch."

I ask her whether the rumor is true that the British premies who served as marshals at the Millennium were armed with guns.

"Certainly not," she laughs, swinging her very long blond hair. "But . . . what if they were . . . would you think it preposterous if they *were* armed? After all, wouldn't *you* arm yourself if you had the task of protecting God on earth?"

The plane is landing, she is gathering her stuff. From the seat ahead of her she carefully unpins the picture of Maharaj Ji which she has been staring at for much of the trip.

"Ah, he has such a sweet face!" she exclaims.

We exit from the plane. At the airport, she waves good-bye.

"See you in the Golden Age!" she cries.

Moonies:
The Heavenly Deception

MAY 1972: Moments remembered from a fortnight of student rallies at Yale University protesting the imprisonment of two Black Panthers who had been charged with contempt of court during their trial:

Among the milder courses of action suggested at a two-thousand-person gathering at Woodbridge Hall: kidnap Yale President Kingman Brewster, shut off the New Haven water supply. A more direct tactic: distribute free guns to whoever wants them. This last suggestion is offered by a Yale dropout who belongs to the Patriot Party, a white radical group whose slogan is "Stop thinking." "Give me some money and I'll buy guns!" he shouts. "I'll stand at the Green and distribute them!"

An equally exotic proposal is brought to the floor by an overwrought law student, who suggests mass suicide: Let each person be allotted a number, he says, and then each day for the following month the person whose number is drawn will give up his life in support of the Panthers.

"Why die?" a student pipes up in the stunned silence.

"To die like a Panther, to die like a man!" the future barrister cries.

The meeting dissolves in an apotheosis of radical guilt and threats of burning down the university; among rumors that 245 pints of liquid mercury (an ingredient used in homemade explosives) have been stolen from the Sterling Chemical Laboratory; among reports that Boston radicals planning to attend the rally planned for the forthcoming weekend had been purchasing guns in Massachusetts, and that 300 Minutemen have reserved motel rooms in the New Haven area; among speculations that if the virology lab was bombed, all its Lassa fever virus might spread through town.

A press conference for the Panther Defense Fund in Center Church. Abbie Hoffman: "We will not let America devour its youth! The Panthers have their breakfast for children program, the Establishment has its children for breakfast program!"

An hour later Jerry Rubin, in tanager scarlet pants, packs them again in Wolsey Hall. "It's you, the white middle-class students, who're the most oppressed class of our society! More oppressed than ghetto children or poor whites! You know what college is? It's an advanced form of toilet training!"

Great stomping, clapping from the audience. "I haven't taken a bath in six months! We're never going to grow up! We're never going to mature! Fuck rationality! It's the alcoholics who're putting the pot smokers in jail! Telling us to stop smoking pot is like telling Jews to stop eating matzohs!"

About to enter Yale University's freshman class that year was a thoughtful, mild-mannered young man called Chris Edwards who remembers attending several similar rallies. I pick up his story several years later, the year after his graduation, when tens of thousands of his generation of Americans, like Rennie Davis before them, were renouncing political activism for the great American pursuits of Community and Selfhood.

H E'D just graduated from Yale with straight A's in philosophy but his girlfriend left him for an Iraqi Marxist. His career at college was academically brilliant and emotionally arid. He was "searching desperately for community." Walking through the streets of Berkeley one summer in the late 1970s, Chris Edwards was approached by a young man his age who invited him to have dinner with "the family" he lived with, "a very loving, very idealistic group of young people." He went to dinner. He was a little perplexed by his hosts' affectionate, constant smiling; but their passionate interest in him seemed like an oasis after "the verbal jousts, the endless mocking and scorning" of his Ivy League life. He was touched by the affectionate way they piled brownies on his plate. They called themselves the Family. They had a country place in Boonville, ninety miles north of San Francisco.

"Since you enjoyed this evening so much, Chris, why don't you join us for the weekend?"

That night they took Chris to the country in a yellow school bus, the sides of which were painted with elephant faces. Plied with hot chocolate and marshmallows ("my boyhood favorite"), Chris continued to feel extraordinarliy loved and appreciated during his weekend at the Family's farm. His initial unease with their frequent God talk vanished during the strenuous program of singing, shouting, and group games the Family indulged in throughout the three days.

"Zip-A-Dee-Doo-Dah . . . Put On a Happy Face . . . Getting To Know You . . . Happy Days Are Here Again. . . ."

"Okay kids, let's go for a dip in the brook, last one in is a monkey!"

Chris is never given a moment to be alone, he's not even allowed to go to the bathroom by himself. He soon experiences "the ecstasy of merging into the mass, tasting the glorious pleasure that accompanies the loss of the ego." As Chris goes to sleep in a dormitory called the Chicken Palace he runs his fingers across the top of his sleeping bag "just as I used to do with my blanket as a child." No drugs, drink, sex, no problems or decisions. Chris signs up to stay for another week at the Family's camp, and then he signs a pledge form for a three-week stay. "Here was the warmth and free acceptance for which I had been searching. How different from college, where you could share a bathroom or classroom all year . . . without truly bridging the gulf between two lonely people."

Throughout these weeks Chris is never told that the Boonville farm is an indoctrination center for the Unification Church of the Reverend Sun Myung Moon. He only knows it as "a wonderful caring community."

In between long group discussions about how the Family is

going to help save mankind—"fulfill God's plan for creation," "create a world where there'll be no crime or poverty"—continuous group activities, just like in summer camp: There's even a camp cheer: "Choo-choo-choo, choo-choo-choo. Yay, yay—Pow!"

> Running like little children, giggling and laughing . . . people high on each other. . . . I could feel myself getting high, high from this smiling group, this happy Family surrounding me. . . .

The only cards he is allowed to write home have little designs of clowns and puppy dogs on them. The only time he is allowed to phone home one of the Family members keeps her ear close to Chris's, listening in.

In college Chris Edwards was particularly fond of Kant, Husserl, "and above all Hegel."

In the fourth week he gives the Family his "one oh oh" (100 percent) and takes particular pride in indoctrinating newcomers to the love-and-brotherhood ethic of Boonville Camp. "God's even here in the *cookie* dough," he tells novices during kitchen tasks.

Barely six weeks after his first dinner with the Family, Chris has been transferred to "city work" and is a full-time Moonie. Through his sincerity and obedience he has joined those of the elect who are allowed to know that God has sent a twentieth-century messiah to earth in the form of a fifty-five-year-old Korean businessman called Sun Myung Moon. To participate in the task of redeeming mankind from the hold of Satan, Chris is lying his way through the streets of Berkeley, selling flowers whose proceeds he says are going to a fund for "deprived children." In fact the hundreds of tax-free dollars that his flower team earns each day are immediately deposited into "Father" Moon's numerous bank accounts in the Bay Area. Chris has been instructed in the doctrine of "heavenly deception." It teaches that since all persons not redeemed by membership in Moon's cult belong to the world of Satan there is no reason to respect their principles of honesty or truth.

Chris has also renounced his natural parents (who are tainted because they're descendants of Adam and Eve's sin) and has chosen as his True Parents Father Moon and his wife, the True Mother. On Sunday mornings he goes to a Prayer Meeting Ground consecrated by Reverend Moon himself and with hundreds of cult members recites the Children's Oath, a long vow to overcome Lucifer and win the entire world over for the new messiah. Scribbled in indelible ink on Chris's knuckles are the slogans "No More Concepts" and "Smash Out Doubt." He has become skilled at the technique of "love bombing," which Moonies are taught to practice upon their prospective recruits—flattery, a constant and loving smile, a gaze specifically aimed at two inches behind the subject's eyes. His group leader has a Ph.D. in behavioral psychology from Michigan and tells him to "actualize" when he's not working hard enough.

Chris actualizes for seventeen-hour stretches recruiting new disciples for selling flowers in streets and late-night bars. At least three more hours of his waking day are dedicated to group chanting, group prayer, and indoctrination sessions from *Master Speaks*, a collection of Moon's sayings. He is constantly exhausted by lack of sleep, often weakened by the malnutrition caused by his high-carbohydrate diet, comes close to have his infected hand amputated when the cult refuses to let him see a doctor until it's almost too late. Whenever he suffers a moment of doubt, exhaustion, hunger, nausea, homesickness, or sexual temptation (intercourse not specifically approved by Father Moon is considered "worse than murder"), he resorts to the inner chanting of an invocation against the Evil One. "Smash out Satan! Smash out Satan!"

The story of Chris Edwards's seven-month stay in the Unification Church, of how this cult managed to turn a highly intelligent young American into a robot, ends with a different sort of terror: Chris returns to his natural parents only after being kidnapped at their behest by the "deprogrammer" Ted Patrick, whom he's been indoctrinated to look upon as "Satan himself." "The Impala pulled in back of the Holiday Inn . . . man opened door . . . ohmyGod, Heavenly Father, save me, save me! big men, two big men climbed in back . . . my arms pinned . . . doors slammed, car flew out of lot . . . futile chanting—SAVE ME, FATHER. . . ."

The Unification Church of Reverend Sun Myung Moon, which has claimed some thirty thousand "followers" and seven thousand "hard-core members" in the United States, differs radically from the numerous other Eastern sects that have flourished in the United States in the past few decades. And in order to assess its particular dangers it must be seen for what it is, a new kind of cult which uses recent methods of behavior modification and corporate management techniques to achieve specific political and economic ends. Whereas other Oriental sects offer ancient Vedic meditations as a road to "higher consciousness," the methods of Moon's church are more akin to those used by twentieth-century totalitarian regimes to indoctrinate dissidents into cohesive loyalty— sleep deprivation, low-energy diets, withholding of information, frequent and disorienting shifts of living quarters, rigid schedules of group activities cleverly interspersed with brainwashing talk fests.

Maharaj Ji and Hare Krishna appealed to the apolitical streak of the post–Vietnam War generation. Moon has preached a grandiosely detailed program of right-wing action which has aspired to influence strongly our domestic and foreign policy, and which has aimed to unite all religions under his leadership into one worldwide theocracy by the late 1980s (Moon: "Separation between religion and politics is what Satan likes best").

Other spiritual cafeterias of the 1970s catered to that generation's rebellion against the Protestant work ethic. Former members of the Unification Church, however, report that they were exhorted to make a minimum of one hundred dollars a day for Moon to earn salvation; and one of them has boasted that she single-handedly made *one quarter of a million dollars* for the cult in her four years of membership. Captain of a six-truck flower-selling team, each truck packed with buckets of sweet william, daffodils, and carnations, Barbara Underwood* drove through numerous states in three months, selling from 7:00 A.M. to 1:00 A.M. in streets, factories, office buildings, and bars. (Father Moon's top aides encourage their acolytes to frequent bars because "people with a few drinks in them buy more readily.") Selling her flowers at a 400 percent markup, she made over sixty thousand dollars a year to redeem the world from Satan's hold, and boasted that she earned more

* Barbara Underwood and Betty Underwood, *Hostage to Heaven: Four Years in the Unification Church, by an Ex-Moonie and the Mother Who Fought to Free Her* (New York: Clarkson N. Potter, 1979).

money in her holy business than her dad, "and he's a lawyer." She was taught that as an "urban guerrilla" for the forces of world redemption she mustn't breathe a word to new recruits about the cult's financial activities and that each client deceived into buying her flowers *has actually taken a step toward heavenly redemption.*

Ambitious and diligent, this devotee has taken her "holy brigade" of sellers as far as Montreal (*"Voulez-vous acheter des fleurs?"*), and resorted to selling little American flags and fortune cookies on a cold winter night when her team was stuck with frozen flowers. Back in Boonville to attend top-level meetings she reports that the so-called "meditation hour" allowed cult members from 5:00 to 6:00 P.M. was also intended to be "the only time for showering, letter writing, playing musical instruments, counseling, reading, or taking a hike." These corporate managers' hectic schedules may make one want to take a bus to the nearest TM camp.

(Samples from the Master's Sayings: "We must reclaim all ownership of money and land from Satan's stolen stockpile." "Do you like to make green bills happy? . . . So many green bills are crying . . . they're all destined to go to Father [Moon].") Team cheers, kindergarten food, "bombing" with "love," rose-selling crusades, Smiley Buttons, Children's Oaths to a Heavenly Family, thirty "Boonville" youth camps spread throughout the United States—such sentimental imagery has appealed to a deeply infantile streak in many contemporary American adolescents, more than a few of whom come from exceptionally "well-educated" and "united" families.

In the past decades the hard-selling activities of Moon's flower-vending teams helped him to do very good business. In New York City alone, his Church was able to buy for a national headquarters the former Columbia University Club on West Forty-fourth Street (right opposite the Harvard Club and the Century Association), as well as the former New Yorker Hotel on West Thirty-fourth Street, the Manhattan Center ten blocks down, and a two-million-dollar building of the Loft Candy Company in Queens. Moon set up his own theological seminary in a monastery once owned by the Christian Brothers in upstate New York. Until 1981, he himself lived with his wife and seven children in the twenty-five-room mansion formerly owned by the Samuel Bronfman family in Tarrytown.

He also owned a fifty-foot cabin cruiser, the *New Hope*, nearly succeeded in obtaining majority holding of the New Diplomat Bank in Washington, D.C., and purchased a vast complex of fishing fleets and fish-processing plants centered in Virginia, Massachusetts, and Louisiana. These made Moon the leading exporter of untaxed fish in the United States, his so-called Church of Unification having acquired the tax-exempt status of all religious institutions. The bluefin tuna caught in Gloucester, for instance, was shipped to the Orient under the pretense that it was a "gift" to his followers there, and was sold in Japan at twenty dollars a pound.

Moon's cult has displayed a shrewd, pragmatic mercantilism, and a commercial genius for imitation and packaging. Moon came from a Protestant family in northern Korea, but was excommunicated from the Presbyterian Church in the 1950s after founding his own cult. According to a *New York Times* report he was arrested several times in Korea, although accounts differ whether the arrests were for political activities or "on morals charges . . . because of 'purification' rites with female initiates." When he sent his first missionaries to the United States in the early 1960s, he made his sect ascetic for American export and Westernized its theology. Although the doctrine he taught in Korea and Japan is based on Buddhism, he shrewdly marketed it for Americans in the form of a Christian Youth Crusade.

What Moon has sold us is a hodgepodge of heretic Christianity, rabid civil religion, and human potential movement practices whose elements are much more familiar and appealing to young Americans than those of any other Asian sect. According to *The Divine Principle*, the sacred book that Moon claims was revealed to him by Christ in 1936, when he was sixteen, God had intended Adam and Eve to have "perfect children" and immediately create God's kingdom on earth. The plan was thwarted by Eve's lapse into sin. When God sent Jesus to redeem mankind the assigned Redeemer bungled his mission by failing to marry and bear perfect children (note the stress on family again). Enter the Second Messiah, who will end the battle fought between God and Satan since the Garden Scene of act I. We are told this Second Messiah was born in Korea in 1920, just like Moon.

As for Moon's civil religion, it has taught politically disaffected young people to look on America again as "God's final bulwark on earth," "the nation which God loves and has prepared the most," the "chosen nation" which must maintain a constant peak of military superiority to win the Armageddon over satanic Communism. Between 1969 and 1974, for instance, Moon's campaign in support of the Vietnam War, the invasion of Cambodia, and the beleaguered presidency of Richard Nixon was masterminded by the Freedom Leadership Foundation headed by Neil Salonen, a former executive of the Dale Carnegie Institute who has served as president of the Unification Church's American branch. To achieve his divine plan, Moon has also stated his intention of infiltrating our political system at its grass roots. ("If the U.S. continues its corruption and we find among the Senators and Congressmen no one really usable for our purposes we can make senators and congressmen out of our members.") The divine plan seemed to demand that Moon maintain very close personal corporate ties to the dictatorship of Park Chung Hee. Moon came to the United States only after he had already become a multimillionaire from a large industrial conglomerate in Korea which produces among other things heavy machinery, titanium, marble bases, shotguns, and ginseng tea. He arrived in 1972, the high point of Nixon's popularity, ready to support the President and his program of "Vietnamization" and to capitalize on the possibility that American youth were starved for family, God, country, sexual restraints, and their lost childhood.

"Conversion," William James wrote, "is in essence a normal adolescent phenomenon, incidental to the passage from the child's small universe to the wider intellectual and spiritual life of society. . . ." All former members of the Moon cult whose testimony I have heard or read cite social pressures which they find unique to our decade, and which makes the rite of passage from adolescence to maturity particularly difficult: the mechanical quality of much of our education, a tightly competitive job market which renders part of that education useless, the painful sense of obsolescence felt by many young adults, the menaces of an overly eroticized society. They all suggest that while cult life serves as a refuge from true adulthood the infantile playacting of Moon's Church can offer a

curiously potent illusion of adulthood. The adolescent's anguish
about being marginal to society is suddenly replaced by a sense of
cosmic purpose and corporate power; Moon's managerial go-getters
are world savers doing holy business; and unlike the members of
any other Eastern cult marketed in the United States, they are
exhorted to be enterprising salesmen in the familiar spirit of the
American Protestant ethic.

The conversion of Christopher Edwards struck me as all the
more troubling because of his evident intelligence and wit. Edwards
describes numerous tactics used by the Unification Church to purge
the recruit of his skepticism after he has been already mesmerized
by "the warmth and caring" of the highly isolated Boonville Camp.

Cult leaders organize confusing group encounter games with
no clear rules so as to make the recruit feel helpless and disori-
ented. Chris is made to play a totally irrational game of volleyball
during which the teams rhythmically chant "Bomb with Love,"
"Blast with Love." He is initially angered by the mayhem, is ordered to shout louder, louder. "As I clapped and shouted I could
feel my tensions slipping away, my sense of involvement growing."
The recruit is constantly rewarded for his compliance with group
activities by additional shows of affection—flattering words, hugs,
gifts of candy. Religious beliefs of a nebulous charismatic nature
are drilled into the recruit in between the bouts of physical activity
which are instilling group cohesion. "God is searching the world
to call His children home one by one. Try praying, Chris. . . ."

Revivalist hysteria takes over. An intense inner conflict is created between the "old" and "new" identities by increasingly stressing the power of Satan. Recruits are forced to confess that their
old lives were worthless. Throughout the nascent converts' stay at
camp, seasoned cult members are assigned to them around the clock
to reinterpret their old lives according to the new beliefs. New acolytes are promised that they will receive gifts of prophecy if they offer the cult unswerving loyalty. They must also follow the Master's
complex dictates on sexual practices: Cult members can only consummate their marriages with Father Moon's specific consent, and
the first three copulations must occur in the woman-above position
in witness to "the woman-dominated fallen state where Eve's seduction of Adam had left us." "What are we going to do about

the matter of homosexuality?" a Moonie asked Moon. "If it really gets to be a problem," the Master answers, "tell them to cut it off, barbecue it, put it in a shoebox, and mail it to me." The Lord of the Second Advent then "roared" with laughter.

Why couldn't Chris Edwards see through such claptrap? Have Moon's behavioral psychologists devised methods of mind control so clever that they can break down all intelligent resistance? Or was Edwards, as he himself seems to suggest, suffering from a new "malaise" that led him to crave instant "relating"—instant intimacy—so intensely that he was willing to swallow any nonsense to feel important and loved? As Chris climbs up the organizational hierarchy of the Moon Church and is indoctrinated with its specific brand of Satanism, his own method of dealing with inner doubts shifts from energetic participation in group activities to the mesmeric devices of "inner chanting" drilled into him by the cult. Satan is blamed, for instance, when Chris fights sleepiness during a lecture by Reverend Moon himself. The pudgy, bald, uniquely charmless guru in a blue business suit addresses his acolytes through an interpreter in shouted Korean, "surveying the crowd with indifference . . . chopping the air with violent strokes," while Chris, trying to keep awake, chants to himself SMASH OUT SATAN, SMASH OUT SATAN.

What is most alarming in such testimony is Chris's admission that his loneliness, his need for community and for a childlike passivity are so immense that he'd rather shout or chant his way out of doubt than scrutinize the cult's methods or beliefs, thereby risking to lose the bliss of "belonging." "Group affiliation is a stronger force than ideology," Edwards writes, "which only justifies and reinforces the affiliation. . . . I who had learned to dwell in solitude was now learning to live . . . in utter obedience . . . a mere heavenly child with no past life, no history."

The sense of infantile dependence, the renunciation of the will to which Edwards confesses are familiar from many other accounts of mystical experience. But what Chris Edwards's experience and that of other former Moonies implies is that the same TV, fast-food generation that turned its back on material and technological values in the 1960s never abandoned the most striking effect of technological values: the search for rapid and sure results. They seem to expect the immediate achievement of certain experiences—"warm relationships," "relating in a close way"—which used to be waited for with more patience and skepticism. Who of us born before 1950 went to college burdened with the psychobabble of the self which recurs in the language of most young cult members—"creating a supportive community," "warm, loving groups," with "people who feel comfortable with each other's needs"? Many of the ex-Moonies so taken with the "closeness" of the Church Family claim to have spent their childhood and adolescence with "close," "caring," "supportive" families of their own. One wonders if they have not confused "family" and "society," and suffer from a regressive desire to prolong into the inevitably cool world of college and career the warmth of family ties.

What about "deprogramming"? Most first-person accounts of cult defection I know of describe it as a harrowing experience. Chris Edwards speaks with painful honesty of the year of psychotherapy that followed his leaving the cult, his recurring states of trance and extreme anxiety. Other studies based on the testimonies of hundreds of former cultists document the hallucinations and "floating" that can pursue them for months or years; their recurring fear of satanic possession; their guilt in all matters sexual; the sense of guilt they also suffer about lying to parents, friends, and strangers; and the confused feelings they have toward the fact that they may never make that much money again as long as they live.

Former Moonies tend to engage in anti-Moon activism with the same single-minded manic commitment they once offered to the Church. They often present us with a phenomenon of reverse Paulinism, apostles turned persecutors of their former faith. After a year of study at the Princeton Theological Seminary, Chris Edwards worked in the anti-Moon crusade as a counselor and lecturer on cults. As for Barbara Underwood, she even married one of her own deprogrammers, but still she found "no community of worship as energizing as the Unification Church." And she left us with this strikingly nostalgic statement about a totalitarian technique that has turned many thousands of young Americans into lying hustlers.

The Church Family offered first of all a sense of belonging to a romantic and intense world that needed each and every one of us . . . brothers and sisters, we were bound in eros, in the instinct for life, but shielded by Church-ordained safeguards against any expression of sexuality. Tired of competitive scholarship, we welcomed community emotion. . . .

As the sect's psychological aggressiveness increased, there were indications its members were resorting to physical violence. In 1979, two directors of Moon's church in Virginia were arrested on charges of shooting at the car of two former Moonies who had gone to their previous cult homes to retrieve their belongings.

Many former cult members have testified that Moon urges his followers to be "willing to die for him." Chris Edwards reported that he received two death threats after his book* appeared. His parents—like those of many defectors from Moon's cult—had to hire a live-in detective for many months because of the harassment—break-ins, trailing of family cars—which occurred after his deprogramming. The detective assigned to one of the defector's families was hospitalized for a week with a concussion after a Moonie allegedly beat him on the head repeatedly with a rock. Former cult members like Chris Edwards fear that this violence might grow as Moon's messianic hopes for world domination fail to be fulfilled.

Yet until 1981 there were ominous parallels between our government's passivity toward Moon's sect and early warnings, also gone unheeded by the State Department, concerning the dangers of the ill-fated People's Temple on the island of Guyana. In 1978, a congressional subcommittee headed by Congressman Donald Fraser revealed the Master's alarmingly close ties to the South Korean dictatorship and the Korean CIA. They disclosed, for instance, that the Master's principal aide and constant companion, Lieutenant Colonel Pak Bo Hi, was entitled to use the direct cable between the Korean embassy in Washington, D.C., and Seoul—a line of communication which only reaches the Korean prime minister, the director of that nation's CIA, and President Park himself.

* Christopher Edwards, *Crazy for God* (Englewood Cliffs, N.J.: Prentice-Hall, 1979).

The Fraser Committee also cited many federal laws concerning illegal use of funds being violated by the sect, and recommended that the State Department and the Department of Internal Revenue undertake an immediate investigation.

But the Fraser Committee's suggestions were not followed for over two years. Throughout the early eighties, Moon continued to strive for increased respectability by such ventures as his International Conference on the Unity of the Sciences. The ICUS was a typically grandiose venture which every year invited some four hundred scholars to seminars at the Washington Hilton, offering them multi-thousand-dollar fees to sit on panels and discuss such themes as "the search for absolute values." Many more academics accepted than refused. And Moon's guest list often read like a little Who's Who in Academe, including many Nobel laureates, and other scholars as distinguished as Walter Kaufmann, the Princeton philosophy professor and biographer of Nietzsche. These impeccably accredited savants, whose intellectual integrity heretofore had never been questioned, seemed to have no trouble taking part in conferences run by a man who presumes to "rule the universe."

The reverend's easy days came to an end in 1982, when he was convicted of income tax fraud, and of other financial misdemeanors relating to a sum of $1.7 million deposited in the Chase Manhattan Bank. He was sentenced to a jail term which he served in the Federal Penitentiary in Danbury, Connecticut. Yet even during his stay in prison his business empire grew substantially, acquiring a Japanese ginseng tea distributorship, a Uruguayan bank, and media properties such as the *Washington Times* newspaper, into which Moon has sunk more than $150 million.

Thus, the cult has been able vigorously to continue its propaganda campaigns, notwithstanding its leader's incarceration. One of the nation's most powerful lobbying groups, Gray and Co., has been hired to polish Reverend Moon's tarnished image. A distinguished Harvard Law School professor, Lawrence H. Tribe, was enlisted by the cult toward the close of Moon's trial, and directed his losing appeals all the way to the Supreme Court. The sect has exploited the notion, shared by some hard-core civil libertarians, that the Justice Department has no constitutional authority to judge the internal finances of any religious group. And Moon's capacity to pay for such expert and persuasive advocacy seems inexhaustible. In 1984 the dean of Washington defense lawyers, Edward Bennett Williams, was recruited to mastermind an unsuccessful attempt to obtain a presidential pardon for the reverend. Another prominent figure, Jeremiah Gutman, president of the New York Civil Liberties Union, was trotted out by the Church to brief journalists on the violation of Moon's civil rights. Full-page ads have been run in *The New York Times*, the *Washington Post*, and other publications, depicting Moon's conviction as a miscarriage of justice. And in 1985 the Unification Church began a four-million-dollar blitz—consisting of books, gifts, six hours of lectures on videocassette—addressed to some 300,000 of the nation's mainstream churches. Emulating its earlier scholars' conferences, it stepped up its goodwill campaign by inviting some seven thousand U.S. clergymen to a series of all-expenses-paid Unification seminars in the Caribbean, Europe, and Asia.

In the face of such zeal, former cult members fear that the Master's imprisonment may have further strengthened the loyalties of his hard-core disciples, and predict that we have not seen the last of Reverend Moon. Even if their fears are not realized, and the United States is spared a resurgence of Moon's protofascist spirituality, the West at large might not be Moon-proof. For if he fails to restore his profile in the United States, there is always the possibility that Moon will shift the focus of his millennial aspirations to another country. "If he finds it impossible to do his work in America," Moon recently announced in that sacral third person he uses in public appearances, "he will go to Germany . . . Germans are trained in totalism [*sic*], so it will be easier to work on his mission there."

God Watching in America
and
Thomas Merton: Man and Monk

THERE is a religious bent in many chapters of this volume. It does not come from a severe religious upbringing but rather from a dearth of it, from the solitude of a lonesome quest. Although my parents have been agnostics, since childhood I have been mysteriously attracted by the Catholic Church and have brought myself up in it more or less alone. Though a totally erratic practitioner, I have been able to remain some kind of a Christian by distinguishing The Church-as-She (rooted in time and never institutionalized) from The Church-as-It (the often corrupt material bureaucracy seated in Rome). My meditations on the Berrigans' witness, on the suffering of Holocaust victims, on the religious symbolism in Margaret Atwood's fiction, on Harvey Cox's spiritual gyrations, or on Thomas Merton's life, may be chapters of an ongoing dialogue with Him/She/It Out There which I have continued to engage in, in great part through the act of writing.

My observations on Thomas Merton in the second of these essays were enriched by these works: *Merton: A Biography*, by Monical Furlong. *Thomas Merton: Monk and Poet*, by George Woodcock. *A Catch of Anti-Letters*, by Thomas Merton and Robert Lax. *Thomas Merton: Prophet in the Belly of a Paradox*, edited by Gerald Twomey.

God Watching in America

I N arriving in the United States, the religious aspect of the country was the first thing that struck my attention," de Tocqueville wrote in mid-nineteenth century. "Strange sects endeavored to strike extraordinary paths to eternal happiness . . . religious insanity is very common in the United States."

The ceremonial prayers heard in Congress, at the opening of every Supreme Court session, and even of Democratic and Republican party conventions have long struck the foreign visitor as one of our strangest curiosities, as exotic as the polygamy or body tattooing of some African tribes. It is ironic that a nation as often accused of materialism as ours remains, in this century, the most profoundly religious society in the Western world. In what other country could nationwide polls still attest that a whopping 96 percent of our population profess a faith in the Almighty, that 75 percent of us would not vote for an atheist, that over 50 percent of Americans regularly attend church services (compared to a mere 10 percent in a church state called Great Britain)? Where else have heads of state felt obliged to invoke the Deity in two centuries of inaugural speeches, an invocation that in most of the anticlerical West could well spell the end of a man's political career? Since the Enlightenment, what nation has been prey to a more widespread hunger for religious ecstasy, more cycles of revivalism, of exotic cults, little and great awakenings?

In the last decades, fervid fluctuations of American spirituality have made the business of religion watching, and the new literary genre of popular theology, more fascinating than ever. And no writer has provided a more accurate barometer of our religious trends than the astute, personable Harvey Cox, professor at the Harvard Divinity School. His book *The Secular City* became, in 1965, the first truly theological best-seller in the history of American publishing.

In the year 1965 Martin Luther King held his largest rally. Father James Groppi began to go to jail for agitating about open housing in Milwaukee, and a nucleus of other Catholic priests nurtured their first plans for radical civil disobedience against the Vietnam War. The fashionable motto among activist clergymen that year was "Picketing is a form of prayer." ("After all," an engaged cleric once said to me, "prayer is a form of picketing.") And the message for most religious liberals was: "Out of the church and into the streets." Celestially in tune with the times, Cox's *Secular City* preached that the truly spiritual modern man is "no longer interested in the mystery of life but in the pragmatic solution of particular problems." The Christianity Cox offered was a secular morality as rigidly scrubbed of ritual and transcendence as the Ethical Culture Society. Referring to all religious myths as "narcotic vagaries," Cox had then offered a fairly classical Freudian exegesis of traditional religion as infantile disorder and urged Westerners to turn away more than ever from metaphysical tutelage. This Harvard-based Baptist minister became the most fashionable (and readable) champion of that ultraworldly Christianity which found its most radical expression in the "Death of God" theology. He saw God as deeply encrusted in humanity's political process and identified His will with highly specific movements of reform and revolution. Most forms of personal mysticism were suspect. The most permissible manner of ecstasy was that found in communal social action, such as political demonstrations.

Indeed, it is hard to forget the elation of those sixties pageants: the teach-ins, the sit-ins, the fasts, the solemn candlelit vigils, the processions winding down Pennsylvania Avenue with all the trappings of religious pilgrimages, often led by black-clad clerics like Harvey Cox, William Sloane Coffin, and Daniel Berrigan, their stark refrain of "All we are saying / Is give peace a chance" sung with the hypnotic monotony of a rosary. The communal ecstasy of these expiatory rites enabled us to channel most of our needs for ritual and liturgy into a prolonged feast of activism.

The decline of that activism—and of its attendant euphoria— was the spiritual fable of the 1970s. Within a few years of *The Secular City*'s militant worldliness, the millennial catchwords of the 1960s—"End the War Now," "Peace Today," "Free All Prisoners"—were being replaced in our storefront windows and on bumper stickers by such placid mottoes as "Occult Power," "Meditate for Peace," "Honk for Jesus." And religion watchers were trying to analyze the erosion of one of our most entrenched progressive myths: For some decades, we had been attributing the West's general disaffection from organized religion to the churches' lack of "relevance," to their incapacity to adjust to the social problems of modern times. But in the early 1970s this interpretation was being negated by the pitiful decimation of the very churches that *had* opted for social relevance and activism; and by the spectacular growth of precisely those sects and cults which were the least tolerant and ecumenical, the most aloof from secular political problems, the most severely demanding of surrender and obedience.

Could it be (this was soon admitted by many of the seventies' chastened liberals) that such churchy activisms as Boycott Grapes rallies, civil rights and antiwar agitation, were being offered in more efficient and more attractive manner by secular groups? Might the liberal churches be committing suicide by deemphasizing the one incentive unique to religion—the offer of Ultimate Meaning, and that sense of the numinous which is only attained by a rigorous practice of liturgy?

Reenter Harvey Cox in the watershed year 1973. (Astronauts are leaving NASA after having mystical experiences on the way to the moon to work in the born-again movement; former militant Rennie Davis becomes aide-de-camp to a fifteen-year-old self-proclaimed Indian mystic.) In a lovely and gullible book published that year, *The Seduction of the Spirit*, Cox reconstructed his vision of human needs on precisely those foundations which he had dismantled in *The Secular City*. Whereas that earlier book had attempted to purge us of the occult, the new one strove to exorcise rationalism. To the surprise of his fans and critics, the diverse salvational, and mystical cults that swept our land in 1973 struck Cox as "a renaissance of spirituality" that would remedy the noxious impact of technological materialism. Cox struck me at that time as a loyal, overimpulsive lifeguard of the sacred, eager to save Christianity by whatever means were at his disposal. Secularization having proved to be a dismal failure, he was swimming to our rescue with life preservers of myth and ritual, preaching a new piety in which the occult regained an almost medieval role. By 1973 he was preaching a syncretic openness that would allow us to feel equally worshipful in the presence of all varieties of ecstatic cults, from yogic mysticism to the hot tubs of Esalen. His group-grope pietism began to make me a little uneasy. I sensed that he was perpetually ready to don a Tibetan Buddhist garment and chant a medieval Slavonic melody while performing a Sufi dervish dance, ending his hybrid liturgy with a consciousness-raising exercise adapted from the human potential movement. I worried about his playfully voracious openness to all forms of Orientalia. Was he forgetting Kierkegaard's warning that "a certain severity is indispensable to the seriousness of eternity"?

But I remained one of his fans, and was happy to see that in his following book, *Turning East*, Professor Cox went on a serious fast after his bout of spiritual gluttony. He learned his new abstinence by going to work full time in the Global Village's Spiritual Cafeterias. He became a full participant in the various religious movements he had earlier admired from a distance, and found many of them sterile, if not totally corrupt. Traveling from Cambridge, Massachusetts ("Benares on the Charles") to Boulder, Colorado ("Tibet in the Rockies") for concrete firsthand experience, he danced with the Sufis, sat with Zen monks, chanted with the Hare Krishnas, and found that many of these imported practices are as un-Oriental as a carryout bucket of chow mein in a Minneapolis diner.

Although he learned a genuine contemplative discipline at a center for Tibetan studies in Colorado, even there Cox's growing distrust of our neo-Orientalism was confirmed by the sight of acolytes striding about the streets in expensive meditation pants, one-upping each other on how long they had been "sitting" with the same pride well-to-do liberals displayed when comparing the number of their overnight jail stays in the Vietnam era. By the late 1970s Cox was predicting that in our society most Oriental cults are bound to be corrupted by consumer greed and by our insatiable yearning for novelty. For in our Spiritual Ticketron, American East-Turners merely co-opted the vocabulary and outward trappings of Eastern religion; they used them to reinforce, rather than overcome, their preoccupation with self-identity, self-actualization, do-your-own-thing individualism—concerns all diametrically opposed to the ideal of self-abnegation fundamental to both Eastern religions and to Christianity.

And so, having grasped the dangers of instant mysticism, by the end of the decade Cox had returned almost full swing to the classical modernist premises of his *Secular City*, and focused again on the Gospel message of social concern and mutual responsibility.

But wait, wait . . . we live in the United States. It seems to be part of our national character to alter our modes of spirituality as readily as Seventh Avenue changes the length of its hems, and Harvey Cox remains an insatiable reporter of our religious fashions. Flash forward to 1984: By then Cox has correctly sensed the occurrence of a totally different kind of religious phenomenon, perhaps the most important one of the century: the return of religion as a formidable political force, both on the Left and on the Right, and on a global scale. In the past few years, *traditional* religion has emerged as a democratizing force in Poland; as a renewed incentive for political fanaticism throughout Islam; as an incitement to revolution among Catholic clergy in Latin America; as a new liberal-activist force in the United States, well evidenced by the Catholic bishops' collective support for disarmament and their condemnation of our government's discrimination against the poor; as a lobbying platform for reactionary politics in North American fundamentalist sects such as Jerry Falwell's. It is this proliferation of recent religious activism which Harvey Cox set out to explore in 1984 in his latest venture, *Religion in the Secular City*.

The new alliance of faith and politics, in Cox's view, is chiefly caused by the demise of that dominant zeitgeist of the past century, "modernism," and by the stirring of a new "postmodernist" era. The analysis rests on Cox's debatable definition of modernism, which he sees as an essentially bourgeois movement which discriminated strongly against blacks, women, the poor and the colonized, and whose central features were the following: unlimited faith in science-based technology as the principal solution to the human problems; the secularization of religion, and a severe distrust of its more mythic aspects; sovereign nation-states as the primary units of the global political system.

One could argue that most of these modernist principles have been displaced in the past two decades by the emergence of transnational political alliances, by the global resurgence of hybrid mysticisms, and, most recently, of traditional piety. Cox predicts that contrary to all earlier forecasts, the "postmodern" age will be an era of religious revival, of a heightened return to the mythic and the sacral. And he has set out to define the contours of a "postmodern" faith which would be better suited to these new social and cultural conditions. He singles out as possible models two powerful Christian movements; however opposite they may seem, they share a deep hostility to the liberal modernist theology which secularized the Gospel to adjust it to twentieth-century needs. The models are Jerry Falwell's self-termed "redneck religion," which wields its political clout through the powerful social programs of the Moral Majority, and the equally activist but left-oriented Liberation Theology influential throughout Latin America.

Ever an optimist, our Harvard-based God-watcher tells us that the first of these models, Falwell-style revivalism, doesn't have a chance of becoming the prevailing mode of postmodern religion. Why not? Cox predicts that current fundamentalism, which thrives on its use of the electronic mass media, carries too great a discrepancy between its media and its message to have any long-range success. It is indeed ironic that the very same brand of ministers who decried the noxious impact of technology on the human spirit, and forbade generations of believers to attend movies, have become masters of cinema's most successful offspring—television. And in Cox's view this discordant tension between high-tech form and old-time Gospel may eventually backfire. The central metaphor used by the German Jewish writer Walter Benjamin in his epochal essay "The Work of Art in the Age of Mechanical Reproduction" is applied here to religion: Cox argues, with Benjamin, that an essential feature of any religious or artistic message is the sense of distance, awe, and authority it elicits, an authority easily lost when technology trivializes it into a consumer commodity. This loss of distance readily leads to the fading of the message's power, to the "decay" of its "aura." Thus Falwell-style spirituality could readily be depoliticized, and even destroy itself, through the very slickness of its vigorously propagated mass media.

If Jerry Falwell is a paradigm for the religious New Right in the United States, the hero of Cox's second and preferred model for a "postmodernist" piety is the Nicaraguan poet and diplomat Ernesto Cardenal. Cardenal, who began his religious life as a Trappist monk under the tutelage of Thomas Merton, exemplifies the faith of the new, lay-controlled religious "base communities" of North and South America. Cardenal's God is a radical opposite of the electronic gilt-edged godhead invoked by the Falwell movement, which, notwithstanding its claims of populism, vigorously supports the interests of capitalism and the entrepreneurial class. It is rather the suffering "dios pobre" of Liberation Theology, a deity whose alliance will always be with the marginals and the dispossessed, with the wretched of the earth. Cardenal is the kind of priest who classifies humanity into exploiters and exploited rather than believers and nonbelievers; who does not so much lament the fact that humanity has ceased praying, but rather that it does not have enough to eat; whose prevalent emotions are not so much nostalgia for old-time religiousness, but anger toward injustice and hope for radical social change.

Cox forecasts that of these two opposite strains of contemporary piety, Cardenal's "premodern" mysticism, unpolluted by electronics and fired with genuine populist goals, will prevail over the Falwellian alliance of high-tech and conservative politics. He describes models of the "base communities" presently mushrooming in the Americas—grass-roots groups which combine worship, Bible study, and multifaceted programs of social welfare. He estimates their number at several thousand in the United States alone, and predicts that they will soon replace the outdated authority of the parish system, which of itself was a nineteenth-century "modernist" phenomenon. Throughout the United States, shelters for the homeless and for battered women, centers for the mentally ill and the addicted, coalitions which lobby for low-cost housing are as often as not being sponsored, or heavily supported, by ecumenical church groups which also meet for communal worship. It is this style of piety, in Cox's view, which will flesh out the making of a postmodern religiousness. Its energy will come from the grass-roots periphery rather than from any traditional center; for it will be principally inspired by the visions of heretofore dispossessed groups—blacks and other minorities, women, Third World visionaries.

But the most novel configuration of this vision is a welding of political activism with a renewed mysticism, a fusion of Cox's *Secular City* worldliness and of his abiding interest in ritual. If Ernesto Cardenal is the archetypal leader of Cox's future spirituality, its ideal acolyte is a young Mexican Cox once observed at the shrine of Our Virgin of Guadalupe in Mexico City: dressed in a Che Guevara T-shirt, he was kneeling in front of the altar devoutly crossing himself over and over again. For one of the many "premodern" elements which Cox envisages for a "postmodern" religion is a return of those cultic practices which we have tended to deride from the time of the Enlightenment—pilgrimages, retreats, mnemonic repetitions of traditional prayers, a host of ritual observances once thought of as "the opium of the people" which still seem to fulfill unchanging needs of the human psyche.

Cox's predicted fusion of mysticism and politics is beautiful and outlandishly optimistic; this time round one hopes all the more fervently that his pulse taking is accurate. If he is right, if mysticism is indeed part of our future religious landscape, its return might be compared to the abiding popularity of narrative, both in literature and in the visual arts: Just as technology had been viewed as a potential destroyer of religious faith, so the new techniques of photography, film, television, were once predicted to abolish the need for novels, poetry, and most other forms of traditional art. But in 1987 all of these millennial enterprises seem to be blooming with unabated health. The writer Isaac Bashevis Singer offers us an insight here which could apply to religion quite as well as to literature: "There is no machine and no kind of reporting and no kind of film that can do for us what a Tolstoy or a Dostoevski or a Gogol did," he said in his 1978 Nobel lecture. "Progress can never kill literature, any more than it can kill religion . . . the more technology, the more people will be interested in what the human mind can produce *without* the help of electronics."

Cox announces the new fusion of politics and mysticism with a warning that this new alliance may well be a mixed blessing. Re-

ligion is an equal source of good and evil, producing "the sublime
and the perverse, Torquemada and St. Francis, inquisitions and
hospitals." Two centuries ago, human freedom demanded a secular
critique of religion. It presently requires a religious critique of the
secular. In the near future, our freedom may once more have to be
rescued by a secular critique of the excesses of faith.

But for the time being, Americans' new acquaintance with
Oriental and other foreign spiritual practices has brought one
major blessing to Harvey Cox and to other thoughtful Christians:
it has stimulated them to reexamine their own traditions; it has led
them to appreciate many contemplative aspects of the Christian
faith—from the stark meditations of the Desert Fathers to the pat-
terned imaginings of Saint Ignatius of Loyola—which have been hidden, or have atrophied, or simply have been taken for granted.
Harvey Cox himself now returns every Sunday to the modest Baptist church around the corner from his home. It is a church which
he has grown to love more deeply than ever, notwithstanding its
uneven preaching and music and its total lack of instant ecstasy,
and which is currently sponsoring programs of social welfare in the
Boston area. Zen Buddhism and most other Oriental practices, Cox
has concluded after his many peregrinations, are religions for innocents and saints. Christians will always need a religion for sinners in
which long periods of spiritual fast, of contrition, are essential.

Thomas Merton: Man and Monk

T HEY found him lying dead on
the floor of a hotel room in the suburbs of Bangkok, the victim of
accidental electrocution. He had apparently touched the live wire
of a faulty electric fan before settling down for his afternoon rest.
Father Thomas Merton was fifty-three years old, the author of
some forty volumes of poetry and prose, the American Church's

most eloquent theorist of nonviolence and its most versatile essay-ist, the man whom Daisetz Suzuki had designated as the most astute interpreter of Zen Buddhism in the West. The date of his death—December 10, 1968—was the twenty-seventh anniversary, to the day, of his entrance into Christianity's most rigid monastic order, a progeny of Benedictinism called Cistercians of the Strict-est Observance, commonly known as Trappists after their eigh-teenth-century reformer, the Abbot of la Trappe.

There was an awesome irony about the conditions of Thomas Merton's death: His fatal trip to the Far East was his first exten-sive venture beyond the monastic enclosure during his decades as a Trappist monk, his first transgression of that oath of "stability" which has been central to the Benedictine rule. For in the sixth century A.D., Saint Benedict set forth the three monastic vows binding on all men who wished to devote themselves to a life of contemplation under his rule: ". . . he shall promise stability, conversion of life and obedience." Stability, perhaps more poi-gnantly than any other vow, expresses the dynamic of renunciation which is at the heart of Christian monasticism. It binds the monk to live within the geographic bounds of his monastery until his death, only traveling beyond them as a great exception, with the permission of his abbot.

Many facts of Thomas Merton's life had been as paradoxical as those of his premature end. In 1946, five years after entering the Abbey of Gethsemane in Louisville, Kentucky, the man who had sought ultimate sanctity by becoming "A worm and no one" (Saint Benedict's seventh degree of humility) was catapulted to national fame by the account of his journey toward self-denial: *The Seven Storey Mountain*, gushingly eulogized by Bishop Fulton J. Sheen as "a twentieth century form of Saint Augustine's *Con-fessions*," sold some 400,000 copies in its first year of publication, running third on the best-seller list behind *The White Collar Zoo* and a book on canasta.

"His face was set in a great and deep peace," so goes the of-ficial report of his death, "and it was obvious that he had found Him whom he had searched for so diligently." There is a saccha-rine piety to those words which might have made Merton uneasy. For still another paradox of this particular contemplative is that he

tended to express himself with his intimates in a wry, self-depre-
cating shorthand that often verged on impudence. "Say that
Merton is dead and never existed," he wrote to a friend when he
was trying to sever himself from the success of *The Seven Storey
Mountain.* "Bogus Trappist exposed. Golf trousers under the cowl.
False priest caught giving candy to widows."

"Though I look through all my pockets," he wrote another
friend when officials of his order accused his pacifist writings of
being "Communist-influenced," "I can't find that old CP card.
Must have dropped out as I was mopping my brow in the confessional."

Several biographical details illuminate Merton's impulse to
enter the most austere of all monastic sects. Merton's Quaker
mother was an obsessionally devoted but demanding, cerebral
woman who kept an extensive diary of Tom's every activity, yet
sent him to bed without supper at the age of five for misspelling
the word which as "wich." She also refused to let her six-year-old
son ever see her again after she'd been taken to the hospital with a
fatal cancer because she felt children should be spared any morbid
scenes. The traumas of Merton's next sixteen years—his wander-
ings through two continents with a nomadic artist father who died
when Merton was fifteen, his misery in French and British boarding schools, his unhappy transient stays with a motley crew of relatives and family friends—are vividly recalled in *The Seven Storey
Mountain.* And his biographers have come close to certifying a
liaison which Merton had during his last two years in England,
before he came to the United States, with a young woman who
bore him a son after he had abandoned her. Both mother and son
were eventually killed in the London air raids, and this could only
add to that deep-seated guilt which, along with an uprooted youth,
are classical psychological incentives for the making of a monk.

Yet it is the general rowdiness of Merton's temperament as a
secular young man that his classmates at Columbia University are
most unanimous about. They remember him in his late teens and
early twenties as a bon vivant who was exceptionally uninhibited
in sexual matters, both in talk and action: Energetic fraternity
man, lusty drinker, girl chaser, and raconteur, editor of college
yearbook and art editor of the *Columbia Jester* (to which he con-

tributed many gifted drawings of bawdy nudes), he cloaked the scars of his nomadic, orphaned childhood with an abundance of high spirits. He had come into the junior class at Columbia after two years at Cambridge, was befriended by such peers and teachers as Ad Reinhardt, Robert Lax, Robert Giroux, Mark Van Doren. They have all emphasized that Augustinian trait of Merton's character—the archetypal reformed rake—which helped make *The Seven Storey Mountain* such a success. Brought up a tepid Anglican, he was converted to the Catholic faith after a brief flirtation with Communism. And in his last two years at Columbia, before his departure to Gethsemane, he seems to have made an interminable series of visits to the confessional booth. Even after his conversion, there was still the rowdy, hard-drinking life, the wild parties with terrible hangovers. "We are potted, potted all summer"—recollection by the poet Ed Rice of a summer spent with Merton in a country house the year before he entered the monastery.

And so there emerges the portrait of a brilliant intellectual who tends to live at a destructive pace, demands those states of intense sensation which can as easily be found in the extremes of self-abnegation as of self-indulgence. After finishing a master's thesis on William Blake with his beloved teacher Mark Van Doren, the rowdy nomadic reveler suddenly turned to the most self-renouncing life available in the West to expiate his sins and those of the world. "Monastic communities are bodies of men reckoned as criminals, men considered by reason of their very state as public penitents"—words of the fanatical Abbot of la Trappe, who drove the already rigorous Cistercian order to still more stringent ways of self-abnegation.

Merton's prodigality as a writer—he averaged at least a book a year in the succeeding decades—is all the more startling in view of the excruciating severity of the Trappist life. With its traditional dedication to silence and to manual labor, the Trappist way combines the routine of hard-pressed peasant farmers with a most demanding liturgical schedule. Merton and his fellow monks rose at 2:00 A.M. to sing the night office, lived on a frugal and sparse vegetarian diet, were responsible for all of the manual labor—hoeing, thrashing, cutting—on the monastery's large farm. Merton was further burdened by his superiors' orders that he channel his literary and linguistic skills into innumerable translations from

Latin and French and countless monographs of obscure Cistercian fathers, and, later, by his pastoral duties as master of novices. He estimated that he never had more than six or eight hours a week to write during his first two decades at Gethsemane.

One must also keep in mind the rigid isolation which prevailed in religious orders until Vatican II, and which allowed no secular periodicals, virtually no news of the outside world, into monastic communities. The monk who was to write more perceptively than any other American cleric about such contemporary sophisticates as Ionesco, Sartre, Faulkner, and Roland Barthes was vowed to silence, and could only communicate with his brothers through four hundred basic gestures of sign language. The man who eventually became the Church's most eloquent commentator on the perils of the nuclear age did not know that a bomb had fallen on Hiroshima until nearly a year after the event.

The central problem which plagued the greater part of Merton's life was that he wished to be both more of a contemplative and more of an activist, albeit in word only, than his order would ever allow him to be. Father Louis (the name given him upon ordination) was haunted by the desire to have a hermitage of his own on the grounds of Gethsemane, or to transgress his vow of stability by moving to a site even more solitary than the wooded hills of Kentucky—Africa, the Far East. These yearnings led him to major confrontations with his superior, Dom James Fox, a Harvard-educated Boston Irishman and former naval officer who had become abbot of Gethsemane in 1948. An enthusiast for old-time piety, Dom Fox had a new motto designed for the monastery which was henceforth rubber-stamped on all its correspondence: "All for Jesus, through Mary, with a smile." Dom James was understandably determined to keep the intellectual star of the Cistercian order in Kentucky. And in the 1950s his machinations to that purpose led him to write a lengthy letter to Archbishop Montini of Milan (later known as Pope Paul VI) which ended with the following words: "Your excellency, before God I say to you, and am ready to meet this decision on the Last Judgement, I can not see the finger of God in Father Louis' desire for a change . . . All for Jesus—through Mary—with a smile."

During years of confrontation with his abbot, Merton often tried the ultimate sacrifice of ceasing to write. He also suffered bouts of excruciatingly bad health which entailed surgery for sinuses, slipped discs, and gastrointestinal ailments. Dom James shrewdly sized up the psychosomatic tensions ruining his star's health, and also the increased contact with the outside world induced by his numerous hospitalizations in Louisville. And in 1962, after two decades of exemplary service as choralist, master of students, master of novices, teacher of theology, Merton finally gained permission to live alone in a hermitage on the grounds of Gethsemane.

One now comes to the final paradox of Merton's brief life: By the time he was granted his long-desired hermit's solitude he had become such a cult figure to a motley crew of Catholic and secular liberals that he spent much of his energy trying to control his flood of visitors. His work had been translated into some twenty languages, his mail was so voluminous that it had to be lugged by suitcase to his hermitage. He'd begun an extensive correspondence with Daisetz Suzuki; Eldridge Cleaver was reading passages of his work at Black Panther meetings; Lenny Bruce often ended his nightclub act by reading Merton's chilling meditation on the Eichmann trial with a heavy German accent; Joan Baez was knocking at his door. Merton's ambivalence toward this unmonastic pace involved the paradox gnawing at the soul of almost any artist: the painfully simultaneous need for both society and solitude. In the Jacoblike wrestling between monk and writer which tortured Merton's life, the artist tended to win over the monk. The curious balance of seclusion and of exposure which marked his last years in the hermitage seems to have inspired his finest works: *Mystics and Zen Masters, Zen and the Birds of Appetite, Gandhi on Non-Violence, New Seeds of Contemplation.* Yet from 1965 on, one notices in Merton an exasperation with the members of his own community, an increased desire to travel to a more tranquil monastic site. "I come down to the monastery only to say an occasional fie upon the commandment and to subvert the troops," he writes a friend. "In my house in the woods I resist war, I resist everything, that is why the hermit life is called the *pièce de resistance.*"

One of the characteristics of this complex, worldly mystic

was his fidelity to traditional ideals of the monastic life. Merton never wavered from the view that the monk plays a central role in perfecting the world by taking on Christ's suffering and self-sacrifice. Upon entering the monastery he had described his Gethsemane as "the center of America," a place which is "keeping the universe from cracking to pieces and falling apart." In the late 1950s, as he turned away from the sometimes self-righteous *fuga mundi* tone of his earliest writings, Merton added a new social dimension to his view of the monastic vocation. He wrote that the monk can be the freest and most efficacious social critic in our society because of the "ultimate compassion" which he receives in contemplative solitude, and thus can identify with crucial areas of contemporary suffering—war, hunger, racial injustice—even more passionately than most laymen. Rebutting fashionable attacks on the "irrelevance" of monasticism in our time, he wryly dismissed the standards of "relevance" imposed on us by the secular world. "We suffer all the needs that society demands us to suffer because if we do not have those needs we lose our 'usefulness' in society— the usefulness of suckers." Merton seems to have exemplified his belief that the most solitary contemplation can lead to the deepest political concern: for his long-awaited life as a hermit also coincided with his period of greatest social outspokenness.

In 1964, Merton led a retreat at Gethesmane entitled "The Spiritual Roots of Protest." It was attended, among others, by the brothers Daniel and Philip Berrigan and by the Catholic activist James Forest. All three of them have recalled that their eventual decisions to engage in acts of civil disobedience—the draft file burnings of the Catonsville Nine and the Milwaukee Fourteen— can be traced in part to the retreat Merton led in the isolation of his hermitage. By this time Merton's writings about racial injustice and the nuclear threat had become so forthright that the Cistercian censors decided to silence him on those issues for two full years. He writes in 1964 to his friend Daniel Berrigan:

> Look, a lot of the monastic party line we're getting ends up by being pure, unadulterated—crap . . . I have been told that I am destroying the image of the contemplative vocation when I write about peace . . . In a word it is all right for the monk to break his ass putting out packages of cheese and mak-

ing a pile of money for the old monastery, but as to doing anything that is really fruitful for the Church, that is another
matter altogether . . .

As for Merton's extraordinary writings on Eastern religions:
What tends to be overlooked is that his insights were much influenced by his extensive studies of the most ancient roots of Christian
spirituality—Cassian, Saint Irenaeus, Origen, the Desert Fathers.
A metaphor used by the Benedictine scholar Brother David
Steindl-Darst is particularly apt: Merton dug so deeply into the
sources of his own heritage that he came out "on the opposite end
of the globe," having discovered all common roots.

Merton's particular affinity to Zen Buddhism can be traced to
other sources: It served him as an intellectual and spiritual ally
against the doctrinal Thomism prevalent in the Catholic tradition
at large, but inimical to the intuitive, experiential Cistercian
temper; the impudent, irreverent aphorisms of the Zen koan were
ideally suited to Merton's own acerbic wit; and the gratuitous nature of Zen illumination is akin to the patristic notions of Christian grace held to by Merton, that ceasing of intellectual process
in which "there is neither word *nor* silence." Even before turning
to the East, Merton, like any true contemplative, had understood
that the principal obstacle to attaining enlightenment is to strive
for it, or to suffer the deception that you have achieved it. When
you think you've got it, you ain't. Or as the ancient Zen saying
goes, if you meet the Buddha, kill him.

Merton's acquaintances have presented him as a man who
throughout his life remained as earthy as he was mystical, as
warmly joyous toward his friends as he was severe toward himself.
James Forest, for instance, has depicted the arrival of two young
Catholics who have hitchhiked to Gethsemane all week without
washing or changing clothes, and Merton's Rabelaisian delight at
the pilgrims' smell. Forest had heard uproarious laughter, "a kind
of monsoon of joy emerging from the guest house. . . . the sound
was coming from a monk on the floor in his black and white robes,
feet in the air, a bright red face, hands clutching his belly . . .
Thomas Merton laughing half to death on the floor. What would

have offended so many others delighted him, our room was like a fish market in a heat wave."

The same playful spirit pervades Merton's voluminous correspondence, which is often couched in a collegiate, semiprivate syntax he evolved over the decades with his close friends. The letters communicate many complexities of Merton's character, most particularly the considerable theological and liturgical conservatism that accompanied his political radicalism, and his openness to the most avant-garde literary experiments. Merton writes his Columbia classmate and close friend, the poet Robert Lax:

> Too much zowie in the Church if you ask me. Let's go back to the old restfulness and the orthos . . . more prayer of Jesus, more gazing at the navel, more kiss of God in the mossy wood . . . Mark my word there is no uglier species on the face of earth than progressed Catholics, mean, frivol, ungainly, inarticulate, venomous, and bursting at the seams with progress in the secular cities and the Teilhardian subways.

Even after he moved into a hermitage at Gethsemane, Merton continued his monastic hours notwithstanding increasing ill health, and rose at 2:00 A.M. to meditate and write. His prodigality was such that some 800,000 words of unpublished writing are said to have been found in his study after his death. His work ranged over an astounding spectrum of ancient and contemporary, sacred and secular, experience. His essays on the work of Ionesco, Sartre, or Flannery O'Connor can be as fluent and lucid as his commentaries on Gandhi, his discussions of such early Cistercian evangelists as Bernard of Clairvaux or Guerric of Igny. But he was a superb prose stylist and a gifted exegete rather than an original thinker, and he was as uneven as he was prolific. Too many sections of works posthumously published, such as *Love and Living,* are commentaries on such themes as Mercy or Christian Humanism which have been much more eloquently expressed in Merton's earlier volumes, particularly in *The New Seeds of Contemplation,* which is destined to remain one of the great spiritual classics of our century. Might it not be wise to let well enough alone after a man has written a devotional passage like the following?

> . . . The Lord plays and diverts Himself in the garden of His creation, and if we could let go of our own obsession with

what we think is the meaning of it all we might be able to hear His call and follow Him in His mysterious, cosmic dance. . . . For the world and time are the dance of the Lord in emptiness. The silence of the spheres is the music of a wedding feast.

In the autumn of 1967 the Draconian Dom James resigned his abbacy and was succeeded by one of Merton's former students, Father Flavian. Dom Flavian was a new young breed of monastic, a man whose cast of mind was very similar to Merton's and who was ready to give Merton all he ever wanted. Most tensions with the order finally came to an end. It was one of the happier years of Merton's life. It was also to be his last, for Dom Flavian enthusiastically agreed that Merton accept an invitation to attend an International Conference on Monastic Renewal scheduled to be held in Bangkok in November of 1968. During his trip, Merton was also to look for a site where a new Trappist monastery more solitary and removed than Gethsemane could be founded.

Like many contemplatives, Merton had eerily accurate premonitions of an early death. I continue to be haunted by the many details, dates, words preceding and attending his end which have a quality of augury. The last phrase of *The Seven Storey Mountain* reads "that you may become the brother of God and learn to know the Christ of the *burnt men.*" "I plan to be struck by lightning from walking in thunderstorms," he wrote a friend early in 1968; "I snap my fingers at life." "I am going home," he wrote in his journal during his flight from California to Asia, "to the home where I have never been in this body, where I have never been in this washable suit." He died the same day as his favorite Protestant theologian, Karl Barth, with whom he had had an intense correspondence. Such coincidences, premonitions, abound. Merton's last recorded words to the world, as he ended his address to the religious congress held in Bangkok an hour or two before his death, were "And now I shall disappear."

There is a letter of Merton's to Robert Lax which breaks me up every time I read it. It is written the day Merton learns about the death of their mutual and beloved college friend, the painter Ad Reinhardt. Merton is preparing to say Mass for Reinhardt the following morning, and offers him the kind of tribute which he might have preferred to any of the pieties uttered about his own untimely end:

Tomorrow the solemns. The requiems alone in the hermit hatch. Before the ikons the offering. The oblations. The clean oblations all round thunder quiet silence black picture oblations. Make Mass beautiful like big black picture speaking requiem. Tears in the shadows of hermit hatch requiems blue black tone. Sorrows for Ad in the oblations quiet peace request rest. Tomorrow is solemns in the hermit hatch for old lutheran reinhardt commie paintblack. Tomorrow is the eternal solemns and the barefoots and the ashes and the masses, oldstyle liturgy masses without the colonels and without the sergeants yelling sit down. Just old black quiet requiems in hermit hatch with decent sorrows good bye college chum.

HOMELANDS

I CAN'T abide most contemporary talk of voyages and voyagers—accounts of the delights of Arctic cruises, of the decline of Siena's *pensiones* and of Burgundy's gastronomy. They tend to degenerate into a recitation of gastrointestinal trivia as predictable and dull—and therefore as graceless—as reports on domestic pets, the state of lawns, or children's performances at school. And when listening to such prattle, which has become a staple of dinner party conversations, I tend to become an uncivil guest. For my attention inevitably swerves to memories of travel narratives I heard as a small child in the 1930s, which inevitably pertained to extremes of political and natural catastrophes—floods, train wrecks, revolutions. There were accounts of a cousin alighting in a small plane in a parched desert of North Africa, rescued from starvation by Bedouin tribesmen; of an aunt who nonchalantly sailed down the Amazon in a kayak to find herself stranded in a village of cannibals; of an uncle who died of a mysteriously rapid cancer growth, shortly after he had broken into an Egyptian tomb upon whose first trespasser (so legend had it) a pharaoh had put a curse three millennia ago. Such tragic hazards have traditionally fueled the best travel writing. For beyond their element of suspense, they circumvent most trivia of hostelry and fare and unmask the essentials of a society, site, national character.

As I look over the list of places I've written about in the past fifteen years, I'm struck by the preponderance of authoritarian regimes and repressive milieus: Prague, the People's Republic of China, decorous and constantly endangered Jerusalem, right-wing French families, paramilitary discipline of African safaris. On almost all these trips, my activities were controlled round the clock by the severe policies of the community I was visiting or curtailed by the political or natural hazards surrounding it. Do I prefer such experiences because they approximate (with considerable safety) that aura of dread I enjoyed in voyagers' sagas of four decades ago? That may be part of it. Yet I note an opposite and equally relevant impulse in my traveling preferences—a specific variety of hedonism which has to do with my love for observing passionately with all senses. There is a state of hallucinatory absorption in a foreign site which I can only reach when liberated from all practical concerns, freed from the hassle of finding meals, arguing with hotel clerks, or haggling about plane reservations.

The key to my oddball taste for authoritarian travel is that my very favorite trips have been to India (hourly dictated by an arduous lecturing schedule for the USIA), Morocco and Sicily (where the tours were totally designed by my husband, and I had the luxury of not making one decision), and most particularly those I have taken to the Soviet Union. There, herded daily into a bus by an often charming and always inveterate liar from the Intourist Bureau who is my nanny for a fortnight, telling me when and where to rise, eat, go to bed, I become a walking receptacle for the most delicate impressions of sight, smell, sound; for every detail of physiognomy and landscape; for every nuance of distortion, ignorance, and fibbing in the conversations of my Soviet mentor and of her peers. In fact, so intense and numerous were the impressions received on my first trip to Russia that a mere two weeks gave me most of the inspiration for an entire novel (*World Without End*). Book me into a severely supervised tour, and I shall need little more than a warm quiet room at night, bread, vegetables, beer by evening to flourish.

What I find equally ironic in the despotic liberty of Intourist-type travel is that it offers the leisure and the opportunity (if admixed with tact and shrewdness) to plumb the minds of one's native guides, learn much about their tastes, prejudices, family life, daily habits. It is totally impossible to coerce a Monsieur Dupont of Grenoble to offer us a recitation of such riches, and his undivided attention, for the span of a fortnight. Whereas Mr. Pavel Crybar of Brno, Czechoslovakia, presumably hired to spy on us (and frequently a very lonely man), in fact becomes our captive and is readily induced to bare his soul and griefs. And so, most paradoxically, the repressively guided visit of a "closed" society can offer us a richer perspective on national character than is gleaned by the privileged traveler enjoying the illusion of "freedom" in the hostelries of Western Europe, where most impressions are culled from talkative waiters, inebriated divorcées, or stray children on beaches. There is also the frequent pleasure of disobedience and adventure, gained by breaking away from such authoritarian groups: The ingenious traveler will plead several migraines, skipping "official" tours of sock factories or puppet shows to make illicit visits to groups of dissident students and writers in Prague, Moscow, or Beijing.

If I were someday forced to confine myself to one literary form, I suspect I would choose the travel essay. For the most treasurable aspect of voyaging is that it becomes the principal erotic experience of one's middle or late years. (This reflection is dedicated to women, whose erotic whims are considerably more restricted by advancing age than men's.) If the essence of erotica lies in the thrill of fresh encounter, the tremor of being newly captivated and seduced, the heightening of desire by the promise of discovery and surprise, the satisfaction of those desires by new chemistries of gratification, and, ultimately, the heightened self-knowledge gained by these aggregated pleasures, then I assuredly cannot think of anything more erotic than wandering to a very novel place.

It is the strong tension between utopia and reality in each of the homelands documented in this volume that originally drew me to the title *Adam & Eve and the City*. Will the Realpolitik of superpowers ever allow Hawaiian activists to recapture the purity of their original culture? Can a romantically authoritarian French family preserve its conservative mores in the permissive climate of the late twentieth century? How far has the state of Israel strayed from the Biblical injunction that it must serve as "a light unto all nations"? This same dissonance between the bliss of the Original Garden and the pragmatism of the Fallen City, between the visionary ideals and prosaic accommodations, informs most of the topics in this book: the quest of American radical Catholics or French Resistance fighters for exemplary p.)test against the crimes of the secular state, the 1970s East-turners' search for their private millenniums, the confusion and conflicts in Thomas Merton's community of monks.

There is another irony about the travels I write about: more often than not, persons I love decided on these sites or else the cities selected me. I went to Hawaii, for instance, quite against my will. My husband was asked to be artist-in-residence at the Honolulu Academy of Fine Arts; since our sons were then nine and ten years old, I was outvoted by a landslide when the family council was polled for a decision. The safari to East Africa was also imposed on me by my three men, at a time when I would have vastly preferred to tour Scotland, Japan, or a half-dozen other countries I had never visited. In a symbolic sense, Jerusalem chose me. I spent two months in Israel upon the invitation of Mayor Teddy Kollek. To this extraordinary leader, my devotion and gratitude.

On Safari

Eighteen years after Kenya's independence, the main bar of Nairobi's venerable Norfolk Hotel is still called the Delamere Room, after Kenya's legendary settler, and is decorated with the mounted heads of His Lordship's trophies. An eager hunter thrice mauled by lions, Lord Delamere used to ride through the streets of Nairobi shooting out the lights of streetlamps with a pistol. He once bought a hotel for the sole purpose of staging window-smashing contests in it, using oranges as ammunition. What a good sport, his fellow settlers said, he bought the hotel first.

Another settler, Major Grogan, walked all the way from Cape Town to Cairo to win his bride. Once married and settled near Nairobi, he held a public flogging of three African rickshaw boys on the ground that they had insulted some European ladies "by holding the vehicle's arms up too high." Grogan was one of twenty children. Traveling through Kenya, one repeatedly hears that its earliest English colonials, who came before World War I, were the younger sons of small landed gentry with large families, the kind of men who in previous years had to settle for modest regiments and parsonages. Were their eccentricities forged in the injustice of the nursery, by that dearth of attention which is often a Benjamin's lot?

□

On the terrace of the Norfolk Hotel, in front of the Dela-mere Room, there stands in desultory splendor a large black lac-quered rickshaw. Its story was told to me the morning I arrived in Nairobi by one of the two Big White Hunters who were about to guide us—a party of family and friends—on a photographic safari of East African wildlife.

"In the old days of Kenya," our guide says, "there was this lovely old bloke who used to keep a sweet tame lion on his lap when he went riding in that rickshaw. When the rickshaw boy pulled too slowly he would tickle the lion's throat, the lion would roar, and the boyee would truly hurry up. Ha-ha!"

The hunter guffaws mightily, slapping his great naked thigh, ruddy and muscled below his khaki safari shorts. He is a hulking, blond, frenetically jovial Englishman in his middle forties, who came out with the British army at Emergency time to quell the Mau Mau rebellion and stayed on in Kenya to hunt big game, marrying into an old white settler family of Major Grogan's circle. His family's land in Surrey was bequeathed to an older brother. His father had also been an army man, a colonel in India's Gurkha regiment. We sit over Pimm's Cups alongside the rickshaw on the Norfolk Hotel terrace going over the schedule of our forthcoming journey.

Our guide has driven us in from the airport past thorough-fares named after many revolutionary African leaders: Sékou Touré, Nkrumah, Lumumba, Nyerere. In the large colonial dining room next to the Delamere Room is spread out a buffet more elab-orate than any I have seen in the States in some decades, com-parable perhaps to Sunday lunches at the Newport Country Club in the 1950s. Africans in red and white livery hover over hams, turkeys, fish in aspic, numerous salads, and a dozen curries set alongside a battalion of puddings that includes some ten varieties of trifle. A few blocks away, in the vicinity of Independence Ave-nue, more than sixty safari firms are in business to serve the quarter of a million tourists flocking yearly to Kenya to gape at the animals of the Pleistocene epoch. Throughout Nairobi, in bars closed to non-Caucasians until a decade ago, old-time British settlers sip their pink gins and curse the proliferation of African bus drivers in the game reserves. One comes here not for revolution anymore, but for nostalgia.

An impulse to restore innocence on the planet we have despoiled, a fantasy of returning to some pacific state of nature. All this strikes me as pertinent to the stampede toward East Africa, and to our predilection for building safari parks in London, Florida, and New Jersey. The peaceable kingdom of Adam and Eve in Eden, before the existence of cities or of any form of violence— Milton put it this way:

> About them frisking play'd
> All Beasts of th' Earth, since wild. . . .
> Sporting the Lion ramp'd, and in his paw
> Dandl'd the Kid; Bears, Tygers, Ounces, Pards
> Gambold before them. . . .

Sweet lion out there, six yards from my minibus, we are friends again! Few men hunt you anymore save some Texans willing to pay a thousand dollars a trophy; we have come to Kenya just to look at you. Dear giraffe, your thick-lashed eyes best answer our longing for innocence, taking us back to that prehistoric purity we search for. You stare back with a gaze of metaphysical surprise which seems to ask all men: How did you reverse the clock of history? I have been here for forty million years. Are you for real, or a joke?

Six A.M., waning darkness, at the Masai Mara Game Reserve where we camp on our first day out of Nairobi. The zipper of my tent is brusquely opened, the ripping sound tears through my sleep. A Kikuyu safari boy, his earlobe deftly looped through a hole in his upper ear, brings a kerosene lamp into my tent. "Jambo memsahib," he booms cheerfully, "chai, memsahib." He puts down a pot of very black tea flanked by large canisters of milk and sugar, and disappears with that faint salaaming gesture that the Arabs have bequeathed to East Africa.

Dawn is the most beautiful time in Africa, providing that glimpse into the world's morning which we have traveled to recapture. A euphoria of cleanliness. The grass itself smells more sweet than a tropical blossom. The trill of the palm weaver bird sounds like spring water gurgling from a narrow-necked jar. Even the dewy hyena loping under the flat-topped acacia trees looks pristinely fresh-coated. I am in an appropriately trancelike state, having slept lightly, woken repeatedly by the distant groan of a lion or the hurried panting of a leopard, and hoping always to hear the subtle sound of the elephants, creatures so soft-footed that they can walk through camp emitting no noise other than the faint rumbling of their digestive tracts.

Our guides—whom I shall call Big Hunter and Young Hunter— herd us into the Land Rover for our early morning viewing of the game. Big Hunter is ever in a state of exuberant cheer, and commences his often salacious commentary on the animals in the same clipped, booming tones in which he trained the Kenya Rifles. "Lovely bushbuck over there, three o'clock of where the zebra is spending a penny . . . look at that splendid ely, five legs and all that . . . we're going to circle the riverbed and look for some more mating lion, the old dears put on quite a show yesterday. . . ." When he is not driving, lecturing us, or diligently organizing camp, our guide concentrates on living up to the myth of the Big White Hunter, which dictates that he be a proficient raconteur and Don Juan, besides being a great shot and an impeccable naturalist. (Hemingway, "The Short Happy Life of Francis Macomber": "Robert Wilson carried a double-sized cot on safari.")

He regales us with a repertory of hair-raising tales that all end with the phrase "And that chap *lived on* to tell the tale!" He boasts of his military expeditions against the Mau Mau, which sound curiously hedonistic and sporting. Being the British army's top star on the East African rugby team, he was picked up in the Aberdare Mountains every Friday by a patrol truck so that he could take part in the weekend games in Nairobi, then on Sunday afternoon he was returned to his command post in guerrilla country. Alternately his wife and his girlfriend accompany him throughout our trip. The women are remarkably civil to each other at their moments of encounter, as if machismo in the bush were part of the safari package, like the assurance of seeing elephants in erection.

Young Hunter, our other guide, is a slender, blond athlete in his early twenties, whose grandparents settled in the Kenya farmlands in 1911. His family still owns twenty-seven thousand acres at the foot of Mount Kenya. There is a strange bitterness about this spoiled and gifted youth who looks as if he had never endured misfortune. He expresses in an extreme form the white settlers' fears for their future after Kenyatta's death. For although our guides regard former president Jomo Kenyatta as "the leader of the Mau Mau" (displaying an astonishing ignorance of their own history), they also look upon him as a man totally reformed by jail, "the greatest African leader, a splendid bloke who was frightfully decent to the Europeans."

"What will happen now that Kenyatta's dead, we might all get thrown out," Young Hunter murmurs to me every few days in that polite Kenya version of a public school voice which barely ever rises above a mumble: "I'll go to Rhodesia or South Africa, only decent place for a white man to live these days. How long do I have there? Ten or fifteen years at the most. But I'd rather get thrown out of Rhodesia after fifteen years of happiness than be miserable in England now. . . ."

A good part of our two guides' conversation is devoted to expressing their nostalgia for the privileges of Preindependence Kenya, to deploring the proliferation of African drivers at the wheels of tourist vehicles, and to cursing that unspeakable day when they will have to share a meal with an African. "Do you know," observes Young Hunter, "I've heard that some European women tourists actually have a drink at the end of the day with their drivers. . . ." Big Hunter shudders: "Bad show, that."

In my tent, I often reflect on the varieties of colonial behavior. The French were less bestial to the Africans than they are to each other. The French and the Portuguese were as carnally drawn to black women as were our own southern plantation owners. Fifteen years after independence, the British managing Kenya's leading industry—tourism—are still rigid with fear of the black man's entering their club.

Still, how bitter it is to have found such beauty and then to lose it! Traveling through Kenya, discovering its splendor and variety, one senses the depth of the settlers' sorrow upon having to leave. Morocco, Mexico, Greece, all other landscapes pale before Kenya's. Besides the game-filled savannas and plains of the reserves there are tropical rain forests heavy with guava and mango trees; austere deserts; rolling upland moors thick with waterfall, trout-filled streams, and fields of heather. There are Indian Ocean beaches rivaling the Caribbean's for their beauty, and lush riverine terrains such as Samburu, where wide streams placidly flow through groves of doum palms, wild lilies, and eucalyptus trees.

The farmland surrounding Mount Kenya, the Olympus of East Africa where the gods legendarily bequeathed the Kikuyus their land, is a farmer's Utopia: On its sumptuous loam, assured of large punctual rainfall and drained to perfection by the land's gentle slope, wheat and oats can be harvested at tenfold the yield of any English field. My favorite landscape is the ascent to Mount Kenya, reached through stands of gigantic cedar and dense groves of bamboo which for many years provided the Mau Maus' safest shelter. Kenya's birds are a microcosm of their land's splendor. Even the starling, the most plebeian of our species, is cloaked there in a glorious iridescence of orange, viridian, and cobalt. Sights of the lilac-breasted roller, the emerald cuckoo, the flame-red turaco, spoil one's bird-viewing for some time to come.

On a March day we cross the Kenya border into Tanzania to enter the Serengeti, Africa's most spectacular national park. We instantly sense an austerity that contrasts with Kenya's opulence. Within the first few hours we observe that shortage of basic staples which can afflict young Socialist countries: no petrol is to be found in the vicinity of our camping site, no soda water or beer to be had in the province, there are no passport forms at the frontier post—the guard has to improvise some on blank paper. Our guides rage at these deficiencies: "Great fun, Socialism, what? Ha-ha!" This is their last time in Tanzania, they proclaim; they've never had anything but annoyance in this bloody Maoist country. "Chinese Communist lorry," they mutter every few minutes, pointing at any vehicle on the road. "Chinese Communist tractor."

We hear that several cheetahs have died of heart attacks in the past months from being chased by tourist vehicles; that lion cubs are going hungry from too much close observations; and that the new African warden of the six-thousand-square-mile Serengeti has forbidden all vehicles to go into the plain, where the best game viewing has traditionally been had. Notwithstanding these restrictions the Serengeti animals live up to legend. In these "photographic blocks" which now make up the major part of national parks and game reserves, where no shooting has been allowed for years and where guides are not even allowed to bear weapons, the walls of our nursery come alive: which is why we are here.

Animals come close and stare, having no memory of aggression on which to base their fear. Buffalo gaze at us trustingly from below their large flat coiffure of horns, noses placidly drooling, making it hard to believe that they are the leading man-killers in Africa, and that one of their species killed Big Hunter's partner just last year during a shooting safari. Another of our guide's best friends was carried off this very year by an elephant in hunting territory. But here the elephants walk closely past us in weightless serenity, allowing us to discover their surprisingly long, flirtatious eyelashes, their trunks affectionately reposing around a tusk instead of trumpeting alarm. And we observe the beauty of the smaller African antelopes—dik-diks, duikers, klipspringers, whose great expanse of liquid eye, nearly half the size of their heads, dominates the landscapes of their bodies like enormous lakes.

Our camping site is in a flat plain filled with euphorbia and the bright yellow-barked acacia, alongside one of the beautiful tree-festooned kopjes, or rock outcroppings, that dot the Serengeti landscape. Ten African safari boys have arrived a few hours before us in their truck and have already completed pitching our camp. They are all Kikuyus, members of that largest and most powerful of Kenyan tribes, numbering over one tenth of the population, to which Jomo Kenyatta belonged. The kitchen fire has already been lit and alongside it the cooks are baking bread in an ingenious oven composed of a flat piece of metal, a large overturned pan, and a strategic sprinkling of smoldering coals. The refrigerator has been plugged into its canister of gas. Each tent is flanked by a small outhouse, in which portable seats are posed over a deep hole. And in the middle of the camping site stands a tented shower which functions smartly on a string-and-bucket system.

Fantasies of primitiveness: Like the camping trip of Abercrombie & Fitch executives who recently spent a week on the rooftop of their Madison Avenue office building, the classiest safaris are the most naturalistic. The cheapest mass tours travel in posh zebra-striped minibuses and confine their clients to East Africa's extraordinarily luxurious hotels. Many treat their groups to a meal at the outlandish Mount Kenya Safari Club, which matches the Westchester Biltmore for its profligate vulgarity. Whereas the more elegant tented safari outfits rumble about in shaking Land Rovers, rigidly avoiding these modern hostelries. Meanwhile we hear of Stavros Niarchos's improvisations on the new primitivism: A private plane daily flies his mail up from Nairobi when he is in the bush, and two large swimming pools are immediately dug out wherever he pitches camp, one for himself and another for his entourage.

The Kikuyus are notoriously gifted cooks, and a typical menu on our safari might consist of a hot fish savory, cream of avocado soup, a roast, three different vegetables, a cold passion fruit soufflé. I read that a modest safari meal in the 1950s, as described by Alan Moorehead on a fairly rough shooting trip, consisted of duck gizzards savory, wild turkey soup, Nile perch, and roasted eland. It is not a question of luxury, since even a billionaire could not conjure up such fare in the disorder of French West Africa. It is rather a Kenyan safari tradition composed of the British talent for importing comfort into wilderness and the East African's prideful need to exhibit his great talents. Laundry is done daily and pressed with immense hot coal irons. One changes several times a day. It is bad form to miss tea.

I visit the cook by his fire as he is deftly whipping egg whites with an old wooden whisk. By him stands the chief steward, a powerfully built Kikuyu who has been in Big Hunter's service for some ten years. The safari boys speak little English beyond the necessities of food and laundry, and earn between one and two dollars a day. "Fair but firm," Big Hunter pronounces whenever he discusses his staff. "I've kept them from joining those blasted new safari unions by being fair but firm." Over dinner one night, our guide tells me that his chief steward is a former Mau Mau. I ask him if he is joking, and he seems offended, swiftly coming to the Mau Maus' defense. "But they're splendid old blokes actually—always were jolly good chaps—I admire them tremendously—admire anyone who's willing to fight for his country. Damn rotten lot, those who don't." Nationalism dominates all, and the former major seems to have as much respect for the Mau Mau he'd come to shoot as he has for the animals he's made a career of hunting.

Today the cook and I chat about the famous Serengeti lions. He tells me that like most of his colleagues he had never seen a wild animal until he started on this safari job. The entire staff is so terrified of animals, he says, that although bwana provides tents, seven out of ten of them sleep jammed together in the lorry to be safe from marauding creatures. Wainugu also expresses great nostalgia for the hunting safaris of old which gave him so much good game to cook. The staff quickly grows despondent, he says, without the sight of freshly shot meat. He speaks longingly of gerenuk, that long-necked and most graceful gazelle of the northern plains, which makes the finest steaks, of Thomson's gazelle chops and impala roasts. Do I really like to just go out and *look* at animals? Wainugu softly laughs. He cannot imagine any thing sillier and more boring.

A few days later we are startled by some unannounced rifle shooting close to camp. We discover that our guides, who nowadays do not shoot more than one or two big game animals a year, have shot an impala and a gazelle to reassure their servants of their sanity and manliness. To Africans—who look upon wild animals as enemies rampaging their crops and herds, enemies to be killed and eaten—a "looking" safari seems the maddest to date of the white man's many mad inventions.

Some items in the *East African Standard*, Nairobi's leading paper: Since independence the term "Big White Hunter" has come into disfavor and they are now called "professional hunters. . . ." Notwithstanding this change of nomenclature the tradition of white hunters is so ingrained that the few Africans or Asians training for the profession will say, "I am becoming an African White Hunter" or "an Asian White Hunter. . . ." Kenya's second largest safari firm bore the unfortunate name of "White Hunters, Limited," and a few years ago was forced to change its title to "Africa Tours. . . ." Among predictions that East Africa will have to accommodate one million visitors by the 1980s, the Kenyan government has declared a policy of "Africanization" in its booming tourist industry. Yet as of 1975, the *Standard* reports, only one safari firm in Kenya (Kibo Tours) was totally African-owned.

With the new policy of Africanization, several European hunters are losing their work licenses on the grounds that they do not employ enough Africans. In an unguarded moment, one white hunter I meet confides to me that in order to ensure the renewal of his license he has made his chief steward a partner in his safari firm. "We did it just on paper, actually," he remarked. "We didn't tell the poor bloke anything about it." Meanwhile, in case Africanization becomes militant and his license is revoked, one of our own white hunters has started a successful grouse-shooting safari outfit in Scotland to fall back on.

Throughout this trip I suffer from extreme claustrophobia, a curious sensation to have in the vast open plains of Africa. Severe laws dictate that the tourist on a "viewing" safari stay inside his vehicle anytime he ventures out of his tiny tented camp, and forbid him to move many yards beyond his hotel room. The tables are turned. *Homo touristicus* is continuously imprisoned behind the metal bars of his Rover, in a new kind of ambulatory zoo. We parade our captivity before the disinterested eyes of the free beast, and apprehend their whereabouts by seeing where other motorized cages have congregated on the plain. Even Africa's most famous hotel, Treetops, is a nightmarish form of prison in which one is incarcerated in an aerial cage, sentenced to stare for eighteen hours at an artificial pond frequented by obliging beasts.

Being addicted to hiking, jogging, and other forms of strenuous activity, I find my physical captivity difficult. It is even more tedious psychologically. I had suspected from the start that the pleasure of the White Hunters' company would be limited. Their racist diatribes, their disdain and ignorance of all things African besides its wildlife, are even worse than I had feared. Young Hunter seldom passes an African farming cooperative without exclaiming, "Poor bastards, they don't know the first thing about land!" Big Hunter cannot drive by an Asian family on a picnic without derisively mimicking the Kenyan Asians' lilting English, and insults African waiters with an imperiousness worthy of Major Grogan.

Young Hunter tells me that Tanzania is so Maoist-dominated

that there are two million Communist Chinese living in that country. Since Tanzania's population is under twelve million, I ask, how is it possible that one out of six of its residents is Chinese? He shrugs his shoulders over his breakfast kippers, and I realize that most of his clients have been trigger-happy Texan hunters only too happy to agree with him. "Are you bringing those smelly objects into my car?" Big Hunter rages when I buy some beautiful Somali and Samburu dolls in a northern Kenya village. "Don't put them on the seat, they're so frightfully filthy." It strikes me as absurd that one should travel to a country with no further purpose than to look at its wildlife, that animal-gaping trips are as narrow and atomized as culinary tours of France, ceramicists' tours of Ireland, or gay liberation tours of South America.

Yet short of renting a private plane, there is no way of leaving the group for a few days if I am to find my family again in Africa. Kenyan transportation is still so primitive that the only road to Ethiopia is an unpaved, blindingly dusty thoroughfare, and the road to Somaliland is akin to a mule track. Altering the schedule by a day or two is equally out of the question, for tourist accommodations are so gorged that hotel rooms and camping sites must be reserved months in advance. African wilderness these days must be booked a year ahead. This trip is remarkably similar to traveling through Russia with Intourist guides, trapped round the clock by tyrannical citizens who command the sole means of transportation, the implacably fixed schedule, and the stupendous array of propaganda.

Although I have been a near vegetarian and a pacifist much of my life, I acquire new respect during this trip for the freedom and the reality of the traditional shooting safari. The twenty or thirty miles of daily walking in order to track an animal, the reciprocity of danger, anything to escape this playhouse fantasy! I entertain macabre notions of learning how to shoot and joining a hunting safari so that I can at least walk on African soil. And at night I pace the confines of the camp like one of those caged animals I have all my life wanted to liberate.

And yet: There is an anecdote Big Hunter likes to tell which sums up that great respect and knowledge of animals which makes him such a good guide to Africa's wildlife, if to nothing else: The year before, a lioness jumped out of the bush at him, and he gambled with his life by shooting at her feet rather than killing her. "There was one chance out of four that it would frighten her—she did turn and run, actually, and I *lived on* to tell the tale." His sentiment toward animals is the essence of the white sport hunter's ethos. It is radically opposed to killing out of hunger, as the African—or any poor man—will do. It is that etiquette of the sport of kings and nobles which is derived from the rich man's leisure and abundance. It is a code based on the ambivalent feelings of loving and respecting what you kill, on the precept that you shoot while also safeguarding the species' young and females, perpetuating the species abundantly for future generations of sportsmen.

Because of the complexity of that code and their precise knowledge of it, white hunters know game as few other men do, and that is why, notwithstanding their odious prejudices, they have been the best guides to African wildlife. We are constantly amazed by our escorts' instinct for when and where each species can be found in the vast reserves; by their ability to identify, with their naked eyes, as a buffalo or impala what to us looks like a dot on the horizon; by their readiness to answer a multitude of questions such as how animals eat (lions every two or three days, when they can gorge on seventy pounds of meat at a time, while elephants need five hundred pounds of grass a day); and by their enormous tenderness and respect for animals, whom they manage to approach without causing the least disturbance or fear. Thanks to their skill we are twice able to observe a leopard—that most savage and solitary animal which few tourists see anymore—staring down at us with its chilling green gaze from the branches of thorn trees in the Serengeti. In the same Serengeti plain—toward the end of the dry season—our guides find the site where the largest migratory herd in years is congregated: a half million zebra and wildebeest move together toward Lake Victoria in search of young grass. From a distance there is no sound but a low dull buzzing on the plain; all scale is lost in such number, one feels submerged in a plague of insects or in a myriad shoal of microscopic fish. The dun, mourning-hued mass slowly palpitates westward, occasionally enlivened by the frail prancing of the young and by a lifted head revealing dumb, muted eyes above the wildebeest's patriarchal beard.

It is the splendor of lions—and our guides' skill at finding them—that dominates my memories of Africa. In the Masai Mara, Big Hunter knows from the wary stance of a vulture in a tree that a kill has been made that day. And he drives us into a thicket stiff with lion, in which a pride of some twelve animals are lying up in the shade after their feast of freshly killed young elephant. Some lift their heads and yawn, gazing at us with trusting eyes. Others continue lying on their backs, paws in the air like pups on a hot day, their white bellies grossly distended by their great repast. Meanwhile fifty yards away from the sated predators a golden-fleeced jackal commences the swift scavenging process that maintains the hygiene of the plain. His ears flared out like antennae, desperately trying to decide whether the lions are sleepy enough for him to get his piece of elephant safely, he darts expectantly toward the feast and prances fearfully back a dozen times, running to and fro like a sandpiper following the turn of the surf on a beach.

Another time we come upon a pair of lions as they are about to mate on top of a huge rock of the Serengeti plain. They stand nuzzling in the sun a few yards above us, their sinews delineated as majestically as in an Assyrian bas-relief. After a particularly affectionate nuzzle the lioness lies down. The lion mounts her, gives a few raging thrusts, and then with an apocalyptic growl bites her in the back of her neck. She swiftly stands up, snarls, and gives him a resounding cuff in the jaw. He looks sheepish, and licks her tenderly. It is intimidating to think that they can repeat the performance some two hundred times in one weekend, about every half an hour.

I think that people are traveling to Africa not only to steep in nature's innocence but also to witness nature's violence. To see predators on a kill is considered to be the great moment of a safari, a new outlet for the blood lust once channeled into hunting. It is the corrida of the late twentieth century, with the animals doing all the bloodletting.

We never once come upon a kill—a failure that pleases me—but the one time we see predators miss their prey is grimly instructive. Driving one evening through Amboseli, at the foot of Kilimanjaro, we see twenty-one minibuses gathered near a clearing to observe three cheetahs stalking. The first cheetah curtly moves through the thicket toward a small herd of impalas, occasionally twitching her ears as a signal for her companions to move on. There is an exaggerated stylishness about these animals' features—extravagantly long, elegant forelegs, outlandishly small, heavily marked faces. These most endangered animals of East Africa—champion runners but unskilled at camouflage, their temperament as open as the plains they frequent—seem only too willing to be movie stars, and cock their heads photogenically toward the tourists.

After we have watched them for several minutes the cheetahs have approached to about a hundred and fifty yards of their prey, coming close to the distance from which they make their famous sixty-mile-per-hour dash for the kill. But as they reach the critical moment minibuses start crashing about them; tourists lean on the open rooftops of their vehicles, cameras poised, and urge their drivers to get the closest possible view of the kill. Startled by the commotion, the impalas race about in circles and cough out their warning message, the baboons' terrierlike barking comes sloughing off the trees. The cheetahs must know better than we that they have lost their chance for dinner, but they go on stalking for a few minutes, as if to finish their pose. And then, amid the clicking of some fifty cameras, the head scout abruptly turns away from the impalas. The three cheetahs slink off into the plain. Their fragile rib cages seem terribly thin in the dusk, the black markings of their cheeks—like rivulets of black tears—seem to express their frustrated hunger.

We are going to kill these animals with sentiment. Having slain and trapped wild creatures for food, domesticated them for our amusement, and hunted them for sport, we are now decimating them by our fantasies of wilderness. How curious that photographic "shooting" is becoming deadlier to game than the ancient pastime of sport shooting. How regrettable that the tourists' most intrusive drivers tend to be Africans. The ancient code of hunting is past, a new etiquette of viewing has yet to be elaborated if the animals are to survive. I turn to Big Hunter, who, along with two other European drivers, respectfully kept his vehicle still during the cheetahs' attempted hunt. "Looking at game may become more dangerous to them than hunting," I say. "Worse than that," he remarks laconically, "it's so bloody rude to the animals."

Briefly escaping from the local Intourist, I visit with some African conservationists in Tanzania. One is the newly appointed game warden of the Serengeti. He receives me in an office that looks like a primitive military outpost: From a line of low barracks attended by rangers dressed in austere khaki, there blares the rash drone of a shortwave radio, the station's only communication with the rest of Tanzania. The warden talks at first with diffidence, probably because of the rudeness with which my type of British guides treat him. As soon as he learns that I am an American and that I frequently write for a magazine which has published a very fine profile of Tanzania's president, Julius Nyerere, he immediately becomes cordial. We chat morosely about the one million tourists a year soon predicted to swarm through East Africa's game reserves. And we discuss the future of his park's three most threatened species—cheetah, leopard, and ostrich—in the light of that invasion. In the past three months alone, Serengeti rangers have reported several cases of cheetahs having heart attacks from being pursued by tourist vehicles, and my tale of the cheetahs' missed dinner seems all too familiar to him.

"Poverty, poverty, it is always a problem of poverty and hunger," the warden says. "The heart of the problem is the poverty of my African brothers and the terrible wealth of the tourists. African drivers are constantly being tipped by tourists to break the rules of our parks and chase its animals. What can you do, our people are poor, it is easier for them to be corrupted. And you must realize that the African has a totally different attitude toward animals from the European. For thousands of years animals have either been food to eat or a pest to kill when it destroys crops, never something to preserve for sentimental or photographic purposes."

However, the young Tanzanian is optimistic about his country's ability to preserve its animal life. Europeans like my guides, he comments slyly, had predicted the extinction of game when

Tanzania became independent, claiming that Socialists were bound
to be indifferent to wildlife conservation. Yet Tanzania has insti-
tuted some eight new game sanctuaries in the two decades since
independence—Serengeti was its only national park previous to
1962. It is also pouring 3 percent of its annual budget into conservation: three times more per capita than the United States allot-
ment for similar programs, and a huge sum for a young nation
where priorities such as schools and hospitals are pressing. The
Wildlife College at Moshi, of which he is a graduate, is supported
by a United Nations grant and is training hundreds of Africans to
be professional wardens and conservationists. Part of the nation's
wildlife budget is going into an extensive audiovisual educational
program that will start at the grade-school level. Its aim is to make
the Tanzanians respectful of the "wild heritage" concept so difficult for most Africans to understand.

In Arusha, seat of the secretariat of the East African Community, I visit the deputy director of Tanzania's national parks,
Albert Mongi. He is in his twenties, and has done all his university
work in the United States: a B.A. at the University of Seattle, followed by graduate work in the wildlife of the Grand Canyon. Since
many naturalists tend to be apolitical, it is curious to hear about
"the problems of psychological decolonization" and "our brothers'
struggle in America" in a modest office dominated by photos of
giraffe, charging rhino, and wading elephants.

Mongi immediately asks me what I find to be the chief difference between Tanzania and Kenya. I tell him of the singularly
narrow character of my trip, and ask him to describe the difference
himself. "The Kenyans remain more colonized than we," Mongi
says proudly. "They are having more trouble acting like Africans;
they are more dependent on the white man and the white image.
That's perhaps why Europeans feel more comfortable in Kenya,
but although we welcome tourists we must *not* alter our character
for the sake of tourism." And then he uses a strange word which,
to the few young Tanzanians I have talked to, seems to mean the
opposite of negritude, decolonization, freedom. "Kenya is more
artificial than we are. Tanzania's leading principle is avoidance of
artificiality."

□

Big Hunter and Young Hunter took exception to my visit with African conservationists, as if I had gone slumming alone at night into dangerous bars. I hastened back to attend our scheduled departure and found that Big Hunter was engaged in searching for his briefcase, which was loaded with passports, money, and all his other indispensables. "This is where they'll steal a briefcase more easily than anywhere else," he fumed, "in Tanzania, with all these locals needing passports." My thirteen-year-old son asked how one of the locals could possibly use a British passport. "They'll take it to some Indian who'll fake it up," Young Hunter answered. "Indians can fake anything." Big Hunter found his briefcase half an hour later at the fruit market, untouched and exactly where he'd left it.

The night before I left East Africa to return to the United States I had dinner with a Kenya-born Asian acquaintance, an intellectual of notably progressive leanings who had been a friend of Tom Mboya's and other leaders of Kenyan independence. When I told him I was determined to return to Kenya to do the same trip from a radically different point of view—with African guides—he expressed great chagrin. "But that would be terrible!" he exclaimed. "You simply might not see any game! Kenya just doesn't have enough properly trained men yet, except the kind of Europeans you traveled with. I assure you that your guides were more liberal than many of their colleagues!"

It would be easier, he said, to arrange the kind of trip I had in mind in Tanzania, where, as the game warden noted, the process of decolonization seemed to have proceeded at a faster pace.

Yet notwithstanding the skepticism of my Kenyan acquaintance, my visits with two impressive young Tanzanian conservationists left me with a new set of questions concerning the future of wildlife in East Africa: questions which would never have entered my mind if I hadn't ventured, however briefly, out of the smug haven of my White Hunters' company.

Shouldn't we radically strip wildlife study of the sentimentalism and fantasizing that have led Europeans to idealize animals—and their parks—as pristine havens? Can we continue to extol the beauty of Africa's wildlife without simultaneously considering the needs of the Africans sharing their terrain? Is it right to divorce the ecology of animals from the sociology of the men with whom they share a nation? Can we continue to trek to game reserves in the company of mastodon colonials who—however knowledgeable they are about animals—are crassly hostile to the aspirations and achievements of Africans?

After my own limited African experience, I sensed that the traditional safari, however nonviolent it appears to be, has a crass lack of curiosity about the problems of the humans among whom the animals live. How about demanding and encouraging a new form of safari which would include visits to conservationist training centers, self-help schools, farming cooperatives? It is precisely the lack of this kind of exposure that shocked me on my trip to East Africa: the segregation of nature from man. It may be a division even more harmful than the much deplored "estrangement of man from nature" because it is far more sentimental, and more based on those false illusions of innocence which are always sure paths to brutality. Anyone with sympathy for African democracy might well consider boycotting Kenya's tourist industry until there exists a new breed of guides who can do well what the former generation of European colonials have done so badly: present the tourist with a view of wildlife in its total agronomic and political—therefore terrestrial—context.

Beyond these human concerns, take it from the point of view of the animals. Anyone consistent about "animal liberation" should extend that principle into the psychological sphere, and protect animals from psychic stress as well as from pain. There are increasingly frequent reports that the close shadowing of lions by overzealous visitors is leading to so many missed kills that an alarming number of cubs are starving. There are growing incidents of cheetah cubs being fatally separated from their mothers by the same kind of aggressive motorized antics I witnessed at Amboseli. Many conservationists believe that the wheels of tourist vehicles are doing more damage to the animals' grazing grounds than the much-maligned Masai pastoralists. And the very boundaries of those parks and reserves used as rich men's zoos are a radical interference with nature which deprive animals of their most powerful measure of survival—free migration.

If our ambivalent and mostly selfish sentiments toward animals are to be revised, we must cease to protect them for our own sake, which is the essence of the White Hunters' paternalism, and has an eventually brutalizing effect on any creature. For if animals remain the victims of our affluent white man's fantasies, there might come a day when we shall have to cease looking at wildlife altogether in order to ensure its survival. We might have to close off African game parks from men as radically as the French closed off the Lascaux caves—to preserve on their walls the ideograms of animals deteriorating in human-tainted air.

Hawaii:
The Sugar-Coated Fortress

Welcome to paradise!" the announcer's voice says on the car radio. Banked by a flare of scarlet plumeria trees and of gold primaveras, a highway sign says PEARL HARBOR, 7 MILES. I am driving through the capital of our fiftieth state with a Hawaiian student dressed in a brown beret and a black leather jacket, in emulation of the mainland's black militants. There is a swell of swooning, saccharine music on the radio, followed again by the ebullient disk jockey's voice: "Aloha to paradise!"

"Aloha to the Pentagon of the Pacific," the young Hawaiian mutters.

"What does 'aloha' mean, Kalani?"

"Hello, thank you, good-bye; mostly these days good-bye."

"How did you feel about statehood in fifty-nine, Kalani?"

"I was nine years old and I knew it was a bummer."

"What's your solution?"

"Simple. Secede."

Kalani hands me a booklet published by a youth congress whose delegates, representing over thirty Hawaii high schools and colleges, have voted to secede from the United States. A quote from their resolution:

. . . secession from the United States of America will be a catalyst to the preservation of Hawaii's land, culture and people. The Westernization, Americanization and colonization of Hawaii has left in its wake pollution, congestion, ugliness on our land; has inflicted economic slavery upon our people. . . . We resolve to take all steps necessary to facilitate the secession of Hawaii from the United States of America.

"What happens if you can't secede, Kalani?"

"Possible violence," Kalani says. "Hey, here come the surf reports."

"Waikiki two feet," the announcer's voice drones, "Haleiwa six feet and fair, Makapuu is breaking at three to four feet and good form. . . ."

"That," says Kalani, turning away from revolution, "makes it perfect for bodysurfing."

Honolulu's Ala Moana is the world's largest shopping center, a fifty-acre complex of 160 shops immersed in soothing music and warm odors of food and flowers. Open seven days a week and often until midnight, continually roiling with humanity, Ala Moana is a gigantic souk, a hymn to American consumerism, a perpetual world's fair. At Ala Moana, Polynesian, Japanese, Chinese, and American-style lunch counters alternate with banks, jewelry stores, tourist agencies, art galleries, Woolworth's, beauty parlors, pet shops, photography salons, Dunkin Donuts stands, souvenir booths, muumuu boutiques, cracked-seed stores, vast emporiums of Japanese, Tahitian, Indian, and other Pacific artifacts. Families gather for meals on Ala Moana's benches and sculpture-ornamented walkways to eat their paper plates full of tempura and raw fish, or poi, or chow mein, or hot dogs. THANK YOU is written in Hawaiian (*Mahalo*) on the streamlined cobalt-blue trash cans of Ala Moana's sidewalks; Japanese calligraphy, alongside Western print, indicates the entrances of rest rooms; T-shirts selling in the sportswear shops bear the slogan VISIT SAIGON, FUN CAPITAL OF THE WORLD; the sign 20% DISCOUNT TO MILITARY is frequently seen. Ala Moana is at its most festive every Friday, the state's Aloha Day, which an association of Hawaiian garment manufacturers has designated as the day for floor-length muumuus. On Fridays, supermarket and parking-lot attendants, housewives, post-office employees, bank clerks, schoolteachers are moving columns of flowered cloth, are hung with real or plastic leis of carnations, orchids, ginger, jasmine. Floral women waft through Ala Moana's alleys, their long clothes incongruous in sunlight, and amid them drift barefoot, bikini-clad teenagers carrying surfboards under their arms, their bodies still dripping from the ocean a block away.

Ala Moana's palatial supermarkets displays vegetables Oriental and American, vegetables of monstrous perfection, vegetables fulfilling the Platonic essence of vegetableness: string beans eighteen inches long and viridian green, two-feet-long eggplants, white turnips the size of melons, ginger roots twisted and ominous as the mandrake's. There is a sense of gigantism, of glandular excess, of beauty coarsened by abundance. There is a glut of orchids. Orchids are rampant on the walls of banks, are treated like parsley sprigs—frilling the bones of lamb chops at the supermarket; orchids are strewn among displays of mangoes and papayas, are afloat in one's glass of orange juice, decorate the shrimp cocktail at Woolworth's lunch counter.

From the upper terrace of Ala Moana's parking lot there is a vast view of the city of Honolulu, on the south shore of the island of Oahu, one of the eight major Hawaiian islands that comprise our fiftieth state. Scores of sugar-white condominiums fleck the violet hulk of Diamond Head crater and the sumptuous rugged green slopes of the Ko'olau Mountains, known as the Pali—the cliffs—behind the city. There are churches in great profusion, vestiges of a missionary society, of an enormous lottery for souls. Christopher Wren spires are surreally flanked by coconut palms and by the crested plumes of the mountain's rain forest. Brief, delicate spells of rain alternate capriciously with bouts of radiant sunshine, festooning Honolulu with rainbows. Los Angeles–style freeways named after Hawaiian royalty encircle and cross the city, their names rendered childish by the twelve-letter Hawaiian alphabet: Likelike, Lunalilo. There are surfboard racks on the tops of the cars whizzing through Honolulu, like ski racks on a New England winter day.

The city's architecture is as hybrid as the humanity which inhabits it. On its west fringe, a block from the ocean, stands Honolulu's business district, dominated by a gleaming complex of bronzed skyscrapers which calls itself the Financial Plaza of the Pacific. It is adjacent to what remains of Honolulu's Chinatown, a shanty quarter of low clapboard houses where gay bars tended by painted transvestites are flanked by pool halls, massage parlors, skin-flick houses. The state capitol is a lustrous structure in the California-Tokyo style which for two decades housed the offices of Governor John Burns, an Irish Catholic former policeman. Across from it stands a pale-gray Victorian folly of a building, Iolani Palace, that was briefly the residence of Hawaii's last kings. Two blocks away, next to a luxuriant tropical park which boasts one of the world's largest banyan trees, is City Hall, a beige stucco structure in the Filipino baroque genre presided over by the mayor of Honolulu, a second-generation Italian from Hartford, Connecticut.

Standing at the top of Ala Moana on a Sunday, one is at the nucleus of the city. The streets are clogged with lines of Datsun and Toyota cars all converging, like the rays of a diamond, toward Ala Moana. In Honolulu, one of the nation's two fastest-growing cities, shopping at Ala Moana has replaced churchgoing, midday dinner, picnics, as a family occupation on Sundays. ("It has to do with the deterioration of the American family as an institution," a prominent businessman tells me, "but it's damn good for our business boom. The further away you are from New York the less you feel the impacts of any recessions. My, the East Coast gets excited so easily about recessions, they're so provincial, so insular over there. . . .")

A student rally two miles east of Ala Moana, at the University of Hawaii, protesting the presence of ROTC. The cream-and-rose-hued campus is heavy with breadfruit and avocados, resplendent with the crimson vulvas of the African tulip trees, the scarlet claws of the Indian coral tree, the purple petals of the jacaranda. It is high noon. Before the microphone stands a bevy of beautiful nisei girls—second-generation Japanese—wearing orchids in their sumptuous waist-length hair, sleek as a black forest pool. "Rotcee is a no-no!" the girls chant, waving their black manes. Their voices waft gently across the somnolent campus. Some fifty students lie stretched out on the grass, interspersed with a few radical professors who talk of taking out Tahitian passports if the United States takes a turn to the right. On the wall of a nearby building is tacked up a small pink poster which says: PLEASE DON'T VISIT HAWAII. DON'T BUY

INSTANT IMITATION ALOHA IN HEAVY SYRUP DISTRIBUTED BY FRIENDLY
SKIES AIR POLLUTION CORPORATION.

A Congregational minister takes his place at the microphone
to protest the presence of the military recruiters. He is a bearded,
six-foot-four California cleric dressed in white corduroys chopped
off high above his athletic thighs, and looks like Charlton Heston
about to play the role of a surfing Christ. "Rotcee is a no-no," the
lovely nisei chant, swaying their hair as lustrous as a mandarin's
silk cape.

"It never stopped being the nineteen fifties here," a mainland
professor standing next to me mutters. "Docility, docility. No hands
raised in the classroom, not a question raised. All those Japanese
students cramming for the top grades—and the rest, you can't get
them off the beach."

The progressive professor has come to Honolulu for his
asthma, and is perplexed. He expresses a commonly heard complaint: "Polynesian paralysis." The Pacific, he says, is like an amni-
otic fluid that lulls all thought and wit out of a man's system. How
are you going to get the students protesting when they're out at the
beach all the time? Living in Hawaii, he quips, is like living with a
beautiful pubescent whore, alternating carnal pleasure with bouts
of terminal boredom.

"Do you know what *I* like best about Hawaii?" says a Honolulu resident who has served successively as president of the University of Hawaii and director of the Hawaii Visitors Bureau. "The
nicest thing about Hawaii is that when we select a beauty queen at
the university we don't have just *one* beauty queen. We have a
Polynesian beauty queen, a Chinese beauty queen, a Japanese
beauty queen, a Filipino beauty queen, a Portuguese beauty queen,
a Puerto Rican beauty queen, a Negro beauty queen, *and* a Caucasian beauty queen. Six, eight beauty queens all in a row. *That's*
what I like best about Hawaii."

We sit in an office in a Waikiki skyscraper flanked by surf-
board-rental stands and souvenir shops selling plastic figurines of
the old Hawaiian gods. To the left stands the Duke Kahanamoku
nightclub, where the state's singing star, Don Ho, bellows out "This
Is America" to busloads of tourists digesting their first Hawaiian

dinner of poi and baked pig. In front of the hotels large, sad-eyed Hawaiians dressed in red loincloths stand as bellhops and doormen.

"The ethnic mix here is the richest in the world," my host continues, "so varied, so interesting to analyze. The Orientals, of course, are the wonder of the island. Look at the Japanese, one third of the population, yet they control over half of the legislature. The Hawaiians, on the other hand, are the big problem, still at the bottom of the economic ladder, dropping out of school all the time. Lots of them on welfare, don't seem to care about getting ahead in the world. . . . And yet the Hawaiian is a very bright, industrious fellow.

"An extremely bright, industrious fellow," he repeats sadly, his eyes quizzical.

"If you want to know why we Hawaiians are at the bottom of the ladder just take a look at this school," Melissa says. She is a seventeen-year-old part-Chinese, part-Hawaiian student at Kamehameha School, which was founded in the 1880s for the exclusive education of children with Hawaiian blood. Kamehameha—Kam for short—is funded by the revenues of the Bishop Estate, which owns one tenth of the land in the state. Its large, drab, barracklike buildings tumble down the side of a steep hill on the northern fringe of Honolulu. "About face!" shouts the leader of a platoon of fourteen-year-olds in military uniform. ROTC training and the wearing of military uniforms have been compulsory at Kamehameha since 1916.

"There are three thousand students in this school which is supposed to preserve the Hawaiian culture," Melissa says, "whatever that's supposed to mean. Ever since Kam was founded, students have been forbidden to speak Hawaiian or even pidgin. Kam hasn't had more than four trustees with Hawaiian blood in its eighty-year history. Until recently they didn't even allow us to dance the hula. Yes, there is an ethnic-studies program in Hawaiian language and culture, but it's so little encouraged that there are about fifty kids enrolled in it. It's not only the fault of the school but also of our parents. Hawaiians of my parents' generation are confused. They want us to do well in the *haole*—the white—culture yet they don't want us to become haolefied. The haole trustees who run this sup-

posedly Hawaiian school are confused too. They want to haolefy us
enough to make us docile, without haloefying us enough to compete
with them."

She is a graceful, angry girl who finds herself isolated in her
rage at the stranglehold which the military has on the state. "One
year, when I was fourteen, I thought of all kinds of plans to bomb
buildings. Not only the draft boards, but also the buildings that
symbolize what the haoles have done to the Hawaiians—like the
Amfac and Dillingham buildings. I was going to do it all by myself;
I didn't know anybody who would join me. Then I calmed down,
I guess there was a big fantasy element to it, you feel so isolated
here as a radical."

"Kam is merely perpetuating the feudalism of our old plantation system," says John Dominis Holt, one of the few impassioned
nationalists of his generation, a writer and scholar in his fifties who
is a direct descendant of King Kamehameha I. Holt, whose life has
been steeped in bitter nostalgia for the loss of his people's culture,
was educated at Columbia College, at Oxford, and at the Sorbonne.
Since his return to Hawaii in the 1950s, he has dedicated himself to
writing about Hawaiian art and history.

"What kinds of vocations are open to Hawaiians when they
graduate from Kam?" Holt adds. "Bellhop, bartender, telephone
repairman. All the income from one tenth of the state's land goes
into the funding of an academy for bartenders. *Quelle belle farce*.
The haoles needed a service class of janitors and concierges and
they created it by picking the brightest Hawaiians of each generation for their lousy school and then breaking their spirit, breaking
their Hawaiian identity."

From the Kamehameha campus there is the most sublime view
available of Pearl Harbor and of the Tripler Army Hospital. One
out of seven residents in the state is an American military man or
his dependent. No state in the Union, Melissa and John Dominis
Holt have both noted, is more dependent on the Cold War than
Hawaii.

"Secession!" Melissa exclaims. "That's the grooviest movement around. It's the only way to get rid of the military and preserve the little that's left of our culture."

□

Shreds of table talk:

"You can't beat us for paradise," says a state official who came to Hawaii as a marine in World War II and loved it so much that he took the first civilian ship back to Hawaii after the war. "Even if you're poor and hungry in Hawaii you can still go to the beach. And we don't have any of those racial tensions you've got on the mainland. Why, the way I was brought up, back in Connecticut, I was taught that the only good Jap is a dead Jap. And now look at me! I'm married to one."

A director of one of the Big Five firms, sitting on the top floor of a skyscraper in the Financial Plaza of the Pacific: "Nineteen fifty-four, that's the year the Oriental began to feel his oats in Hawaii. You had them coming out of your ears, all those Japanese going through college and law school on the G.I. Bill and then taking over the legislature. It got kind of tiresome, that monkey legislature."

A Caucasian professor, formerly active with Hawaii's Communist party: "I have anti-Hawaiian prejudices because of their lack of realism. They've blamed their woes on everybody else and never faced up to the failure of their own chiefs. They're stuck in the politics of nostalgia. The only thing they do well is fornicate and drink."

Kalani Ohelo: "Kill Haole Day, that's the most satisfying thing around. That's when our high-school gangs go out and beat up some military men."

"When's Kill Haole Day, Kalani?"

"Christmas, Sunday, tomorrow, anytime."

Kalani Ohelo and I are driving around Mount Tantalus, on whose steep slopes thrives one of the most luxuriant rain forests in Hawaii. At the bottom of the mountain, in Papakolea, are lands belonging to the Hawaiian Homes Commission, an agency founded in 1920 through which the U.S. Congress allotted 200,000 acres of land to be leased for minimal fees by persons of at least one-half Hawaiian blood. Fifty years later only some 12 percent of the acreage has been awarded, most of it totally uncultivable; some seventy-five hundred Hawaiians are still wait-listed for a homestead; many of them have been waiting over thirty years.

Halfway up the mountain are the homes of some of Honolulu's most elitist haole and Asian millionaires. Driving below, through the Hawaiian Homes Commission land, Kalani points to a clapboard house, flanked by obese breadfruit trees, on the stoop of which sit two round-cheeked, nut-brown children.

"Here are our ghettos," Kalani said proudly. "Are they much worse than the ghettos on the mainland?"

"Oh, no, Kalani, they don't begin to be as bad."

He looks disappointed. "Then I don't want to go to the mainland," he says. "I'm enough of a flaming radical already."

He makes a growling sound. "We Hawaiians used to be a very violent people," he says, "and we can become violent again."

Kalani's luscious eyes try to glimmer fiercely in his big, kind face. Kalani never liked school and seldom read a book until he was nineteen, when in the span of one month he read *The New Indians, Manchild in the Promised Land, The Autobiography of Malcolm X,* all of Rap Brown, all of Eldridge Cleaver, and every other book he could find on the Black Power and Brown Power movements. The tourist industry has created an image of the docile, smiling, sleepy, ukulele-strumming Hawaiians; but soon, he warns, the haoles will learn that the Hawaiians are not so gentle.

We are halfway up Mount Tantalus, crossing into a rain forest heavy with avocado and banyan trees, redolent with ginger, guavas, eucalyptus. Kalani takes a long, appreciative whiff.

"Hey, smell that ginger," Kalani exclaims. "When I smell that ginger I become less of a flaming radical."

On a February day in 1779 Captain James Cook fell face down on a shelf of black lava at the edge of the cobalt-blue sea on the island of Hawaii, killed by a native's blow. His death had come during a skirmish when the Hawaiians stole a cutter from one of his ships. Trembling, pale-green branches of the feathery kiawe tree brush the black lava upon which fell the greatest explorer of the eighteenth century. The site of the incident, at the edge of Kealakekua Bay, is very beautiful and has changed little since Cook's death. It had been inconspicuously marked until 1874, when the British government was ceded the land by the Territory of Hawaii to build Cook a pompous white obelisk. Employees of the British consulate come every few years to repaint the solitary, rarely visited monument. To this day there is no road or footpath to approach this memorial to one of the few white men in history ever killed by a Hawaiian. One can travel to it only by boat.

On the face of the obelisk is engraved: "In memory of the great circumnavigator, Captain James Cook, R.N., who discovered these islands on the 18th of January in A.D. 1778, and fell near this spot on the 14th of February A.D. 1779."

In 1970 I noticed that some bold graffiti in scarlet paint had been added to the left face of the monument: "To the memory of the great Hawaiians," the scribbling says, "who discovered Hawaii in the year 1200. All power to the people."

The date is wrong: Hawaii was probably settled by a migratory wave from the Marquesas Islands between the years 300 and 700, and by a second migration from the Society Islands around 1200. But no matter. John Holt, Kalani Ohelo, and other nationalists say that the Hawaiians have to become proud before they can become historical.

Captain James Cook was killed partly because he was taken for a god, and was expected to behave like one. There prevailed at the time of his arrival the bittersweet myth of the god of agriculture, Lono, whose character is very Hawaiian in its combination of Hamlet and Samurai, of tenderness and fierceness. Lono, as the story goes, had killed his human wife, whom he suspected of infidelity. Later, when he realized that she had been innocent, he sailed away in grief, promising to return someday when he had purged his guilt. It was in Lono's honor that the Hawaiians every winter used to hold the great Makahiki festival, a weeks-long celebration of feasting, athletic and artistic contests during which Lono's symbols—large wooden sticks hung with swaths of white *kapa* (bark cloth)—were carried around the islands. When James Cook first landed on the Hawaiian island of Kauai in 1778 on his way to search for a northwest passage to the Atlantic, he arrived at the time of the Makahiki festival; the sails of Cook's ship, the *Resolution*, seen from afar as pieces of white cloth fluttering on the wooden post that was his mast, strikingly resembled Lono's symbol. For reasons in part political, the priests of Lono, in a quest for increased power, pronounced Cook to be the god returned. The explorer was worshiped with all the ceremony and bearing of gifts appropriate to deities.

One thinks of another destroyer of a culture, Cortes, arriving in Mexico two hundred years earlier with the attributes of Quetzalcoatl. But the considerably more benign Cook had the misfortune to be twice mistaken for a god. A year later, when he landed a second time in the Hawaiian Islands—this time at Kealakekua Bay on the island of Hawaii—he again arrived at the time of the Makahiki festival. But this time the festival was drawing to a close and the natives' enthusiasm for Lono was waning. It was on this occasion that the Hawaiians stole one of Cook's cutters; the explorer, giving in to one of his famous bursts of temper, fired his musket into the crowd in an attempt to recapture the boat. At the height of the squabble between his men and the Hawaiians, Cook was struck at the back of the neck and fell at the water's edge, and then was stabbed and clubbed to death. To be sure, the islanders took certain precautions just in case he was a god. A few Hawaiians are said to have helped themselves to his potential *mana*, his sacred power, by eating his entrails. Cook's bones were scaped of flesh and given a decent godlike burial in a place of total secrecy, as Hawaiian custom requires for the burial of all great chiefs.

Probably standing at the scene of Cook's death, and he may have given a few blows himself, was a shrewd young chief called Kamehameha. Some accounts have it that he kept Cook's hair, and that its mana was responsible for his extraordinary rise to power. For Kamehameha was an upstart, a chief who rose to absolute kingship within three decades of Cook's death through the barrels of white men's guns. He has been called the greatest political genius of the Polynesian people, the Napoleon of the Pacific. He was the only leader in that vast third of the planet's surface who ever managed to unite any chain of islands into one kingdom.

The few portraits of King Kamehameha I executed during his lifetime show a powerful, squat face in which the shrewd eyes contrast strongly with the compassionate, anxious mouth. One thinks of his life as a nightmare of narrow options. The Maori of New Zealand chose to fight the white men unto death, and retained part of their land and a good part of their culture. The great Kamehameha chose the opposite course. He welcomed the white men, and used them as tools to attain absolute power over his rival chiefs; the intruders, in return, took advantage of his calculated generosity to gain control of his islands. By 1800, white men had become the principal advisers at Kamehameha's court. He treated them like precious, exotic pets, married them to women chiefs, and gave them the choicest foods. For a few decades Kamehameha's cunning welcome was rewarded. Having broken the power of the *ali'i*—the chiefly caste—by appointing white men as governors of his most strategic islands, by the time of his death Kamehameha had total control over the eight major islands of the Hawaiian chain—Oahu, Kauai, Maui, Molokai, Hawaii, Lanai, Niihau, and Kaho'olawe.

Settled later than any other major Polynesian islands, devoid of a single contact with strangers for six centuries, discovered by European explorers later than any other Pacific civilization, Hawaii lies two thousand miles away from the nearest other island group. It is the most isolated archipelago in the world. Most quirks of its history flow from its isolation. Precisely because they had never been challenged by any foreign values, the concepts of mana and tabu which pervaded all of Polynesian society existed in Hawaii in their most rigid form. Because they were so rigid, it was there that their abolition would leave the deepest scars on the natives' psyche. There were *kapu* (tabu) people, places, times, objects. Any profanation of their sacredness—a misdeed as minor as crossing the shadow of a royal person, or dropping the royal spittoon upon the ground—was punishable by death. The mana of the highest chiefs was so powerful that they avoided walking in the daytime for fear that their shadows might harm a subject, or that they would make the ground kapu and barren. The fabled corpulence of Hawaiian ali'i was in part caused by the fact that they were carried by attendants from childhood on so that their feet would not make the ground kapu. Through this theocratic kapu system the Hawaiian chiefs, their lineage traced to the Gods, were adulated by their people as in few other civilizations. "The ants weep, pebbles rattle, bivalves mutter indistinctly, birds wither, smoke lies low, the rainbow arches, rain rains, rivers flow, the horned coral flows up upon the land, the mournful cry of spirits wail loud . . . these are the witnesses of a great chief." Thus an ancient Hawaiian poem describes the ali'i's divine right over man and nature.

Yet Hawaiian society was less oppressive, in some aspects, than many of the Mediterranean civilizations that are the predecessors of our own. Accumulation was unknown in this self-sufficient, isolated culture devoid of any commerce beyond its own interisland trade. The most honored social attributes were those of largesse and hospitality. Its most central value, infusing the Hawaiian ethos to this day, was the sacredness of the land, 'aina, which the gods had entrusted for communal holding rather than individual ownership, and which men must live with in a relationship of harmony instead of domination.

Such were the features of many societies of the Pacific. The major trait which differentiated the Hawaiian from other Pacific islanders was a passion for innovation which could be interpreted as a trait of high intelligence, and which made him swiftly throw away his stone tools upon the sight of a white man's iron nails. The ferocious Maori had showered the first European intruders with arrows from their shore, but the inquisitive and ebullient Hawaiians greeted the first ships with a joy and excitement displayed by few other Pacific islanders. And it was their appetite for Western technology which destroyed the delicate balance of Hawaiian society. If the men on Cook's ship received two pigs and several loads of fish from the Hawaiians in exchange for one iron nail, one can imagine the extravagant abundance of crops and animals which the islands' chiefs forced commoners to produce from 1780 on. As a growing number of trading vessels anchored at the islands a non-competitive economy of subsistence was rapidly, brutally, transformed into a forced economy of trade. Labor conditions became increasingly oppressive in those very decades when the Hawaiian people were being decimated by the white man's diseases. Lacking immunity because of centuries of isolation, Hawaii's native population fell from an estimated four hundred thousand to half that number in the forty years between Cook's arrival and 1820. It was further depleted by the white man's alcohol, which would remain the islanders' curse.

A singular trait of the Hawaiian culture was its tendency to theocide, its extremely pragmatic bent to create, destroy, resurrect its gods at will according to the gods' accomplishments. The destruction of this success-or-else religion occurred several months before any Christian missionaries arrived. The kapu system had discriminated stringently against women (they were looked upon as the dark, contaminated half of humanity, were forbidden under penalty of death to eat with men or taste the islands' choicest foods) and women brought about its destruction. The leader of this revolt was an astute three-hundred-pound beauty who had been one of the great surfers of her day and was the favorite of Kamehameha's twenty-one wives. Her name was Ka'ahumanu. Six months after her husband's death she managed—with the aid of another of Kamehameha's widows, the mother of the new young king, Liholiho—to destroy the kapu system in one stroke. The two queens scheduled an enormous feast and invited the weak and dissolute new ruler to break one of the most sacred kapus by eating with the women. Liholiho acted as several future Hawaiian monarchs would act when faced with a serious decision: A few days before the scheduled feast he went to sea with a boatload of liquor to consider the issue. Returning to the women's quarters in time for the repast, he wavered a few moments, then lurched to the women's feast and ate voraciously. This violation triggered a considerable rampage. In the next months Ka'ahumanu's followers swept through the island destroying temples and burning their ancestral idols, which included some of the most superb wood carvings in Polynesia and its most exquisite featherwork. Thus Hawaii's religious institutions were destroyed by its chiefly caste—a rare phenomenon, since the dissolution of religion typically starts at the bottom of primitive societies and not at their apex.

The first companies of Protestant missionaries arrived from Boston several months after these events and took advantage of the process of destruction which the Hawaiian royalty itself had instigated. Ka'ahumanu ruled as regent of the Hawaiian kingdom until 1832, and further accelerated the transformation of Hawaiian society by becoming the missionaries' most ardent supporter. The native religion continued to be observed by a minority of Hawaiians—mostly commoners—and went underground. Whatever temple idols remained were hidden and worshiped secretly. The most enduring of the ancient beliefs has been Hawaiians' reverence for their 'aumākua—spirits of deified ancestors who often assume the shapes of sharks and numerous other creatures and serve as guardian angels to the living. It is a tradition which still reinforces Hawaiians' primordial loyalty to land and *'ohana*—the extended family that cuts across all bonds of kinship—and their view of salvation as communal.

Diderot: "One day the Christians will come, with their crucifix in one hand and their dagger in the other, to cut your throats or force you to accept their customs and opinions." It is unfortunate that the evangelizing of Hawaii should have fallen to Calvinists, one of the more intransigent of Christian sects. The company of missionaries led by Reverend Hiram Bingham were earnest, dedicated, tragicomic figures whose search for sin was as passionate as J. Edgar Hoover's hunt for Communism. They saw it in most traditional details of Hawaii's brilliant culture: in the recitation of native poetry; the playing of Hawaiian games and music; in the most inoffensive hula, a sacred dance whose creation was attributed to the goddess of forests, Laka, and which was a principal means of communication between humans and gods.

The first white clapboard houses which the missionaries built and in which they lived under most arduous conditions, often packed ten or twelve to a tiny room, still stand intact in downtown Honolulu. They are a testament to their suffering, their dedication, and their comic intransigence. With the same doggedness with which they continued to wear long-sleeved New England garments in a sweltering climate, and exhorted the natives to do likewise, they built low-ceilinged rooms to retain the heat of their Honolulu fireplaces; and to teach their tropical flock to read, they used alphabet books with pictures of children skating, sledding, and chopping pine trees in a snowy New England landscape. Unlike Enlightenment explorers, the missionaries had little admiration for Polynesia's noble savages, only that most dangerous of loving concerns which expresses itself in evangelism. They played a major role in the process of cultural genocide by making Hawaiians ashamed of being Hawaiian.

The Polynesian Hawaiians are the most dispossessed people of our island state, suffering from the lowest levels of education and technical skills, the highest incidence of disease, crime, suicide, of any ethnic group. And it is clear that their troubles stem from the great schizophrenia instilled in them by the first missionary companies—the neutralization of their identity, a national death wish. This island people weakened by centuries of isolation lacked the psychological antibodies, as well as the physical ones, needed to survive such sudden contact with the white man.

To this day the Hawaiian, John Dominis Holt tells me, has an uncanny way of predicting his own death. "I shall die next Thursday," he might tell his relatives. And die on Thursday he does, without doing physical violence to himself or showing symptoms of any disease.

The beautiful Princess Nahienaena, a sister of Kamehameha III and his favorite concubine, was torn between her passionate and very traditional love for her brother and the sense of guilt imposed upon her by her missionary teachers. Weeping and laughing in turn in the royal pews of the churches, alternating between bouts of debauchery and fits of the deepest Calvinist piety, she died in 1834 shortly after her brother's child was born to her. She still lies buried at Lahaina, on Maui, a few blocks away from the psychedelic bikini shops of a hotel-studded resort that has become the St.-Tropez of Polynesia.

In the following decades of the nineteenth century the "missionary monarchy," as the white power structure was called, was responsible for an equally tragic restructuring of Hawaiian society which deprived the Hawaiians of most of their land.

In 1850, under the terms of the "Great Mahele," the extensive division of land forced upon him by white settlers, King Kamehameha III gave up his rights to much of his property. He kept certain estates which became known as crown lands; a few hundred high chiefs received a million and a half acres which they proceeded to sell, lease, or give away to foreigners with unmatched insouciance (Kamehameha IV sold the entire island of Niihau for ten thousand dollars to a family of Westerners whose descendants still own it, strictly barring it to visitors to this day). Of some seventy-two thousand Hawaiians still alive in mid-nineteenth century—diseases had again reduced the population by half in the decades since the missionaries' arrival—only about ten thousand received land. And it amounted to less than 1 percent of the islands' total acreage of four million. Hawaiians had become gypsies in their own country, deprived of that one substance—'aina, beloved earth—which had given them spiritual meaning and material security. "The missionaries told us to look up to heaven," so a saying goes, "and while we did so, they stole our land."

The Gospel has never excluded greed. The redistribution of property effected by the missionary monarchy was responsible for the amazing centralization of real-estate ownership, begun by the founding of immense sugar and pineapple plantations, that still prevails in contemporary Hawaii. An estimated one third of the officers of the Big Five—the cartel of companies that would totally control the islands' economic and political life until the 1950s, and still owns over one half of its arable terrain—have been direct descendants of the islands' missionary families, or related to them by marriage. In the 1890s the missionary-planters' power clique would also play a principal role in the high-handed coups d'état which overthrew Hawaii's last monarch, Queen Liliuo'kalani, and five years later forced its annexation to the United States. Condemned by President Grover Cleveland as an "unlawful act of war" against "a friendly and confiding people," the seizure was carried out in an outlandishly illegal manner. Never approved by the two-thirds-majority Senate vote our Constitution requires, it was effected with the help of marines never authorized by the U.S. government, solely engineered by a few hundred Americans protecting their wealth, which already comprised some four fifths of the islands' cultivable land.

Traveling through the Hawaiian Islands during my six months' stay on Oahu in the early 1970s, I found that part of their great magic lies in their geological infancy, the sense that we are still witnessing an active process in the history of creation. Nowhere is this newness more keenly felt than on the "Big Island" of Hawaii, which is still being sculpted by the eruptions of Kilauea crater. Hawaii Island's savage lava shores and snow-capped volcanic domes, reaching nearly fourteen thousand feet, reflect the island's extraordinary youth—a mere three quarters of a million years. Kilauea erupts every few years, forging new coastlines, cloaking the island with miles of lava fields that solidify into a brilliant, brittle crust of metallic blue-black hue pierced by vents of sizzling steam. Walking through volcanic areas of the Big Island one is thrust back to our world's infancy. Lichens, mosses, tree ferns—the planet's earliest vegetation—sprout from fields of lava poured out a decade ago. As in the other islands, a prolific variety of flora and fauna makes Hawaii a veritable laboratory and showcase of evolution, a microcosm that still displays the development of earliest continental life. (Due to its extreme isolation, 95 percent of the state's native flora and fauna occurs nowhere else in the world, and there are nearly ten thousand species of insects which are unique to the islands.)

On the island of Kauai, on the slopes of the three-thousand-foot deep Waimea canyon, which ranges from russet to violet according to the whims of the capricious Hawaiian sky, I admired groves of the scarlet-spiked *lehua*. Sacred to Pele, goddess of volcanoes, it is a tree which many Hawaiians still dare not touch. And I sensed that notwithstanding their ravage of Hawaiians' souls, the missionaries did not manage totally to eradicate the islanders' original beliefs. The ancient art of the *kahunas*, medicine men and healers, has never ceased. John Dominis Holt, in the middle of an erudite discussion of Baudelaire's poetry or Verdi's operas, will still throw his head back and chant the genealogy of his kingly ancestors, stressing the fact that they were descended from the gods. There are families on the outer islands who continue to offer their first fruits to deities of fishing and planting, still know the legends of every stream, cove, rock formation, in their community. This aura of pantheistic sacredness is most pervasive to me on Maui, at the dormant Haleakala volcano, a majestic bowl of copper, black, and purple volcanic dust punctuated by monumental cinder cones and the violet flowers of the extremely rare silversword plant. Twice the size of Manhattan island, lying in awesome stillness ten thousand feet above sea level, Haleakala crater was a place of pilgrimage for the ancient Hawaiians, a site for meditation and revelation. It retains the magic aura of the world's great sacred spaces: Delphi, Olympia, Uxmal.

Soaring waterfalls abound throughout the Hawaiian Islands, as in many terrains shaped by recent volcanic eruptions. Some are narrow, diaphanous, feminine effervescences of spume, others are broad and vigorously masculine torrents bounding out of dark ravines of black rock. Watching them cascade into pools fringed with wild lantana, bamboo, mango, banana, pandanus, avocado, and breadfruit trees, their vapor creating innumerable rainbows in air redolent with the fragrance of ginger and frangipani, one senses that there have been few more blessed landscapes on our planet.

And yet one senses the waning of a dream. For notwithstanding its reputations of luxurious abundance, Hawaii is a chain of precipitously steep, volcanic islands in which only 15 percent of the terrain is arable. Its dearth of cultivable land, the fragility of its narrow ecosystem, its consequent vulnerability to outside forces are as crucial to its history as its unique isolation. Numerous areas in the islands are becoming the ecological nightmare which mainlanders come to Hawaii to avoid—sprawling concrete shopping centers, automobile dumps, heaps of refuse washed up on beaches, foully polluted shores and streams. The greed of out-of-state developers—the Big Five's Amfac, several of the mainland's airline companies, an increasing number of Japanese firms—are at fault for the growing urban sprawl. In few places has the American ideal of unlimited growth, of an endlessly receding frontier, wrought more havoc. Hawaii's resort hotels and condominiums, planned with thoughtless optimism in the last decades to remedy the financial crisis created by the demise of the pineapple and sugar industries, are proving to be a very unstable base for the Hawaiian economy. They have often concentrated on Hawaii's most verdant sites, contributing to the disaffection of an indigenous population increasingly deprived of access to decent land. And the alienation of many young Hawaiians has been compounded by the growing encroachment of the United States' military presence.

Proponents of Hawaii's annexation to the United States, in the 1880s, had argued that Hawaii could serve as "the Gibraltar of the Pacific." Their predictions came spectacularly true. Hawaii's Schofield Barracks was already the biggest Army post in the United States in the years between the two world wars. In 1941, at Pearl Harbor, the Japanese confirmed Hawaii's strategic importance. In the succeeding years, after the fall of China and the rise of the Cold War, Hawaii became the Pentagon of the Pacific as well as its Gibraltar. Today the Pacific Command, still based at Pearl Harbor, has become the most powerful defense headquarters in the world.

It surveys 40 percent of the planet's surface, and oversees over three hundred thousand military personnel, on bases or on ships in various areas of the Pacific. It controls more than one quarter of the land on the main island of Oahu, accounts for one out of seven of the island's residents, and employs a greater amount of the civilian labor force (some 8 percent) than in any other state in the Union. Since World War II the U.S. military has also controlled the entirety of another major island, Kaho'olawe; once verdant and inhabited, Kaho'olawe, the seventh largest island of the Hawaiian chain and the site of many sacred *heiaus*—ancient shrines—has become a wasteland exclusively used for shelling and bombing practice.

Notwithstanding its awesome might, the military presence in Hawaii is barely visible, hence all the more sinister. It has been forced to covertness because of the traditional tensions symbolized by the high-school gangs' Kill Haole Day fantasies, and by memories of the notorious Massie trial. (In 1931, three American military men were pardoned by federal authorities after having been found guilty of murdering a young Hawaiian; the youth had earlier been found innocent in court of the allegation that he had raped one of the servicemen's wives.) The case has remained a symbol of the deep-seated racial tensions that exist in the islands' much-touted melting pot, and of the resentment felt by some native Hawaiians for Oahu's vast military population. Due to these pressures, servicemen have been under orders since the time of Eisenhower's directive never to leave base in uniform. Sending their children to schools on base, living in enormous military ghettos, playing golf at military country clubs, swimming at military beaches, wandering through the honky-tonks of Waikiki with their families in pineapple-print shorts, they are indistinguishable from all the other transients who come to the islands on a holiday.

A sense that Hawaii reaps all the disadvantages of statehood and pitifully few of its benefits, a resolve to restrict mainland encroachment, has recently spread through many levels of Hawaiian society. Yet whatever resentments the vast defense industry may cause, it has been largely responsible for the enormous economic boom Hawaii has enjoyed since World War II. Given the islanders' ambivalent feelings toward this source of prosperity, most resentment toward the military presence on Hawaii is confined to a small group of radically inclined citizens. ("If someone doesn't stop the military from retiring in Hawaii," John Dominis Holt grumbles, "in twenty years half of the state's population will be living in condominiums with German shepherds and armed guards in the foyer.") The state's more conservative citizens focus on environmental issues, and a few adopt the broader motto "Don't Visit Hawaii."

"If I were elected governor," says the aristocratic, part-Hawaiian president of one of the Big Five firms, "I'd put it on a plank to send everyone back who hasn't been here for fifteen years."

As for the nationalist movement just nascent on the islands, it has focused on a more immediate grass-roots problem—the dearth of land available to the Hawaiian people.

On a sunny, hot winter afternoon in January of 1971, Kalani Ohelo and a tiny group of activists—some twenty of them—were picketing the state legislature in Honolulu to ask for more land for native Hawaiians. Specifically, they were protesting the "rip-off" of Kalama Valley, one of the few places left on Oahu's south shore where Hawaiians could still make their living as small farmers—raising pigs, sheep, or vegetables on small plots of leased land. Kalama Valley belongs to the Bishop Estate, whose revenue is intended to fund the Kamehameha Schools and other educational programs that offer "such useful knowledge as may tend to make good and industrious men and women." It was being cleared to make way for a new thirty-thousand-person housing development which, as the protesters stressed, would only serve the growing numbers of upper-income mainlanders settling in Honolulu. A few families had already been evicted from their homes in the valley. And the state authorities were threatening to bulldoze the homes of the remaining families. Kalani and his fellow protesters, who included several haole militants, called themselves Kokua Kalama, "Help Kalama." They had come to the legislature to see Governor John Burns and ask for a moratorium on the Kalama housing development. The Kokua group carried signs which said IMUA! (Forward!), HULI! (Overthrow!), HAWAII FOR HAWAIIANS, and WHERE HAVE ALL OUR PEOPLE GONE?

The protesters received the same response they had received

during their few previous protests. The governor was busy, or away; and one of his chief aides, a polite nisei in a bright floral shirt, had come down to say that the governor could not receive them. Kalani Ohelo's little group disbanded, as it had several times before, with a show of clenched fists and a last shout of *"Imua Hawaii!"*

And I wondered: Seeing the Haiwaiians' often tragic tendency to docility, to what extent can such reformist groups engage the passions of the islands' original people? When asked how the Kalama movement came to be started, a part-Polynesian member of Kalani Ohelo's group looked sheepish and answered, "A haole mainlander suggested it. At first when he started pushing and prodding us to start this protest movement about our land I said to myself, 'Oh oh, here comes another haole to exploit me.' But later I began to trust him, and he helped me to get confidence in myself, because that's what we Hawaiians need most: self-confidence."

But it is not only self-confidence that Hawaiians have lacked when confronted by the possibility of militant action. Also at cause is the islanders' avoidance of any divisive issue that might upset the unity of the tribe. John Dominis Holt tells me that Hawaiians have a parable about themselves: They are like crabs in a basket; as soon as one crab tries to climb up and stand out, the others pull him back in. In the sociologists' lingo, Hawaiians continue to be affiliation-oriented rather than achievement-oriented, as they were in pre-Cook times. Whereas residents of Honolulu's Japanese district salute each other according to the delicate hierarchy of their motor-car status—the relative chic of their Datsuns, Toyotas, or Buicks—the Hawaiian tends to find greater pleasure in remodeling a 1962 Ford with his friends and relatives. Swift-witted and formidably gifted at learning all manner of skills, Hawaiians will put out gigantic amounts of labor if they are allowed to work with a group of peers and set their own pace. One of the most interesting institutions of island life is the *huki pau,* or "work together till you're finished," system pioneered by the garbage collectors' union, which is more than half-Hawaiian. Under its terms the workers are free as soon as they have finished an assigned route, whatever number of hours they may have put into it. Garbage in Hawaii is collected with prodigious efficiency, neatness, and speed. The garbage collectors are often through by noon, and think the rest of the world is mad for working any other way.

"Hawaiian life-style," Governor John Burns said to me during a visit in his office at the state capitol, his voice cynical and paternal. "Fine if you want to be a beachcomber. Work *huki-pau* to go *ula-ula*. I too, when I was young, worked *huki-pau* to go *ula-ula*." Ula-ula means to have a good time. The haole liberal who was the principal lobbyist for Hawaiian statehood, the Japanese-American legislators with whose support the governor restored the Democratic party's dominance, have often been very insensitive to the original Hawaiians' needs. And the Burns machine's central commitment—to create an economic boom through unlimited expansion of land development and tourism—can only deepen the ecological crisis and aggravate Hawaiians' alienation from what they most need—access to the 'aina, their beloved land.

I leave the islands aware of widespread discontent on environmental issues and increasing unrest among native Hawaiians, sensing that the fabled Aloha spirit might be facing extinction. (It had always been, in good part, an invention of the tourist trade, as false as it saccharined distortion of the mercurial Hawaiian character—which is humorous but proud, in turn genial and aloof, circuitous and brooding.) After three decades of urbanization, Hawaii has a renewed aura of provincialism and hostility toward the outside world. In this society of subtly covert racial tensions where the poverty of underprivileged groups such as the native Hawaiians is masked or assuaged by good climate, and to which the defense industry has brought considerable prosperity, environmental issues tend to obscure all other national or international problems. Only in Hawaii could a protest group called Save Our Surf (S.O.S. for short) be so powerful.

For many years S.O.S.—the bumper sticker seen most frequently on Hawaiian cars—has been led by a Marxist-oriented surfer and body cultist, John Kelly, who has agitated with admirable stamina against the gradual closing off of public beaches by hotels and residential complexes. A demonstration of hundreds of barefoot, bikini-clad S.O.S. members at the state legislature, holding surfboards under their arms, is a totally normal occurrence in Honolulu. Kelly's slide show, which he has shown to tens of thousands of Hawaii residents, simplistically but triumphantly links the closing of beaches to uncurbed capitalistic profitmaking, to the encroachment of the U.S. military, and to the imperialistic suppression of Polynesian culture. "Who do our beaches belong to?" John Kelly asks his acolytes after his slide show. "The people!" roars the audience. "Who does the surf belong to?" "The people!" they roar again, as in a tribal catechism. Issues of beach and surf, Kelly has found, might be the best way to politicize a society which, until the advent of a very grave threat, will remain profoundly hedonistic and insular, a sugar-coated fortress, a plastic paradise in which the militarism and racism of the American empire are cloaked by a deceptive veil of sunshine and of flowers.

1971

II

Hawaii: 1986

Friendships seem particularly loyal and deep-rooted in our fiftieth state. Meeting with Kalani Ohelo the day after I'd returned to Hawaii, fifteen years after my last visit, we embrace and reminisce and talk as if a mere month has passed. Kalani is now a very large, hulking man with a rolling gait and a long bushy beard. Since I've last seen him he has obtained a university degree in political science and has fathered seven children.

Kalani Ohelo's ancestry is half-Hawaiian and also part Spanish, Portuguese, German, Chinese, and Filipino, "a Molotov cocktail," as he calls it. He came to life in the slums of Honolulu thirty-six years ago. Due to a difficult forceps delivery he was born club-footed and nearly blind, and also made nearly mute by a paralysis of his facial muscles. His sight was given up for lost until the age of six, when during a family outing he suddenly spoke out his detailed impression of the landscape. His childhood handicaps still mark him with deceptively violent features—a gruff, immobile face, a guttural speech. The son of a bus driver, in his teens Kalani ran the streets with youth gangs, had problems with drugs and alcohol. When I last saw him, at the end of my first stay in Honolulu, he had begun a clean life with the 1960s Movement, and was working alongside young mainland radicals in the cause which has obsessed him since adolescence—the restoration of land to thousands of homeless Hawaiians.

Over a long lunch we share on the day of our reunion I become acquainted with Kalani's wife, Kawahini, a stately beauty with radiant warmth and a very quick wit. I learn that they are living on Oahu's east coast with an assortment of relatives equally hard-pressed by Hawaii's extravagantly high rents, the second highest in the nation. Kalani and Kawahini are sharing a five-room house with twenty-seven other adults and children, pooling resources to pay their landlord $895 a month.

Kalani and Kawahini have "tested the system," they tell me, by applying to the Hawaiian Homes Commission for a homestead on the island of Molokai. After a five-year wait they were granted an acre in one of the state's most barren sites; the closest accesses to water or electricity were some twenty miles away. "We tried to rough it for a year," Kawahini tells me. "We lived in a tent, surviving on our taro patch and the fish and seaweed we got from the ocean. But without water or electricity it was hard on the babies during the damp rainy seasons, so we had to move back to Oahu with my parents."

In 1985 Kalani and his wife resumed living in tents, this time in way of protest. Leaving their children with grandparents, they camped out with ninety-six other Hawaiians on Oahu's east coast, on a beachfront that belongs to the Hawaiian Homes Commission, to protest the fact that the site had been made into a public park. They remained there for six months, daily threatened with eviction by state police, until they were forcibly removed. Toward the end of our lunch Kawahini lifts Kalani's shirtsleeve, showing me two four-inch-long scars: He suffered a compound fracture of the upper arm while being dragged into the paddy wagon by "terminally rough cops." I ask Kalani how he is spending his time when he is not helping out with his large extended family or getting busted in "The Struggle." He says that he is learning Hawaiian and spending several hours a day in the University of Hawaii's libraries, still studying. But he is no more into Marx or Cleaver "or anything Western-oriented"; he is engaged in a comparative study of all the treaties made between colonial powers and indigenous populations of the Pacific. He hopes it will help him better to understand "all the illegalities that had occurred in the United States' theft of Hawaiian lands, and why other Pacific cultures have remained more intact."

The big news in the fiftieth state, in November of 1986, is that the first elected governor of Hawaiian descent in Hawaii's history, John Waihee, is about to take office. What about your first Hawaiian governor? I ask Kalani and Kawahini before we part. They seem both proud and diffident. "We worked for him hard, but very secretly," Kawahini whispers. "It took me awhile to convince Kalani that we must still try the system, too many of our friends have given it up."

As we drive downtown, making dates for the following weeks, Kalani and Kawahini reveal one more detail of their lives which strikes me as very novel. When I last saw Kalani fifteen years ago he had been a hard-core Marxist atheist, but recently he and Kawahini have begun to observe many ancient rituals of the Hawaiian religion. Kawahini describes one such practice in detail: When each of their last four children was born, Kalani wrapped the baby's placenta in *ti* leaves and swam out to sea to offer it to the ocean. It is a custom which even their parents had forgotten, which Kawahini learned from *kupunas*—wise elders—whom she met in the Hawaiian Struggle. This ritual has come to symbolize something very important to Kawahini and Kalani: "It's a way of giving back to the elements what they've given us and introducing the baby to its *'amakua*, its ancestor guardian angel, a way of saying *mahalo*, thank you."

I have turned often to Kalani, out of affection and admiration, and also because the evolution of his entire life is analogous to the growth of the nationalist movement which he helped to found at Kalama Valley: Growing from blindness and crippledness to partial healing and restored sight, from apprenticeships with haole mentors to native tactics purged of Western influences, informed by a return to ancestral values of family and religion—this, indeed, is a precise summation of the stages through which the Hawaiian Movement has passed in the last fifteen years. From an inchoate group of disaffected youths spouting SDS and Black Power slogans, it has spread to most sectors of the Hawaiian people—fishermen, shopkeepers, housewives, aging *kupunas*—and can summon thousands to its protests; its religious revival has been accompanied by an unprecedented renaissance of Hawaiian culture—language studies, native music, ritual dance, and crafts; and it is now being led by highly articulate citizens—doctors, lawyers, academics—who like Kalani are inspired by numerous other indigenous groups throughout the world struggling for self-determination. My old friends Kalani Ohelo and John Dominis Holt would remain the principal mentors of my second Hawaiian journey.

A few days after my return to Honolulu, a joyous crowd of some eight thousand gathers on the lawn of Iolani Palace in the blazing winter sun to watch the inauguration of Governor John Waihee III, another direct descendant of King Kamehameha I. The vast floral mural surmounting the officials' dais is composed of two hundred thousand bougainvillaea and chrysanthemum blossoms spelling out the phrase *Ho'ohui*, "Let us Unite." I sit next to John Dominis Holt, with whom I'd also had a ritual Hawaiian reunion on the day I arrived, and whose feelings about the new governor are very strong. "What do you think, one of our very own people in power, at last, at last!"—these were his first words as he strung my shoulders with the traditional lei of greeting, a wreath of fragrant pikake, and asked me to wreathe his own shoulders with a lei of green *maile* in exchange.

John Holt, whom I last knew as an isolated nationalist struggling to preserve his people's culture, is now hailed as a prophet and doyen of the Hawaiian renaissance. He has grown statelier and even more imposing in these happy years; today his fedora hat is wreathed with a talismanic band of iridescent feathers, reserved for the most august occasions, that is meant to ward off evil and beckon the mana of beneficent spirits. He must translate and explain many of the inaugural festivities to me, for over half of them are being held in Hawaiian, and are resplendent with ancient ceremonies. The hulas being performed below the dignitaries' dais by solemn-faced beauties in traditional *pā'ū* skirts are not the coarsely simpering tourist horrors prevalent a decade ago, but awesome and darkly majestic rituals, miming, as they did of old, offerings and supplications to wrathful gods. They are followed by a young Hawaiian who sings the *mele ma'i Hālala*, a "genital chant" celebrating the sexual

powers of King David Kalakaua. ("He was reputed to have a magnificent one," Holt whispers.) And one of the songs played toward
the ceremony's end is "The Queen's Prayer," composed in 1893
by Queen Liliuo'kalani, while she was imprisoned in her palace, to
protest the American settlers' takeover of her islands.

After the lei-wreathed young governor offers his inaugural-
speech pieties ("We offer a new tomorrow," "We shall open the
doors to all the people,") one last song is performed with that tribal
warmth unique to these islands. The audience of eight thousand
friends and strangers joins hands as in some peace protest or church
ritual and sways together to the grave strains of "Hawai'i Aloha"—
"O Hawaii, sands of my birth, My home, my native land." Still
more leis are piled upon the stocky shoulders of John Waihee, who
exits from the podium alongside his icy-featured mentor and protector, outgoing Governor George Ariyoshi. I join the festive thousands who have been invited to a multiethnic feast on the grounds
of the state capitol a block away. Lining up at the free-food booths
amid the smiling, compliant crowds, I pile my paper plates with
Okinawan fried donuts, Korean *yak kaw* and *kang jung*, Japanese
sushi and *takuwan*, Chinese noodles and spring rolls, Filipino
rellenong, bangus, and *lumpia,* Hawaiian breadfruit, taro, and *aku
poke,* Portuguese bean soup and milk bread. I sit in the sun and
stare beyond the bacchanal at the plume-crested skyline of the
mountains, viridian green this afternoon against a cobalt sky, driven
to the verge of tears by the abiding beauty of the Hawaii before
me. Despite ecoterrorists' dirges about growing pollution and high
rises, Honolulu continues to strike me as the nation's sweetest and
most gracious city. I still abide by the custom of shedding my shoes
at hosts' doorsteps, remain dazzled by the ardor of their welcome
and by the sunny aloha of cabdrivers, shopkeepers, clerks, savor the
Asian courtesy that assuages much of the community's tension or
bitterness.

And yet, and yet: I sense that this floral mask might be even
more deceptive than it was a decade and a half ago. Observing the
beaming features of the new governor, I had wondered whether
the idealism of his early years (as a student on the mainland he
had been an antiwar militant, a community organizer in black
neighborhoods, a devotee of Saul Alinsky's) has endured enough

to solve the monumental problems confronting him: In a state which has both the highest cost of living in the nation and its ninth lowest median wages, one out of four native Hawaiians is living below the poverty level. This economic duress is blamed for the state's tragic "brain drain": Almost a third of its citizens under thirty-five years of age have left the islands to seek gainful employment on the mainland. The unemployment toll of native Hawaiians is twice higher than the statewide average. In Honolulu, once the most pacific of our cities, the per capita crime rate is now the third highest in the nation, and the crimes are predominantly aimed at visitors. It is being blamed, in good part, on Hawaiians' hostility to the extravagant growth of foreign-owned enterprises and of tourism, which now accounts for nearly six million travelers a year, six times the islands' population. These are only a few of the problems confronting a forty-year-old Hawaiian governor recently groomed by the party machine inherited from John Burns, by a Democratic power clique still deeply committed to its corporate interests in real estate and tourism development. How soon would this canny young politician, John Waihee, be able to meet his people's urgent demands? The most striking and unexpected change in the fiftieth state, I had found, was the increased power and eloquence of the nationalist movement challenging its first truly native leader to redress centuries of wrong. And during my stay I did little else than listen to these new Hawaiian voices.

"It's going to be even more difficult for us with a Hawaiian in the state capitol," says Professor Haunani-Kay Trask as we sit on a lawn at the University of Hawaii's Honolulu campus. "Instead of one or two Uncle Toms, we'll have a government full of them. Now it's the Hawaiian brothers who'll come to drag us away from our land."

The lush campus is ablaze with tropical blossoms, redolent with smells of frangipani, just as I recalled it from my last stay; but the somnolent aura of the early 1970s has quite vanished. Bulletin boards are pinned with announcements of antimilitary and antidevelopment demonstrations at various sites in the state, bumper stickers on students' cars plead for A NUCLEAR FREE AND INDEPENDENT PACIFIC, the university's Hawaiian studies curriculum is growing, with many of its courses taught by Haunani-Kay Trask.

Full-fleshed and amber-skinned, reminiscent of the beauties in Gauguin's *Arearea*, Haunani-Kay often accentuates her Polynesian features with shoulder-baring *kikepa*-style cotton vestments. She is a Phi Beta Kappa graduate of the University of Wisconsin, where she received both her undergraduate and doctoral degrees in political science and American studies. She returned to Hawaii in 1976. And like many others she was inspired to militancy by the civil disobedience actions which began that year on Kaho'olawe to protest the U.S. Navy's bombing of the island, "the first aggressive acts of protest in centuries Hawaiians have dared to indulge in."

Beginning in 1976, groups of Hawaiians began to make illegal landings on Kaho'olawe. Some of their most inspirational leaders were aging *kupunas* who were protesting the desecration of the island's *heiaus*, sacred shrines; and when the trespassers came to trial they pleaded their right to freedom of worship. One of the most quixotic aspects of the Kaho'olawe epic is that the U.S. Navy was forced to commission an archaeological study of the island: A team of three mainland scientists soon reported that there was a greater density of sacred sites on Kaho'olawe than on any other island of the Hawaiian chain. The Kaho'olawe actions galvanized Hawaiian nationalism as no other issue has, fusing the concerns of cultural revival, demilitarization, and land reform. The island was henceforth listed on the National Register of Historic Sites; the Navy has had to give Hawaiians several days of legal access a month to the island, and Hawaiian ritual practices were recognized, for the first time, as elements of a true "religion." Haunani-Kay has often joined the dozens of islanders who now sail forth every month to the island to perform ancient rituals: In the third week of January, for instance, they celebrate the end of the Makahiki festival dedicated to the god Lono, the very same religious celebration through which Captain Cook met his end two centuries ago.

Haunani-Kay typifies the newly urbane Hawaiian activist, frequently traveling to attend reunions of American Indians in Canada and Eskimo tribes in Alaska, human rights congresses in Geneva, or month-long seminars on indigenous populations and international law in Strasbourg, France. She would like to see a Hawaiian movement analogous to West Germany's Green party, one that would fuse even more forcefully the issues of land reform and de-militarization and enforce severe curbs on tourist-related industries, which employ more than half of the islands' population. Tourism, in Haunani-Kay Trask's view, has created "a new feudalism" that offers few opportunities for advancement or for learning specialized skills, decreases the Hawaiians' social mobility, and perpetuates their submissiveness. She is considerably less sanguine than John Dominis Holt, or even Kalani, about Governor John Waihee's commitment to "decolonizing" Hawaii. She points out that he has spoken in favor of the construction of a new spaceport on the Big Island; and that he also supports the building of a geothermal plant which would despoil native forests and "drill right into the heart of Pele," desecrating the volcano goddess's terrain. Haunani-Kay adds that Waihee has opposed a "Right to Sue Bill" which would enable Hawaiians to litigate against the state government on matters concerning all native land trusts. "Perhaps it's good that people expect so much of Waihee," she concludes in a classically revolutionary tone. "The more he disappoints them, the angrier they'll get."

A few days after the governor's inaugural I lunched with an equally cosmopolitan scholar, a native Hawaiian lawyer named Hayden Burgess—an ironically Wasp, mainland name for a dedicated secessionist. Along with John Waihee, Burgess graduated in the first class of Hawaii's only law school, which was not established until the 1970s. He has brought the Hawaiian cause into a wide international forum through the World Congress of Indigenous Peoples, founded in Canada in 1976, of which he is vice-president. In the mere span of two years, between June of 1984 and October of 1986, Burgess has traveled to the following places to confer with other native movements and present the case for Hawaiian independence: to Switzerland, on three separate occasions, for meetings with the United Nations Commission on Human Rights and with its Working Group on Indigenous Populations; to Sweden and Norway, on four occasions, for conventions with the Minority Rights Group of the Swedish International Development Agency; to Alaska and to Canada, six times, for conferences with various American Indian and Eskimo coalitions; to Strasbourg, France, for meetings with members of the European Parliament; to Fiji, Colombia, Australia, West Germany, and Denmark, for discussions with still other human rights agencies. Burgess's principal problem at such international forums, he reports, is that their participants often resist the inclusion of a Hawaiian delegate: "A society as dependent as ours on tourism and the military is a succinct model of the way *not* to go."

Burgess is a soft-spoken, cheerful man in his early forties who has refused for a few years to pay his taxes on the grounds that he does not consider himself a legal citizen of the United States. (The tactic is not popular with all of his peers. "With our people making up seventy percent of the state's prison population we can't afford one more brother in jail for tax evasion," Haunani-Kay Trask says.) Burgess's refusal of citizenship rests on two principal grounds: the United States' illegal annexation of his country, to which no statute of limitations applies ("We do not pay taxes to the invader," "We cannot ask a thief to administer our justice"), and the religious freedom granted by the First Amendment. His definition of "What is an American?" or "What is a Hawaiian?" is rooted on cultural, religious principles, analogous to those allegiances of the American Indians that enable them to define themselves as "a nation." When his plans for Hawaii's secession are accused of being utopian, Burgess gives a radiant smile, answering that the same allegations were made of Gandhi's plans for independence and of our own thirteen colonies' aspirations in the early 1770s; he goes on to cite more contemporary models in the Pacific—Vanuatu (once New Hebrides), Fiji, Western Samoa, Kiribati, Nauru, Tuvalu—former British, American, or New Zealand colonies which in the past two decades have all become independent nation states.

In a 1978 documentary film Haunani-Kay Trask often shows to her Hawaiian Studies classes, one of the Kaho'olawe trespassers is shown testifying in the state legislature. He is followed to the speaker's podium by a young state representative of Hawaiian descent, Henry Peters, who bursts into tears as he pleads with his colleague lawmakers to honor the protester's demands. "The life of the land," he says between sobs, trying to quote the motto of the fiftieth state, "is preserved in righteousness . . ."

Since then Peters has become one of the wealthiest native Hawaiians of his generation through his seat on the Bishop Estate's board of trustees, which in 1986 earned him an income of over $300,000 a year, part of it tax free. And during my visit with Congressman Peters I noted little in his demeanor related to the emotional, committed young legislator I saw in the film made a decade ago. "I am very *patient*," said Peters; "I don't sit on doorsteps and go 'knock, knock, bowwow.' I too grew up in a slum district, in Nanakuli, I too heard stories of how my mother was beaten at school for speaking Hawaiian. I too have memories of my mother resorting to making patterns of the Hawaiian flag on her quilts, that was the only place you could afford to show your allegiances to the 'ohana, making a little quilt which you kept at home under the covers. . . . But I look around me now and think: Those who expect things immediately or too fast are going to be dangerous in their disappointment; the kind of people who say 'We want it *now*' are the ones who end up breaking things."

I quoted a familiar figure from Hawaiian Homes Commission sources: Some ten thousand Hawaiians have been waiting for decades for a piece of land on which to live. Peters pointed impatiently to the view from his office window, *mauka*, toward the mountain. "They're all applying for land in Papakolea, right here in urban Honolulu . . . of course everyone wants to live there, it's closest to where the work is. But there's barely any land left to build on in Papakolea . . . *that's* why you hear so much about people waiting for Hawaiian Homestead land."

(His exaggeration was amazing. Only some 7 percent of the families currently wait-listed for homesteads on Oahu have specified Papakolea as the desired site. I listened on.)

"We have a good system," Peters continued; "it may seem slow because we are getting almost no help from Washington, but it will eventually work. I represent a community that's forty-five percent Caucasian, and only twenty-two percent Hawaiian. As a legislator I can't work from the perspective of any one *segment* of my constituency; I don't have the luxury to make Hawaiian issues the number one priority. We have a saying in pidgin: 'If the bugger no broke, no fix it.' So don't let anyone throw up their arms and say 'We quit.' I am a realist, I am a patient man."

□

"Are those gorillas in our legislature telling me to be patient while I witness the genocide of my people?" Mililani Trask, Haunani-Kay's older sister, exclaims when she talks about the cautious centrism of many Hawaiian legislators. Mililani is a Honolulu lawyer in her late thirties who wears her long hair in two severe schoolgirl braids down to her waist. She is quick to cite the disturbing health statistics concerning native Hawaiians: the highest infant death rate of any ethnic group in the state, 50 percent higher than the statewide average; the lowest life expectancy, seven years shorter, and the highest suicide rates, some 70 percent higher, than that of any other group.

Educated in California universities, Mililani specializes in children's custody cases and in land issues. One of her principal crusades has been for the Right to Sue Bill, a version of which was passed in 1986 by both the state Senate and state House; it was vetoed by Governor Ariyoshi, a move which increased the growing hostility of the Trask sisters and other nationalists to the "Nisei Bureaucracy" which has been ruling the state for two decades.

The Right to Sue Bill is one of the more crucial issues in contemporary Hawaii. More than a third of the land set aside for native Hawaiians in the Homestead Act of 1921 and many later statutes has been leased out for federal or county use—airports, highways, harbors—with no reparations to Hawaiian agencies. Hawaii is the only state in the union in which a certain amount of land was set apart by *state* law for indigenous people. These stipulations were made at statehood, in the 5 F clause of the 1959 Admissions Act. They were elaborated at the state's Constitutional Convention in 1978, which ruled that Hawaiian agencies have the right to 20 percent of all the revenue earned by the lands which the United States seized in 1893—about half the acreage in the state. Yet like much legislation relating to the Hawaiian people's welfare these laws have never been fully implemented. "When are we going to get revenues from the Hilo airport on Big Island, built on land leased from the Hawaiian Homes Commission?" Mililani Trask demands. "Or from the two thousand acres of Hawaiian Homes land on the Waianae coast leased out to the U.S. military for ammunition storage—bombs, missiles, God knows what other high explosives? Both the state and the feds are in breach of trust; how do you expect us to abide by laws dictated on every level by lawbreakers?" Mililani has corresponded with the Justice Department to press for federal support for the Right to Sue Bill, with no success. She feels frustrated and very angry about the "total invisibility" of Hawaiian issues in the nation's capital. "The East is still provincially, deeply Europe-oriented, quite deaf to most Pacific issues; we'd need twelve full-time lobbyists before our needs even begin to be heard."

Talking to this dedicated nationalist, it struck me that the islands' activists have gained power by blending militancy and mysticism, by both exteriorizing and interiorizing their Hawaiianness. While gaining an increasingly international perspective, they have relearned their original language and recaptured ancient cultural and spiritual values (like most of their peers, the Trask sisters started studying Hawaiian some five years ago, when sacred and secular concerns were being fused in the Kaho'olawe actions). Mililani now honors all three religious strains in her ancestry—Hawaiian, Buddhist, Christian. She observes the meditation practices of Vipassana Buddhism, a dominant sect of Southeast Asian nations. She does her Christmas and Easter duty at the Roman Catholic church in which she was brought up. She is particularly dedicated to certain observances of the ancient Hawaiian religion. She performs ancient rituals of cleansing in the ocean, and in the fumes of Kilauea crater on Big Island: She sits over a steam vent, "bathing in the breath of Pele." Once a month, at sunrise, this sophisticated lawyer and scholar goes to heiaus on the Big Island to bring offerings to Lono and to Papa, an earth-mother deity, and has earned ritual white robes bestowed upon the most faithful acolytes of these traditions.

"I'm not sure about all this religion business," Kalani grumbles to me during one of our visits when Kawahini is out of earshot. "Eldridge Cleaver always said 'Keep your gods hidden, they muddle the political issues.' I just don't know anymore."

"It's always the women who bring it back, isn't it?" he adds. "I'll only capitulate to it on my deathbed, to be sure I get a good deal next time round."

"Did you know that the mother of Representative M. is one of our most powerful kahunas?" John Dominis Holt says to me over dinner another time, citing the name of a prominent Hawaiian legislator. "Why, there was once a bothersome pig on her property messing up the vegetable patch, and I saw her kill it with just *one* gesture of her arm. No one in the state capitol better mess with *her* son."

John Holt laughs gleefully, projecting fantasies of other Hawaiian mothers giving the evil eye to members of the state legislature who oppose measures proposed by their offspring, killing bills right and left with ancient magical gestures and incantations.

Such reports of primordial practices have again become a commonplace in contemporary Hawaii. Is this refuge in neoprimitivism analogous to the revival of orthodoxy among Basques, Catalans, Bretons, Welsh, the Moslem nations, our own Falwellian fundamentalism? How much genuine religious emotion is involved in these reconversions, to what degree are they inspired by a need for increased political clout? How far will subnationalist movements such as Hawaii's be allowed to progress before the centers of power attempt to suppress them? These are issues often discussed among my friends, in conversations which make Hawaii a considerably more vibrant place than it was a decade and a half ago.

Driving by West Beach on Oahu's leeward coast, on the way to Waianae, I admired again one of the world's most idyllic landscapes: delicate palm trees fringing crescent-shaped, sugar-white beaches on which I'd picnicked with my family in the 1970s, bougainvillaeas and hibiscus in scarlet bloom against the dun violet of the mountains. This is the site where Hawaii's new lieutenant-governor, Ben Cayetano (the first man of Filipino descent ever elected to Hawaii's legislature), recently broke ground for the building of a gigantic and controversial resort community designed to accommodate some thirty thousand persons. Financed by Tokyo-based firms, West Beach has become still another rallying ground for Hawaiian nationalists protesting the encroachment of mainland and foreign companies: Some 40 percent of the state's gross revenue is attributable to out-of-state investments; roughly half of the hotel units in Waikiki are already owned by Japanese concerns.

Driving by the bulldozers assembled at West Beach, saluting

its beauty in farewell, I reflected on the changes in the kinds of "bashings" native Hawaiians have indulged in. Until the late 1970s their resentments had been directed at the haole missionaries who'd destroyed their culture, the haole Big Five firms who'd stolen their land. During my last stay there had also been some "Kam bashing," young radicals who took it out on King Kamehameha I for opening the islands to white men. But a decade later Hawaiians, as the brutal local lingo puts it, are "into Jap bashing." Entrepreneurs from Japanese corporations are now seen as the thieves ruining Hawaiians' land, beaches, homesteads, through their billion-dollar real-estate investments; island-born Japanese are the icy, Creonlike bureaucrats in the state capitol vetoing the bills designed to redress the Hawaiians' ancestral rights, ordering police to jail them when they squat on Hawaiian land, brainwashing young Hawaiian legislators into equally impersonal efficiency. "You know what my husband wants to do more than anything else in the world?" an acquaintance from Molokai, a social worker married to an alfalfa farmer, said to me over dinner. "He'd like to hire a Japanese worker one morning, and fire him the same night."

Driving by the West Beach development, I was on my way to Waianae to meet with Adelaide (Frenchy) de Soto, a remarkable woman in her sixties who had just been elected to be a trustee of the Office of Hawaiian Affairs, known as OHA. OHA is a five-year-old organization, unique of its kind in the nation, upon which many Hawaiians pin their hopes for a better future. John Dominis Holt has described its founding as "the sixth great event influencing the life of native Hawaiians in the past two hundred years." Granted authority by a constitutional amendment approved in a statewide referendum, it is an autonomous agency founded to "promote the betterment of conditions of the Hawaiian people." OHA's most arduous task is to help implement the laws, already described, which endow Hawaiians with 20 percent of all revenue earned by leases on native land trusts. Because many state and federal agencies—the U.S. military, the Department of Transportation, airport authorities—have failed to pay the legally stipulated share of their earnings, OHA has rarely been able to collect more than half of the revenue legally due to the Hawaiian people.

It was a trustee of OHA who first conceived the notion, now

officially proclaimed by the state government, of celebrating Hawaii's booming cultural renaissance by designating 1987 as "The Year of the Hawaiian." (The plan was uncannily prescient, having originated many months before John Waihee's election to the governorship was assured.) OHA's nine trustees are chosen by statewide election, voted for by anyone of Hawaiian descent. Frenchy de Soto, who was elected to her second term on the OHA board with a larger margin than any other candidate, is described by Kalani Ohelo as "the political genius of our movement." She is a tall, majestic woman in her late fifties whose powerful presence and eloquence of diction blend the most magisterial traits of Coretta Scott King, Toni Morrison, and Bella Abzug. The oldest of four orphans who were given out for adoption in infancy, she spent her first decade as a stray child in the slums of Kalihi, escaping from each of her foster families to search for her siblings in the streets of Honolulu. Arrested repeatedly and sent on to still other foster homes, Frenchy was mostly on her own by the age of nine, shining shoes, begging for food, riding with motorcycle gangs. After her marriage, while educating herself in community colleges and holding a variety of jobs as clerk and janitor to help support her family, she bore six children and had the energy to adopt four more, in the ancient island tradition of *hānai*—adoption—which even the poorest Hawaiians practice to extend their family bonds into the 'ohana, the kinship of all humanity.

Frenchy de Soto applied to the Hawaiian Homes Commission for a homestead in her husband's native Waianae shortly after her second child was born, when she was twenty years old; she was granted it thirty-seven years later, at the age of fifty-seven. "The first application, they said after eight years, was lost," she recounts laconically. "The second, they told me after still another decade, was accidentally burnt. The third they couldn't find any more excuses for, and I just kept reapplying. It wasn't exactly bitterness I felt each time, but some deep, savvy cynicism about the hopelessness of any bureaucratic system through which Hawaiians have tried to find redress."

Unlike Hayden Burgess or the Trask sisters, Frenchy de Soto has faith in Governor Waihee's ability to improve the lives of Hawaiians, and keeps a guarded but hopeful outlook on OHA's potential as her people's first efficient organization for self-help. The younger activists I had talked to all brought up the considerable inner dissents plaguing the Hawaiian Movement, sometimes citing the ancient ali'i caste system as responsible. Frenchy de Soto admits to the divisions, but detests being asked if there is a Martin Luther King in sight who might heal them. "Oh oh, there we go again, the black syndrome," she said impatiently when I raised the question. "Please don't compare us to the civil-rights movement—black leaders united to press for the *making* of new state laws to improve their plight, laws that would enable them to vote properly and sit in the same buses and schoolroom with whites. We're asking access to resources that have been *legally* ours for decades. We've got most of the laws and statutes we need, we're asking to have them *implemented*; that process can cause much more complex problems of leadership than the *making* of laws."

She waved out of her window, toward the rickety Hawaiian dwellings of Waianae—unchanged in squalor since my last stay on the islands—in which a major part of Oahu's juvenile delinquents are raised. "There isn't much time left to change those young men's cynical outlook toward the law. You patted us on the head like children, you raised us and said 'Be good little law-abiding Hawaiians,' and yet *you don't abide by the law.* How do you expect our kids to react to such hypocrisy?"

"So here we are, about to celebrate The Year of the Hawaiian," Frenchy de Soto added as we parted. "I live daily in the pain of my people." As I drove back to Honolulu, I reflected that Frenchy and the Trask sisters typify the amazingly powerful women who have come to lead the Hawaiian Movement since my last visit, a phenomenon for which one could venture a variety of reasons: Hawaiian women are not yet being sought for positions of great power, are hence less corruptible than their men. Generations of Hawaiian men have been emasculated from childhood on by haole planters; Japanese schoolteachers, Japanese bureaucrats, are often afraid of joining the struggle because they're afraid of losing face; women, in Hawaii as elsewhere, don't have that much face to lose. And as Kalani Ohelo points out, whenever a culture has been decimated the women are usually the ones to remember and resurrect it.

□

Frenchy de Soto's troubled Waianae district is represented in the state House by Peter Apo, a Hawaiian legislator whose background is considerably more militant than most of his colleagues'. A 1962 graduate of the University of Wisconsin, where he majored in psychology, he remained on the mainland for a decade after college, playing guitar with an itinerant jazz band. He immersed himself in the land struggle when he returned, and in 1975 he was a member of the first group to make an illegal landing on Kaho'olawe. The following year, unable to pay the exorbitant Hawaii rents, he camped out for fourteen months on Makua Beach, a site on the western coast of Oahu where generations of penniless or homeless Hawaiians have sought refuge. But a decade later, a third-term legislator recently elected majority leader of Hawaii's House of Representatives, he finds incisive arguments against many of the complaints put forward by his more militant contemporaries.

Apo, for instance, qualifies much criticism of the Hawaiian Homes Commission's misuse of land. This agency, he notes, is highly dependent on land leases to remain solvent. "Are you going to cut off your nose to spite your face? The homestead program would become powerless, would be disabled from giving out *any* land whatsoever if it did not *lease* out half its land to different island interests." Apo also challenges the notion that the work options offered native Hawaiians by a tourist-based economy are demeaning: "The winter I was living in piles of orange crates on Makua Beach I started as a busboy at the Hawaiian Village Hotel, and within a year I ended up being manager of the dining room. There's fully as much opportunity for advancement in the tourist industry as in any other."

A large, handsome, athletic man, Apo, like many islanders of predominantly Hawaiian blood, has such innate eloquence that he could convince me of most any point he made. "Look, I've been a hard-up hard-core activist, and I know a lot of the activists *could* have homes and jobs if they wanted to. Since the demise of our sugar by overregulation, the demise of our pineapple through Mexican competition, tourism is our only temporary resource. We turned from a preindustrial, agrarian society into a postindustrial, information-oriented society; we had a big gap to fill during that time, and we could only fill it with tourism: it's here to stay, and we've got to do the best with it." However Apo continues to have passionate feelings against the bombing of Kaho'olawe and about the Hawaiians' need for a Right to Sue Bill. "We're going to introduce that bill again and again. Frankly, the last time round I was disgusted by the mixed signals we got from Governor Ariyoshi. What's been totally lacking up to now is a desire on the part of our executive to see Hawaiian issues as number one priorities, but with OHA on its feet I hope that's all going to change around with John Waihee."

A few days after I returned to Honolulu, the Kilauea volcano on Big Island began one of the most spectacular phases in an eruption begun four years ago, spouting some six hundred thousand cubic yards of lava a day, flowing in eight-mile-long spurs to the Pacific Ocean, demolishing dozens of homes in its wake. I flew to Hilo to revisit "Madam Pele," as erupting volcanoes are referred to in honor of the goddess, and walked as far into the flow as the police would allow me. I stood on a bed of still-hot lava, traversed by long steaming fissures, that had invaded a two-mile stretch of highway. Standing over one such vent, staring at the molten rock still glowing red within it, I dropped the green leaf of a banana frond which I had picked from the roadside and watched it shrivel to a crisp brown strip. Within a few minutes my sneakers began to smell ominously of burning rubber. The lava's day-old surface had been deceitfully comfortable under my feet; destruction lay a few inches below its surface. And that, I thought, was the reality of contemporary Hawaii: soothing splendor of its nature, consoling hopes for the new regime expressed by such dedicated Hawaiian officials as Peter Apo; smoldering forces of anger and bitterness lying underneath those deceptive surfaces, taking paths as unpredictable as the lava's flow.

"A nippy day in paradise!" the announcer's voice says on the radio. "Blustery winds up to thirty miles an hour, temperatures tonight dipping down into the low seventies."
I am driving toward Lanikai, the town on Oahu's north shore where I lived in the 1970s, with Kalani, Kawahini, and their youngest child, three-week-old Ku'ike. Kalani is softly rocking his son

against his chest, saying, "Are you going to be my big labor organizer? Are you going to be my big boy community leader?" Kawahini
is telling me the names of their children and what each name means:
Kamalu, peaceful. *Sanoe*, mist. *Pamai*, gentle. *Ahonu*, patient.
Ku'ike, prophet. She is also recounting how she and Kalani met, a
decade ago, at a demonstration about Kaho'olawe. Kawahini had
helped to plan the Kaho'olawe landings from the mid-seventies on,
when they were still illegal. She cooked the food and organized the
boats and the supplies of bottled water which had to be secretly
stored on the island before each expedition. That is how she met
Aunty Emma de Fries, a very wise *kahuna* in her late seventies who
participated in each of the illegal trips, who had adopted thirty-five
children besides her own eleven, who began to reinstruct Kawahini
and her contemporaries in many of the old Hawaiian rituals and
practices. Someday before I return to the mainland, Kawahini prom-
ises, she and Kalani will take me to see the different sites on Oahu
where Kalani offered their babies' placentas to the ocean; that too
was a ritual she had relearned from Aunt Emma. . . . "Are you going to be my big boy Saul Alinsky," Kalani is cooing to his infant
son, "are you going to be my big activist?"

"You love children, Kalani," I say. "How many do you plan to
have?"

"Till we run out of gas."

"Did you go on any of the trips to Kaho'olawe, Kalani?"

"Nope, I hate tourism. I'll wait till it's really ours again, and
then I'll go and have a big party."

One day in Honolulu I went to visit a haole tycoon in one of
the gleaming new skyscrapers on Bishop Street, the heart of
Honolulu's business district. His opinions on Hawaii were so vastly
different from those of anyone else I'd met during this visit that
they were downright exotic, making me feel as if I had been flown
to another planet for a tea party. Francis Morgan is a fifth-generation
haole islander who after some prosperous decades as chairman of a
Big Five firm started an independent sugar-producing company on
thirty thousand acres of the Big Island.

After expressing his apostolic faith in the continuing viability
of the sugar trade and the medical benefits of sugar consumption

("Look at the way it goes zoom to the brain and raises your energy levels. . . ." "It's the low-sugar diet that will do you in and *keep* you fat"), my genial host expressed some more general views on contemporary Hawaii and Hawaiians:

"Hawaiians . . . well you know I grew up among them as a child, worked alongside them in the cane fields, there's no smarter, quicker worker in the world. So much more proficient than us that when some new piece of technology would arrive we'd joke and say, 'Don't show it to the Hawaiians or they'll run us off the island with it.' "

He smiled ever so warmly, and I believe he truly loves them, in his way. Then his face darkened. "But all this hubbub about Hawaiian lands, all this nonsense of giving them back land or offering reparations, that's the biggest phony around. What outrage! The Hawaiian people never owned that land! Their *former* government owned it, the king and chiefs; and now their *present* government owns it, the United States. Such a fine, hardworking, industrious people! How belittling and rude to humiliate them with handouts; it would take away their sense of dignity. . . . It's just another rip-off, but then everyone is trying to get a rip-off these days, isn't that the name of the game?"

Many equally quixotic encounters can occur in the span of a few weeks on the islands, on either side of the political spectrum.

On a November morning I was invited to attend a Thanksgiving liturgy on a farm property in Waianae which is owned by the Catholic diocese and shelters some of the most successful self-help projects on Oahu—a women's support group, alternative education programs, a large communally owned vegetable garden. Some sixty persons were there to celebrate, sitting under a large makeshift tent. Bishop Joseph Ferrario, the leading Catholic prelate of the state, sat on a little wooden chair facing the congregation, alongside a few other parish priests from Oahu and a much loved pureblood Hawaiian kupuna. Next to the bishop there also sat the farm manager who had obtained the land from the diocese, a now defrocked former priest, affectionately called Father Gigi, who had been exiled from the Philippines by the Marcos dictatorship. The former priest's Hawaiian-born wife and two young children, often waved to by the cordial bishop, sat in the front row.

After a message of welcome from Father Gigi, various invocations and Gospel readings offered by Catholic curates, there appeared a triad of voluptuous young hula dancers dressed in brilliant yellow strapless tops and the traditional skirts of *hau* bark strips, holding offerings of brilliant young green taro shoots. They looked particularly beautiful and Gauguinesque from where I sat, their swaying bodies outlined against the moody, rainbowed sky. It was five days before the beginning of Makahiki, Lono's festival. Accompanying themselves with a powerful, driving drumbeat, the hula dancers performed a traditional fertility ritual, a majestic and somber dance to Lono replete with many gestures intimating the act of procreation. The scarlet-capped bishop smiled appreciatively throughout, and at the end of the dance gave a sensitive sermon on the sacredness of land in the Hawaiian culture, the close analogies between the ancient Makahiki festival and our own Thanksgiving. Led by the bishop, the former priest turned diocesan farm manager, and the kupuna, the congregation of worshipers then proceeded to the taro fields and stood in a circle, hands joined. In one of the more syncretic rituals I've witnessed, the bishop blessed some large fronds of banana leaves with holy water and handed them to the kupuna, who chanted another long incantation to Lono, waving the fronds over the field. Still headed by the jovial bishop, we then returned to the tent for a large and delicious potluck luau of baked pig, Filipino kidney stew, Chinese noodles, and other ethnic delicacies.

Only in Hawaii, I thought, can gods be so casually resurrected.

Visiting in my hotel room with Kalani and Kawahini, we watch numerous videotapes of recent protest actions. In 1982, several dozen Hawaiians, holding signs that say FIRST YOU TOOK OUR RELIGION, THEN OUR CULTURE AND OUR LAND, are taken to jail for refusing to leave their dwellings on Makua Beach, where Peter Apo had once squatted, where bulldozing was then beginning for the building of a public park. Earlier, in 1979, a similar eviction from Sand Island, a strip of state-owned land near Pearl Harbor used for decades as a garbage dump which several dozen families (one of them had been waiting for land from the Hawaiian Homes Commission since 1947) had reconverted into a self-sufficient community of fishermen. In 1985, eviction of ninety Hawaiians from Waimanalo, the action in which the police fractured Kalani's arm.

In each of the evictions, tearful priests invoke blessings on the community of dissenters; the group joins hands in a circle around the protested site and sings Hawaii's state anthem, "Hawai'i Pono'i" ("Royal father, Kamehameha, We shall defend With spears"); the raising of clenched fists is interspersed with more prayers and chantings of "Jesu Kristo" and "Amene" while impassive, predominantly nisei policemen herd the trespassers into vans. Like the Thanksgiving liturgy at the Waianae farm, the slogans pinned on many of my friends' floral shirts, "The Struggle's" lingo and antimilitary bumper stickers, these events hauntingly recall the 1960s and early 1970s on the mainland, when all in Hawaii was still so quiet, and radical professors complained that the state was still mired in Eisenhower's fifties. It is as if this warmhearted Pacific treasure of ours were destined to relive most of our upheavals and traumas, in indigenous form, a decade and a half later.

And yet the activism in contemporary Hawaii is anything but a déja vu. In the Hawaii of the late 1980s, one is confronted with a wealth of information about the politics of the Pacific barely familiar to mainland residents. In the company of the most informed friends, we will hear next to nothing about the reshuffling of NATO alliances, Poland's Solidarity movement, or some student rebellion threatening to topple the French government. We hear spirited discussions, rather, about the antinuclear struggle on the Micronesian island of Pelau, the first community in history to stipulate a ban on nuclear reactors and weapons in its constitution; about the escalation of the Cold War in the Pacific, the promulgation of the Rarotonga Treaty and the United States' condemnation of New Zealand's ban on warships. At the yearly film festival at Honolulu's East-West Center, I saw a documentary on the Conference for an Independent and Nuclear Free Pacific held in 1983 in Vanuatu, now an independent nation-state, formerly New Hebrides: Delegates from twenty-four Pacific states—among them Guam, West Papua, Tahiti, East Timor, New Caledonia, Hawaii—resolve to "turn back the tide of development," secede from their colonizers and return to self-sufficient economies based on native taro, coconut, and fish; they pledge their solidarity to each other in "Doing It the Pacific Way" and stand in a circle singing "We Shall Overcome" after planting twenty-four taro shoots into one small patch of Vanuatu land.

Every one of these Pacific communities has its own tragic history, its own set of martyrs. And the emotions attending public discussions of Pacific issues can be bitter, such as the one I heard after the showing of a fine Dutch documentary called *The Pacific: Paradise in Pain*, which focuses on the struggle for self-determination and denuclearization in three Pacific communities: New Caledonia, Pelau, and Hawaii. In this last segment, Hayden Burgess is filmed amid his lawbooks, predicting that by 1991 Hawaii will be an independent state, liberated from the encroachment of tourism and of the military complex. Burgess is sitting in the audience, and after the film showing several soft-spoken haole liberals ask him whether his plan is not, really, very utopian. "They said the same thing about Gandhi, and about our thirteen colonies," I hear Burgess repeat.

A loud voice with a faint foreign accent suddenly interrupts the good-natured exchange: "I can't believe what I'm hearing!" a man in the audience exclaims. He is white, has the style of a radical professor, is very angry. "Didn't we all see the same film? Didn't we see those Kanaks in New Caledonia being shot down by French bullets? And all you can talk about is Hawaii, where all is luxurious abundance and freedom! I'm from New Caledonia, where dozens of people are killed every year by white men's bullets!"

"There are many ways of death," John Dominis Holt gently replies from a back row of the screening room. "Over the centuries half of our original people have died from the pain of having their culture obliterated. Hawaiians have the highest rate of lung cancer of any ethnic group in the world, the second highest rate of hypertension, heart attacks, circulatory diseases . . ."

The audience stirs to leave. The discussion is over, as well it might be. "Such comparisons should not be made," John Holt says as we ride home. "Such comparisons are as dreadful as those which ask which is worse, Stalin's purges or Hitler's holocaust."

However flawed its arguments, the incident indicates the Hawaiian nationalists' growing solidarity with other indigenous and pacifist movements mushrooming throughout the Pacific. At Governor Waihee's inaugural, for instance, a young Hawaiian executive of the Office of Hawaiian Affairs, Malcolm Chun, sat in the section assigned to the diplomatic corps as the official delegate of the Maori community of New Zealand. Unable to send one of their own leaders to the inaugural because its date conflicted with an important tribal conference, the Maori had delegated a Hawaiian friend.

Lunching a few days later with Malcolm Chun, who is considered to be one of the finest scholars of the Hawaiian language in his generation, I learned more about the Maori's influence in our fiftieth state, and his own intense relationship to their culture. Chun, who is in his late twenties, spent a year in New Zealand on a research grant in the early 1980s to study the many historical factors which enabled the Maori to retain their ethnic identity. (Ironically, many of those beneficial factors are traceable to the traditional racism of the British colonial system—British taboos on buying land from the Maori, on intermarriage and most other forms of social contact.) The principal gift Malcolm Chun has received from his study of the Maori, he says, is "a heightened aggressiveness." Hawaiians could also benefit from the Maori example, he adds, by concentrating on relearning the skills of material survival—farming, fishing—and the mainstay of spiritual survival—religion. Too many activists, he believes, are "using Hawaiian religion as a political expedient" without having relearned it properly, and are debasing it through lack of genuine feeling.

Mightn't this be the case, I asked, with much renascent piety throughout the planet—in Poland, Islam, Latin America? Doesn't the element of autosuggestion present in all religions make them ever available to pragmatic ends? Malcolm Chun often wears an ancient pendant made of a whale tooth that invokes mana. He pointed severely to the talisman, saying, "I don't trust exterior means or ends; we must truly interiorize our religion so as to make such tokens of it unnecessary."

Toward the end of my last stay on Oahu, a celebration took place which was quite as meaningful, to many Hawaiians, as Governor John Waihee's inaugural: the investiture of the new trustees of OHA, the Office of Hawaiian Affairs. It was held in historic Kawaiaha'o Church, in the same building in which the Christian instruction of the islands' original people had begun. Standing on the church's sun-drenched steps, a young Hawaiian blew resounding tones on a *pu*, a large conch shell traditionally used in pre-Cook times to gather an important assembly, and the dignitaries proceeded into the sanctuary. An enormous temple drum whose frame of coconut burl also predates the arrival of Captain Cook, so heavy it had to be carried by five men, stood below the pulpit from which haole missionaries once preached fire-and-brimstone sermons against pagan ways. The nine trustees, wearing ceremonial robes and many leis, dominated by the grandiose stature of "A. Frenchy Keanuenueokalaninuiamamao de Soto," as she lists herself, stood gravely at the side of the sanctuary. The entire ritual was performed in Hawaiian, and John Dominis Holt, adorned with insignia and decorations bestowed on his grandfather by Hawaii's last king, David Kalakaua, was again at my side to offer a translation.

The ceremonies were begun by Kamaki A. Kanahele III, the chairman of OHA, a very tall, stately Hawaiian with resplendent shoulder-length hair. Kanahele gave a long, lilting chant of welcome, transmitted to him from generations of his ancestors on the island of Niihau. It was a secret family chant which, according to John Holt, had never been performed in public before. Kanahele was offering it as a very special gift to the new trustees of OHA, to a community which he felt was in need of strength and nourishment. "The gods greet you, the wind, the rains, the heavens greet you on this auspicious occasion," so John Holt translated the verses to me later. "You from Molokai, from Oahu, from Kauai, from Kaho'olawe, the mana is all collected . . ."

The next chant, performed by a famous teacher of hula known as Aunt Sally Wood, invoked Laka, the goddess of forests who had first taught the hula to the Hawaiian people. It celebrated a few of the numerous trees, plants, and flowers that are exclusive to Hawaii—the koa tree, *eaea*; the Hawaiian bamboo, *'ohe*; the Hawaiian fern, *palapalai*. "Like these plants," Aunt Sally sang, "the human beings gathered here have a chance of developing, of growing . . ." Aunt Sally danced a slow, mournful hula as she sang. Her mellifluous arms mimed the motions of tree branches and *maile* vines swaying in the breeze, of flower blossoms slowly opening, of seeds being scattered in the wind.

After the hula performances held before the sanctuary, the new OHA trustees stood below the altar. Mr. Kanahele, chanting an incantation in Hawaiian to each trustee, placed about their shoulders a ceremonial cape traditionally reserved for the chiefly caste, the ali'i, in token of their new leadership, authority, responsibility.

The festivities after the investiture, held in the nearby parish house, were as merry as the former proceedings had been solemn. A ukulele band played swift-paced music while the guests feasted on a buffet of dozens of traditional Hawaiian delicacies—marinated raw fish, breadfruit, baked taro, baked pig, raw sugarcane. And toward the end of the banquet, a stone's throw from the church in which Hiram Bingham urged Hawaiians to give up their pagan rituals, their songs and dances, Aunt Sally performed the hula again, a very different one this time, a bawdy and very sexual hula. Her body became that of a young woman's as she swayed and twisted her hips, her audience laughed lustily as she rolled her eyes to many innuendos, as her arms caressed the body of her imaginary lover, "Let me touch it, let me hold it," she sang in Hawaiian. And no one was laughing harder at those verses than Hiram Bingham's successor, the Hawaiian pastor of Kawaiaha'o Church, Reverend William Kaina. Reverend Kaina, who sat across from me, was stomping his feet and laughing so hard at Aunt Sally's bawdy hula that he could not finish his lunch. "No no, not that way, let me put it in," Aunt Sally sang. Reverend Kaina had taken a bite of sugarcane and was seized with merriment, his head was bent down below the level of the table and his body shook uncontrollably with wonderful, lusty laughter at the sound of Aunt Sally's libidinous verses. Looking at the merry pastor, I suddenly remembered the memorial monument to Hiram Bingham that stands a few steps from the parish house where the banquet was being held, and is inscribed with these words: "He preached the first sermon ever delivered in this City on April 25, 1820, from 'Fear not, for behold I bring you glad tidings of great joy.' Here he taught confiding kings, queens, and chiefs . . ."

Only in Hawaii, which I have come to love as I never could before. And now I shall always return.

In the hours after the OHA ceremony Kalani, Kawahini, John Dominis Holt, and I went swimming together in a pool on John's Pacific Heights estate. Afterward we sat in a hot tub together, old friends sharing thoughts, enjoying the city of Honolulu shimmering below us, the beauty of the indigenous plants John has nurtured in his garden—*kukui*, red-flowered *ohi'as*, *koa* trees.

We talked about the beauty of the OHA ceremony, about that amazing gift Kamaki Kanahele had offered, the secret chant previously unheard by anyone outside his family.

Governor Waihee had not attended the investiture of the new board of OHA. John Holt was very sad that he had been absent. "If he turns into another cold bureaucrat he'll break my heart," he said, "he'll break many hearts."

"He might be confused about his Hawaiianness," Kawahini ventured. "We're all still so colonized."

"You know," Kalani suddenly said, "it strikes me that colonization is like alcoholism. The first step is to admit that you're powerless. And then you've got to detoxify. And how are you going to do it without rituals and prayers, just like in Alcoholics Anonymous. What I'm saying is that you need liturgy to decolonize."

The day before I left Hawaii, Kalani and Kawahini took me for a drive around Oahu, as they had promised, to show me the different places where Kalani had returned their babies' placentas to the elements. We stood on a cliff below Koko Head and watched the surf pound the rocks from which he had offered one baby's spirit to its guardian angels. We drove a few miles north toward Waimanalo to a beach where he had offered still another. We also stood on a desolate, wind-torn beach on that eastern tip of Oahu which is particularly loved by Kalani because it is the site nearest to Kaho'olawe, the military and sacred island which has rallied so many Hawaiians to fight for their land and for their culture.

"I wrapped the baby's placenta in ti leaves and swam out toward Kaho'olawe," Kalani said, "because for centuries that is where our spiritual leaders have gone to cleanse themselves and restore their energies. I swam out there to strengthen our baby's mana, to ensure it a fruitful, protected, and clean life. I rendered the baby's energy to the bigger Energy out there, I rendered its spirit to the elements and offered my gratitude. I said mahalo and aloha for Ku'ike, mahalo and aloha Lono, aloha Papa, aloha Ku, aloha Laka . . ."

"What the heck," Kalani added in his fierce gruff voice, "I also said aloha Buddha, aloha Shiva, aloha Jesu Kristo; these days you need all the help you can get."

A Family of France

O_N February 6, 1934, my uncle
André Monestier joined my father and forty thousand other Frenchmen at the barricades to preserve the honor of France and overthrow a government which they thought inept and corrupt. Like
most other patriots of their time, they looked on their nation as supreme unto all others in the glory of its culture and its political and
military might, "Mother of arms, of arts, and of laws" (a phrase
drummed into them since infancy). And in the winter of 1934 that
image was being sullied by a number of political scandals which
had culminated in the Stavisky affair, a heist brought off by a foreign adventurer who had robbed France of billions of francs, impli-
cating some of the country's most prominent men.

At the cost of several dead and many wounded, most of the
militants confronted the police at the Pont de la Concorde, near
the Chamber of Deputies, and forced the resignation of the Daladier government. My uncle and father, however, belonged to a
quixotic right-wing organization called Croix de Feu, "Fiery Cross,"
which had decided to avoid all physical violence. They remained in
front of the restaurant Lasserre, just off the Champs-Elysées, and
were satisfied to tear out the metal pickets that surrounded Lasserre's lawn, brandishing them as symbolic weapons. When policemen asked them the purpose of this singular gathering, my two rel-

atives cried out: "We are here to shout subversive words! We are shouting '*Vive la France!*' "

"*Vive la France*, subversive words!" my uncle repeated with relish as he related the incident to me during a recent summer. "I've always been proud of that answer, one barely hears those words anymore. . . ."

We were seated on the terrace at La Croze, his summer property in the Gorges du Tarn, a savage, mountainous site in southern France where I've been visiting him since early childhood. My uncle André, now in his nineties, is the only relative I have left who has witnessed the changes that have swept France in our century. Six foot two and massively built, he is as lucid, vigorous, and idealistic as ever. He was born in this very region, the Lozère, and traces his ancestry to thirteenth-century Albigensian dissenters who were forced to flee their ancestral village of Monestier, close to Albi. And earlier that day I'd teased him with the notion that he had been made a true patriot by his more heretical traits—Utopian optimism, audacity, rebelliousness.

"Right," he'd quickly answered, "too much passivity these days, people are always waiting for a leader . . . never wait, just vote for the least imbecile of the lot and continue griping and create whatever microcosm of perfection you can in your own life. . . ."

Below us, as poplars gleamed on the sunny bank, a large wooden crate, strung on cables, was slowly traveling above the river Tarn, carrying *Le Figaro* and a load of groceries from the nearby village. My uncle's summer retreat, which he bought in 1935, had struck me since childhood as a microcosm of romantic perfection. La Croze is a complex of rustic gray stone buildings that can only be reached by boat, perched on that steep, rocky side of the Tarn canyon on which there is no road for many miles. And the region itself, the Lozère, is one of France's most untamed, close to where the Wild Boy of Aveyron is said to have been raised by wolves, the only part of the country in which wolves are said occasionally still to roam.

"The age of leaders may be over," my uncle was saying. "It already was over in 1914. Do you realize that World War One was the first major war in history which did not bring forth one great man? Not one military genius? Led by total dunces who wasted men left and right? I was there, in the Somme. . . ."

I had originally started visiting La Croze because Uncle André's wife, Aunt Simone, was a cousin of my father's, and the three had become inseparable by the time I was born. They shared interests in philosophy, maverick politics, and exotic places thought bizarre by their conventional, provincial relatives. After being wounded and highly decorated in World War I, Uncle André had graduated from a competitive *grande école*—Polytechnique. He had settled in the Paris region, and with a fairly modest capital investment—the equivalent of six thousand dollars today—he had started a small chemical factory that provided him with a comfortable living for some decades. Every few winters, he and my aunt set out on audacious trips considered outlandish by habitually cautious French travelers—they descended the Amazon into the wilds of Brazil, skied in the Carpathians, sailed through the Norwegian fjords.

Aunt Simone was an indefatigable, high-spirited redhead with a vigorous need to nurture, shelter, spread cheer. The Monestiers had yearned for ten children but had never been able to bear more than one daughter, Claude, a decade my senior. During my summer vacations at their eccentric hamlet, La Croze, they treated me as a second child, putting me to bed in their own room when the house was overcrowded with guests. Their boldness and largess remained unabated with the decades. During the years of the Nazi Occupation, after my father had died with the Free French and I had immigrated to the United States, the Monestiers repeatedly risked their lives to shelter whatever underground fighters came their way. After the liberation, my uncle was elected mayor of La Malène, the impoverished village closest to La Croze. During his decade as mayor, he organized the first boatmen's union in the region, and lobbied relentlessly in Paris to provide his constituents with their first public water system.

Two decades later, when he and Aunt Simone were close to seventy and their own finances were decimated by the forced sale of their chemical factory, they persuaded the Alliance Française to back their several trips to India where they gave lectures on Teilhard de Chardin. They lived in an ashram in Pondicherry for several months of the winter, rising at 5:00 A.M. to work and pray with the rest of the community. And back in Paris, my uncle published a book entitled *Teilhard or Marx?* My aunt busied herself with Jungianism and graphology, supplementing income by analyzing handwriting samples at thirty dollars a shot.

By the age of ten, in the middle of the war, I had settled in the United States with my mother. But the deep love I had for the Monestiers, and theirs for me, remained undiminished by time or distance. After the war, returning to France every few years for a summer visit, I was increasingly fascinated by their views, which were as quirky and original as their avocations. Devout Catholics and Gaullists, they had come to believe that "Communism is a manifestation of the Devil, a satanic event"; yet they declared themselves to be Christian Socialists because "capitalism is based on usury, which is forbidden by the Gospel." Despite their love of travel and their great admiration for American character and customs, they never came to the United States because they judged it to be "too similar to France, equally part of the materialistic West." Radically ecumenical, my uncle could write and publish the hazardous opinion that "Christ has been present, through His Holy Ghost, in each religion since the world's beginnings," yet defend every pope that came to power.

In the last decades, the Monestiers' longing for a large family has been amply fulfilled. By 1980, the five children of their daughter Claude, who had married during the war, had given them twenty-one great-grandchildren. Claude's husband, Jean de Laromiguière, had spent two years in Dachau for his work in the Resistance, suffered many nervous breakdowns, and was frequently absent from home, leaving the Monestiers all the more in charge. Every summer the entire clan congregated loyally at La Croze, which teemed with little ones. And as I watched my adopted parents aging amid proliferating youth, I feared that I was seeing an aspect of France threatened with extinction. They belonged to a generation infused with the unquestioned authority of *travail, famille, patrie*; yet they also exemplified that spirit of idealism and risk that, until World War II, had constantly revitalized the nation, inspired its mavericks and visionaries, from the Curies to de Gaulle, from Cousteau to Teilhard.

Could this balance of rootedness, daring, and chivalry be maintained by their progeny? How did the sense of "being French" differ in 1985 from what it had been in 1934, when my father and uncle took to the streets to help overthrow a corrupt government? What are the French thinking today about such issues as religion, family, French-American relations, the threat of Communism, the atomic bomb? How has France's traditional sense of superiority been affected by its diminished status as a great power? These are some of the questions I'd set out to explore as I stood by the Tarn river on a recent July afternoon, waiting to be ferried across to La Croze. I had driven up from Montpellier, some three hours south, and parked my car in the family lot that lies below the D907 *bis*, the tortuous public road across the river from La Croze. I'd given my decades-old shout, *"Traversez!"* and been answered with the traditional *"On arrive!"* I inhaled the thyme and lavender on the hot air, stared at the gray garland of houses that lies nestled on the rock-crested mountain like a nation unto itself. I looked at the site with particular sadness and urgency, for my beloved Aunt Simone had died of a heart attack just five weeks before, aged eighty-seven. And my uncle, so I'd been told the day before on the phone, was in his bed at La Croze, suffering from bronchitis and a fever of 102.

Two bikini-clad beauties, Claude's fourteen- and seventeen-year-old granddaughters, whom I had last seen when they were six and nine, pole across the Tarn to fetch me, the wooden rods thudding softly against the stony riverbed. My cousin Claude stands on the other side and runs forward to hug her welcome, a large, exuberant woman who has inherited her mother's tumultuous vitality and warmth. This particular afternoon she wears a green-and-white T-shirt inscribed with the words TUPPERWARE—FRANCE, the American company for whose Paris branch she has worked for over two decades. My uncle, she immediately reassures me, is improved today, and I can see him for a very short visit. In residence at La Croze, she adds as we climb the steep path to the house, are twenty-seven members of the family—four of her five children, fourteen of her grandchildren, several cousins. "It's a great disappointment," she says. "We'd planned to be thirty-five." Missing from the reunion is her husband Jean, who "is again in crisis." "It's been a very sad summer," she sums up as we reach the house, "but a wonderfully quiet one. Imagine, none of us has crossed the river more than once, on Sundays, to go to Mass!"

"Oh well, the very best times are those when there is a priest vacationing here," says one of her granddaughters, "and then we can spend weeks without crossing, except to fetch guests!"

"*C'est ici qu'on se ressource*," gravely adds her fifteen-year-old cousin—"We're renewed, refueled here." And I sense that the mysterious force of tribal roots is exerting itself as fully as ever on the new generation.

Uncle André greets me from his bed, a biography of Pope John Paul II in hand, effusive and lucid despite his illness. Do I notice that he's wearing the red bathrobe I'd sent him for Christmas a decade ago, which he hasn't gotten out of since? No one must worry about this silly fever, don't we know what powerful stock he comes from? His ninety-two-year-old sister, the retired nun, is playing bridge tournaments in Lyons, having lied about her age to get into the tournaments. . . . The room, sparsely furnished with rustic chairs and chests of fruitwood, left almost cave-dark by the narrow seventeenth-century windows that pierce the walls of rough-hewn stone, has barely changed since I slept in it as a child. I'd been determined to remain stoic about Aunt Simone's death, but at the sight of the half-empty bed my eyes flood with tears.

"Come come," my uncle says gently, touching my cheek. "It's sad but not *so* sad. What's life but a passage to more important things?" The faith of the phrase threatens to set me off again, so I hasten downstairs to the terrace, where the immense family always congregates when it isn't pouring rain, the one indoor public room being constantly used as a bedroom by some member of the clan.

As I join my cousins, they are finishing Sunday lunch, a frugal, American-style meal prescribed long ago by Aunt Simone so that no one would have to cook on the Sabbath: a self-service buffet of hot dogs, rolls, and red wine, a selection of Popsicles for dessert. After the emotional mayhem of greetings, the queries about the health of my family back in the United States, the introduction to each child born since my last visit, my relatives sink into their

"chaises relax" to take their coffee. From now until five, when everyone will descend to the Tarn for the ritual late-afternoon swim,
the air hums with the clicking of knitting needles and the snipping
of scissors. Most of the women are making a garment for another
member of the family—evening dress for a sixteen-year-old niece,
bloomers for a four-year-old nephew—while the rest of us sit on the
lawn, stringing beans for supper. Yves de Laromiguière, Claude's
youngest son, sits apart with his brothers-in-law and nephews, planning next morning's work. All the upkeep of the property is done
by the men of the family—there is always a leaking roof to be re-
paired, a generator to be serviced, brush to be cleared in many
fields.

As the shadows lengthen and everyone prepares for the evening swim, a five-year-old passes his cousins and siblings the basket
holding the afternoon snack—dark chocolate nestled in thick chunks
of white bread. I follow the clan down the steep path to the Tarn,
and we all wade into midriver to a small, pebbly island some twenty
feet wide and forty feet long that I find strikingly uncomfortable
and claustrophobic. The family favors it because it offers shallow
water on one side for the little ones, more adventurous depths on
the other side for the adults. They remain there until close to suppertime and continue the family banter started over lunch, two
dozen relatives supremely content with each other, seeking out for
the evening hours an enclave even more intimate and crowded than
the one they have spent the day in. As I watch this tribal spectacle,
it strikes me that they might be re-creating, in these compulsive
yearly gatherings, a micro-France of bygone years, indulging in a
nostalgic fantasy of that superior, united, self-sufficient nation that
their patriarch had already battled to preserve a half-century ago.

Of the adults gathered on that crowded island, I have chosen
six who might express how that sense of France has changed.

Chantal de Bussac, Claude's second-oldest daughter, a very
handsome, outgoing woman of forty-two, has amply inherited her
grandparents' forthright warmth and intellectual gifts. Before her
marriage she taught mathematics and physics to the senior class of
a girls' school in Paris. For the last fourteen years she has lived in
Clermont-Ferrand, her husband's native city, which she prefers to

the capital because "it provides better quality of life for the children." Soon after the last of her four offspring was born, she began to feel restless and became interested in the theories of personality development formed in the United States by the psychologist and author Carl Rogers. For two years, she spent part of each week in Lyons, leaving her husband in charge of the children, learning "la méthode Rogers." Using its techniques of consciousness-raising, she now runs group seminars in which she teaches women to "fulfill their identities, express themselves more eloquently, abolish their sense of powerlessness."

Although Chantal is still uncomfortable with the "feminist" label, she admits that her work involves "a quintessence of nonconfrontational feminism." She has also been active in a nationwide organization, Accueils des Villes Françaises, which helps women adapt to their surroundings when they move to a new city. Chantal feels that a recent blossoming of volunteer organizations is one of the most striking developments in contemporary France, and that it has to do with a great loss of faith in the state as an agent of change. She heartily welcomes this new public-mindedness. "We're at last crawling out of our traditional shell, the home, and reaching out to others." The de Bussacs also do a great amount of volunteer work for their parish, including a weekly counseling session for couples who are about to be married. ("Can you imagine, some of them tell us they've already been living together . . . that would have sounded very startling ten years ago!")

Pierre de Bussac, Chantal's husband, is the most cosmopolitan of my cousins. A slight, pensive man approaching fifty, he is a graduate of a competitive *grande école*—Ecole des Mines. He spent a year in the Soviet Union in the 1960s, overseeing the installation of French machinery in Soviet chemical plants. He speaks and writes Russian fluently and speaks English well, though he is very shy about using it. After a stint with the American firm Armco, he now directs a small company that makes computer printout paper in Clermont-Ferrand. "*Etre Français, c'est être contre,*" Pierre says— "To be French is to be against." But he senses that his compatriots are dissatisfied with a larger variety of issues than ever before, and that they are engaging in an unprecedented amount of self-criticism. Pierre's particular obsession is the "downright pathetic state" of France's scientific research, which lacks any systematic or adequate funding. "Americans might seem overly specialized to us, but you're the ones getting the Nobels."

Pierre feels that the French are undergoing a crisis of identity that was originally triggered by the student uprisings of 1968, when all forms of traditional authority were put into question. Like every member of the Monestier-Laromiguière clan, he is militantly opposed to Mitterrand's Socialist government and to all forms of leftism. Yet he does not totally share his in-laws' condemnatory views of the 1968 rebellion and believes it was a great benefit to French family structure. "It made better parents of us; it finally taught us to listen to children's opinions as the most interesting and precious we can hear, it transformed the table talk of French families . . . it is at table that everything happens." In Clermont, Pierre's favorite recreation is to see American films, particularly those of Woody Allen. He dismisses all allegations of American cultural imperialism abroad as "more misguided leftist nonsense." He believes that French culture "needs to turn outward in every possible way, and would benefit by emulating American models of business management, scientific research and philanthropic funding."

Catherine de Maistre, Chantal's younger sister, is a delicate, elegant woman with a striking resemblance to the young Zizi Jeanmaire. Her sinuous, feline charm is ill-matched to her grimly disciplinarian views. During a short walk we took together, she said that "1968 was a watershed year for me because I was in the last year of school and my brother Bruno and I were tempted to join our classmates and go to some demonstrations. But Mother put her foot down and said, 'I've worked my heart out to support you, don't you dare go out there or you can't come home.' It was blackmail on her part, virtual blackmail, but I've always been grateful to her for it. . . . She taught us then and there the supremacy of family duty and patriotic values, of order, order above all . . . and I've tried to instill the same values in my children."

For a decade Catherine had fervently hoped to bear a son who might continue her husband's illustrious name: Alain de Maistre is a direct male descendant of Joseph de Maistre (c. 1753–1821), the prominent archconservative thinker whose writings opposed the Enlightenment philosophers, deplored the progress of science, and acclaimed public executioners as the guardians of social order. Catherine and Alain bore four daughters in a row, and a few years ago rejoiced at the birth of their first son.

The de Maistres shun their local parish in fashionable Neuilly because it is "close to being Communist," and travel a distance to attend Mass at which they listen to "marvelously old-fashioned authoritarian sermons which hold even the youngest children spell-bound." Catherine has recently stopped reading *Elle* magazine because of its support of legalized abortion and switched her loyalties to *Madame Figaro*, which she considers the most "B.C.B.G."—*bon chic, bon genre*—fashionable and proper—publication in France. Catherine says she would be "deeply shocked" if one of her daughters admitted to having sex before marriage. Like her sister Chantal and her brother Bruno, Catherine came to spend some weeks with me in the United States in the mid-1960s. She was "overwhelmed by Americans' hospitality and warmth." And notwithstanding her qualms about the permissiveness of our mores ("one intake of marijuana in school and you get hooked for life on stronger stuff like cocaine and heroin"), she wishes fervently that each of her children might enjoy a similar stay in the States when they come of age.

Alain de Maistre, lanky, six feet two, did his military service in France's most elite paratroop corps, stayed on a few extra years, and almost decided to make a career of it. He is the director of an advertising agency that handles financial accounts, including that of the Banque Nationale de Paris. He is more publicly active than his home-loving wife, and his great cause is the Boy Scout movement. He recently spent seven years as scoutmaster, giving the movement a dozen hours a week. He trained for the paratroop corps in several different countries and the happiest times of all were spent in Germany, the country for which his generation and that of his children feel the most sympathy. "I found no difference whatsoever in human values, in any point of view, between our group and our German colleagues." The most unhappy days of Alain's paratrooper training were spent in England, which my cousins unanimously agree is that country in the world which the French dislike the most. "The British forced our unit into total isolation. The British will never become Europeans; they'll always remain insular, a culture of their own."

Like every one of my relatives, Alain and Catherine have intense admiration for Ronald Reagan, as they had for Richard Nixon. ("How lucky you are to still have such great leaders! Magnificent men!") Alain says that he inherited a negative view of the United States and only began to admire it in his late teens, when his Scout troop was taken to the World War II museum in Normandy. "I learned there to my total amazement that the U.S. forces had participated in the liberation of France—in all our history courses we were taught that the Free French alone had liberated the country."

Yves de Laromiguière, Claude's fifth and youngest child, is the family's political activist. For the first five years of his marriage, he lived near Amiens, where he ran for the Chamber of Deputies on Valéry Giscard d'Estaing's ticket. He is tall and heavyset, like his grandfather, with a ready smile and a voluble gift for conversation. He now lives in Brussels, where he directs the Belgian branch of a French wallpaper concern.

One of Yves's favorite political topics is the need for a united European community. "France can't go it alone any more than Great Britain or Italy can. If we don't destroy our outdated boundaries and create Europe, the decline of Western civilization will be as total as that of Egypt or other ancient cultures. The first step is to create one single European monetary unit; but like other tasks in building Europe it can't be done through the political system. "The notion of abandoning French currency is an abomination for the average French deputy and his constituents. So we have to lobby for it, create a massive grass-roots movement which will impose the notion on our politicians. The situation is already serious, dangerous; Europe is becoming poorer by the day. . . ."

Yves enjoys Brussels because "it's marvelous to live in a country which has no complex of superiority." He looks upon that particular trait of his countrymen as "an escapist delusion kept alive for too many decades by de Gaulle and not yet eroded enough." His devout Catholicism is an interesting mixture of liberal and conservative. He shares his grandfather's belief in the equal sanctity of all religions, and finds it abominable that the Church of Rome still retains the word "Catholic" in the Nicene Creed: "One Holy, Catholic and Apostolic Church." "The word 'Catholic' should immediately be dropped to make a statement of universal salvation," Yves says. Yet like most every member of the family, he and his wife go to confession once a month. And last fall the couple has accompanied Yves's mother, Claude, on a pilgrimage to a site in Yugoslavia where the virgin Mary is said to be appearing daily to six young peasants.

As with the rest of his kin, the central priority of Yves's life is his children's education. He is very critical of both the Belgian and the French educational system. "They cram you with facts and don't teach you how to use them," he says. So, notwithstanding his profound dislike of the British, Yves has sent his oldest son, Louis, nine, to a Jesuit boarding school in England. During one of our lunch conversations, Yves said that if he were doomed with some illness and had only a few months to live, he would spend all his time writing letters to each of his four children, "a fundamental letter for each year of their growing up until they reach the age of twenty-one." Every member of the assembled family enthusiastically agreed that they could not conceive of a better way to spend their last days on earth.

"What do you think of Allen Ginsberg's 'Howl'?" Yves's wife, Sybille, asked me in her near-perfect English on one of my mornings at La Croze. She is a seductive, green-eyed redhead with a spunky sense of humor and has graduate degrees in British and American literature from the University of Amiens. She taught her subject in a private school while bringing up four children. Her reading in contemporary American literature, which seems to go up to 1960, includes Henry Miller, Arthur Miller, and Truman Capote. She yearns to return to the United States, where she once spent a summer on Long Island.

Unlike my other relatives, Sybille thinks it wrong for Catholics to impose their views against abortion on the population at large and is opposed to the growing movement to repeal legal abortion in France. Sybille is militant, however, on the issue of preserving the freedom of private church schools. She and Yves traveled from Brussels twice in 1984 to attend rallies protesting government legislation that threatened to curtail that freedom and which drew unprecedented crowds of a million and a half people. Sybille is also adamant on the issue of premarital sex. "I'm particularly disturbed when unmarried teachers have sex together. *Il faut avant tout ne pas choquer"*—"Above all, one must never shock."

Both the American television imports "Dallas" and "Dynasty" are unanimously shunned and derided by the family (*"C'est pour les ploucs"*—"It's for the simpleminded";) and the children are forbidden to view them because of their "low moral caliber."

My relatives have not read, or seen, and have barely heard of: Roland Barthes, Jacques Derrida, Marcel Ophuls, Marguerite Duras, or most other persons who have recently served as cultural bridges between France and the United States. Being little aware of discussions about the mediocrity of current French culture and its consequent colonization by foreign talent, they are indifferent to the fact that a Chinese-American architect is about to build a pyramid in the courtyard of the Louvre, that an Italian was commissioned to design the interior of the new Quai d'Orsay museum, and that a Canadian architect is designing the new opera house at the Place de la Bastille.

My relatives' names sound ancient and romantic but their means are modest, and their talk seems totally centered on Confucian concerns for family and on issues of immediate survival—how best to take care of Grandfather Monestier now that he is widowed; the threat posed to Pierre de Bussac's business, where production has been cut by 30 percent because of several strikes by the C.G.T., France's largest union; the precarious finances of Yves's older brother, Bruno, who must support six children on the meager salary he earns from an American automotive company whose French branch has fallen on bad times; how to pool the money direly needed to maintain La Croze, the upkeep of which they finance jointly.

Along with their obsession with the children's education, they are, above all, immersed in the cultivation of harmonious family bonds; their concept of "self" seems virtually nonexistent outside of the communal context of their extended family. These dutiful, cautious lives may strike Americans as constrained, class-conscious, tradition-bound. Yet one cannot help but admire the remarkable cordiality, tenderness, and deference that is maintained between siblings and cousins, parents and children, and most striking of all, between husbands and wives. It is a family in which women have considerable influence and power and often express themselves in strong language, as they did on a recent summer afternoon:

A young married couple, only vague acquaintances of my family clan, had waded across the Tarn for a visit. The aggressive, loquacious husband sat by my uncle talking of the abandoned shepherd's house he had just bought on one of the neighboring *causses*, the barren stony plateaus that dominate the gorges of the Tarn and of other neighboring rivers. He planned to live there with his bride five months of the year. He was rebuilding the walls and roofs of the house with his own hands. He had just started his own lumber business in the area; no more of the capital's *"métro, boulot, dodo"*—roughly "subway, the office grind, and off to bed"—current shorthand for the hassle of Parisian life.

"And do you have any employment, madame . . ." my uncle courteously asked the waifish, very silent young wife. "Hell no, I wouldn't let her," the husband interrupted with a lewd wink. "Who'd want a wife who's all tired out at night?"

"That man is a walking phallus!" Sybille exclaimed as soon as the uninvited guests had started wading back to the opposite bank.

"Must be a beast in bed," my cousin Claude remarked.

"Odious machismo!" Catherine added.

"Poor pretty girl," my ninety-year-old uncle said; "she'd be better off with me."

"The finest wine for my lunch!" Uncle André called out from his bedroom as his lunch tray was about to be brought, "none of our local everyday swill! And a *poire* with my coffee!"

By the third day I was at La Croze, my uncle's fever had abated and I was able to visit with him for a few hours of the afternoon. He sat in his armchair by a window that overlooked the Tarn, shoes impeccably shined, the Legion of Honor rosette blazing in the lapel of his tweed jacket. He had discovered my predilection for serious talk when I was about six years old, and as in our meetings of past decades, he began with a little theme that he wished me to ponder. This time, it had to do with the twentieth century as analogous to the Book of Job.

"It is simply not normal," he began, "for God to send us as many plagues as he has since 1914. At just about that time, as I see it, God and the Devil had one of their big executive meetings, and the Devil said, 'You think they're worthy down there? Let's test them out with some real trouble and we'll find out.' And sure enough the Lord sent all those plagues to test our faith, the decimation of World War One, Hitler, Stalin. . . ."

"My heretic ancestry!" He pointed his cane toward the windows and mountains. "You've always thought that's my source. . . . Well, I do grow increasingly Manichaean as I get older. I sense that a force of Evil has been pitted against Good since the Creation. And in 1985 God sits up there, still challenged by the Devil, pretending He's dead, pretending He's abandoned us, testing us, testing. . . ."

He paced the room slowly, his eyes benign under the bushy black brows even when he wished to look threatening. "Well, we deserve His abandonment, we asked for it. Pope John Paul put it best: Christians have failed the Gospel, capitalism is totally unjust toward the working class. But we might just be able to come out of it. I feel we're at the end of the Great Temptation. Mind my words, the twenty-first century will be *the* spiritual century, or it will not be at all. . . ."

It had been two hours since the younger generations had been in the patriarch's room. They had been admonished to respect his afternoon rest. Now they started crowding in as they do every midafternoon, bringing their hugs and kisses, their presents of butterflies and leaves, their admonitions to him to avoid *"courants d'air"* and to move about less. Tea was brought in, and somehow we all fell to talking about heroes. Which public figures did we particularly admire or uphold as heroes, either past or present?

"Dear God, all the heroes I was brought up to revere as a schoolboy!" Uncle André exclaimed. "Archetypes of patriotic valor: Vercingetorix, Roland at the pass, Napoleon. Later on I also adulated Clemenceau, Poincaré, Teilhard, and still later Gandhi, the great pacifist Lanza del Vasto. . . ."

"Well those of us who came of age during the last war never admired military men," my cousin Claude said. "*My* heroes are Renoir and Berthe Morisot, those passionate, sensual artists who can fill our lives with joy and warm colors. Oh, I'd crawl through the Sahara on all fours to own one. . . ."

"I admire most those who work above and *beyond* politics," said Claude's daughter, Chantal. "Like Mother Teresa."

"John the Twenty-third," Catherine said.

"Mozart, Bach, Chopin," said Anne, Claude's silent, pensive, oldest daughter, who seldom participates in group conversation.

I turned to the generation of my uncle's great-grandchildren, who were gathered together in the back of the room. "I balk at the very *notion* of heroes," said eighteen-year-old Arnaud, Chantal's eldest child. "Well . . . perhaps Einstein."

"The only heroes I have are fictional," said Christelle, his seventeen-year-old sister, "like Julien Sorel."

"But why *have* heroes?" exclaimed her seventeen-year-old cousin from Tours, Valerie. "Our generation refuses heroes! That's our motto, no more heroes! We've all seen the obverse side of the coin, we all know the shoddy seamy side of geniuses and public men!"

"We don't even have any more leaders," she added defiantly. "*Et je trouve ça très bien*"—"I think it's all to the good."

"Look, magic!" Claude exclaims, lifting up her Tupperware plastic rolling pin for everyone to see. "Impeccable pie crust in sixty seconds without a moment of sticking! And now I transfer my dough into the pie plate . . . see, even the rolling surface is intact!"

Claude joined the Tupperware corporation some two decades ago, shortly after it had opened its first office in Paris. She was the eleventh dealer in France. "Tupperware of America!" she exclaims to anyone not acquainted with the company: "An enterprise of genius, branches in thirty-three countries!" Today she is giving me a Tupperware demonstration on the terrace of La Croze, and a score of her progeny have assembled for the umpteenth time to watch her. "Here's the secret!" she continues. "A *hollow* plastic rolling pin which we fill with ice-cold water to avoid any sticking!"

The very way in which Claude joined Tupperware seems providential. It was in 1962, and her husband, Jean de Laromiguière, had just undergone the second of the major nervous breakdowns that he would suffer after his return from Dachau. With five children to support, Claude's finances were desperately strained. She economized by going to Les Halles at five every Thursday morning to do the entire week's marketing. A friendly merchant expressed concern that Claude's groceries might spoil, and showed her a streamlined new kind of plastic container which, she claimed, ensured week-long garden freshness. Claude immediately coveted the containers and was dismayed to learn that "le Tupperware" is sold only "en salon"—at demonstrations in private homes.

But the merchant promised to arrange such an event, and within a fortnight my cousin was watching a Comtesse de Chambure ("proprietor of a splendid château in the Somme") sell several hundred dollars' worth of the American miracle in one afternoon. Broke and energetic, Claude immediately decided to join the circle of Parisian women making independent incomes through the plastic wonder. She found her first clientele through her hairdresser, who invited Claude to perform in an apartment building of a working-class suburb.

"All the women there were members of the C.P.," Claude recalls. "They launched me, and I owe them eternal gratitude. With the Communist ladies, I'd doubled my sales quota in a fortnight. The secret? Communists love presents, and Tupperware offers a free gift with each purchase."

Twenty years later, Claude directs a Tupperware concession that covers a few hundred miles north and west of Paris and supervises more than four hundred sales personnel. In the last two decades, she has "seen the world, thanks to Tupperware," attending conferences and visiting branch offices in nineteen countries, including Ireland, Senegal, Indonesia, and the United States, where she spends most of her time at the company headquarters in Orlando, Florida. She speaks no more than a few words of English. She admires, above all our other institutions, the Thanksgiving holiday, "a sign of the profound religiosity of the American people."

In the 1970s, when Claude's deranged husband began to leave home for months at a time, she drew strength from still another American import—the "speaking in tongues" manifestation of the charismatic movement which had recently migrated from United States churches to those of Europe and was making spectacular inroads into French Catholicism. It is also called Le Mouvement du Renouveau, somewhat analogous to our term "born again." Claude learned about it from a colleague at Tupperware's office in Nantes and discovered "a form of prayer which is all the deeper because it abandons logical linguistic symbols."

In the last few years, this daughter of the country gentry has become one of the charismatics' most active street evangelists. On Saturday mornings, she meets a dozen colleagues in front of a prosperous branch of the Félix Potin grocery chain in Neuilly. The group stands on the sidewalk, reading and chanting texts to a guitar accompaniment and urging any passerby who approaches them to "read and spread the Gospel." Claude sees the charismatic movement as one more way in which staid, conservative French adults are joining in voluntary organizations, taking to the streets to fulfill their needs and aspirations.

"And wait till you see our new Ultra Twenty-one line," Claude says as she brandishes a soufflé mold at the end of her Tupperware demonstration. "Tupperware for the twenty-first century! A revolutionary new brand of plastic that can go straight from the freezer into a three-hundred-and-fifty-degree oven!"

"Formidable!" Even the athletic teenage grandsons applaud. "Mother is so persuasive," Catherine says proudly. "She could sell you a bag of rusty nails even if she'd told you they were rusty."

But Claude's oldest daughter, forty-three-year-old Anne, has knitted dourly throughout the performance, her eyes cast down on her clicking needles, as she sits through most of her days at La Croze. She is a brooding woman with a great gift for music, which she was never able to fulfill, and a broken marriage. And as she angrily knits on the terrace at La Croze, I am forced to recall that she is that child of the Monestier-Laromiguière clan most profoundly marked by the traumas of World War II.

Anne was a one-year-old in 1942 when her mother and father, Jean de Laromiguière, a brilliant and eccentric graduate of Saint-Cyr, undertook one of the most perilous tasks of the Resistance: they turned their small Paris apartment into a shelter whence Free French and other members of the underground were guided to the Spanish frontier. The resisters' hiding place was a small bedroom reached through Anne's nursery, its door hidden by a curtain. The

Laromiguières's escape network was eventually infiltrated by a Gestapo informer, and Jean was sent to Dachau. During the following
months, Claude shifted homes every few days with her tiny daughters, Anne and Chantal, to avoid her own arrest.

Anne was four when she saw her father return from Dachau,
a dour, silent invalid weighing some seventy pounds. He had repeatedly suffered floggings and solitary confinement for agitating
in behalf of fellow inmates. She was twelve when her father had
his first total breakdown.

For a decade, a series of French doctors, hardly known for
their contribution to the field of mental health, tried to cure Jean
with a combination of drugs and sleeping cures, which entailed
being put to sleep for months at a time. During one such treatment, he fell off his bed while unattended and lay hours on a
freezing hospital floor, contracting double pneumonia and suffering
setbacks of mental illness. Lithium drugs were made available in
France in the late 1960s, and these periodically enabled Jean to resume some kind of family life. I saw him at La Croze in 1974 and
1977. Plump and numbed by the drug, my once razor-witted cousin
spent most of his time wandering about the property, keeping company with the youngest of his grandchildren, dusting their toys,
pushing their swings. During periods when he refused treatment,
he would leave home for stretches of up to two years, begging hospitality in different provinces from relatives and friends.

Since his most recent cure he often comes to Paris to lunch
with Claude. "The independence I've gained through my Tupperware work gives me courage," she has told me, this summer. "The
charismatic movement has strengthened the faith I need to pray
for his total healing."

"And you know," she adds with her brave, luminous smile,
"they both came from the United States."

"He is the crucible for our memory." That is the phrase with
which seventeen-year-old Arnaud de Bussac describes the missing
member of the yearly family reunion, Jean de Laromiguière, his
recurringly ill, absent grandfather. "He has forced us to remember
the past, to a far greater degree than most of our generation. And
one must remember in order not to start again; it is forgetfulness
which could start another war. . . ."

And yet, I note, Germany is the country for which he and his relatives feel the most affinity. Doesn't his grandfather's suffering, begun at Dachau, make it particularly difficult for his family to feel close to Germans?

"The first thing Grandpapa said when he returned from camp is this," says Arnaud's fourteen-year-old brother, Nicolas: "We must remember, but we must also forgive."

"Anyhow, we must all outgrow our sense of national boundaries," says Arnaud, who is cramming for the admissions examination to his great-grandfather's school, the prestigious Polytechnique, and whose words are heeded with reverence by his peers. "I feel just as 'European' as I feel 'French.' There is much more affinity these days between a French and a German than there is between a Breton and a Parisian."

The six youngsters, whose ages range from fourteen to seventeen, nod approvingly. Arnaud, two of his siblings, and three of his cousins are dining with me at a small restaurant at La Malène, the village a few miles upstream from La Croze. In the first half hour, they've already confronted me with two myths which I destroyed as well as I could. One, "In the States everyone informs you of their annual salary the second they meet you." Two, "Americans publish no news about France whatsoever in their newspapers; they don't even bother to study French anymore, everyone's learning Japanese."

I'd asked them about their future vocations. Arnaud is one of *"Les happy few"* whose scientific career would be assured by his admission into a *grande école*. His sister Christelle would like to work in the business management of some international couture or perfume industry, "ideally like Hermès." Valerie, seventeen, is studying at the Ecole du Louvre, aspires to be an art dealer, and detests any art more recent than the Impressionists. Nicolas, fourteen, wishes to start his own business enterprise. ("Good luck, old man," the others jibe at him. "It's not like the old days when great-grandfather could set up a factory on a pittance. These days the government stifles all initiative.")

All of these youngsters fear that their schools' outdated curriculums, and the general rigidity of French society, could pose severe obstacles to their goals. "We can't seem to succeed according to our gifts anymore, as you still can in the United States."

"Our country is too withdrawn into itself, our economic system seems unable to find any source of renewal." "Our schools only cram us with facts with which to pass exams; we need a more complete formation which would include computer techniques, arts, sports."

Do they feel threatened by the possibility of an atomic war? "We're much more afraid of pacifists and demonstrations and protest movements than of the bomb," Nicolas says defiantly, and the group nods vehemently in assent. Their favorite musicians are Michel Sardou, Pink Floyd, and Simon and Garfunkel. The only American actor they care for is Gregory Peck. Their favorite French stars are Isabelle Adjani, Miou-Miou, and Marlène Jobert. They are in unanimous accord that their parents are "absolutely fair and liberal" in their ways of imposing discipline, and that their private schools, most of which are church schools, "do not give a rigorous enough religious formation."

And their favorite moments of the year are spent at La Croze, where there is nothing much to do beyond engage in family banter, do maintenance work on the property, take a daily swim in the Tarn and a weekly trip to La Malène to go to Mass and enjoy many visits with Great-grandfather Monestier ("The most extraordinary man we'll ever know." "A magnetic force." "A source of inspiration to each of us.").

"It is uniquely serene here at La Croze." "It is so romantic." "We are renewed here," one of them says, as a cousin had said earlier that week. They have helped me to learn that of that once sacred triad, "*travail, famille, patrie*," *famille* is the only one that remains undiminished and intact.

For the sphere of *travail* has been made more precarious than ever by a society in which social mobility seems not to increase, by a fragile Socialist experiment whose vision has seemed limited. The issue of *patrie* is being increasingly blurred by the aspirations for a European community; by an unprecedented lack of faith in the central government; by a cosmopolitanization that is affecting the entire planet, but particularly affects the French because their identity so depended on their sense of superiority and uniqueness. So, amid the tarnished, tenuous concepts of work and nationhood, the narrow pleasures of family life may provide all the more seductive a refuge for the young. I could not perceive one chink in the reverence and admiration my young relatives have for every generation of their family, for its authority and rituals. Their docility struck me as downright scary.

Many things happen in France at lunchtime, if one allows the symbols to take over.

Uncle André had fully recovered from his flu. And just before lunch one day he indulged in one of the yearly rituals, the bestowing of the Grand Ordre de La Croze. It is an honorary society whose ranks, from Chevalier to Grand-Croix, duplicate precisely those of the Legion of Honor. It has been awarded for decades by my aunt and uncle to those members of the family who "with good humor and diligence" (as one citation reads) "have helped us to preserve this privileged site, La Croze, and contributed to its improvement."

We all stood in the sunlight to watch my uncle elevate the new Chevaliers. This year the decoration—a rustic metal cross hung on braided string—was awarded to fourteen-year-old Nicolas de Bussac "for having completed the restoration of the wheat bin and the renovation of the boat." His fifteen-year-old cousin Alain was equally honored for having "participated most efficiently in the clearing of the threshing floor and the collection of trout." The towering old man, wearing his own Legion of Honor rosette, beamed with pleasure as he kissed each youngster and hung the decorations around their necks. Everyone clapped. A few parents wiped tears. A regional aperitif, walnut wine, was served to all.

We were picnicking on the *causse* above La Croze, and I asked to hear the words of a song Aunt Simone had taught me when I was a child. The loyal, loving couples, the loyal, handsome adolescents, joyously burst into song, raising their glasses of red wine to the sun:

> "*Buvons un coup*
> *Buvons en deux*
> *A la santé des amoureux,*
> *A la santé du Roi de France* . . ."

> "*Let's drink a glass,*
> *let's drink two*

to the health of lovers,
to the health of the King of France."

And then—I knew why I needed to hear it again: the refrain was ageless in its loyalties and hatreds:

"Et merde pour la Reine d'Angleterre
Qui nous a declaré la guerre."

"And shit to the Queen of England
Who has declared war on us."

Another day, after the habitual Sunday lunch of hot dogs and Popsicles, my uncle decided to "celebrate a very beautiful day" by setting off his cannon. The cannon stands at the edge of the terrace that overlooks the Tarn, a decrepit seventeenth-century specimen he'd bought decades ago in some local antique shop. Yves and Alain went to get the gunpowder, and we closed our ears. Off it went, a thunderous and meaningless explosion over the gorge, clouds of putrid fumes rising into the air, groups of amazed tourists stopping their cars on the road across the river to stare at the eccentric little nation wreathed in smoke.

"One of my patriotic fantasies," my uncle said with a mischievous smile. "Just another of my little follies."

Some time later, one of my four-year-old cousins, seated on her mother's lap, asked: *"Qu'est-ce que c'est, 'La Marseillaise'?"*

Outbursts of indignation. "Doesn't she know yet? What *are* they taught these days?" "Let's teach her right now."

And a dozen voices sang again, right through to the last brutal verses: *"Marchons, marchons, qu'un sang impur abreuve nos sillons"*—"Let us march, let us march, let impure blood drench our fields."

Everyone was quiet for a few seconds. Then Catherine spoke softly: *"Comme c'est beau."*

It was said with sadness, with emotion, with longing and regret, with a certain defiance.

In Jerusalem

CLIMBING up the Via Dolorosa. In that stretch where it traverses the markets of the old Arab city and is flanked by arrays of copper bowls, caftans, woven baskets, baklavas, a group of pilgrims are making the Stations of the Cross. They are led by a brown-robed Franciscan friar who walks up the street backward, gesturing to his flock. They are speaking Spanish. Two of the pilgrims carry a gigantic wooden cross. A man in front holds the top of it. At its base is a woman in spike-heeled shoes and a satin dress, her harrowed face haloed by a mop of brilliantly dyed red hair. Fellow pilgrims trudge up very slowly, following. The friar stops at the plaque marking the eighth station, where Christ told the women of Jerusalem to weep not for Him but for themselves and for their children. He folds his hands upon his rope-belted waist, closes his eyes, begins an oration. The pilgrims' voices weave a rivulet of whispers beneath the garrulous stream of the Arab vendors' calls. Her eyes closed, her mouth moving in prayer, the woman in the satin dress staggers under her burden.

I follow the Via Dolorosa past more markets selling more caftans, hunks of lamb, tooled leathers, to the Church of the Holy Sepulchre. It is administered by four of the twenty-eight Christian rites that officiate in Jerusalem. Many parts of this holiest spot of Christendom are a shambles of scaffolding, abandoned ropes, overturned cement, and paint pails. There is a tiny crypt in the western rotunda that is hung with a profusion of beautiful Byzantine lamps. It stands over a slab of stone which that influential archaeologist, the Empress Helena, mother of Constantine, declared was the tomb of Christ and the center of the world: *Umbilicus Mundi*. Hovering over this site for which so much blood was shed, an aging Greek Orthodox priest stands askew, his body tilted at a crazy angle to the crypt's wall, pointing to his plate of coins and softly repeating in English, "Holy shrine, ancient shrine, body of Jesus, Holy shrine . . ."

A few hundred yards farther on I approach the Temple Mount, Jerusalem's most disputed and beautiful landmark, the third most sacred site of Islam. The golden-cupolaed Dome of the Rock is built over a vast, rugged ledge—its surface visible inside the mosque— on which Abraham is alleged to have prepared for the sacrifice of Isaac, on which Jesus is claimed to have preached, from which Muhammad is said to have risen heavenward on his horse. The indentation left by the Prophet's foot is still displayed by Arab guides, as is a hole in the rock through which the sacrificial blood of animals allegedly flowed from the altars of early Jewish temples. Here all is primeval moment, nature worship in the raw, elemental passions thrusting back to that time when generations of men deified the more awesome sites of nature—mountains, rivers, trees, rocks as numinous as this one.

I get to the Western Wall shortly before dusk, when the just lit floodlights and the waning sun drench its pale stone with a gleam of blondness. Boxes of cardboard yarmulkes stand at the entrance to the men's section. I pick up a cotton headscarf at the adjoining women's gate. Taking a multilingual prayer book from a table in the center of the women's section, I twice scan the same psalm, beginning "Let me be overwhelmed by thy might, O Lord." Dusk's edge at the wall: Muffled whimpering of the women's prayers, the men's more raucous plaints rise over the screen that separates the sexes, occasional shouts of demand or remonstrance to the Almighty, purring of doves nesting in cracks at the upper reaches of the rugged wall, rising and falling of incantations in rhythm to the quick ritual bobbing of worshipers' heads, rustle of more prayer petitions being shoved into the crevices of the honey-hued stone. This morning, I saw an Israeli soldier on the other side of the screen take off his prayer shawl and his phylacteries, fervently kiss the leather bands, wind them elaborately onto their boxes. Now, before me, a woman in her late teens, finely booted, discreetly eye-shadowed, is bowing and bowing as she ululates her prayer. Five o'clock, winter dusk. The vigorous tolling of Christian church bells is accompanied by the lilting commencement of the muezzin's voice from the minaret: *"Allahu akbar Allahu, akbar . . ."*

Click. The muffled metallic click of the tape on which the muezzin's voice is recorded slices through the church bells and the women's whimpering. A bell, and then the tape again: *"La' ilaha 'illa 'Llah, Muhammadun rasulu 'Llah. . . ."*

By the wall of the Old City—rebuilt by Suleiman the Magnificent in the sixteenth century, when the Ottomans captured the Holy Land after four hundred years of Crusader and Mameluke rule—I pass an Armenian funeral. The beaked face of the deceased rises, fierce and scornful, above the sides of the open coffin decked with flowers. A score of boy musicians in knee pants precede the coffin, playing a mournful tune on trumpets and drums. They are slowly followed by the square-hatted, white-bearded patriarchs. Three laughing Israeli soldiers saunter alongside the cortege on their way to a bus stop, their submachine guns swinging from their shoulders.

Deepening dusk in Jerusalem. The lights of the capital are going on, defining its settlements in graceful bands upon the skeletally pale Judean hills. This city desired by too many nations, generations, remains as pure and pale as a cloistered nun, pledged only to its surrounding desert. A line of John Donne's obsesses me at this hour: "A bracelet of bright hair about the bone . . ."

But over dinner an Israeli friend describes Jerusalem in a very different manner: "Don't you understand, she is like a beautiful savage woman who will always prefer to be a mistress to being a bride, who will never want to be owned by one man. Our entire land is that way."

At two o'clock on a December afternoon the Jewish mayor of Jerusalem, Teddy Kollek, takes a small group of foreign visitors

to the Christmas Eve lunch given annually by the Arab mayor of
Bethlehem, five miles to the south, in former Jordanian territory.
Kollek is stocky and ruddy-faced, and braves the sunny forty-degree
weather without an overcoat. He says, "I'm Teddy," shakes hands
and thrusts his hands back into his pockets, scrutinizing his guests
with a blunt, bemused gaze. We drive to Bethlehem through a
surf of Judean hills ablaze with the low winter sun. It is predominantly a town of Christian Arabs, ten minutes outside of the capital and the 1967 borders. I am one of five women at the lunch
held at the town hall, along with some two hundred men—men in
fezzes, city dignitaries in Western dress, Bedouins in burnouses
and traditional kaffiyeh headdress. The youthful Israeli commander
of the Administered West Bank sits at the place of honor upon
the dais, next to the mayor of Bethlehem. The commander is a
storybook Israeli general: longish and poetically uncombed hair,
rumpled khaki fatigues casually opened onto a white undershirt,
mud-caked boots. The Jordanians at my table are members of the
Bethlehem City Council who also teach at the local high school.
When I ask them what history texts are used in Administered
Territories they correct me suavely: "You are in *occupied* territory."
It is my first venture into the etiquette of these euphemisms. We
go on to banter courteously about New York subways and American television programs ("Hawaii Five-O" and "Kojak" appear in
prime time here).

The so-called Green Line that divided Palestine into Israeli
and Jordanian territories until 1967, slicing through the heart of
Jerusalem, remains omnipresent. It looms in psychological form
if not in the shape of barbed-wire fences. One constantly crosses
borders between, for instance, the exquisite and circuitous courtesy of the Arab world and the guileless forthrightness of the Israelis, whose plainspokenness often verges on the brusque.

"I bring you much love from your friend H— F—," my husband had said earlier today upon first meeting Teddy Kollek, men-
tioning the name of a New York lawyer.

"Tell him I don't need his love," Teddy snapped back, "I
need his money."

Tonight we take our two young sons to a restaurant for Christmas Eve supper. A tableful of Americans are making a fierce din
in the back of the small room. A very sober Israeli dining at a table

in front has been looking increasingly annoyed at the noisy tourists. Suddenly, he punches the table mightily with his fist and yells, "Silence!" Glasses clatter, a saucer falls to the ground. The room is pleasantly hushed for the duration of our dinner.

Everywhere in Israel, a frontier manner: This is a threatened place, identify yourself. Precisely *who* are you? My Israeli host sits me down with a drink, draws his chair up very close, looks at me straight in the eye, and says, "Well tell me all about yourself, what do you *do*?"

"I'm a writer et cetera. I write for this and that magazine et cetera."

Details are expected to be plentiful: "How often do you publish? How long does it take you to write twenty thousand words?" Same cross-examination of my husband and each of my sons. "I'm a painter." "I'm a high-school student." "I'm in school, too." We had been subjected to this sort of detailed interrogation two hours before, over tea, by a distinguished professor who had lost his eyesight in the War of Independence, and we assumed that this searing questioning was his only way of communication. Yet here it is happening again at the home of a professor with perfect eyesight.

Drinks are offered. Jerusalemites are conspicuously abstemious; nine out of ten guests have asked for juice or soda. I feel like a degenerate when I ask for a second glass of wine. The women— a few grandes dames of the capital among them—dress with stark elegance; there is a notable absence of jewelry. Three out of the seven men present bear visible wounds—one limps, another has an eye crazily askew, still another has a scar near his left ear. At ten-thirty sharp the hostess, having glanced at her watch several times in the past half hour, goes to the kitchen and prepares a tray of coffee, tea, and cake, and announces firmly that the cake is *home-made*. (A cake is some crucial symbol of hospitality and honor. Even on kibbutzim where housing units have no kitchens, most families own an eighteen-inch-wide minioven just large enough to bake a cake.) Halfway through the sweet course the hostess looks at me straightforwardly, "Well? You haven't told me how you like my cake?"

I murmur a compliment while the conversation swirls.

"When I was in the Haganah . . ."

"You must meet my daughter soon, she's coming home on leave from patrol duty in the Golan, where it is getting exceedingly uncomfortable. . . ."

"There was that time in forty-eight when I was standing patrol on the Tel Aviv road," the hostess recalls. "We were so low on ammunition we had to pass a machine gun among four of us, and barely did I get the gun in my hand when I saw the enemy and opened fire. . . ."

"I shall never get over the beauty of those first years when we were totally pure and frugal and austere," says a woman who owns one of the most elegant houses in town. "Ah, the beauty of those days when we had nothing but a little water and vegetables for weeks on end!"

There ensues talk about the wars of Israel, the faltering economy of Israel, the landscape of Israel, the corruption rackets growing in Israel, the eroding Socialist dream of Israel (and the Tel Aviv nouveaux riches grown fat on the 1967 war), the military service in Israel (a compulsory three years for men, twenty months for women). There is nostalgia for the beloved early years of independence, "when everything was much more difficult but so much less complex." At some point, there is, inevitably, talk about the atrociousness of the Israelis' driving. The nation follows only Jordan, Sri Lanka, and Syria in the rankings for the world's worst highway-death rate, even though an exorbitant fine—a thousand pounds, or a hundred and thirty dollars—is imposed on anyone who drives without a seat belt outside the Jerusalem city limits.

The suicidal perilousness of the Israelis' driving—regularly involving triple passing, insane tailgating, and speeding around blind curves—is a ritualistic item of the Israelis' conversation, like wines in France or the weather in England. It is a subject that enables them to indulge their immense appetite for self-definition, and it receives a wide spectrum of interpretations. "We're killing each other on the roads because we spend too much time in the army, where we have constant right of way. . . ." "Nothing to do with the army, it's our tendency to inner dissension, and that's what's going to destroy us, not the Arabs. . . ." "Of course, it's the profoundly anarchic streak of our character. . . ." "It's because we're so impatient. . . ." "It's because of the political anxiety; with all those borders closed we're like bees in a hive. . . ."

"Actually," a guest announces, "it all stops when there's a war on. It's quite wonderful here in wartime: Israelis drive nice and carefully, no one screams at anyone else, cars stop to let you cross the road, drivers apologize to each other, women stand at street corners handing out delicious little buns. Everything is so beautiful and quiet, it's the only time this country acts civilized."

The party disperses in an aura of great cordiality, with a new invitation extended to the foreign visitor to "come to us next Sabbath at nine-thirty." There is a frugality in this late hour socializing well suited to a city where most women work until seven, where one wishes to include those religiously observant friends who limit the traditional Sabbath meal to their immediate families, and where visible servants are viewed askance. (The one hostess I know who has a maid pass canapés is the butt of some ridicule.)

Street life of Jerusalem: not a pornographic film or bookstore in evidence. A handful of barely frequented discotheques. The little prostitution that exists is said to center in one of the larger hotels. The cracking of an off-color joke would be as poorly received here as in North Korea. After ten days of Jerusalem's propriety, I happen to go to Tel Aviv to lunch with a chic leftist journalist on Dizengoff, the city's main drag. Men are drinking hard in the middle of the day; women wear flashy clothes and eye makeup; call girls in spike heels and Dynel wigs strut on the sidewalk; bleary-eyed reporters keep coming up to my host to whisper rumors about who did what with whom; the flushed men keep drinking into the afternoon. I feel like a fourteen-year-old convent girl taken by her dissolute uncle to visit a red-light district.

"Ah, but Jerusalem is a very holy city," says the young Israeli housewife of Moroccan origin who sits next to me in the bus going back to the capital.

Should a religious Jew be allowed to listen to a woman singing on the radio? The chief rabbi of Jerusalem is about to hand down a ruling on the matter. According to the Talmud, "A woman's voice may be seductive."

And yet even the Israelis of Jerusalem can lack discretion.

The bar of the Intercontinental Hotel recently advertised dancing until 4:00 A.M., "with a spectacular view of the Mount of Olives." The Hilton coffee shop boasts of a dessert called Banana Split Masada.

A bitter political demonstration recently occurred at Hebrew University. The issue: whether the university's six hundred Arab students—who are not allowed to bear arms, since Arabs (except for members of the Druze sect) do not serve in the Israeli army—should be forced to do guard duty at the dormitories alongside Jewish students. Eight Arab students who have refused to do guard duty have been ordered to vacate their dormitory rooms. A handful of leftist Jewish youth came to support the demonstrating Arabs. A handful of right-wing Jewish youth, from the National Religious Parties, staged a counterdemonstration. The only violence occurred when two of the right-wing Jews called each other Fascists and a fistfight ensued.

I speak at the "H.U." cafeteria with a group of Israeli students who vote Moked (the Zionist Socialist party left of the ruling Labour Party) and sympathize with the Arabs. They are intent on explaining why they did not attend the demonstrations. We are at the newest of the university's three campuses—Givat Ram, an ultramodern complex whose opulence and luxuriant vegetation are faintly reminiscent of Berkeley.

"Do you realize how long it takes us to do our studying?" asks one of the students, a tall, red-bearded Sabra—native-born Israeli—of Lithuanian origin. He holds up a paperback entitled *Metaphysics Series: Space and Time.* "Do you realize that we have to do almost all of our studying in English, since Hebrew textbooks in science and humanities barely exist? I come from a working-class family, I had no English at home, and high-school English is so badly taught it barely counts. . . . This textbook, for instance; it takes me ten minutes to read one page, then this afternoon I have to translate it in my mind to write an exam about it in Hebrew."

"You think that's bad!" his companion interjects, a recent immigrant from Rumania. "I came from Europe only three years ago, and I had to learn English and Hebrew sumultaneously to study here."

"So we sympathize with our Arab brothers," the Sabra says with a gentle smile. "But demonstrate? We have so little time. We can't even start our education until we're twenty-one, when we get out of the army."

Unlike the older generation of Israelis I talk to, they are exceedingly cynical about the notion of more *aliyah*, or immigration.

"We have so many intellectuals, engineers, and doctors we don't know what to do with them," the Rumanian immigrant says. "And at this point, all we'd probably get if we begged for more aliyah is more reactionary Russian immigrants, and that might swing the country even faster to the right."

"Why expose more people to the insane danger we're facing here?" the bearded Sabra asks.

One afternoon I go to Knesset—the Israeli Parliament—to talk to Geula Cohen. She is a member of the right-wing Likud party. She is also the Knesset's most ardent supporter of Gush Emunim (literally, "the bloc of the faithful"), the paramystical, ultrachauvinist grass-roots movement that has been creating unauthorized new settlements on the West Bank and the Golan Heights—sometimes clashing with the Israeli army—with the active support of some of the ministers of the government. Starting with the Samarian settlement of Sebastia, and capitalizing on the deep-seated religious notion that the Chosen People were given the right—through Biblical revelation—to all of Palestine, Gush Emunim has illegally settled several thousand Israeli Jews in Administered Territory. Although a few of its leaders are from the right-wing religious parties, Gush Emunim has numerous adherents from the secular Israeli right, and easily draws twenty thousand people to its rallies. Gush Emunim's tactics—which had been a major source of new friction between Arabs and Jews in Israel and a great source of instability in the Israeli government—have been to create Jewish settlements in Administered Territory substantial enough to inspire strong popular sentiment against the return of any of those territories.

Geula Cohen meets me in the spacious Knesset cafeteria, which seems perennially filled with a large number of snack-eating, coffee-drinking, heatedly arguing parliamentarians. She is a large, warm-mannered woman of Yemenite origin with a Rita Hayworth mop of dark hair. She shakes my hand affectionately upon meeting me and announces in a clarion voice: "I was a member of the Stern Gang!" (The Stern Gang was the illegal terrorist organization of the 1940s responsible for the murder of many British officers. After a fortnight in Jerusalem one is used to Israelis identifying themselves with equal brusqueness: "I'm from Auschwitz." "I was a guerrilla in Uruguay.")

"For twenty years after the Stern Gang was dissolved, I was a commentator for the most right-wing paper in Israel," Geula Cohen continues. "I published a book called *Women of Violence.* It came out in 1966 in your country—Holt, Rinehart and Winston. So I've fought them with my gun, I've fought them with my pen, and now I'm fighting them with my voice! Gush Emunim is the only movement which shows there is still power left in the people of Israel. . . ."

"Tell me about the areas that Gush Emunim has recently occupied," I say.

"No, no, dear, not occupied, *liberated*," she corrects me, with a warm squeeze of my arm. "That land belongs to us. It belongs to us because the Bible says so. The very day in 1967 when we won the Six-Day War, that was the day we should have truly annexed all those territories. Our troubles were born that very day, because we did not annex them. Listen, every generation has one group that bears the torch to light the way for the people behind them. And just the way the Stern Gang was the torchbearer for the underground, so now Gush Emunim bears the only torch."

"If you annexed the territories," I ask, "how would you deal with the issue of the Palestinian people?"

"Ai, who *are* the Palestinian people? Listen. *We* are the Palestinian people, not the Arabs! In 1947, they had the opportunity to settle in this country, to halve the land with us. But only the Palestinians were opposed to accepting that land, only the Palestinians were against a Palestinian nation. Why? Because they are not a people!"

She bangs the table with one hand for emphasis, and squeezes my arm with another.

"In forty-seven I was against partition, too, but then if we

Jews are given land we'll run to take it, even a yard. That's why we accepted Israel without most of what we had the right to—without Galilee, without Bethlehem, without Negev, without Sinai—it's because the Jews *are* a people."

Throughout my stay the ubiquitous Israeli submachine gun brushes my elbow in front of the detergent shelves, swinging from the shoulder of the soldier at the supermarket; it jabs me gently from the knees of the soldier asleep next to me in the bus; I sometimes worry about it going off as the hitchhiking soldier climbs into a car in which I'm riding. At first, my lifelong hatred of all firearms made me stare with a perverse, infantile fascination at the weapons that continually accompany every soldier in this army-saturated country. For the first time in my life I wished to understand a gun, hold one, study its details. I learned that the weapons carried by the Israeli soldiers are either Czech Kalashnikov rifles, or, more frequently, Israeli-made Uzis which have a switch button alongside the trigger that can convert them from single-shot to repeat. I once asked a young Foreign Office employee why this large and ominous arm was given such omnipresent visibility—why a good pistol was not enough. "We estimate that in Vietnam only one out of ten thousand of your shots reached its destination," he answered suavely. "We're too poor for such luxury. We can afford only one accurate, all-purpose weapon."

After a fortnight or so I lost my fascination for these objects of death and defense; they became as familiar as hats, boots, gloves, as natural as the almost hourly gesture of opening my pocketbook for inspection at the entrance of every supermarket, department store, movie house, museum. The bearded young guard who sleeps every night in the lobby of our guesthouse occasionally sets his Uzi on top of a coat or newspaper I've forgotten on the coffee table there. I gingerly lift it up and slip my possession out. The gun can be theatrical. The guard is a recent immigrant from Russia, and he carries his weapon in a briefcase filled with nineteenth-century Russian classics, and whispers long, secretive telephone conversations at 7:00 A.M. that go "You will be therrrrre at four o'clock . . . you will be therrrrre alone . . . Ah, not alone . . . then I shall come at five. . . ." with a conspiratorial air worthy of Peter Sellers in a spy role. The gun is historic. It is a token of that state of siege in which the Jews here have been living for some eight decades—of that garrison mood which was abated in the golden days between the Sinai War of 1956 and the Six-Day War, but which has been vastly intensified in the past decades by the issue of Administered Territories, the concurrent resurgence of terrorist attacks, the hostility of an increasingly powerful and wealthy Arab world.

The gun, finally, can become casual. "We simply refer to it as *hamatzav*—the Situation," a young immigrant from England tells me in the supermarket this morning. "I mean all the weapons, the constant state of siege. It's horrible, but you get used to it very fast, really." She received a degree at Oxford and lives in an all-vegetarian village in Galilee—a community limited to those who can prove that they have been vegetarians for two years. (I can't for the life of me get it out of her how anyone can offer proof of two-year vegetarianism. Much in Israel is as fey as it is surreal.)

Masada is the Herodian clifftop where in A.D. 73 some Jewish zealots who had made a last stand against the Roman occupiers of Palestine slew one another in an act of mass suicide rather than fall prisoner to the Romans. The event is recorded by the Roman Jewish historian Flavius Josephus. It has become a symbol of historic Israeli valor and defiance, and, more recently, of fanatic or suprachauvinistic politics. Youth movements stage emotional pageants at Masada. All recruits to Israel's armored corps are taken there to take their oath of allegiance. Meanwhile, Gush Emunim's zealot tactics of settling the Golan are referred to by Israeli doves as "Masada politics." The Dead Sea lies just below Masada, the pale green of crushed mint in the beautiful pink stretch of the Judean desert. We decline the modern cable car that climbs Masada's 1400-foot peak, and walk the fairly arduous "snake path" behind our guide. He is a British immigrant who came to fight in the War of Independence, remained to farm, and has fought in every subsequent conflict. At sixty-one, he persuaded the army to let him drive an ammunition truck in the Yom Kippur War. Every second Israeli I meet who is over combat age tells me that he begged for permission to fight in that war. The patriotism is exuberant, harrowing, incessantly expressed. "If this country ceased to exist, there would be no more reason for me to live," a friend said to me recently over dinner. She is an artist, on the Left—a militant dove married to a university professor who is outspokenly critical of his government. "What about your children?" I asked. "There would be no reason for them to go on living either," she answered.

"This nation was founded to finally give Jews a normal society," the novelist Amoz Oz says, "to normalize the life of the Jews, to protect them from the physical danger and the constant anxiety of the ghetto. But the cycle has come full round. Since sixty-seven we have been reghettoized, both by the Arab world and by our own stiff-necked policy on the Palestinian issue and the occupied territories. The two reinforce each other in a vicious circle. The present government seems to look forward to a policy of constant confrontation, with no end in sight. . . ."

Oz has lived for the past few decades—since the age of fifteen—on a kibbutz halfway between Jerusalem and Tel Aviv. His book *My Michael* sold some forty thousand copies in Israel in the first year of its publication. (A similar per capita sale in the United States would come to over three million.) His presence is very monastic, his face very beautiful, his manner has a courteous reserve that is more Brittanic than Israeli. He writes in a tiny cubicle of Spartan neatness and frugality, seven feet square, in his two-room complex on Kibbutz Hulda.

"This garrison state may last years, decades. We are going precisely against what the Zionist fathers had wanted, we are infinitely perpetuating the state of siege conditions we came here to abolish. But perhaps this ghetto mentality is a deep habituation, a drug in our system, I don't know whether we can ever be disintoxicated. . . ."

(A French Dominican priest—an immigrant from France who became an Israeli citizen some years ago—said to me during this visit: "Isn't that the most mysterious aspect of the Jewish personality, its constant need to recreate a ghetto. . . .")

"I wake up in the morning and I don't know whether to read Flavius Josephus or the morning paper," Yoram Kaniuk says. "It's all the same, we're more surrounded than ever." Kaniuk, along with Oz, is one of Israel's two or three most distinguished novelists, and he is also a columnist for the labor newspaper *Davar*. He has a grim and witty face, framed by longish gray hair. He is always dressed in blue jeans and turtleneck, and he walks with a slight shuffle, one leg having been damaged by a grave wound incurred in the War of Independence. He has come to exemplify for me the quintessential middle-aged Sabra intellectual: pessimistic; increasingly depressed by the Situation; sublimating his anxiety by torrents of apocalyptic philosophizing; made claustrophobic by his beleaguered society but never willing to leave, even for a visit abroad, because of his deep concern for his country.

"When I read the American papers or see Americans here who talk about women's liberation or civil rights for gays, I say, 'Very refreshing but like going to Shangri-la.' Here there's nothing to talk about but resistance, death, the possibility of survival. Look, the essence of our present dilemma is this: Until forty-seven the Jews had only known drama, which is the pitting of a wrong against a right. We lived two thousand years trying to be good in a bad world that harmed us and killed us; we believed that ultimately our suffering would be justified by the triumph of our goodness, that we would be a mission unto the evil world, an example of the most moral society in history. That was drama. But, beginning in forty-seven, with the founding of the state, we began to know tragedy, which is the pitting of two rights against each other. We had a kind of right to the land and the Arabs had an equal right. That is not Hebrew history anymore, it is Greek tragedy."

By the time I make my second trip to Yad Vashem, the grim and muted memorial to the six million Jews who died in the Holocaust, I am keenly aware of the Israelis' constant need to remind themselves of their suffering. It is as if they were afraid that their children will forget it, that this forgetting might erode the very basis for Israel's statehood. After each visit to Yad Vashem I see in the face of every Jerusalemite I pass on the street the helpless eyes, the eyes beyond despair depicted in its hundreds of photographs of concentration-camp victims. Tourist sites stressing struggle and suffering are not confined to Yad Vashem. They are spread throughout the country. Overturned tanks—*objets trouvés* of the War of Independence—are artfully displayed alongside the Tel Aviv–Jerusalem road. In western Galilee, Kibbutz Lochamei Hageta'ot, founded by the survivors of the Warsaw ghetto, has a museum offering elaborate documentation of the Warsaw resistance; survivors give guided tours; postcards are available. Yad Mordechai, north of the Gaza Strip, offers the most complete display: Egyptian tanks, artillery, and life-size cast-metal figures commemorate the siege in which eighty Jewish men and boys held off six thousand fully equipped Egyptian troops for one entire week of the War of Independence. Taped explanations of the siege are available in several languages. Guidebooks urge the tourist to "visit our handsome snack bar and our impeccable rest rooms."

One afternoon Teddy Kollek drives me, at terrifying Israeli speed, through Jerusalem in his tiny white Audi. He talks about the problems of being the mayor of a "cultural mosaic." "I'm under fire from two directions," he says. "Many Israelis find me too pro-Arab, and some Arabs say I haven't done enough of this or that. But just look at the simple problem of building a hospital for the Arabs. They badly need their own hospitals, but they're not even allowed to be touched by a female nurse; after all it's still a society in which even an engaged couple doesn't have the right to see each other without the presence of the family. I recently had a meeting to plan for such a hospital, but none of the well-to-do Arabs asking for this hospital were there. I had to meet privately with a handful of their doctors. They're terrified that their slightest cooperation with Israel might be publicized. They're afraid that if they eventually decide to move to Amman or Damascus they will be discriminated against for having cooperated with an Israeli municipality. They also need a university badly. Since the Arab countries don't recognize Israeli degrees there are no more than two or three students from the West Bank at Hebrew University, but the same problem of collaboration exists there. . . . Okay, here's the most blatant example: A few years ago our municipality was accused of forcibly evicting Arab families from a site in the Old City, near the Armenian quarter. But here's the way the reasoning goes in the mind of each Arab head of household: If I accept the compensation and willingly move out I'll be called a collaborator and my cousins in Amman or Damascus will be persecuted for it; on the other hand, if I make a fuss and refuse the compensation and the Israeli police come to drag me away, my cousins and I are safe."

The car lurches to a stop in front of a brilliantly hued, ultra-modern playground in East Jerusalem. "Look at that," Teddy says. "In some cases it works out after all. In this case, a Dallas Presbyterian, in memory of a Baptist friend, gave money to me, a Jewish mayor, to build a playground for Arab children. That's the way *this* was built."

On the third Sabbath I spend in Teddy Kollek's city, I begin to look forward to the peacefulness, the utter stillness of the weekly observance. I even come to love those Sabbath laws—derided by many young Israelis—which have been imposed on the nation by the religious parties: no newspapers are published, no buses run, all airline traffic ceases inside the country, many hotel elevators are stopped, smoking is forbidden in public places, no omelettes can be ordered in whatever coffee shop remains open, because of the law that forbids the lighting of fires. After dusk one night, looking for the house of an acquaintance on a quiet residential street, I rang a wrong doorbell, and entered a scene of extreme beauty. In a high, vaulted, bleached room of the early twentieth century Arabic style common to Rehavia, a Sabbath table was exquisitely laid out on a gleaming lace tablecloth. A ceremonial gold-embroidered white satin napkin was folded over a plate at the head of the table, a silver tray held wine and delicate glasses, the matzoth were daintily laid out. An aging man—no doubt the grandfather—sat dozing over his newspaper at the far end of the room. His yarmulke was a bright Chagall blue, as was that of a middle-aged man who sat at the front of the room, turning the pages of a large dark book very gently, so as not to wake the dozing patriarch. The woman of the house and her son, with great courtesy, took me to the library to look up the address I was seeking. They walked on tiptoe, they spoke in whispers. In their paneled library, heavy with the scent of sandalwood, the telephone had been taken off the hook.

On another Sabbath afternoon I needed medicine for my younger son. I took the twelve-minute walk into East Jerusalem—or "into Jordan," as I romantically put it to myself—to find a pharmacy. Dead stillness on King David Street and the first blocks of Hativat Hatzanhanim, where the wall of the Old City juts sharply eastward. Not a car, barely a face, many blinds down, metal screens drawn over storefronts. And then, abruptly, beginning at the precise street corner, near Damascus gate, where Administered Territory begins, taxis honk, cars screech, torrents of humanity throng the streets, vendors' stalls spill their wares out upon the pavement, radios blare out the ululations of Arab melodies.

After a few weeks in Jerusalem, one is amazed by the absence of "Jewish humor." One soon realizes that such humor belongs to the Diaspora; that this defense mechanism of a persecuted community was eroded by the austere radicalism of the Socialist Zionist founders, and dissolved when the Jews became a majority in a country of their own. Almost the only jokes I have heard are based on curt, deadpan allusions to the high combat losses of the past thirty years. Examples: "The survivors of the Seventeenth Armored Division will hold their yearly reunion in the phone booth at the corner of Yafo and Ben Yehuda." "The 1967 graduating class of Haifa High School will hold their yearly reunion on the memorial plaque of the administration building."

There is one more—a gentler tale of Chasidic origin told me by almost every Israeli friend I have:

God has decided to bring a final deluge to the world to punish mankind for its evil, and sends the archangel Gabriel to announce the forthcoming disaster to the Western world's three major religious faiths. The pope asks for one final favor for his people before they face destruction: that his priests be allowed to have all the women they want. The head of the Islamic faith, in Mecca, asks that his nation be allowed a great feast of pork and wine before the final deluge. When Gabriel goes to Jerusalem to announce the news, the chief rabbi asks for no favors. He only wants Gabriel to answer one question. "How deep will the waters be?" he asks. "Sixty meters," Gabriel answers. The rabbi muses, and says: "It will be difficult living under sixty meters of water."

A high-school teacher tells me that her teenage children and her students are in the habit of saying, with grim irony: "If I grow up I'll be a doctor," "a lawyer," or "an engineer."

□

On our return from a drive along the West Bank one evening, we give a ride to a young hitchhiking soldier. Although English is compulsory in Israeli high schools he pretends to know none beyond "thank you," and does not talk to us. This has been true of the dozens of hitchhiking soldiers we have had in the car for the past weeks. They smile gently whenever one smiles at them, they emanate great warmth. My younger son once fell asleep with his head against a soldier's shoulder. Our passenger stroked his head with great sweetness, but he did not talk. The soldiers all seem extremely shy. Their manner is radically different from that of their outgoing, exuberantly loquacious parents.

"Yes, the young Israelis are very shy," Yoram Kaniuk explains, "the under-forty generation is quite introverted, quite silent. It's not because you're a foreigner. When I pick up a soldier, I can barely get a word out of him. I've lectured in about a hundred and fifty kibbutzim in the past two years, and I know how much some of these young people love me, they adore writers, from one year to the next they remember how I like a certain kind of chocolate or a fish cooked just this way, but they barely talk to me. Even though they've read every Israeli classic in print, they sit there during our meetings, every man with his gun beside him, and just stare at me with their great sad eyes. It's got to do with the trauma of too much combat duty—three wars in ten years if you include the War of Attrition—and a certain rebellion against the endless sloganeering and verbal hairsplitting of their Zionist Socialist grandparents. I know they love me but they are so silent, so grave, that sometimes when I've said all I have to say on Israeli literature their silence is so heavy that I have to walk out of the room . . . the next week they phone me to come back, and the same pantomime starts again."

Yoram and I have been driving through northwest Galilee. We walk into the dining room of Kibbutz Eilon, two miles from the Lebanese border. Yoram taps on the shoulder of a young man eating alone at a table. A head of straight, thick honey-colored hair slowly turns, the eyes rest guardedly, ever so wearily upon the visitor. There is so little expressed pleasure, so little recognition in the gaze that I assume that he is a bare acquaintance of Yoram's. But he turns out to be the very man who is such a fan of Yoram

Kaniuk's that he constantly phones to invite him to Eilon. He stands up and shuffles ahead of us to another, cleaner table, and we all sit down. He gazes tiredly at Yoram for a few minutes while an older kibbutznik, with a shaven head and a sunken face reminiscent of Buchenwald, slowly rolls a metal tray full of soup bowls past us. Our host's face is chiseled and elegant; his cap of honey hair reminds me of the soldiers in Uccello paintings. After a minute he shrugs his shoulders and the corners of his mouth curl up ever so slightly, as if to acknowledge the weight of his silence. Yoram turns his eyes briefly away from his friend's, with a reflective "Nu?" He taps the wall, which is made of handsome two-inch-wide glazed tiles. He turns to me and says "Mosaic. This is what they've evolved here for their old people to do. Brilliant. Slow, gentle work you can do until the day you die." He turns back to his friend, and by catching the word "Katyusha"—rocket—I realize that he is questioning him about last Tuesday when the region had been shelled again from the Lebanese border. The younger man's blue eyes become annoyed, he eats his cabbage soup as he does everything else, ever so wearily, and then gruffly barks back a few sentences in Hebrew. "He says they've been shelled so often here how can they remember one shelling from another," Yoram reports. "I say to him, 'The one last week,' and he says, 'How can you ever expect me to tell the one last week from the week before from the year before that?'" I stare at the young man's eyes, which have the sad aloofness of one who lives with great pain and very minimal pleasure, as with a drug addiction. Later that afternoon, when I convey this impression to Yoram he says, "These children have all been brought up in bunkers. This constant danger we've been living with *is* a drug, like any other."

A kibbutznik with a pistol in the back pocket of his blue jeans passes around pieces of apple cake. I ask the young man about his courses. His English seems fluent, but he answers monosyllabically, with no particular need to communicate. We walk out into the grounds of Eilon. The men are in khaki fatigues and almost every one of them carries an Uzi or a Kalashnikov under his arm. "If you think you're seeing guns you should go to any northern kibbutz at night," Yoram says. "Thirty men at a time standing guard, floodlights whirring around, like an armed camp." His friend goes to get his own gun and we set out for the five-minute ride to the Lebanese border. There is something defiant about the young man's silence, something of a defensive theatrical pose. We stand at the border, where a three-meter thicket of barbed wire separates us from a stretch of no-man's-land, and stare at the dry, spruce-fringed Lebanese hills beyond. The two men talk. His friend is saying, Yoram reports, that this particular valley is one of the few places in Lebanon where Arab and Christian villages coexist in peace, but who knows what will happen next week? Suddenly, with a big smile, the young man speaks to Yoram, in English, "I never promised you a rose garden." They both laugh. Then he points to the border and addresses me for the first time in two hours, saying, in good English, "This is where their haschisch ends and ours begins."

Yoram is lecturing that night at still another kibbutz—"a South American one, full of very radical Venezuelans," he says. And I take a succession of three *sheruts*, at Nahariya, Haifa, and Tel Aviv, to get back to Jerusalem. At Haifa a couple with two young children board the cab with me, chattering sweetly in Russian. The woman is slender and very erect, with prettily arranged, short red hair and a smart tweed coat. Two gold teeth gleam in an upper corner of her mouth when she smiles. She smiles often. She sits in the backseat next to two Israeli soldiers, holding a cherubic three-year-old boy in her arms. Her little daughter sits quietly on the jump seat between me and her father. We begin to talk in Russian when I offer to hold one of their bundles. They are both engineers, and came out of Russia just last year, via Vienna. They are happy although they do not get along well with the other Russians they have met in Haifa, because of a difference in attitude toward Israel. *Those* Russians, they say, are not finding enough of the kind of socialism they want—are not being totally taken care of by the government. Neither are they finding enough of the kind of capitalism they expect in Israel—consumer goods. Very sad, this criticism, Anya and Yuri comment. It is creating anti-Russian feelings in Israel which they themselves suffer from deeply.

We babble in a combination of my basic Russian and their faltering English, which Yuri occasionally spices with sonorous French. He has a kind, jolly face and loves poetry.

"I am no frustration in Israel," he says. "You like?" "I adore," I say. But I am upset by what I have seen that very day at the border kibbutzim—the tension, the children brought up in the bunkers, the men living with machine guns under their arms.

"*C'est la vie*," Yuri shrugs. "*Tout est* better than *la Russie*. You read Mandelstam, our greatest twentieth-century poet?"

We go on to discuss Esenin, Akhmatova, the death of Mayakovski. We sweep past the lights of Herzliya—the posh Tel Aviv suburb where the nouveaux riches of the post-'67 boom built their villas. "She loves you yeah yeah yeah" the Beatles croon on the *sherut* radio. Each of us accepts a stick of chewing gum from the driver. The two young soldiers are asleep in the backseat, their machine guns cradled in their arms. At 6:00 P.M., *bleep bleep bleep bleep*—a radio signal announces the hourly news. Israelis are news-obsessed. The driver turns the volume on full, the soldiers wake up and lean forward on their guns, straining to hear if anything is happening on the borders. I have been told that young couples making love in cars sit bolt upright at two minutes before the hour, turn the radio on, and resume their embraces after the news is over. Tonight, nothing special. The prime minister is leaving for the United States. A spokesman for Gush Emunim defends the group's right to settle in Administered Territory. It is the eve of Sabbath. All the way to Tel Aviv, soldiers swarm on the roadsides, looking for lifts to get home for the family meal. "Look, a lieutenant, a captain," Anya cries, pointing at Israeli soldiers on whose rumpled fatigues yellow shoulder bars denote officers' ranks. "This is wonderful! The officers hitchhiking right along with the soldiers!"

"*C'est la démocratie*," Yuri says.

Arriving late for an interview at the Knesset one day, I walk into the guardhouse at its gate like a surrendering guerrilla, passport thrust forward, arms up to facilitate the searching. That way the pretty woman soldier can begin to frisk me immediately, while the policeman writes out the identification slip that will get me through the next three or four shifts of guards.

Upon one visit an M.K. offers me a particularly striking metaphor for the origins of the situation.

"Here's how the tragedy began," she tells me. "Up until 1967

we were a marvelously strong little David. The Six-Day War transformed us into a big, sloppy Samson—Samson seeing everything
out of proportion, running after the Delilah of size and power.
Well, the Yom Kippur War was our haircut. The trouble is that
Golda and her circle never went through the proper psychological
metamorphosis away from the minority mentality. She never lost
the terrible pessimism of our people, she never seemed to fully accept the fact that we are here in a majority, in a state of our own
with an incredibly strong army and police. . . . When she went to
see the pope that time and he asked her why she wasn't nicer to
the Palestinian refugees, all she had to say was 'I was once a refugee
from Kiev.' Ever since the Golda tragedy our government has been
so afraid of falling that it has been equally afraid of acting, of
taking any leadership on the issue of the Palestinians. That's why
there's all this current retreat to mysticism, groups like Gush Emunim running around quoting the Bible and invoking God as a basis
for making new settlements that aren't even legal . . . the people
of Israel live in a trauma and are confused, they have the right to
be confused, but our leadership has no right to its confusion."

Every member of the Knesset enjoys enlarging on his colleagues' Biblical metaphors, disagreeing with them, offering new
ones. Another dovish M.K. offers an apocalyptic variation: "It
wouldn't be so bad to just have a haircut, as my colleague says.
I'm afraid that if we don't soon make a peace settlement we may
get to the next stage of the Samson story—when Samson says 'Just
give me one more burst of strength, dear God' and he pushes out
upon the pillars and brings the whole roof down upon himself and
his enemies. And if that happens, then there won't be any more
Tel Aviv or Damascus or Beirut or Cairo. There are a lot of people
here with that mentality who are saying, 'Let the roof fall on us
and our enemies together.' "

This parliamentarian has fought in seven wars, written a score
of books, and speaks perfect, often colloquial English. "The Israelis
were led on a collective LSD trip by Golda and Dayan, and after
all these years we're still—how do you say—cold-turkeying, suffering
such withdrawal symptoms that our vision is impaired. Do you
know what could happen in the next war, at the very *best*? We'll
be victorious, and we'll take more land, with more Arabs on it who
want to annihilate us."

There is also the moral argument of my friend, the writer Yoram Kaniuk.

"I am trying to say something very simple, but it drives me crazy," he says. "We come to Israel and tell the Arabs 'Move over a little.' Well, since this whole situation is based on a tragic contradiction—right against right—we can only be saved by breaking the deadlock of that tragedy, by doing the only moral thing, which is to give the Arabs of Palestine their own state, even if it's impossible to keep the peace forever. You know, it's easy enough for you American liberals to say to us, 'Give back all your territories.' How would you feel about giving back Michigan if a Chinese army was massed in Canada? I do see some of the dangers in an Arab state alongside us but . . ."

He gives a characteristic shiver, pessimistically hunched up, rubbing his hands, as if a cold wind were perpetually blowing on him.

"But for moral and political reasons I shall fight for a Palestinian state, even though it may be the end of me. Even if we only exist for a few years side by side, for once since forty-seven we shall have gotten rid of the contradictions and we shall have been moral. We'll have an Israel which for the first time will be truly beautiful, truly clean. This is my Utopia, I can go to Nablus and cross the Palestinian border there and say 'Hello, Ahmed,' and he stamps my passport and we kiss each other. Anything else will be like Masada. Except that there's a big difference. Masada was a heroic suicide and the Romans survived, whereas I fear that after Auschwitz the Jews cannot know heroes anymore—only revenge—and this time we'll slaughter first them and then ourselves, and no one will survive except for a few Arabs in the desert."

"We're treated like second-class citizens," the young Arab student cried out. "We're considered suspect, we're treated like a fifth column!"

His name was Nabeel, and he was a graduate student in biochemistry. He was sitting in the office of the vice president of Hebrew University, and a dean—the university spokesman—was sitting next to him. Nabeel perched on the edge of his seat, gesticulating dramatically as he poured out his griefs. The expression in his large, long-lashed eyes was gentle, contrasting sharply with his voice, which was loud and harsh, and his manner, which was inflammatory.

"We can be put into jail at any moment for any amount of time," Nabeel continued. "We are not Jews, therefore we are not full citizens. This is a racist state. When I want a teaching certificate, I have to wait three months for it and fill out seventeen forms, and then the school board still spies on me in my village to be sure I will behave okay. . . ."

The dean—whom the two Arabs called by his first name— stared at the ceiling or out of the window most of the time, his arms over his head, and his fingers softly tapping the wall behind him. He was a small, square man, with reddish hair and a suffering face. A photograph of Harry Truman hung on the wall, as it does in many offices in Jerusalem.

"Even at the university, we are so mistrusted that we are not allowed to take courses in physical geography," said Dakwar. He was a tall, slender Arab Israeli law student with the luminous, bearded face one sees in Fayoun portraits.

"Now come on, come on, Dakwar," the dean interrupted, with a glance to me that seemed to say "I hear this seventy times a day." "You are *not* forbidden to take courses in physical geography. It may be that there have been no Arab students registered in that course for a few years, but that does not mean there is a law against it."

"The facts are there, Benny," Dakwar said gruffly. "The facts are there. And what about your policy against our rooming with Jewish students? Many of us would like to room with Jews. There's a joke among Arabs at H.U. which goes 'If you want to be sure to be denied a place in the dormitory, insist on rooming with a Jew.'"

"That is not a policy but a preference, geared to the new immigrants," Benny said patiently. "Look, you have all these *olim* arriving from all over the world who are going to have a very hard time adapting to Jewish culture. Doesn't it make it easier on them to have a Jewish roommate?"

"That points out even more clearly that Israel is a racist state!" Nabeel exclaimed. "Do you know how much more money the government hands out to Jewish municipalities than to Arab ones? Do you know that in my hometown I can't move without being watched by my *muktar*, who's been asked by the government to watch me? But it so happens I don't like my *muktar*, I don't get along with him. . . ."

Nabeel and Dakwar were Christian Arabs from villages in northwest Galilee. I had asked them one direct question—about their position on the issue of the Arab university guards going on strike. They had offered me a half hour of sociopolitical background on the griefs of the one-half-million Arab Israelis living within the 1967 borders. Every ten minutes or so, the dean had touched one or the other of them gently on the arm and said, "You are not answering her question." But one or the other had barked back, "Come on, Benny, I desire to give the background," and continued. The dean had frequently apologized to me. "Not at all," I'd said at one point. "I am observing an excellent example of Israel democracy at work." Benny seemed very pleased by my reply. After forty-five minutes, he left us to go to an administrators' meeting. What interested me most about this interlude was the way the Arab students' bodies and voices changed the instant the dean left the room. They leaned back and relaxed, their faces flooded with luminous, gentle smiles. They spoke in very soft, courteous tones. "He's not a bad man," Nabeel said, almost in a whisper. "We give him a hard time."

We decided we wanted to talk at greater length off campus, and we met a few hours later in a small Arab restaurant in the Old City, near the Jaffa Gate. Nabeel and Dakwar had brought along a friend, a quiet, intense Druze law student, with a face both gentle and fierce and the taut body of a cat about to pounce. (The Druze—some twenty thousand strong in Israel—are members of a sect that broke off from the mainstream of Islam in the eleventh century. In addition to serving in the Israeli army, they follow various other rules of their own.) I offered them a drink, apologizing as I did so, since the young Druze might follow some Moslem precepts. They all smiled broadly, saying that their generation of Israeli Arabs was "highly secular" and regarded all religion as "highly counterrevolutionary." "We're strongly for the liberation of our women, too," the Druze said with some militance. "That is very important for the radicalization of all society." We ordered a bottle of wine.

Nabeel and Dakwar agreed jokingly that the complaints they had voiced in the dean's office were not likely to get them in trouble, because Israeli intelligence was so busy in occupied territory. They stated their determination to remain in Israel even after an independent Palestinian state was created on the West Bank. They expressed dislike for King Hussein ("We hate him more than Golda Meir") and also expressed a guarded, resentful irony toward the large Arab nations. "Of course, they used us as pawns," Dakwar said. "They forced us to suffer. They refused to improve conditions in the refugee camps for precisely one reason—to radicalize us for their own purposes. What is a better school for guerrillas than a refugee camp?" Yet these very intelligent and reasonable young men laid down certain conditions for their future which would pose severe economic and social problems for Israel. They believed that every one of the three-quarter-million Palestinians who had left his home in 1948, at the time of the Israeli independence, should either be allowed to return or be compensated for the land that he had abandoned. And they said that they would continue to fight for equal rights with Israelis, which could only be achieved when their nation had become "a secular, non-Zionist state."

One morning I sat in the living room of an Arab Christian woman whom I shall call Elena, on the outskirts of a town in Administered Territory fifteen minutes from Jerusalem. It can be difficult to find people to talk to on the West Bank. Many Israelis are reluctant to share their West Bank acquaintances with foreign visitors, and many West Bankers—like any group living under a military occupation—are justifiably cautious about expressing their views. But after several weeks I had met a generous Israeli journalist eager to share his West Bank contacts with me, and I had called Elena forthwith.

Elena is known as a "fire-eating supporter of the PLO," though some of my earlier Arab acquaintances say that is in part "a pose," that she "plays with radical rhetoric," that she is "one of the many coffee shop PLOs on the West Bank." She is a short, pretty, very courteous woman in her middle thirties. She is wearing a carefully matched pants and sweater set, and has savvily applied makeup on her swift green eyes. It is a motley crew that has ended up in her living room this morning. Two Americans beside me who are professional "peace people" employed by New York pacifist groups; a quiet, rather anti-Zionist young British television reporter doing a story on the West Bank; and a gracious Israeli pacifist in his sixties whose organization is the Israeli parallel of our War Resisters League, but—because of the strength of Israeli patriotism—claims no more than some fifteen members.

Elena's house is a fairly elegant two-story villa, with a spacious glassed-in veranda that overlooks the bleak, terraced Samarian hills. Shades of Westchester in the 1950s: there are simpering china figurines in glass-fronted cabinets, philodendrons and rubber plants, a few Picassoesque lithographs, gladiolus on the imitation-green-marble coffee table. A ceiling-high Christmas tree richly hung with ornaments still gleams in a corner of the living room. Elena frequently barks out orders at a fat, kerchiefed maid in carpet slippers who is cleaning her house, and then turns to us with a radiant smile to offer us tea, cake, fruit, nuts, sweetmeats. "You are welcome, you are welcome," she frequently repeats.

The Israeli pacifist is saying that in order for peace to come to the world all nation-states must be dissolved, and the Middle East, in particular, must become a confederation of pan-Semitic states—based on the Swiss canton system—that will comprise Iraq, Saudi Arabia, Syria, Israel, Jordan, Libya, and the new Palestinian state. "So all the rest of the world has had its turn at nationalism!" Elena cries out. "You want to deny it only to us. And what will our little canton of a state consist of?"

"The West Bank and Gaza, of course," he says.

"So," she growls, "you give us the bones and Israel keeps the meat. The PLO people I support won't accept a return to the sixty-seven borders. How can we have a Palestinian state without Galilee? We have just as much right to Galilee as the Jews. We want to return to the forty-seven borders. We want a secular state in *all* of Palestine, in which Palestinians and Jews can live in peace, if the Jews will let us!"

Several times during the morning, we hear a distant boom in the valley below and all run to the window, led by Elena, who each time cries, "There is something, there is something!" We stand and look for five minutes, searching the landscape. "I guess there is nothing," she says, seeming disappointed. "There is nothing," we repeat, and we sit down again. The town Elena lives in is one of those Arab communities where my Israeli friends have advised me "not to drive after dusk unarmed," and which has had many demonstrations. But by noon we realize that the recurring boom is caused by the blasting at a construction site. Elena asks me, in an aside, what other residents of the West Bank I plan to visit in the following days, and expresses considerable dismay at my contacts, referring to them as "corrupt," "bought out," and "quislings."

After two hours the other visitors leave, having decided to accompany the British journalist to the town of Nablus, where, it is said, there may be a demonstration. Five minutes after they leave, a woman of Elena's age, but with long schoolgirl hair and dressed in a T-shirt and blue jeans, appears. Her name is Fatima. She is a Moslem. Elena and Fatima open a bottle of wine, and from then on it is hopeless for me to try to talk about political matters, for all they wish to discuss is the condition of the Women's Movement in the United States. How do we organize? What are those consciousness-raising meetings like? Is there any new legislation? Are men's chauvinist attitudes changing? Fatima has gone back to college in her middle thirties and has written two books, which were published in Beirut, where most of the books originating in occupied territory are published. They are acquainted with the work of Betty Friedan and Germaine Greer. What else are American women writing? I tell them about Juliet Mitchell, Erica Jong. They are both perched on the edge of their seats.

"Ai ai ai ai," Fatima cries, raising her glass. "Intercourse! They write about intercourse! Ai ai ai, marvelous, like D. H. Lawrence," she exults.

"Maybe like Henry Miller!" Elena says.

"I wish we had the time to organize women's meetings," Fatima says. "But, you see, we can't revolt against everything at the same time."

"Do you know what it *means* for a woman to be a political activist in the Arab countries?" Elena asks me. "To be put out in the streets, talking to strange men, handing out leaflets, being arrested, as I was last year? My husband almost divorced me."

"I am divorced," Fatima says. "I have a child and must live with my parents. Do you know that when a man comes to call on my brothers, if he is not a friend of twenty years I must remain in the kitchen or the bedroom? I am not even allowed to go into the same room with the visitor!"

"Palestinians are in the foreground of the Women's Movement," Elena announces proudly. "The PLO has an important program to liberate women. Maybe because in those refugee camps we had to live at close quarters for the first time, men and women together."

"The kind of suppression we've been living under," Fatima says, "it will give us a lot of explosive power." She swigs her wine down defiantly. "We are like volcanoes."

"Do you realize," Elena asks, "that Fatima has been divorced three years and she has not had a relationship."

"Maybe she doesn't want to," I interject.

"*Tsatsa tsatsatsa*," Fatima chides me, "that is not the issue. The issue is that I am not allowed to."

"Can you have freedom without sexual freedom?" Elena asks. "What is it like to live in a place where you will lose all respect—then where are you?"

"I have a daughter," Fatima says proudly as we part in an effusion of handshakes and "you are welcomes." "Our daughters will be different. They will change the world."

One of the West Bank residents whom Elena disapproves of—a journalist—receives me later that afternoon in his office, in East Jerusalem. It is in an old building by Herod's Gate and is totally unheated; I secretly stuff sheaves of paper from my notebook into my shoes to keep my feet from freezing. We drink mint tea. The journalist, a handsome man in his late thirties, with a mustache and glowering eyes, is considered one of the best columnists in any of the three Arab-language newspapers published on the West Bank. When I ask him to compare life under the Jordanian and Israeli regimes, he answers: "If I have to choose between keeping silent and being watched, I prefer being watched. Under Israeli occupation, I am merely watched." Israeli censorship on the West Bank, he explains, is very strict on security and military matters, but he and his colleagues can rant all they want against the Knesset or any member of the government. He smiles slyly. "The Israelis must pay the price of their democracy."

I ask him whether he feels that there is a substantial moderate element in the PLO. He answers with characteristic circuitousness: "There is an old Arab song that says, 'You swear to me that you adore me. Yet when I look at your behavior I am astonished.' If there are moderate elements, why don't they speak up?"

We discuss the notion—widely held by Israeli centrists—that Hussein's supporters on the West Bank are the small wealthy land-owner class; the PLO support comes from the slightly larger, uni-versity-educated middle class, they say, and the allegiance of the large majority is impossible to gauge. The journalist seems to have no sympathy for either Hussein or the PLO. He prefers this rather surprising solution: The occupied territories would be administered for a substantial period by an impartial power—not the United States, perhaps some Scandinavian nation—while its inhabitants elect constitutional bodies and achieve a firm base of parliamentary self-determination.

Toward the end of our talk, the journalist slams his fist on the table and says, "The problem is, who cares about my feelings about a Palestinian? The Palestinians have become the new wandering Jews. It is not totally and entirely the fault of Israel, as the PLO claims. I am fed up with the Arab world's flowery speeches. I am fed up with the Palestinians saying what they don't want, now is the time they must say what they do want. I am fed up with being an Occupied-Territory-Jordanian-Israeli-Palestinian Arab. I'm ask-ing to be recognized as a citizen, as a father, as a man with a back-ground of my own. If the world continues to neglect us, then the really fierce Palestinians will emerge from the occupied territories, and the world will pay for it."

Bir Zeit is an Arab college of several hundred students on the West Bank, in the Samarian hills, half an hour north of Jerusalem. I am guided through it by a tall, thin, mustached young Palestinian who works there as an instructor, and who received his philosophy degree from a German university. He immediately asks me whom I have seen on the West Bank and expresses horror for those two compatriots of his—Elena and the journalist—whom I visited the previous day. "*Tsatsatsa*, please do not tell them that you know me; they are both very dangerous to our cause." We sit in the Bir Zeit cafeteria, a littered, unheated room with rickety furniture, which is as different from its counterpart at Hebrew University as a cafeteria at a community college in Harlem is from a college dining hall at Yale. I shall call the young instructor J. He gathers several students to talk with us over a cup of tea. Unlike the Arabs I saw yesterday, they immediately take great pains to stress that they support those more moderate elements in the PLO they feel have implicitly recognized an Israeli state and acknowledged readiness to dialogue with it. "It is Israel that is making it hard for the moderate elements in the PLO, by not acknowledging their overtures," J. says. The students' political ideologies seem to run a spectacular gamut—from Syrians strain of Ba'ath Socialism through anarcho-syndicalism to conservative social democracy—but they declare that they are trying to forget ideology for the time being, "for the sake of building Palestinian nationalism."

Throughout the hours we spend together, J., who is wearing a thick navy-blue sweater, keeps pulling the top of it up toward his chin, and he talks in a hoarse, barely audible voice. He often points to his throat, referring to his hoarseness, and claims that the Israeli police tortured him terribly during two months he has just spent in jail on charges of organizing political demonstrations. They had imposed the "water torture" on him, he says, which can ruin one's throat for years. I express interest in his jail stay and he delectates in telling me more about it. The Israeli military police whipped him, he whispers; they dragged him so roughly across a cobblestoned yard that he broke three ribs. They even took away his Palestinian flute and thrust it into his body. He makes a graphic gesture.

"That I don't believe," I say.

J. pulls the top of his navy-blue turtleneck over his mouth and looks at me very mournfully out of his thickly fringed eyes.

"What do you think of Hussein?" I ask.

J.'s voice rises by five tones, and becomes quite loud, losing all its hoarseness. "Hussein!" he shouts. "A bastard! I hate him more than Gush Emunim! He has suppressed the West Bankers, he has given us away, he has made us into slaves!"

□

The acting dean of Bir Zeit College, a graduate of the University of Beirut, is a stately, pale-faced man in a conservative pin-striped suit. He sits in his office, with an assistant in a chair by his side. She is a large, handsome, angry-faced woman in her thirties, dressed in slacks, who often speaks up. The dean is exceedingly courteous, but is obsessed by the idea that the majority of New York City's population is Jewish. Our one altercation occurs over this issue. There is a sizable percentage of Jews in New York, I say, but certainly not a majority.

"Oh, no, you're wrong," he says. "You'll see when you return. New York is more than fifty percent Jewish."

"It can't be, Professor. There are eleven million people in New York and only three million Jews in the whole of the United States."

The dean and his assistant are eager to disabuse the Israelis of the notion that the PLO has no support in the working class of the West Bank. Yet unlike J. or the students, the dean and his assistant are sympathetic to Hussein, and do not see support of the PLO and of Hussein as mutually exclusive. Hussein, they stress, is putting most of the West Bank exiles into positions of power in his government, partly in an attempt to create a detente with the PLO. And these two cautious, intelligent Jordanians are also careful to point out that they see the PLO as a highly transitional structure, one which might not be giving enough representation to the new culture that had developed on the West Bank.

"We West Bankers are involved in a critique of the Arab press, of sexism, of education, of family structure, of a variety of cultural attitudes," the dean's assistant says. "We want self-determination, like all other nations. The critical point is whether the PLO can make its way here as a symbol of the new Palestinian identity. If it can't, it is in trouble."

"We support the PLO because it is the only vehicle for the establishment of a Palestinian state," the dean says. "But once our state is established, the PLO can wither. It can only be seen now as the most provisional of government."

His assistant says later, as she ushers me out, "Perhaps when you come back to see us next time, we shall already have our state."

"We are a patient people," the dean says, bowing. "We shall wait."

□

I am scheduled to return in a few days to the United States. Yoram Kaniuk and I sit in the courtyard of the American Colony Hotel, a beautiful building in East Jerusalem erected a hundred years ago by a Chicago lawyer. It is one of those sunny winter days in Jerusalem when I can pretend, if I am sheltered from the wind, that spring has arrived. The walls of the American Colony's patio are high, the sun is hot, and we sit coatless beside a lemon tree which is luxuriantly in fruit—enormous lemons outlined against the sapphire blue sky. Yellow and blue, bold and dazzling complementary colors—Jerusalem colors, the hues of the golden Dome of the Rock outlined against the sky.

"I believe in God," Yoram is saying, "and I think He is anti-Semitic. Here we are, a people who followed His law like no other people ever followed God's law, a people driven by the *Halacha*, the legalism in which you do fifty little things a day to be worthy of God's love, down to every little detail—eat this way, don't eat that, the dishes here, the dishes there, in Danzig in the freezing weather we celebrated Middle Eastern rituals based on a desert climate. . . ."

A tourist desperately yearning for the sun lies in a chaise lounge a few yards away from us, white cream spread on her cheeks, a triangular object perched in the middle of her face to shield her nose. She holds a little portable radio that has been playing some old Beatles' songs.

". . . Right into the nineteenth century, observing His law like no other people," Yoram says, "and look what He does to us. If I could meet God, I would kill Him."

"*Bleep, bleep.*" A crisp, Britannic male voice: "Good afternoon, everyone. You are tuned to the two o'clock news, broadcast from Jerusalem. The Lebanese state radio reports that large-scale clashes are raging in Beirut and other regions. In Jerusalem, the defense minister reiterated this morning that Israeli government's earlier warning . . ."

"Oy," Yoram says. "Thank God you're getting out tomorrow. War next week . . . Tuesday or Wednesday at the latest."

The day before I flew back to New York I received a visit from an Israeli poet whom I shall call Chaim. He has very soulful eyes. We talked for several hours. He did not see the Situation in sociopolitical terms, like a journalist, but in that subtle, more tortured psychological perspective which poets, novelists, playwrights seem to bring to historical events. He spoke in short, interrogative, aphoristic bursts.

"The solution is never, never totally political; it must always be seen in a spiritual perspective, mustn't it? The founding of our state has not solved the Jewish question, has it? Perhaps it has complicated it. Who are we, who is a Jew? That is the question. The Israeli cabinet has twice fallen on that issue. Perhaps that is the most crucial problem for our country, more crucial than the Arab problem—to continue probing for our spiritual identity."

The poet went on to say that only once in his life had he known something that he could truly call "freedom." It was in 1948; he was twenty-five years old. He had been sent to Paris with a delegation of the Palmah, the shock troops of the Jewish underground resistance, to organize aid for the new state. Once, during that visit, he had been to a nightclub called the Taboo. "There, at the Taboo, beyond all prophets, beyond all dangers, *that* was freedom!"

He continued: "We are an obsessional people who always seem terrified of free choice. Will it always be that eternal motto for us, *Ein Brera*, no alternative? Is it part of the Jewish condition to always re-create solitude, the state of siege, the garrison state? We always return to a state of siege, don't we—we, with our profound historical pessimism? That was what the ghetto was, wasn't it? Like our country today—a Jewish place under constant menace of persecutions. Shall we always have to live with this illness?"

He banged the table angrily.

"I ask you, are we a ghetto? Or a mission?"

WOMEN'S LIVES

WE took it for granted as schoolchildren memorizing Tennyson: "Come, my friends / 'Tis not too late to seek a newer world. / Push off, and sitting well in order smite / The sounding furrows . . ." From Ulysses to Captain Ahab and the protagonists of John Updike's novels, many of our favorite literary heroes, at different stages of life, suffer spiritual crises that can assail humans blessed with all material trappings. They leave prosperous homes and loving families in search of some mysterious deeper fulfillment. And this archetypal leavetaking has been labeled in our critical literature as "a search for transcendence," "a quest for deepened identity," and even "a search for secular salvation."

But neither in literature nor in real life have these exalted phrases greeted the women who resolve their fear of mortality by undertaking similar journeys. Until recently, our unease before the restless female protagonist created one of the more severe double standards in contemporary culture. Satisfied by their husbands, baffling their psychiatrists, exhausting their lovers, heroines who leave their men for some solitary quest have evoked little comment beyond the jaded chorus of "What do women want?" Whereas heroism has ranged the world, heroinism remains fixed and static, Homer's Penelope being its ideal. With an implicit and cynical suggestion that women, unlike men, can live by bread alone, what has been known as the hero's search for transcendence has tended to be headlined in the heroine's life as a case of cabin fever.

This brings me to one of the most perplexing factors in the liberation of women: the fact that there exist two extremely different types of misogyny which result in very distinct kinds of oppression. Misogyny

One, prevalent in Teutonic cultures, is the prejudice which views womanhood as a perniciously sensual, primitive power that tends to undermine moral values and the progress of rational thought (D. H. Lawrence's hocus-pocus, Freud's view of women as a force "retarding the work of civilization"). This style of disparagement makes us clearly unfit to rule in courts of law, handle microscopes, wield surgical knives, or—God forbid—imperil the planet by roving it, unleashed, in quest of the White Whale of selfhood.

Misogyny Two is a considerably subtler form of prejudice and therefore can be even more pernicious. It idealizes woman as the purer, more spiritual gender, as the guardian of ethical standards whose function is to civilize man's cruder, more primal energies. It seems easily buttressed by a cult of the Virgin Mary, for it abounds in Roman Catholic societies and in some areas of the Slavic cultures, Dostoevski's women being a case in point. Misogyny Two mythifies us into creatures of such delicacy and refinement that we would do a disservice to society by tainting ourselves with its more arduous business. And more covertly, deviously than its Nordic variant, it has implied that our functions as a civilizing force must be accomplished within the confines of the home or at least the immediate community.

It is this attitude which has enabled men to place us on pedestals, and watch us suffer, while they continue to gloss us with such flattering tributes as diligence, sensitivity, modesty, a capacity for nurturing said to be uniquely ours. Gunnar Myrdal used to refer to women as the first Negroes of the human race; but unlike the blacks, we are the only exploited group in history ever flattered into powerlessness. Misogyny Two does not shout out, "You're not intelligent enough to be a doctor or a lawyer, you're too weak and dissolute to travel alone." It pleads, "You're too fragile and precious to survive out there! You'll get mugged on the way to the subway! Careful when you cross the street. Don't forget you have a home." And so Miso I and Miso II shout in unison (albeit for different reasons), Do not let women loose, Do not let women roam.

So the following pages are dedicated to women who have dared to defy these restraints and have set forth, like Odysseus and Ahab, on the inevitably solitary search for the White Whale of self. They celebrate women, real or imagined, who have set firsts, set standards, left home for God or for each other, who have broken the ancient patriarchal rules and avoided punishment; to early prodigies of the outré, rummy androgynes, deviant nomads, metaphysical tramps who have not feared the marks of precipitous decline; to women who have ceased to practice their millennial ploys of pleasing and seducing, who have married desert sheiks or trapezists three decades younger than they, who have said no and become voyagers.

But these pages are also dedicated to the women who have said I'll try and stay: dedicated to the George Sands of banking and commerce, the Jane Eyres of bartending, the Emma Goldmans of aviation, the doctors and lawyers who must go home to breast-feed their infants; to the professors of microbiology, philosophy, and Sanskrit who still delight in growing fastidious vegetable gardens, to the fortieth and 327th woman train conductors, to the twelve grandmothers who will succeed Sandra Day O'Connor. For to these pioneers and deviants and virtuosos of our perennial balancing act we and our progeny will owe our liberation and our loving gratitude.

On Friendship

I saw Madame Bovary at Bloomingdale's the other morning, or rather, I saw many incarnations of her. She was hovering over the cosmetic counters, clutching the current issue of *Cosmopolitan*, whose cover line read "New Styles of Coupling, Including Marriage." Her face already ablaze with numerous products advertised to make her irresistible to the opposite sex, she looked anguished, grasping, overwrought, and terribly lonely. And I thought to myself: Poor girl! With all the reams of literature that have analyzed her plight (victimized by double standards, by a materialistic middle-class glutting on the excesses of romantic fiction), notwithstanding all these diagnoses, one fact central to her tragic fate has never been stressed enough: Emma Bovary had a faithful and boring husband and a couple of boring lovers—not so intolerable a condition—but she did not have a friend in the world. And when I think of the great solitude which the original Emma and her contemporaries exude, one phrase jumps to my mind. It comes from an essay by Francis Bacon, and it is one of the finest statements ever penned about the human need for friendship: "Those who have no friends to open themselves unto are cannibals of their own hearts."

In the past years the theme of friendship has been increasingly prominent in our conversations, in our books and films, even in our college courses. It is evident that many of us are yearning with new fervor for this form of bonding. And our yearning may well be triggered by the same disillusionment with the reign of Eros that destroyed Emma Bovary. Emma was eating her heart out over a fantasy totally singular to the Western world, and only a century old at that: the notion that sexual union between men and women who believe that they are passionately in love, a union achieved by free choice and legalized by marriage, tends to offer a life of perpetual bliss and is the most desirable human bond available on earth. It is a notion bred in the same frenzied climate of the romantic epoch that caused countless young Europeans to act like the characters of their contemporary literature. Goethe's *Werther* is said to have triggered hundreds of suicides. Numerous wives glutted on the fantasies of George Sand's heroines demanded separations because their husbands were unpoetic. And Emma Bovary, palpitating from that romantic fiction which precurses our current sex manuals in its outlandish hopes for the satiation of desire, muses in the third week of her marriage: Where is "the felicity, the passion, the intoxication" that had so enchanted her in the novels of Sir Walter Scott?

This frenzied myth of love which has also led to the downfall of Cleopatra, Juliet, Romeo, and King Kong continues to breed, in our time, more garbled thinking, wretched verse, and nonsensical jingles than any emotion under the sun: "All You Need Is Love," or as we heard it in our high-school days, "Tell me you'll love me forever, if only tonight." As Flaubert put it, we are all victims of romanticism. And if we still take for granted its cult of heterosexual passion, it is in part because we have been victimized, as Emma was, by the propaganda machine of the Western novel. It was the power and the genius of the novel form to fuse medieval notions of courtly love with the idealization of marriage that marked the rise of the eighteenth-century middle class. (By "romantic love," I mean an infatuation that involves two major ingredients: a sense of being "enchanted" by another person through a complex process of illusion, and a willingness to totally surrender to that person.)

One hardly needs a course in anthropology to realize that this alliance of marriage and romantic love is restricted to a small segment of the Western world, and would seem sheer folly in most areas of this planet. The great majority of humans—be it in China,

Japan, Africa, India, the Moslem nations—still engage in marriages prearranged by their elders or dictated by pragmatic reasons of money, land, tribal politics, or (as in the Socialist countries) housing shortages. Romantically motivated marriage as the central ingredient of the good life is almost as novel in our own West. In popular practice, it remained restricted to a narrow segment of the middle class until the twentieth century. And on the level of philosophical reflection, it was always friendship between members of the same sex, never any bonding of sexual affection, which from Greek times to the Enlightenment was held to be the cornerstone of human happiness. Yet this central role allotted to friendship for two thousand years has been progressively eroded by such factors as the nineteenth-century exaltation of instinct; science's monopoly on our theories of human sentiment; the massive eroticizing of society; and that twentieth-century celebration of the body that reaches its peak in the hedonistic solitude of the multiple orgasm.

To Aristotle, friendship can be formed only by persons of virtue: a man's capacity for friendship is the most accurate measure of his virtue; it is the foundation of the state, for great legislators care even more for friendship than they care for justice. To Plato, as we know, passionate affection untainted by physical relations is the highest form of human bonding. To Cicero, *Amicitia* is more important than either money, power, honors, or health because each of these gifts can bring us only one form of pleasure, whereas the pleasures of friendship are marvelously manifold; and friendship being based on equity, the tyrant is the man least capable of forming that bond because of his need to wield power over others. Montaigne's essay, along with Bacon's, is the most famous of many that glorify our theme in the Renaissance. And like the ancients, he stresses the advantages of friendship over any kind of romantic and physical attachment. Love for members of the opposite sex, in Montaigne's words, is "an impetuous and fickle flame, undulating and variable, a fever flame subject to fits and lulls." Whereas the fire of friendship produces "a general and universal warmth, moderate and even," and will always forge bonds superior to those of marriage because marriage's continuance is "constrained and forced, depending on factors other than our free will."

A century later, even La Rouchefoucauld, that great cynic who described the imperialism of the ego better than any other precursor of Freud, finds that friendship is the only human bond in which the tyrannical cycle of our self-love seems broken, in which "we can love each other even more than love ourselves." One of the last classic essays on friendship I can think of before it loses major importance as a philosophical theme is by Ralph Waldo Emerson. And it's interesting to note that by mid-nineteenth century, the euphoric absolutes which had previously described this from of bonding are sobered by many cautious qualifications. A tinge of modern pragmatism sets in. Emerson tends to distrust any personal friendship unless it functions for the purpose of some greater universal fraternity.

Yet however differently these thinkers focused on our theme, they all seemed to reach a consensus on the qualities of free will, equity, trust, and selflessness unique to the affection of friendship. They cannot resist comparing it to physical passion, which yearns for power over the other, seeks possession and the state of being possessed, seeks to devour, breeds on excess, can easily become demonic, is closely allied to the death wish, and is often a form of agitated narcissism quite unknown to the tranquil, balanced rule of friendship. And rereading the sagas of Tristan and Iseult, Madame Bovary, and many other romantic lovers, it is evident that their passions tend to breed as much on a masturbatory excitement as on a longing for the beloved. They are in love with love, their delirium is involved with a desire for self-magnification through suffering, as evidenced in Tristan's words, "Eyes with joy are blinded. I myself am the world." There is confrontation, turmoil, aggression, in the often militaristic language of romantic love: Archers shoot fatal arrows or unerring shafts; the male enemy presses, pursues, and conquers; women surrender after being besieged by amorous assaults. Friendship on the other hand is the most pacifist species in the fauna of human emotions, the most steadfast and sharing. No wonder then that the finest pacifist ideology in the West was devised by a religious group—the Quakers—which takes as its official name the Religious Society of Friends; the same temperate principle of fraternal bonding informs that vow demanded by the Benedictine Order—the Oath of Stability—which remains central to the monastic tradition to this day. No wonder, also, that the kind of passionate friendship shared by David and Jonathan has inspired very few masterpieces of literature, which seem to thrive on tension and illicitness. For until they were relegated to the dissecting rooms of the social sciences, our literary views of friendship tended to be expressed in the essay form, a cool, reflective mode that never provided friendship with the motive, democratic, propagandistic force found by Eros in novel, verse, and stage. To this day, friendship totally resists commercial exploitation, unlike the vast businesses fueled by romantic love that support the couture, perfume, cosmetic, lingerie, and pulp-fiction trades.

One should note, however, that most views of friendship expressed in the past twenty centuries of Western thought have dealt primarily with the male's capacity for affection. And they tend to be extremely dubious about the possibility of women ever being able to enjoy genuine friendships with members of their own sex, not to speak of making friends with male peers. Montaigne expressed a prejudice that lasts well into our day when he wrote, "The ordinary capacity of women is inadequate for that communion and fellowship which is the nurse of that sacred bond, nor does their soul feel firm enough to endure the strain of so tight and durable a knot." It is shocking, though not surprising, to hear prominent social scientists paraphrase that opinion in our own decades. Konrad Lorenz and Lionel Tiger, for instance, seem to agree that women are made eminently unsociable by their genetic programming; their bondings, in Lorenz's words, "must be considered weak imitations of the exclusively male associations." Given the current vogue for sociobiology, such assertions are often supported by carefully researched papers on the courtship patterns of Siberian wolves, the prevalence of eye contact among male baboons, and the vogue for gangbanging among chimpanzees.

Our everyday language reflects the same bias: "Fraternity" is a word that goes far beyond its collegiate context and embraces notions of honor, dignity, loyalty. "Sorority" is something we might have belonged to as members of the University of Oklahoma's bowling team in the early 1950s. So I think it is high time that the same feminist perspective that has begun to correct the biases of art history and psychoanalysis should be brought to bear on this area of anthropology. We have indeed been deprived of those official, dramatically visible rites offered to men in pub, poolroom, Elks, hunting ground, or football league. And having been brought up in a very male world, I'm ashamed to say it took me a decade of feminist consciousness to realize that the few bonding associations left to twentieth century women—garden clubs, church suppers, sewing circles (often derided by men because they do not deal with power)—have been activities considerably more creative and life-enhancing than the competition of the poolroom, the machismo of beer drinking, or the bloodshed of hunting.

Among both sexes, the rites and gestures of friendship seemed to have been decimated in the Victorian era, which brought a fear of homosexuality unprecedented in the West. (They also tended to decrease as rites of heterosexual coupling became increasingly permissive). Were Dr. Johnson and James Boswell gay, those two men who constantly exhibited their affection for each other with kisses, tears, and passionate embraces? I suspect they were as rabidly straight as those tough old soldiers described by Tacitus begging for last kisses when their legion broke up. Since Freud, science has tended to dichotomize human affection along lines of deviance and normalcy, genitality and platonic love, instead of leaving it as a graduated spectrum of emotion in which love, friendship, sensuality, sexuality, can freely flow into each other as they did in the past. This may be another facet of modern culture that has cast coolness and self-consciousness on our gestures of friendship. The 1960s brought us some hope for change, both in its general emotional climate and in our scientists' tendency to relax their definitions of normalcy and deviance. For one of the most beautiful signs of that decade's renewed yearning for friendship and community, particularly evident among the groups who marched in civil-rights or anti-war demonstrations, was the sight of men clutching, kissing, embracing each other unabashedly as Dr. Johnson and James Boswell.

Which leads me to reflect on the reasons why I increasingly turn to friendship in my own life: In a world more and more polluted by the lying of politicians and the illusions of the media, I occasionally crave to hear and to tell the truth. To borrow a beautiful phrase from Friedrich Nietzsche, I look upon my friend as "the beautiful enemy" who alone is able to offer me total candor.

I look for the kind of honest friend Emma Bovary needed: one who could have told her that her lover was a jerk.

Friendship is by its very nature freer of deceit than any other relationship we can know because it is the bond least affected by striving for power, physical pleasure, or material profit, most liberated from any oath of duty or of constancy. With Eros the *body* stands naked, in friendship our *spirit* is denuded. Friendship, in this sense, is a human condition resembling what may be humanity's most beautiful and necessary lie—the promise of an afterlife. It is an almost celestial sphere in which we most resemble that society of angels offered us by Christian theology, in which we can sing the truth of our inner thoughts in relative freedom and abundance. No wonder then that the last contemporary writers whose essays on friendship may remain classics are those religiously inclined, scholars relatively unaffected by positivism or behaviorism, or by the general scientificization of human sentiment. That marvelous Christian maverick, C. S. Lewis, tells us: "Friendship is unnecessary, like philosophy, like art, like the universe itself (since God did not *need* to create). It has no survival value; rather it is one of those things that give value to survival." And the Jewish thinker Simone Weil focuses on the classic theme of free consent when she writes: "Friendship is a miracle by which a person consents to view from a certain distance, and without coming any nearer, the very being who is necessary to him as food."

The quality of free consent and self-determination inherent in friendship may be crucial to the lives of twentieth-century women beginning their vocations. But in order to return friendship to an absolutely central place in our lives, we might have to wean ourselves in part from the often submissive premises of romantic passion. I suspect that we shall always need some measure of swooning and palpitating, of ecstasy and trembling, of possessing and being possessed. But, I also suspect that we've been bullied and propagandized into many of these manifestations by the powerful modern organism that I call the sexual-industrial complex and that had an antecedent in the novels that fueled Emma Bovary's deceitful fantasies. For one of the most treacherous aspects of the cult of romantic love has been its complex idealization and exploitation of female sexuality. There is now a new school of social scientists who are militantly questioning the notion that Western romantic love is the best foundation for human bonding, and their criticism seems much inspired by feminist perspectives. The Australian anthropologist Robert Brain, for instance, calls romantic love "a lunatic relic of medieval passions . . . the handmaiden of a moribund capitalistic culture and of an equally dead Puritan ethic."

What exactly would happen if we women remodeled our concepts of ideal human bonding on the ties of friendship and abandoned the premises of enchantment and possession? Such a restructuring of our ideals of happiness could be extremely subversive. It might imply a considerable de-eroticizing of society. It could bring about a minor revolution against the sexual-industrial complex that brings billions of dollars to thousands of men by brainwashing us into the roles of temptress and seductress, and estranges us from the plain and beautiful Quaker ideal of being a sister to the world. How topsy-turvy the world would be! Dalliance, promiscuity, all those more sensationalized aspects of the Women's Movement that were once seen as revolutionary might suddenly seem most bourgeois and old-fashioned activities. If chosen in conditions of rigorous self-determination, the following values, considered up to now as reactionary, could suddenly become the most radical ones at hand: Virginity. Celibacy. Monastic communities. And that most endangered species of all, fidelity in marriage, which has lately become so exotically rare that it might soon become very fashionable, and provide the cover story for yet another publication designed to alleviate the seldom-admitted solitude of swinging singles: "Mick Jagger Is into Fidelity."

Jane Bowles Reconsidered

I CAN'T live without her, not for a minute," a heroine of Jane Bowles's *Two Serious Ladies* says about the teenage whore she has taken as a companion. "I'd go completely to pieces."

To which one of her serious friends replies: "But you *have* gone to pieces, or do I misjudge you dreadfully?"

"True enough," says Mrs. Copperfield, "I have gone to pieces, which is a thing I've wanted to do for years . . . but I have my happiness, which I guard like a wolf, and I have authority now and a certain amount of daring which, if you remember correctly, I never had before."

Women's right to self-determination-at-all-cost (even at the cost of going to pieces) has been a dominant theme of feminist literature ever since Charlotte Brontë's chaste *Jane Eyre* was attacked by male critics for "fostering Chartism and rebellion at home." And I sense that most male readers continue to resist the vision of women who are truly independent from men—spiritual, nomadic, asexual women—as powerfully as they thirst for explicit firsthand accounts of nymphomania. One of the ironies of the current porn chic is that it reinforces the ancient and comfortable male myth that we are nothing but a bunch of dependent sexpots. How much more threatening to the male psyche is the celibate freedom of Jean Rhys's heroine when she exclaims, in *After Leaving Mr. Mac-*

kenzie, "I wanted to go away with just the same feeling a boy has when he wants to run away to sea!"

Of the twentieth-century novelists who have written most poignantly about modern women's independence from men—Colette, Doris Lessing, Kate Chopin, Jean Rhys, Jane Bowles come immediately to mind—the last three are consummate artists who have each spent several decades buried in oblivion. Though totally devoid of prurience, Kate Chopin's *The Awakening* (1899), in which a woman artist turns her back on marriage and motherhood because they do not satisfy her search for happiness, was banned from public libraries for scores of years for its explicit statement of female autonomy. Jean Rhys's two finest novels, which deal with willfully single women trapped in the solitude of urban poverty, were only resurrected in 1966, after twenty years of obscurity. As for Jane Bowles, whose oeuvre also concerns a redefinition of female freedom, a considerable silence has attended her work since the production of her play *In the Summer House* thirty-five years ago, notwithstanding the critical acclaim she has received. (Alan Sillitoe called her "a landmark in contemporary literature"; and Tennessee Williams, perhaps a trifle gushingly, describes her as "the most important writer of prose fiction in modern American letters.") Since the publication of a complete anthology of her works (*My Sister's Hand in Mine*), Ms. Bowles has begun to receive the belated recognition accorded not too long ago to Ms. Chopin and to Ms. Rhys. Our struggle against the forces of misogyny has finally favored the acknowledgment of these three important writers.

If there is one common denominator in Ms. Bowles's work, it is women's relentless search for autonomy and self-knowledge, for release from all conventional structures. And a demonic, frenzied search it becomes in Ms. Bowles's hands. In "Camp Cataract," one of her finest short stories, a spinster who lives with her two sisters chooses to lapse into madness rather than remain in the suffocating shelter of her siblings' domesticity. Holed up in a summer camp in the company of a fat waitress whose greatest ambition is to own a garage, she reaches a dubious new level of freedom, when, refusing to return her adoring older sister's affection, she drives her to suicide. The denouement of *In the Summer House* deals with a woman engaged in an equally ruthless task of self-definition. The alcoholic Mrs. Constable is left bereft of her daughter, whose independence she had tried to destroy for her own selfish ends.

Two Serious Ladies, Ms. Bowles's only finished novel, documents the decline into debauchery of two very different but equally staid women. Miss Goering is a wealthy spinster who has been made solitary since childhood by her ugliness and her severe mystical inclinations, while Mrs. Copperfield is trapped in the most respectable and prosperous sort of marriage. Miss Goering eventually sells her worldly possessions to work out "her own little idea of salvation"; she moves to a small nasty house on Staten Island and commutes to the mainland to lead a new life of bar crawling in which she ends up as a high-class call girl. Mrs. Copperfield, a casual acquaintance of Miss Goering's, accompanies her restless, penny-pinching husband to Panama, and leaves him to take up with a band of loose women she has befriended in Colón. She eventually returns to New York with a teenage half-breed prostitute called Pacifica, admitting, in the same breath, that she has "gone to pieces" but has found a new brand of independence and happiness that she guards "like a wolf."

The theme of women's independence, and its frequent coefficients of solitude and potential destruction, have more often than not been limned with Lessingesque earnestness in a sociorealistic setting. So Ms. Bowles's oeuvre is all the more unique because of its Grand Guignol hilarity, its constant surprises, and a blend of realism and grotesqueness that occasionally recalls Ronald Firbank. There is a constant tension between the sturdy, supernormal physical world she describes and the gloriously unpredictable, fantastic movements of the eccentric personages who inhabit it. These superstraight middle-aged women going to pot in their ball gowns, leaving home to make war on their inhibitions in landscapes of photographic literalness, speak, move, and acquiesce to debauchery as they would in the dream freedom of a Delvaux painting. All "normal" logic of social behavior is disbanded. Total strangers decide to move into one another's houses after their first cup of tea together. Railroad conductors forbid passengers from talking to one another, under threat of calling the police. The siblings in "Camp Cataract" are so unskilled at domestic niceties that they can barely get out of their dining room without crawling under tables. And Ms. Bowles's lithe, feverish dialogue has a blend of surreal candor and deadly precision often worthy of Lewis Carroll.

"I don't like sports," says the salvation-bent Miss Goering. "More than anything else, they give me a terrific sense of sinning." "It is absolutely nonsense to move physically from one place to another," a friend of Miss Goering's remarks, "because all places are more or less alike." "You call yourself an artist," a father chides his son, "and you don't even know how to be irresponsible."

Upon reading the enthusiastic reviews that *Two Serious Ladies* received in 1943, I was startled to see some critics comparing it to *The Well of Loneliness*, perhaps the only novel in the English language to have previously touched on the issue of lesbianism. Ms. Bowles's acerbic genius for the outré does not leave it any grounds for comparison with Radclyffe Hall's sentimental tale. Neither are her heroines' precipitous declines caused by any preference for lesbianism, for they seem as asexual as they are independent and nomadic, turning to the flesh as a symbol of independence without appearing to enjoy one moment of it. Their uninhibited carousing, their voluptuous liberation from all male discipline ("You'll get indigestion . . . good God!" Mr. Copperfield keeps saying) has much more to do with a return to the permissive sexual androgyny of juvenile bonding than with any sexual preference. It is this very childlike playfulness that gives Ms. Bowles's work its fey power and its originality, and that may disconcert readers fond of predictably "female," "mature" heroines.

The little we know about Jane Bowles's life intimates that it was as feverish and singular as that of her heroines. Left lame in her teens by a riding accident, she was married at the age of twenty to the composer and author Paul Bowles. She finished *Two Serious Ladies* at the age of twenty-four, and settled in Tangiers in 1947. At the age of forty, she suffered a cerebral hemorrhage that made reading and writing impossible for her. She died in a convent hospital in Málaga, Spain, in 1973. In several interviews, Paul Bowles has disclosed some more details about the last decades of Jane Bowles's life: She drank to excess, and had a passionately dependent relationship with a Moroccan woman servant who, according to Paul Bowles, is suspected of having poisoned her food over a period of years with hazardous Moroccan drugs.

"No one among my friends speaks any more of character," Mrs. Copperfield says in *Two Serious Ladies*. "What interests us most, certainly, is finding out what we are *like*." In Jane Bowles's work, the traditional novelistic struggle between weak and strong characters ends inevitably in a draw. The rigorous pursuit of autonomy, and a rueful acceptance of its often tragic consequences, is the only heroic goal. For even the strongest are unmade by their failure to take into account "the terrible strength of the weak," and follow an equally drunken downward path to wisdom. There is a severe avoidance of all moralizing. We are left free to determine whether Bowles's heroines were better off in the shelter of their repressive marriages and inhibited spinsterhoods than in the anarchy of their libertinage. I quote from the concluding paragraph of *Two Serious Ladies*, in which Miss Goering reflects on her new-found freedom after leaving one of her one-night stands on the fringes of the underworld:

" 'Certainly I am nearer to becoming a saint, but is it possible that part of me hidden from my sight is piling sin upon sin. . . .' This latter possibility Miss Goering thought to be of considerable interest but of no great importance."

Margaret Atwood:
Nature as the Nunnery

Ｉ<small>N</small> an early passage of Samuel Richardson's *Clarissa*, the heroine laments the fact that there are no more nunneries left where she can seek refuge from an obnoxious suitor. And her complaint offers an important insight into the ultrasecular nature of the literary form that Richardson was pioneering and into the consequences of this secular vision for women.

In the widest historical sense the eighteenth-century novel reconciled the values of medieval courtly love (and its complex romanticizing of female sexuality) with the Puritan idealization of marriage. Through this curious wedlock it participated in the demise of the monastic ideal that had prevailed in Europe until the Reformation and had suggested that women's first allegiance is to a divine order, rather than to any patriarchal rule. The novel, in Georg Lukacs's words, is "the epic of a world forsaken by God." It has described a society in which the theater of salvation—most particularly for women—is centered exclusively in the home, in *Kinder* and *Küche*.

One wonders whether the novel's origins in this narrow worldly ethic, and its courtly presentation of the female as sex object, have helped to make the novel impervious to the theme of women's spiritual quests. In what classical work does the heroine seek religious or mystical fulfillment with the intensity, for instance, of Dostoevski's Alyosha, Bernanos's country priest, or even the hero of Somerset Maugham's *The Razor's Edge*? The rarity of such a search is all the more striking because it flies directly against the reality of history. The experience of mystical vision is fully as frequent among women as among men. Catherine of Siena, Juliana of Norwich, Teresa of Ávila, Joan of Arc, and in our time, Simone Weil, are only a few of the names that come to mind in a long history of women mystics.

The nature of "female" mysticism and its barely explored literary possibilities have recently received increased scrutiny from a new generation of feminist theologians. Mary Daly and Rosemary Reuther, among many others, have attacked our Judeo-Christian tradition for its exclusively masculine imagery. And they have questioned the adequacy of such figures as Father and Son for a contemporary expression—either liturgical or literary—of women's spiritual quest. Since this new awareness, the woman novelist who also happens to be a feminist and who seeks to depict a religious vision uniquely "female" in character is not likely to have her heroine discover the predominantly male cast of the Judeo-Christian pantheon at the end of her spiritual pilgrimage. She would tend to seek vision in traditions endowed with richer female symbols of ultimate reality. She could turn, for instance, to Eastern models such as the male-female pairing of yin-yang in Taoism, or the Shiva-Shakti of Tantric Buddhism; she could return to prehistoric images of the Great Mother cults; she could even resort to the heretic medieval tradition of Meister Eckhart, which refuses to attribute to the Godhead any human characteristics, sexual or other.

The interest in women's religious experience has become so intense that feminist historians are currently inclined to draw a distinction between what they call "the novel of social quest" and "the novel of spiritual quest." The theme of social quest, which has amply endowed literature from Charlotte Brontë and Colette to Margaret Drabble and Alice Munro, shows heroines acquiring a heightened sense of identity, purpose, vocation, power, by risking a temporary alienation from society. In the novel of spiritual quest, however, which until recently had mostly been tackled by Doris Lessing, the protagonist undertakes a journey whose purpose is to attain a new relation to cosmic power, to some manifestation of transcendent deity.

The centrality of woman's search for religious vision in Margaret Atwood's *Surfacing* (one of her first and finest fictions, published in 1972) makes it a novel unique in our time. And the singular prophetic power with which she depicts her heroine's quest makes it, for me, one of the most important novels of the last decades.

"Flow backwards to your sources, sacred rivers, and let the world's great rivers be reversed. . . ." The primeval, matriarchal direction of this women's chorus in Euripides is clearly the one Atwood has taken in her quest for religious symbols. The protagonist of *Surfacing* returns to the island in the Canadian wilderness where she had lived as a child to search for her father, a lone forest-dweller and student of American Indian lore who has been mysteriously missing for a month. The novel's religious imagery makes it clear that she has also returned to search for some power of communion with nature that her father failed to teach her fully, some way of contact with the primeval gods originally worshiped on her island. She is accompanied on this journey by three contemporaries, a woman and two men: decadent urban bohemians, knee-jerk Canadian nationalists who deplore the "American capitalistic pig's" encroachment on their wilderness yet have themselves lost all sense of contact with nature.

Woman as visionary, protector, and provider: Atwood reverses the Western stereotypes of male and female behavior more radically than any other novelist who comes to mind. Her nameless heroine is the one who teaches her male companions to fish, to hunt, to split logs, to build fires. Her lover is totally dependent on her, domestically in need of sex and household. She, on the contrary, is only seeking vision. The annoying social task of choosing a male to live with is "like buying a goldfish or a potted cactus plant." Identifying her body with the virgin wilderness threatened by male technology, she sees sexual contact as "a sacrilege," a profane threat to her visionary powers.

The stages of the heroine's quest are starkly archetypal: She descends, like Persephone, into the world of the dead; she tests, like Perseus, the extreme limits of human endurance; she finds her ultimate vision in self-enforced solitude. By plunging repeatedly into the glacial lake by the side of which she spent her childhood she reaches the first stage in her search and finds the body of her drowned father. Atoning for a previous abortion, she reaches the next stage of her quest through a reconciliation with nature: She decides to conceive, in accordance with primeval rites, "with the full moon over my left shoulder," a child whom she will bear by herself, "squatting on dry leaves," without the aid of male technology. "I'll lick it off and bite the cord, it will be covered with shining fur, a God, I will never teach it words."

Surfacing is laced with religious allusions. And its Christian symbols, handled with the cool, offhand, collagist style that informs much of Atwood's fiction, are relegated to the dross of our technological civilization, to "the logic that failed." The handless arm of a woman shopkeeper is "miraculous like the toes of saints or the cut off pieces of early martyrs." The Western ways of worship are "no more use now than silver bullets or the sign of the cross." "The animals die that we may live, hunters in the fall killing the deer, that is Christ also." Atwood substitutes naturalistic epiphanies of a prehistoric character: "The Indians did not own salvation but they had once known where it lived. Their signs marked the sacred places, the places where you learned the truth."

In the terrifying last stages of her transformation, the protagonist dismisses her friends to remain alone in the sacred, tribal space of her father's house and loses much of her human identity. She enters a stage of savage hallucination, prowling through the island on all fours, feeding on roots and wild berries, sleeping in relays like a bobcat, kicking earth over her droppings so as not to show her traces, waiting to see "the fur growing" on her body. At the book's end, Atwood's metaphors blur all distinction between nature and humanity. "I lean against a tree, I am a tree leaning . . . I am not an animal or a tree, I am the thing in which the trees and animals move and grow." Finally, coming out of her trance, facing her matted hair in the mirror, returning to so-called civilization, opening a can of beans to nourish her starved body, she decides to take her transformed self, and her new knowledge, back to the city. And she marks her new selfhood with a message that must remain the common denominator of all genuinely feminist works: "This above all, to refuse to be a victim . . . give up the belief that I am powerless."

The debate that *Surfacing* has provoked among contemporary scholars is almost as fascinating as the novel itself. *Signs*, for instance, the journal of women's studies, devoted an issue to an examination of Atwood's religious symbolism. The following questions were raised: Are the overwhelmingly pantheistic symbols of Atwood's vision, and her archaic identification of woman's body with the forces of nature, a legacy of oppression or a potential source of wisdom and power? Might not her symbols of female naturism, with all the biological determinism they imply, reinforce the dangerous stereotypes that assign "earthiness" and "instinctualism" to females, and "transcendence" and "abstract thought" to the male?

But Atwood tends to transcend these debates. For her naturalistic epiphanies are of a strictly mythic nature and never tend to stereotyping or separatism. The female religious vision that she presents in her remarkable book has also marked the surfacing, I believe, of a future tradition of religious quest in women's novels. From Emily Brontë's moors to Doris Lessing's forbidden velds, women authors have turned to nature not only in search of heightened perception but also as a refuge from the patriarchal order. Atwood stands in that particular tradition. "For the woman who has not fully abdicated," Simone de Beauvoir wrote, "nature represents what woman herself represents for man . . . a kingdom and a place of exile." Until all forms of sexual dominance are abolished, nature may be the only form of nunnery left to us, the only sacred shelter remaining in that desacralized world which gave rise to Clarissa's sorrows and to the great power of the novel form.

Clare Boothe Luce
and One of Her Admirers

In 1952, six years after her conversion to the Roman Catholic Church, Clare Boothe Luce edited a remarkable anthology called *Saints for Now*, published by Sheed and Ward. The company of authors she persuaded to contribute to this volume reminds one of the Luces' famous dinner parties, at which "Winnie" Churchill and "Bernie" Baruch were names as familiar as those of their household pets. Evelyn Waugh was called to perform on Empress Saint Helena, Rebecca West on Saint Augustine, Vincent Sheehan on Saint Francis of Assisi, D. B. Wyndham Lewis on Pope Pius VI, Whittaker Chambers on Saint Benedict. But a still more striking aspect of the book is Mrs. Luce's pious introduction. The saint for whom she expressed the greatest affection in these pages is that most self-effacing of all Catholic role models, Saint Thérèse of Lisieux. "Hidden from the world in a Carmelite monastery . . . Thérèse seeks to become little and helpless and hidden, like the infant Divinity."

The "little" Thérèse, paragon of anonymity, patron saint of anticelebrity, is a curious choice for a woman who achieved a greater degree of fame than almost any other woman of her generation, and whose protean career (society hostess, satirical essayist, managing editor of *Vanity Fair*, popular playwright, war correspondent, congresswoman, ambassador to Italy) was struck by a plague of firsts. First woman to give the keynote address at a majority party convention, first woman member of the House Military Affairs Committee, first woman ambassador to a major nation, first woman to receive West Point's highest honorary award. The proselytizer for Saint Thérèse de Lisieux's "little way" would eventually end up number two on the list of The American Women You Most Admire, nosed out only by Eleanor Roosevelt; and number four on the list of The Ten Women You Admire Most in the World. And she would remain on the Best-Dressed List for several years. Even her conversion to the Church—an event most advocates of anonymity would not splash out to the media—was rendered as public as every other aspect of her life: Clare Luce felt compelled to state in *McCall's* magazine her reasons for becoming a Catholic in a three-part essay that remains, to this day, one of the most popular reprints that magazine has to offer.

"A force of nature," one might call her. Her facility and competitiveness seeped awesomely and abundantly into the athletic field, the drawing room. Her skill at swimming once led her to try out for the U.S. Olympic team. She took up scuba diving at the age of fifty-four and descended more than fifty feet, publicizing *that* experience in a three-part article for *Sports Illustrated*. She wrote an introduction to a book called *Backgammon to Win*. Clare Boothe Luce was so skilled at all parlor games that one of the subtler ruses she is said to have employed during her thirty-two-year marriage to Henry Luce was to lose to him at Scrabble.

Such proficiencies have created the image of a woman made almost superhuman by ambition and talents; of a shrewd, icy climber akin to the snippy bitches she described so well for the stage in *The Women*. Her portraitists have either been star-struck by her motley gifts (Faye Henle's malicious but fawning *Au Clare de Luce*, Stephen Shadegg's official but soapy hagiography) or have depicted her as a greedy arriviste (Helen Lawrenson's wickedly biased recollections). The Clare Luce presented in Wilfrid Sheed's witty, protective book* is 80 percent angel and 20 percent Dragon Lady; but it is the first which begins to decant the private, complex human essence contained in the sacred monster Clare chose to strut out onto the public stage. It meanders along a chron-

* Wilfrid Sheed, *Clare Boothe Luce* (New York: Dutton, 1979).

ological sequence of Clare Luce's life but makes no pretense at being a biography. Yet it is more than a memoir or an essay. It is a meditation on a woman and her times; or, in the author's own words, "a meditation on what a smart girl had to do to get ahead in the twentieth century."

Sheed begins at the moment of his first meeting with Clare, on a summer evening of 1949, at the Luces' house in Ridgefield, Connecticut. He is eighteen. He has been invited for the weekend but ends up staying for the better part of the summer. Clare has recently become a friend of Wilfrid's remarkable parents, the publishers Frank Sheed and Maisie Ward, through their mutual and passionate involvement in all things Catholic. Sheed's first forty pages—ironic, winsomely self-deprecating—are the most charming in the book. They describe the awe of a young man raised in a family of frugal, high-minded Catholic intellectuals ("my parents refused to spend unnecessary money on themselves as long as there was one empty rice bowl in India") suddenly faced with the opulence of millionaire media stars. After Clare has maternally checked on the propriety of his tie, young Wilfrid nervously sits through dinner parties that are like a "Pan American board meeting." He is amazed by being able to ring for breakfast and see it delivered to his room with four newspapers, wonders why the famous beauty should be bothering with a "flotsam like me," a polio-stricken adolescent who had little to offer his hostess save his precocious expertise in her most recent acquisition—the intricacies of Catholic theology.

The famous CBL monogram emblazons every towel and matchbook in the opulent house; Clare's dressing room is exclusively hung with photographs of herself in every one of her public roles, and Wilfrid continues to brood on why this near stranger is offering him the most extravagant hospitality he's ever received. Could young Wilfrid have been the new convert's Good Cause for the summer? Could her kindness be related to the main tragedy in her life—the fact that she had lost her only child five years before? According to the author, there was more to it than that. Clare seems to have had "the unique distinction of being interested in other people's children. . . . I satisfied a deep passion in her, which was simply to instruct." One more revelation, at the summer's end, proves a secret capacity for altruism which will win Sheed's loyalty for life. Every August 22, the birthday of her late daughter, Clare was in the habit of offering someone a surprise present. It could be accepted only on the condition that it never be mentioned to anyone. And at the end of his stay with the Luces, Sheed became the happy recipient of a brand-new Oldsmobile. "That summer," the author muses, "I was part of St. Thérèse's 'little way.' "

Behind success as phenomenal as Clare Luce's there usually lurks a mom, and studying this life, one witnesses the enormous impact of Clare's mother on her daughter's career. Ann Boothe was a former chorus girl and the granddaughter of a stable owner in Hoboken, New Jersey, which was then the social equivalent of owning a trucking garage. She had been abandoned by Clare's father, an unsuccessful fiddler, shortly after her two children were born. Ann, Clare, and Clare's older brother David lived in a near tenement on Columbus Avenue in New York where Clare remembers bathing in the kitchen sink to a smell of cabbage. The stage-struck, romantic mother tried to compensate for her own failed career by dragging her delectably pretty blond daughter to numerous screen tests which never yielded anything more substantial than a brief job as understudy to one of Mary Pickford's more obscure roles.

In a striking reversal of early twentieth century values which may have fueled Clare's cyclonic invasion of male vocations, Ann Boothe continued grooming her daughter for success and stardom while giving little thought to the advancement of her son. (She'd even dress him up in Clare's clothes on occasion, saying, "See—you're a girl, you're a girl.") Fortunes rose when Clare's mother married a well-heeled doctor and was able to take her on their first trip to Europe. On the way home, through an adroit movement of deck chairs, Mom placed Clare in the vicinity of Mrs. August Belmont. It was through this introduction that Clare eventually met George Brokaw, the murderously violent millionaire drunkard with whom she was to spend six miserable years as a battered wife.

"A woman is compromised the second she's born." "Men—you can't let them out on a leash." "The first man who can think of how he's going to stay in love with his wife and another woman

is going to get that prize they're always talking about in Sweden."
Lines from Clare Luce's film version of her play *The Women*. I
was struck, during a recent viewing, by the author's prophetic
brand of man-wary feminism, and most particularly by her autobiographical stress on the unique trustworthiness of mother-daugh-
ter love. "Never confide in a girlfriend," the protagonist's mother
advises, meaning "only trust me." Clare's love for her own mother
was a particularly deep and passionate one, so much so that she
tried to fulfill Ann Boothe's high expectations by abiding at dangerous lengths with her mother's advice to "hang in there gamely
until [your husband drinks] himself to death." For Clare had a
few miscarriages during her marriage to George Brokaw. And notwithstanding his strong distaste for melodrama her most recent
biographer believes that they were probably caused by Brokaw's
physical violence.

Clare eventually received an alimony settlement of twenty-six-
thousand dollars a year for life, a handsome sum in 1929, which
made possible her swift rise as one of New York's leading literary
hostesses. Running a salon in those days was only a step away
from editing *Vanity Fair*, one of America's most fashionable magazines.

Frank Crowninshield, Clare Boothe Brokaw's boss at *Vanity
Fair*, had immediately sensed the wit, cleverness, and formidable
industriousness of this young divorcée whose formal education had
consisted of three years at mediocre high schools. He described
her as "a creature combining the various capacities of a super-
fortress, a battleship, and a tank." Other survivors of *Vanity Fair*
describe the ruses with which she'd cajole celebrities she'd never
met into dining at her Beekman Place flat in New York. ("Hello,
this is Clare Boothe of *Vanity Fair*," she'd say to Constance Bennett. "I'm having a little party for Maurice Chevalier and he suggested that I call you. . . ." A few minutes later: "Hello, Mr.
Chevalier? I'm giving a little party for Constance Bennett and she
suggested I ask *you*. . . .") It was done with such assurance and
style that John Mason Brown, George Jean Nathan, John O'Hara
were all as charmed as Wilfrid Sheed upon their first visit, and
remained friends for life. One of Clare's most important coups was

the capture of Bernard Baruch, with whom she had a long romantic interlude and who introduced her to the realpolitik of the two-party system. Still other survivors of *Vanity Fair* report on the motto that stood on Clare's office desk: DOWN TO GEHENNA OR UP TO THE THRONE. HE TRAVELS FASTEST WHO TRAVELS ALONE. The motto is worth noting because it testifies to her obsessive and wily search for stardom and success, and to the suffering and solitude that preceded and even attended her rise to power. The one masterstroke that seems relatively devoid of shrewd planning was Clare's capture of Henry Luce, the result of love at first sight on his part the minute he met the loquacious blond beauty; he proposed to her upon their third meeting. And a few months later he had divorced his wife of fifteen years.

So Clare marries tycoon. Clare goes to Broadway, becomes war correspondent, goes to Washington, to Rome. Her apologists will always attempt to cleanse for liberals the reactionary political image she had acquired. "Her cold war alarums were simply translations of Churchill into American," Sheed writes. Her vehement conservatism on foreign policy, as he sees it, was amply compensated by her liberalism on domestic issues. "She called for a soak-the-rich tax scale to the level of confiscation in order to pay for the war . . . She made uncalled-for pitches for black rights. . . ." Such an admirer inevitably stresses that Clare had been an ardent New Dealer before marrying Luce, and might even be charmed by her kittenish rationalization for changing parties ("You married Harry, you became a Republican.").

Clare Luce's eccentric streak was made evident by her quixotic ambassadorship to Rome and her subsequent retreat from public life. Her ambition to advance in diplomatic ranks was evident, but she flubbed a potential ambassadorship to Brazil by not curbing her malicious tongue ("Wayne Morse was once kicked in the head by a horse," she quipped about the senator who had led the opposition to her confirmation). In her next and most unexpected incarnation Clare retired to Arizona, where she took to painting, ceramics, and LSD. Harry followed her into Lotus Land and reported having communicated with God on the golf course. One of the more mysterious aspects of her career, left unexplained in any of her writings or interviews, was her decision to retire to Hawaii after Luce's death.

I once visited Clare Boothe Luce in Honolulu, in 1970, with press credentials from *The New Yorker*, and the spell she cast on me for an hour helps me to understand the spell she cast on many others for life. Her translucent beauty—with her golden hair, and immense pale blue eyes, she had the air of the princess in some Nordic fairy tale—was still there; she was sixty-seven. Her charm was made all the more mysterious and hypnotic by an intense attentiveness toward her visitors (feigned or genuine, how can one know?) and by a floating serenity of manner which made her look as if she'd never done a strenuous thing in her life. There were two other persons in the room. One of them—a visiting professor—said, "It's quite extraordinary, Mrs. Luce, but I don't see any black people walking around Honolulu." "Yes, isn't it marvelous, there are so few!" she answered dreamily. "Let's continue to keep them out by keeping the plane fares high, and raising the hotel room rates."

Sheed also traveled to Honolulu, in 1977, to document his book. For years he had been unsuccessfully defending Clare and finally decided to commit to print a portrait of his heroine that his numerous liberal friends had not allowed him to express in table talk. " 'She's really a nice woman,' I'd say: and a quick survey of eyebrows would tell me, he's showing off again, pretending to know something. Mae West is really chaste, oh sure." So Sheed and his wife were flown by Clare to Honolulu ("the ancient secret charity is still there," the author muses) to be her guests in her flower-filled lanai. Sheed finds her "sunny and gentle and life-size," regretting little except the loss of her looks (looking in a mirror becomes "a summit conference with the enemy"), and he also finds her valiant. She is half-blind, after nine cataract operations, but the schedule continues the Connecticut routine of thirty summers ago: work in the morning, swimming in the afternoon, good talk in the evening.

The talk returns to Saint Thérèse. Clare admits that she had once tried the saint's way of getting through the day anonymously and perfectly, but had realized at the end of twenty-four hours that sanctity was "too strenuous" for her. She has taken to the new détente with Red China surprisingly well and does not blurt out an unkindness about anyone except Otto Preminger. Later, comparing Clare to the Roman matrons of classical times, Sheed sums her up with a historically questionable generalization: "All the famous Roman women were villains. It was the price back then, too. The *virtus*, the *pietas*, the stoic virtues are all there, shining fiercely in this seventy-seven-year-old lady: love them or leave them, but they are not tacky." For "not tacky" read "high style."

None of Clare Boothe Luce's biographers have been willing, or able, to document the central episode of her drama: the link between the death of her daughter, Ann Brokaw, and her conversion to the Church. This connection is only touched on by Clare herself in the torturously self-probing series for *McCall's*, "The Real Reason." In January 1944, on the day before her death, Ann Brokaw was walking down a street in San Francisco with her mother, and when they passed a small Catholic church Ann suggested they go in. Clare followed her daughter's impulse, and they stayed through Mass.

Ann died in a freak car accident the following morning near the Stanford campus, where she was attending college. Upon hearing the news Clare rushed out of the hotel and went to the church in which she had attended Mass with her daughter the previous day. She spent a half hour there and returned to her hotel in tears.

A few hours later she asked her secretary to call for the priest of the church she had just visited. The bewildered cleric, whose answers to Clare's questions she found "too pat, too shallow," was swiftly dismissed.

It was time to run for Congress again, and Clare responded to her sorrow by burying herself in the congressional campaign more vigorously than ever. Her nascent interest in Catholicism was not resurrected until the following year, after her reelection to office, when she phoned a Jesuit with whom she'd had a long correspondence (he'd originally written her a fan letter about a laudatory article she'd written on Madame Chiang Kai-shek). The Jesuit, as terrified of Luce's searing questions as the parish priest she'd run to some months before ("I can't accept hell, father"), passed her on like a hot potato to Fulton Sheen, then famous for inspirational radio broadcasts. She was in Sheen's office the very next morning. The monsignor shrewdly offered his notoriously talkative catechumen a format in which he could speak for five minutes and she could answer for an hour. When it was time to find a confessor, she asked Sheen for "someone who has seen the rise and fall of empires." She was confirmed in Saint Patrick's Cathedral in February of 1946.

The chance visit to the church which occasioned her first impulse to conversion, her sublimation of that impulse to win a congressional campaign, her choice of the greatest media star of American Catholicism for instruction, her need to describe her conversion in three-part magazine installments—all this is vintage Luce. But this histrionic streak is balanced out by less controversial qualities: her furtive generosity, her capacity for friendship (especially with men), the androgynous charm that enabled her to build her career. For alongside her talent for vocations that were thought of as "masculine" she retained throughout her life an old-fashioned coquettishness, rather like "a southern belle," in Sheed's words, "for whom a certain flirtatiousness is simple good manners." It was this kittenish grace that enabled her to learn from the many successful men whom she seduced into her orbit, and who taught her almost everything she would need to advance her career, from the problems of farm parity to the intricacies of international relations. That "passion to instruct" which led her to befriend young strangers such as Wilfrid Sheed was part of a passion to *be* instructed which was the central obsession of her life.

How would this seductive establishment feminist fare in our own times? Have we come to expect "women achievers" to be blunt and tousled? Have we lost that gallantry that once made us cherish the deeply female qualities possessed by the perennially soignée Clare Boothe Luce? One should keep in mind that the New Left of the sixties treated its women considerably less well than the individualistic capitalists of the previous generation treated Clare. For one of the ironies of her career is that her very femininity enabled her to move into men's worlds that most women were scared even to touch, and to make clearings for other women in the future.

Henry Luce called his wife Mike. He had a passion for reading aloud in the evening, and on nights when they were alone he read aloud to Clare. Even as ambassador to Rome, the Dynamo might have listened, bent over her needlework.

Chanel: What Is "Style"?

REMEMBERING Coco Chanel as I saw her in the 1950s, I associate her with blackness, often chastened by a trim of white: the large number of black dresses brightened with a white starched collar or ruffle; the flat grosgrain bows and white gardenias posed on her models' heads; the black tips of the cream sling pumps which became one of her signatures; the black lacquered chinoiseries and black coromandel screens in her living room; the often-told anecdote that upon the death of one of her lovers she had had her bedroom totally redesigned in black, down to sheets and pillowcases (a few days later she had it redone in pink). Even the downstairs boutique of her shop in the rue Cambon, suffused with the dark-flower scent of N° 5, had a smokiness about it that contrasted greatly with the shrill cream-and-gilt decors of Balmain and Dior. And there was the blackness of Chanel's hair, the coal-black glint of her very mean eyes.

She once graced me with her sarcasm, the only time I was at her dinner table. It was in 1955, when I was spending a misguided year writing fashion copy for the French magazine *Elle*. (The ultra-Spartan nature of her dinners was considered to be very chic. That night it was codfish and boiled potatoes, the menu most admired for its daring bleakness.) Someone asked me what it was like to be a young American journalist living in Paris. "She's not a journalist," Coco snapped. "She's just a poor *child*."

□

"She has the head of a little black swan," Cocteau once said. "And the heart of a little black bull," Colette added. Any one of us who ran minion's errands to the rue Cambon in those years could witness the autocracy and vitriol which she could even pour into the making of her collections: Mademoiselle Chanel—then in her seventies—attacking the fitting of each dress with her bare hands, clawing and pawing at the fabric; jamming in pins, tearing out seams, cussing at the imperfections, pitilessly forcing her team to work eight hours without a break, driving seamstresses and doe-eyed models into fits of tears. With the same tenacity this consummate snob fabricated her own very self, tore at the fabric of her life to cut out whatever traces of her past did not serve her.

To some of her friends Gabrielle Chanel used to say that her nickname—Coco—was given her by her father when she was a tiny child. To others, that she earned the name because she went horseback riding at early dawn, rooster-crowing time (*cocorico*). In fact, it was bestowed on her, at age nineteen, in a low-class music hall by a group of raucous military officers who used to hear her sing the following song about a Parisian courtesan who has lost her dog.

J'ai perdu mon pauv' Coco, mon chien que j'adore, dans le Trocadero. . . . Qui qu'a vu, qui qu'a vu Coco? Eh, Coco!

She said that she had been brought up by two aunts who raised purebred horses, that her father was a well-to-do country squire who made a fortune in the United States. In truth, her father was a ne'er-do-well drunk of peasant origins from the Cévennes, an itinerant vendor of shoelaces and handkerchiefs who abandoned her to a convent orphanage upon her mother's death. The essence of Chanel's style, that taste for unadorned essentials which revolutionized the century's fashions, can be traced to two well-hidden secrets of the designer's youth: her life as a convent girl and her life as a cocotte.

Chanel learned to sew exquisitely in that convent, an austere thirteenth-century edifice in the town of Moulins. Between the ages of twelve and eighteen she lived in a world of long white corridors and whitewashed walls, staring at the starched white wimples on the nuns' black gowns, helping them to stack away tall piles of white ruffwings, wearing the black, belted smocks and box-pleated skirts of orphans' uniforms . . . the very germs of Chanel's poor little girl look, of her exquisite "Less is more" asceticism.

As for the other source of Chanel's revolutionary style—abolition of corsets and waistlines, feminizing of masculine fashion into the lean-hipped gamin look—they are readily found in the chintzy treatment Chanel received from her first lover. Etienne Balsan, a wealthy but stingy horse freak, was one of the music hall admirers who used to shout "Coco!" for encores in the garrison town where she worked daytimes as a seamstress after leaving the convent. He set her up as a second-string girlfriend in a minor guest room of his château, on the side of the stables. The humiliation of being a mistress, at the age of twenty-two, without being the mistress of a house incited Chanel to avoid all possible associations of sluttishness.

Coco did not want to be a cocotte. She cultivated a tomboyish *jeune fille* look, dressing in strict tailor-made suits and a boater, inventing costume parties so she could attend them in her lover's clothes. This transvestitism became the backbone of her style. Throughout the next forty years she would raid her men's closets and bureau drawers for inspiration, copying the slim straightness of their polo shirts, the gilt buttons of their sailing blazers, the cavalry braid and sleeve edging of their military uniforms. For along with its convent austerity, there was at the heart of Chanel's fashion that androgynousness which conferred to her clothes their notorious timelessness, the staid unchangeability of "menswear."

To assess the importance of Chanel's impact on our present view of dress, one need do no more than leaf through any illustrated history of early twentieth-century costume: long skirts, tight skirts, corseted waistlines, those cumbersome hats on which reposed so many an innocent fowl. All such restrictive trappings have been signs of female servitude as blatant as the deformed, bandaged feet of the women of Old China. The stylish women of Edwardian times—that very decade in which Chanel began to effect her revolution—were the last generation to brutalize their bodies and endanger their health by submitting to such tyrannies. Stumbling on the tasseled hems of their hobble skirts, choked with pearls, stabbed with osprey feathers, unable to exit unaided from carriages, known to faint when they saw a woman in the same dress across the room, their finery chiefly served to prove the wealth of the men who supported them.

For until Chanel, vestments would still center on a celebration of abundance, on a display of rigorously defined social status, and on a vision of woman as man's chattel. Compensating for the sober anonymity that the new work ethic had imposed on menswear, the sumptuously restrictive costumes of *la belle époque* glorified the idleness of a female elite who did not work either within or outside their homes. No wonder that the symbolic gesture of the feminist movement, in the first decade of our century, was to substitute bloomers for corsets and restrictive skirts. No wonder that the collective psyche of this newly suffraged womanhood was given its first stylistic expression by a female of equally revolutionary vision.

Chanel shocking crowds by wearing her lover's tweed coat to the races, surrounded by belles still stumbling on their silks and brocades, or riding to the hounds wearing all her pearls under her pullover ("Jewels are only elegant," she once said, "if one pretends they're junk"). Chanel putting an end to the ostentatious role of vestments by declaring that true *chic* is to never take clothes *seriously*, that an evening dress must be worn as casually as a tennis skirt. Chanel effecting the ultimate democratization of fashion by cutting the newest, most proletarian of fabrics, jersey, into vestments inspired by the jackets of Normandy sailors.

So to Chanel, who did more than anyone else to eliminate this frippery of bondage, twentieth-century women owe considerable gratitude. Yet a feminist view of Chanel involves considerable contradictions. Yes, she enabled us to breathe and move more freely, she shortened skirts to abolish the obscene thrill which the sight of our bared ankles used to offer men, she lived a dazzling series of "open relationships," she claimed independence, saying she never wanted to weigh on any man "more heavily than a bird."

Yet her styles of living, her business decisions, were extraordinarily dependent upon her lovers. Her existence was one long succession of heartbreaks at the hands of the conservative playboys whom she wished to marry, and who left her for death, for other women, or for God. The one who kept leaving her for God, the poet Pierre Reverdy, spent years shuttling between Chanel's bed and the austere Abbey of Solesmes. But what an empty-headed collection of jocks most of the rest were.

After Balsan (who read only horse-racing weeklies, and enjoyed playing tricks such as apple-pie beds and shaving-cream assaults on his weekend guests) there was the British polo star and diplomat Arthur Capel, "Boy" for short. It was Boy who installed Chanel, in 1914, in a shop in Deauville where she first ventured beyond hat design, and sold the loose sailor jackets of machine-made Rodier jersey which launched her fame. Tortured by his own striving for respectability (he was a bastard with a drop of Jewish blood), Boy eventually married a peer's daughter while managing to retain Coco as his mistress. He was killed in a car crash in the tenth year of their considerably passionate love affair.

After she had founded her rue Cambon empire with the help of Boy's money, Chanel's liaison with Grand Duke Dmitri of Russia ushered in a "Slavic" period. In 1921 she presented to an astonished Paris a collection of belted muzhik blouses with discreetly embroidered bands on cuffs and collars. Soon afterward the grand duke married a rich American heiress. He might have done better to wait for Chanel. Nº 5 alone—the first synthetic perfume in history, usable in much smaller amounts than earlier floral scents because of its greater tenacity—netted her fifteen million dollars in the next few decades. And by the 1930s Chanel was the mogul of a four-business conglomerate—couture, textiles, jewelry, perfume—that employed some 3,500 workers.

From 1925 to 1930 it was the duke of Westminster. England's wealthiest peer was once described by his schoolmate Winston Churchill as a man "deeply versed in all forms of animal sport." Four times married, this tall, blond frolicker was also known for his love of pranks, but his were amiably expensive—hiding diamonds under his mistresses' pillows, sending Chanel a walnut-sized emerald in the bottom of a bin of fresh vegetables. He was nicknamed Bend'or, after his grandfather's prizewinning horse.

Pursuing her man throughout Europe, as usual, with the élan of the perpetual arriviste, Chanel desperately tried to have a child by Westminster at the age of forty-six, dragging herself through gynecologists' offices and a series of "humiliating acrobatics" recommended by midwives to achieve pregnancy. Never did Chanel collections show so many English-country-house-style sweaters as in that decade, so many tweed suits "to wear to the races," so many sport coats "resolutely masculine in cut," all copied from those hanging in Westminster's closet. But like Boy, Bend'or left her for a peer's daughter. And with the thrift of a French housewife making pot-au-feu out of last week's table scraps, Chanel copied in fake stones the treasures he had left her, thus pioneering the famous costume jewelry she sold.

Great love N° 5 was a chauvinist right-wing cartoonist and journalist called Iribe. He depicted Chanel's face on his drawings of "Marianne," symbol of the French nation, threatened by radical, subversive forces (Daladier, etc.) and died on the tennis court. She had loved him truly, and went into a flurry of designing patriotic blue, red, and white ball gowns. That was in 1939, the last year decent French people danced.

What light, youthful nicknames her lovers had, epithets that give away the trivialness she sought in men: Boy, Bend'or. And then, upon the Occupation, the tall German spy called Spatz—sparrow. He adored to dance, and was thirteen years her junior. They lived on an upper floor at rue Cambon, where the combined threats of war and of Schiaparelli's triumphant ascendance over Paris fashions had forced Chanel to close her *salon de couture*, but where bottles of N° 5 continued to be sold to German soldiers.

In the postwar years Chanel had much evidence to destroy, much silence to buy, from the records of her early orphanage to the memories of the SS men who had been her intimate friends: the story of her life. Her carefully stitched myths worked well enough, for a while. Her comeback in 1954 was barely tinged by political rancor (the French are not long on political memory) and within a year she made a spectacular fashion success. "Those men who can't sew," she called Dior and other postwar male couturiers, who tried to imprison us again with waist pinchers, wired bras, heavily lined skirts, the frippery of lace and ribbons. "They're good for nouveaux riches whores," she jibed to a fashion reporter in the fifties. "Let them turn a few hundred women into overstuffed armchairs, and I'll dress them decently by the tens of thousands."

It was Chanel's simplicity and freedom that prevailed and became historic. For throughout the centuries and well into the first decades of our own, sumptuary laws had restricted each class of society to a rigorously distinct costume, punishing with high fines the burgher who attempted social mobility by wearing the dress of noblemen, censuring the aristocrat who mystified his station by wearing workmen's clothes. Part of Chanel's genius was to give functional expression to democratic ideals by extolling the sparser, pared-down dress codes of the working classes, and to capitalize on the mass production methods of the Industrial Revolution by bringing such previously humble materials as jersey into the full repertory of couture. If there is one phrase that sums up the ultimate elegance of our time, it is her motto "One must suppress, suppress." It reminds one of the equally prescient credo spoken by the greatest fashion arbiter on these shores, Diana Vreeland: "Elegance is refusal."

Compared to such revolutions, any attempts at novelty in the succeeding decades—Dior's New Look, the sixties miniskirt, Saint Laurent's yearly caprices—seem like abortive palace coups. Only in Chanel can one find the true seeds of contemporary style: the cult of health and open-air comfort she pioneered and that presently overrides all modish dictates; the vogue for antifashion, such as the worldwide fad for the ubiquitous American blue jean, which began in her incessant raids on male vestments, including farm laborers' and bellhops' (Patou used to complain that Chanel's slouching, flat-chested mannequins looked like starved Western Union messengers). And that stupendous eclecticism—incipient in Chanel's stress on the wearer's casual *attitude* toward fashion rather than fashion's *content*—that presently enables us to go out for dinner wearing most anything under the moon: embroidered shepherds' jackets from Sri Lanka, fastidious satin copies of workmen's overalls, football-shouldered duds of forties' vintage acquired in thrift shops.

There is yet another aspect of Chanel's character—her bisexuality—which may have helped to give her work its prophetic character, and to precurse the "unisex" trends of our own time. Her thirty years of erotic friendship with Misia Sert was as casually flaunted as her liaisons with Boy, Bend'or, or any of her other male lovers. And along with her abrasive, autocratic character, androgyny is the most striking trait to emanate from the thousands of photographs that remain of her: Coco in an oversize man's vest, her sharp hips thrust forward flapper style, her arm nonchalantly slung over the shoulder of a woman friend. Chanel in a sailor's vest, slouching in her roguish hands-in-pocket stance, a Gauloise hanging from a corner of her mouth, her mean and handsome little face thrust forward like a young bull about to charge. And throughout all images of her, that mordant, boyish charm which Chanel retained into her eighties and to which the French give the untranslatable epithet of "chien."

Yet, however liberating the vision of Chanel's artistry, one must face the reality of her profoundly Fascist views. "France should have a monarchy again," she was heard to say in the 1950s. "The Jews and Socialists in the thirties, then that brigand de Gaulle allowing Communists and Jews into his government again. . . ." It is clear that Chanel's espousal of Nazism was not a moral *crime passionnel* inspired by her lust for a German body, but the result of ingrained political beliefs. One has only to look at Chanel's earlier lovers: Westminster's arguments for a negotiated peace with the Nazis made his childhood friend Winston Churchill see red. Iribe was director of the Fascist-leaning paper *Le Témoin*, which she alone financed, and which indulged in such slogans as "Blum's Judeo-Masonic Mafia."

Chanel was clearly not one of those numerous *honnêtes gens* who collaborated mildly to save their skins, and whom it is hard for Americans to judge because they have never confronted the moral problems posed by a foreign occupation. On the contrary, Chanel was clearly part of that right-wing industrial bourgeoisie—she entered it on the profitable fumes of N° 5—which was rendered so hysterical by the rise of the labor unions and the "Red Threat" that it took as its motto "Rather Hitler than Blum." For one as miraculously endowed as Chanel was with the French qualities of rationalism, self-survival, tenacity, material greed, and *méfiance*, it must have taken firm conviction in Fascism as the wave of the future to become a hard-core collaborationist. But these odious beliefs do not minimize her gifts any more than Baudelaire's shocking sexism and proto-Fascism diminish his genius.

☐

Whenever I recollect Chanel, I have a strange flashback to her salon at 31, rue Cambon. I recall that final entrance of the bridal gown which, for many decades, had been the last item on any Paris designer's showing. Costing several thousand dollars, in it came amid torrents of applause. It was marvelously chaste, high-necked, as virginal as first communion vestments, reminiscent of that asexual poverty of her convent childhood which it had been her life's aim to destroy, and her genius to recapture.

Mother Love:
Madame de Sévigné

PARIS, March 3, 1671. One of the most admired noblewomen in France stands by a window on the top floor of her mansion, contemplating suicide because her recently married daughter has driven away to join her husband in a distant corner of Provence. The Marquise de Sévigné's life is devoid of any other trace of sorrow that could lead her to such action. Forty-three years old, renowned for her beauty and her wit, she has been courted by, and has refused, some of the greatest peers in the realm. The Duke de La Rochefoucauld, the Countess de La Fayette, the Cardinal de Retz cherish her company above that of any other friend. Her intelligence and charm are so famed throughout the kingdom that the abbess of a convent has recently refused Mme de Sévigné's visit as a form of self-punishment. But for the next thirty years none of these graces will assuage the central torment of Mme de Sévigné's existence—her recurrent separations from her life's "most adored object," her oldest child, the Countess Françoise-Marguerite de Grignan. She will only be able to sublimate her sorrow by a torrent of correspondence, which will eventually become one of the treasures of French literature.

There was certainly an obsessional streak, perhaps a neurotic one, in this maternal love; and it might be readily traced to the author's childhood losses. By the time she was ten years old, Marie de Rabutin-Chantal, the future Marquise de Sévigné, had mourned the death of her father, her mother, and her maternal grandparents, who adopted her after her parents' death. She was educated by a regiment of doting, bookish uncles whose affection, however genuine, could not replace her need for some form of maternal bond. Her brief marriage did not allay her solitude. Henri de Sévigné was a dissolute roué whose liaison with Ninon de Lenclos gave him little time for his wife; he met a scandal-ridden death dueling over the favors of a considerably less elegant whore called La Belle Lolo. Mme de Sévigné's infatuation with her daughter, all the more pathological because it was so faintly reciprocated, was intensified by the humiliation she suffered from her husband in her only heterosexual relationship.

She was widowed at the age of twenty-five and left with two small children, a great name, and little other means of survival beyond an education which was unique among her peers. At a time when the schooling of women was so minimal that some of Louis XIV's cousins could barely write a letter without the help of a scribe, Mme de Sévigné was well-versed in Latin and Italian, able to quote Tasso, Saint Augustine, Montaigne as effortlessly as she could cite a line from a current hit of Corneille's. Until her daughter came of age as a great beauty (at which point she began to refer to her as "the prettiest girl in France"), there's no evidence that she had any unusual affection for her children. She was too busy capitalizing on her intellectual gifts to establish a central position in Paris society. "Your brilliant mind lights up and embellishes your countenance," Mme de La Fayette once wrote her, "to the point that there is no one in all the world as charming as you are when you are in an animated discussion . . . your presence enhances every occasion, and every occasion enhances your beauty."

A thorough reading of the Sévigné letters, however, discloses a personality far more complex and contradictory than the salon charmer limned in that portrait. They reveal a woman whose need for solitude creates a constant tension with her love for society; a devout Catholic whose Jansenist brand of faith tends to austere pessimism; a bonne vivante whose conversation leans toward the bold and racy; a flirtatious coquette addicted to spa cures and dietary fads to maintain her figure; a flirtatious tease who enjoys men's attention and yet is reported to be sexually frigid. The Sévigné letters disclose, in sum, an ardent temperament which was made all the more complex by its strong distaste for heterosexual lust, and found its only outlet in a morbidly excessive maternal love.

But Mme de Sévigné had two offspring, two love objects to choose from. And psychoanalytic literature about possessive, sexually repressed mothers has led us to expect that such women choose sons rather than daughters as the center of their fixations. Moreover the extravagantly affectionate, devoted, ever-present Charles de Sévigné, unlike his aloof, secretive sister, looked to his mother as his closest confidante. So much so that we see him running home to mom to tell her about his moments of sexual impotence, sharing the news in a tone of bantering candor which makes contemporary family relations seem rabidly repressed. "My son came yesterday from the other end of Paris to tell me about that accident that befell him," Mme de Sévigné writes her daughter; "a favorable occasion had presented itself and yet . . . 'He could not get his dada up at Lerida.'" (The quote comes from a scabrous limerick concerning one of the Prince de Condé's sexual fiascos.) "The cavalier made his exit, in disarray . . . he could not wait to tell me about his mortification. We laughed uproariously. . . . He laid the blame on me, telling me that it was from me that he had inherited his frigidity."

Some critics have offered a pretentious Proustian theory ("One loves only what one cannot wholly possess") to explain why Mme de Sévigné favored her elusive, unresponsive daughter to her effusively tender, communicative son. The arrogance and hauteur of the daughter led one contemporary to comment that "she will make as many enemies as her mother had made friends." Although her beauty surpassed her mother's, her aloof, overbearing manner kept her from finding a suitable husband until she was twenty-three—a perilously belated age in that century. "At long last," Mme de Sévigné wrote a cousin, "the prettiest girl in France is marrying . . . one of the most distinguished men in the kingdom: he is Monsieur de Grignan." He was indeed the only scion of one of Provence's noblest families, a gentle, loyal man whose previous two marriages had yielded no male offspring. What Mme de

Sévigné could not have predicted is that soon after the wedding, Louis XIV appointed her son-in-law to serve as governor-general of his native province. The Grignans were forced to leave Paris for their ancestral estate many hundreds of miles from the capital, where they would ardently strive to continue the family name.

Mme de Sévigné began her writing career at the age of forty-three, as a way of surviving the pain of this severance. During the next three decades the many hundreds of letters she wrote to her daughter were postmarked from her Paris mansion (now the Musée Carnavalet) where she indulged her taste for society; from the nearby Abbey of Livry, residence of one of the worldly clerical uncles who had educated her, where she spent much time in meditation; and from the castle of Les Rochers, in Brittany, inherited from her husband, whose lands and produce were her principal source of revenue, and where she spent a considerable amount of time to satisfy her need for rural solitude.

"Still weeping, still swooning with grief . . . I look in vain for my dear daughter," so begins the immortal correspondence when Mme de Grignan leaves for Provence after spending her first two married years under her mother's roof. "Oh, what a cruel separation it is! . . . I spent five hours . . . sobbing incessantly . . . I went to Mme de La Fayette's, who only intensified my grief by sharing in it."

Par for the course in this most lachrymose of centuries, when the expression of excessive sentiment was elevated to a moral virtue. But this particular mother's correspondence has a tone of erotic possessiveness unusual in any epoch. One is struck by the keen sense of rivalry Mme de Sévigné expresses toward her son-in-law, her desperate attempts to prove that she, the mother, should remain the center of her daughter's affections. "Why hold back the truth? It is by me that you are truly loved." We immediately sense her voyeuristic interference in her daughter's sexual life; her morbid fear of the countess's often ill-fated pregnancies (attributed by later historians to a syphilitic condition inherited from the Grignan side); her constant pleas for a curbing of the couple's marital lust. "I implore you, my darling, do not be overconfident about sleeping in separate beds. The temptation is still there. Have someone else sleep in the same room."

The sixth of the month, date of the countess's strikingly punctual menstrual cycles, is referred to time and again as a way of inquiring whether she is "sick" or "well." The word "sick" is reversed from its habitual association to denote pregnancy, "well" denotes menstruation. "The youth, the beauty, the health . . . the very life of the lady," she writes the count, "will be destroyed by frequent relapses of the malady you bring on her." "How distressed I am at this misfortune!" she exclaims upon learning of Mme Grignan's third pregnancy. In view of the Grignans' obsession to give birth to a son who might save from extinction one of France's most illustrious names (only one of their sons survived infancy), the words "misfortune" and "malady" are curiously unfeeling. "Do you think I gave her to you to kill her, to destroy her health, her youth, her beauty. . . . I will take your wife away from you."

This last threat is not a raillery. Every two or three years, during the countess's stays with her mother in Paris, Mme de Sévigné's nagging and snooping became so possessive that relations between the two women could be strained to breaking point—so strained they sometimes communicated by letter from room to room, across closed doors, rather than face another violent confrontation. In this eccentric erotic triangle, it is the courteous count who emerges as the only hero, dealing ever patiently with a great spirit and a great writer who was also a nightmare of a mother-in-law.

Most of the Countess de Grignan's correspondence was destroyed by her descendants, and not enough letters of hers survive to give us any objective view of her character, or of her responses to her mother's prehensile love. She only echoes back to us through her mother's pen, and the extent of her coldness is thus subject to a spectrum of interpretations. The many malaises that plagued her between pregnancies could be attributed in part to a deep sense of guilt—guilt at not returning her mother's love fully enough, guilt at retaining her husband as a natural center of her affection. The intensity of maternal love, in turn, created considerable spiritual problems for Mme de Sévigné. From the beginning of their separation, she senses that her passion for her daughter may amount to idolatry, and threatens to ruin her relationship with God. "I found myself so wholly preoccupied with thoughts of you—my heart so incapable of any other love—that I was denied permission to take the sacrament at Pentecost," she writes the countess. Earlier, concerning a conversation she has had with her spiritual director: "He scolded me severely . . . he told me . . . that I was an outright pagan, that I had set you up as a idol in my heart, and that this sort of idolatry was as dangerous as any other kind. . . . In sum, he told me that I had best give thought to my immortal soul."

Concentrating too exclusively on these unusually forceful maternal obsessions, the reader would run the danger of overlooking Mme de Sévigné's remarkable talents as a social, political, and literary chronicler. It is a talent only equaled in her century by Saint-Simon. Be they addressed to her daughter or her two other principal correspondents, the Marquis de Pomponne and her cousin Philippe Emmanuel de Coulanges, the Sévigné letters deal with a dazzling spectrum of objects and events: the intrigues that accompanied Louis XIV's shifting of affections from Mlle de la Vallière to Mme de Montespan to the future Mme de Maintenon; the public execution of a mass murderess who had poisoned numerous patients of charity hospitals and seven male members of her family; the costumes, coiffures, jewelry, games, and conversations displayed at the court of Versailles, which Mme de Sévigné visited once or twice a year; the trial on charges of treason of her "poor dear unfortunate friend" Jean Fouquet, Louis XIV's superintendent of finances, an event on which she lavished forty letters that offer as detailed an account as we have of the daily court proceedings of seventeenth-century France.

She is estimated to have written between twenty and thirty pages a day. The ironic, vigorous terseness with which she describes the death of the Duke de La Rochefoucauld, and the grief experienced by Mme de La Fayette, his companion of many years, is characteristic: "Yesterday morning he did not see Mme de La Fayette because she was weeping and he was taking extreme unction. He sent, at noon, to inquire about her. Believe me, my daughter, it is not in vain that he did so much thinking all his life. Approaching his last hours on earth in the same manner, they held nothing strange or new for him."

Many of Sévigné's depictions are gleaned from secondhand accounts, but described with such imaginative precision that one feels in the presence of a great writer searching for a genre: If she had lived a few decades later she might have brilliantly mastered the novelistic form which was only budding in her lifetime. The death of seventeenth-century France's greatest military man, Maréchal Turenne, is rendered as vividly as any of Tolstoy's battle scenes. And it is thanks to this passage of her letters ("a random shot rips his body half in two . . . imagine the cries, the tears of the army!") that generations of Frenchmen know the details of the hero's end. In Sévigné's historicized accounts, the more ridiculous aspects of the Sun King's reign are described as brilliantly as the sublime. Such is her tragicomic rendering of the Prince Royal's chief cook, Vatel, who committed suicide during a *fête* at Chantilly upon learning that the shipments of seafood he had ordered might not arrive in time for lunch. "Vatel goes up to his room, places his sword against the door, and runs it through his heart— although not until the third try, the first two wounds not being mortal . . . he falls dead. The shipments of seafood begin to pour in from all directions. They look for Vatel to distribute it. They go to his room. They try to open the door; they burst it open; they find him drowned in his own blood. They rush to Monsieur Le Prince, who weeps in despair. . . ."

"I would have wished to marry the daughter," Joseph de Maistre commented a century later, "if only to receive the letters from the mother." He had particularly admired those passages which show the marquise in her moments of brooding religious introspection, such as the following: "I must leave this life, and this thought shatters me," she wrote when she was forty-six, in the bloom of health. "And how will I leave it? By what door? In what manner? Will I suffer a thousand and one agonies which will bring me to death in desperation? How will I appear in the sight of God? Will it be fear and extremity which will bring me back to him? Will I feel no other emotion but fear? What can I hope for? Am I worthy of paradise? Is hell my just desert? What an alternative! What a perplexity!"

Death, when it finally came to Mme de Sévigné at the age of seventy, might well have been graced by the spiritual peace she'd desired throughout her life. For it occurred in the proximity of her daughter, her "unvariable taste," during one of her rare visits to the Grignans' castle in Provence. Mme de Sévigné spent the last two months of her life nursing her daughter back to health from a long illness before falling ill herself. Her end was marred by an irony as complex as her obsessional love, and may have caused more speculations than any other event in seventeenth-century French literature. For during the two weeks of the illness that carried her mother away, the Countess de Grignan never set foot into her mother's sickroom, and she never even attended the funeral.

Over the centuries, the countess's descendants have set forth several theories to deny her reputed heartlessness. It has been conjectured that she was not fully enough recovered from her own illness to visit her mother; it has also been surmised that she was enough recovered to have been away on a trip at the time of her mother's death. Both theories have been discounted by contemporary historians, who tend to trace her absence to the psychological complexities of the two women's relations. The prevailing view is the following: Obsessed by the idolatrous nature of her maternal love, and wishing to make one great and final penance, it was Mme de Sévigné who forbade her daughter to come into her room for a last visit. Facing her last hours, she made the supreme sacrifice and denied herself her life's greatest treasure—her daughter's presence—as a requisite to entering the presence of her Maker.

It is striking that even the least introspective of great writers, Saint-Simon, uses the word "idolatry" when writing about Mme de Sévigné's death. He writes in an entry of his *Memoirs,* upon hearing of her end: "Madame de Sévigné, a most amiable woman and the best of company, died . . . at the home of her daughter, whom she idolized, despite the fact that such idolatry was scarcely merited."

Black Mountain:
The Breaking (Making) of a Writer

At eight thirty tonight John Cage mounted
a stepladder and until 10:30 he talked about
the relation of music to Zen Buddhism while
a movie was shown, dogs ran across the stage
barking, 12 persons danced without any pre-
vious rehearsal, a prepared piano was played,
whistles blew, babies screamed, Edith Piaf rec-
ords were played double-speed on a turn-of-the-
century machine . . .

THIS journal note of mine, record-
ing what is said to be America's first "Happening," is dated August
1952, Black Mountain College, North Carolina. I have long felt
a need to pay tribute to this visionary community of men and
women, and particularly to Charles Olson, the poet who might well
be responsible for my becoming a writer.

Black Mountain originated in 1933, in the same decade of
educational ferment in which Antioch, Bennington, Sarah Lawrence, and the University of Chicago designed their progressive
curriculums. I signed up for my first summer session there in 1951,
at the age of twenty, having gravitated to it for reasons that then
seemed eminently objective: how captivating, in the span of two
months, to study painting with Ben Shahn and Robert Mother-
well, dancing with Merce Cunningham, music with John Cage,
writing with Charles Olson. A dissolutely aesthetic adolescent, I

was drawn to each of these possible vocations and several more; I
had received one of those antiquated European educations which
encourages young women to draw landscapes, play the piano, ex-
ecute basic ballet steps as fluently as they read and write.

I arrived at Black Mountain straitlaced by many other conventions: the protocols of France's diplomatic corps and of its
impoverished aristocracy (my father's world); the decorum of my
mother's fashionable salons and of my American schools—Spence,
Bryn Mawr, and Barnard, where I'd begun a major in medieval
philosophy. I brought these inhibitions to a community pledged
to rebel against all traditional modes of behavior, in life as in
art. And it took me a few months to realize that I had gravitated
toward Black Mountain not for detached aesthetic purposes, but
out of an instinctual need to purge myself of much ancestral
folderol, to engage in that symbolic parricide without which none
of us can become totally adult. It was with equally blind instinct
that of all the alluring mentors Black Mountain was offering in the
summer of 1951, I gravitated to the most iconoclastic and dicta-
torial of the lot, Charles Olson.

Charles Olson was born and raised in Gloucester, Massachusetts. After receiving a Ph.D. in American Civilization from Harvard (the first doctoral candidate in that department), he worked
as a fisherman and a mail carrier between brief stints of teaching.
He came to Black Mountain in 1949 at the invitation of the artist
Joseph Albers, then the rector of the college, and soon afterward
succeeded him as rector when Albers moved on to Yale. It now
strikes me as odd that he was only forty-two when I met him, for
he emanated an awesome, oracular majesty (in part innate, in part
shrewdly cultivated) which one only associates with the most seasoned shamans. He was a mountain, a giant of a man, measuring
six feet seven inches and 250 pounds. Thick lenses floated above
his walrus mustache, giving his steel-blue eyes a perpetually ferocious, irate gaze. The balding pate of his enormous head was
fringed with a mane of graying hair that flowed to his shoulders, like
that of some Indian sage. Just before coming to Black Mountain
he had lived in the wilds of Yucatán studying the Mayan culture,
and a Mexican wool serape was magisterially draped over his huge

shoulders, even when he was bare-torsoed on the hottest North Carolina summer day.

1951: Olson's rebellion against all traditional literary forms, his militant insistence on subjectivity, self-expression, self-exposure—these were the first aspects of his teaching that struck me as revolutionary. The confessional journal engaged in with full sincerity was an infinitely nobler art form, in Olson's eyes, than any of those courteous short stories published in *The New Yorker* which have been the model of our literary taste. There was much of American revivalism in Olson: bear witness by baring your soul, be redeemed by the sheer authenticity of your individual emotions. The uniquely American ideal of "finding oneself" (a phrase whose equivalent might not exist in any other Western language) was expressed by Olson in the most native populist style: each aspiring writer in his workshop must realize "what is his or her *ground*, get to that, citizen, go back there, stand on it, make yrself yr own place, and move from that."

So whenever Olson was pleased by a student's particularly intense self-revelation (I cite another instance from my Black Mountain journals), he slowly rose from his chair to tower over its author:

"*Sí*, Victor, *sí!*" Olson shouted. "You have it, Victor!"

And he glared at the newly loved writer with fierce affection. In the case of Victor, Olson's fancy was caught by this visceral, reductive line: "I finger my innards for the truth."

"*Sí*, Victor, you have it!" Olson announced. And Victor was held up as the workshop's hero for the rest of the week, until another equally raw metaphor of self-revelation caught the master's ear.

Like all introspective writers who have theorized about their craft, Olson was obsessed by the loss of energy between the rich immediacy of our emotions and the relative poverty of our scripted words: "The dodges of discourse," as he called it, "the distinction between language as the *act* of the instant and language as the act of thought *about* the instant." His infatuation with the Mayan culture came from the directness of its hieroglyphic writing, whose signs "retain the power of the objects of which they are the images." There was also much neoprimitivism, much redneck yahoo posturing in this Harvard-educated scholar who preached that we would not be free "until we have completely cleaned ourselves of the biases of westernism, of greekism, until we have squared away at historical time."

Olson proclaimed that traditional concepts of linear time must make way in our writing for a native American concept of "space." Stated in the very opening of his best-known prose text, *Call Me Ishmael:* "I take SPACE, to be the central fact to man born in America, from Folsom cave to now. I spell it large because it comes large here. Large, and with no mercy." The ideal contemporary text, in his view, was a "space-field" organized by an idiom of shared Americanness, an optimally direct, colloquial vernacular. As in his own verse:

> It ain't dreamt until it walks   It talks   It spreads its green
> barrazza
> Listen closely, folks, this poem comes to you by benefit of its
> own Irish green bazoo. You take it, from here.

The lectures Olson delivered in his writing workshops were equally iconoclastic and antilinear, random shards of culture as purged of any historical coherence as the elements of John Cage's Happenings (which Olson hailed as one of the glories of the twentieth century). His classes averaged four hours and could last six or eight, and sitting through them was like seeing an archaeologist throw a tantrum in a richly endowed museum. Within the span of one summer class we might be assailed by snatches of Sumerian history, of Fenollosa's theories on Japanese art, of Heisenberg's *Principle of Indeterminacy;* by passages from D. H. Lawrence's *Studies in Classical American Literature,* Dostoevski's *Notes from Underground,* Leo Frobenius's books on African rock painting, Pausanias's *Descriptions of Greece* ("more valuable than Plutarch . . . because of its careful localism"), and from Ezra Pound's *Guide to Kulchur* ("just because it razzledazzles History"). We would be simultaneously assaulted by lines from the medieval poet Cavalcanti and Renaissance poet John Skelton, and from Olson's more recent idols—Blake, Melville, William Carlos Williams.

Olson's collagist approach to culture, his stress on the spontaneous and instinctual, tended to breed a mayhem of narcissistic mumblings among his students; it led to adulation of several texts as idiotic as Ezra Pound's *ABC of Economics,* and more self-expression than there were selves to express. Yet his presence was magically fructifying because he did not so much engage in Oedipal rebellion against contemporary fathers, which would become the curse of the 1960s, as in a reappraisal of revolutionary great-grandfathers: "Big O.," as we called him, transferred to us the momentum of his gigantic, archaeological curiosity for all forms of "immediate" discourse, past and present. The fineness of his ear had few equals in his generation. No teacher I've ever had put greater stress on tonal texture, on the notion that in all literary forms "it is by their syllables that words juxtapose in beauty." He forced us to realize that prose is only as good as it approximates the condition of poetry—that state in which not a particle of sound can be changed without upsetting the entire page. And the lines of classical verse he battered us with most frequently had a haunting, reductive musicality whose repetition would make anyone into a better writer: Blake's "Ah! Sunflower! weary of time!"; the medieval lyric "O western Wynd, when wilt thou blow / And the small rain down shall rain"; these lines from Marvell's "The Garden": "Annihilating all that's made / To a green thought in a green shade."

How did I fare in this scheme of things, an adolescent girl skilled at all Olson most detested—Aristotelian abstractions, European proprieties? Parachuted into this virulently Yankee, predominantly male community whose favorite mottoes were Ezra Pound's "Make it New" and William Carlos Williams's "No ideas but in things," I fared with mixed results. Several aspects of my brief past made me somewhat suited to Black Mountain: I'd been a pacifist lefty and World Federalist since my early teens, I was a tomboy who had always identified, in art as in life, with male heroes. Once in college, I'd concentrated so heavily on my philosophical abstractions that I'd never taken a literature course beyond freshman English, thinking I was smartass enough to read all of it by myself; and Olson thought that was particularly fine. "Girl," he'd say, pressing his five fingers hard into my scalp until it hurt, "if you get the high-falootin' Yurrup and *poh-lee-tess* and stuck-up schools out of that noggin and start playing Gringo ball you'll be okay."

That was a lot to get rid of in two months. And I'd brought along some equally unsuitable possessions to Black Mountain: my first short stories, in which I was always an adult male facing situations I knew little about—my favorite persona was a middle-aged alcoholic actor seeking salvation in a Bowery church. Olson was equally capable of abysmal rudeness and of ambassadorial courtesy, and I've always been grateful that he never assailed these texts' atrociousness publicly. He reserved his ire for our tutorials. "Girl," he bellowed at me after reading my trash, "this is pure shit! You're going to do nothing but keep a journal for a year, an hour a day minimum, come back next summer and show me what's in it!"

So I went back north and obeyed Big O. and kept my journal through the rigors of senior year of college, where I'd changed my dissertation thesis from medieval themes to a more irreverent topic, "Kierkegaard's Views on the Demise of Christianity." Throughout that winter I scribbled recollections of early childhood in my journal, noting one incident curiously akin to the one I'd just lived through with Olson:

In Paris in the 1930s, at the wish of my father, who deplored the laxness of twentieth-century education, I'd been tutored at home from the age of five by a tyrannical governess. The two of us traveled once a week to a correspondence school where we were doled out lessons for the following week, Gallically rigid homework (memorization of Asian capitals and Latin verbs, codifying of sentence parts) which was hardly conducive to a fertile imagination. But when I was eight an unprecedented event took place— a new teacher came in and gave us the following assignment: "Write a Story about Anything You Wish." Filled with excitement and terror by this novel freedom, I began as a severe minimalist:

> The little girl was forbidden by her parents to walk alone to the lake at the other end of the long lawn. But she wished to visit a green-eyed frog who would offer her the key to freedom. One day she disobeyed her parents and walked to the lake, and immediately drowned.
>
> **The End**

"Pathetic dribble!" the Father stormed on his daily visit to my study room. "You dare call that a story? What will become of you if you never finish anything!" He grabbed the paper from my little desk and tore it to shreds. It was a May evening of 1939, fourteen months before he died in the French Resistance. My father had been the love of my life, and he'd warned me that I should never write again. Always these male censors, silencing, silencing me . . .

During my senior year at college I also returned, in my journal, to impressions of the past summer at Black Mountain:

Supercool pose of silence or monosyllabic utterances, bare feet, men's dark glasses and long hair, easygoing nudism and bisexuality—fads of the just nascent Beat Generation, precursors of the 1960s Movement style. (I hadn't skimped on Black Mountain's brand of unisex macho, chopping off my hair as short and jagged as a contemporary punk's.)

Everyone aping Olson's Yankee-phonetic spellings and punsome divisions: waz, enuf, luv, kulchur, yrself, lawd, abt, ga-wan for "go on," Ru-man-tick, egg-zack-tly. All taken secondhand from 1920 vintage Pound.

The girl who danced in front of the mirror in the main hall from 7:00 A.M. to suppertime, stopping only to feed the baby braying in a basket by the exercise bar. She did not take any courses, she never spoke to anyone, she simply moved about ten hours in a row, staring at herself in a mirror.

Olson, a serape flung over his naked torso, sitting in the dining room next to John Cage, always most formal in a black city suit and tie and very shiny pointed black shoes, punctuating the cultivated laconism of dinnertime with his tinkling, Zen monk's laugh as he mused about his next Happening.

Accompanying the poet Jonathan Williams to the Asheville, North Carolina, draft board in 1951 when he refused induction into the U.S. Army on grounds of conscientious objection: that was as important a political education as any I had received from family or college.

I returned to Black Mountain in 1952 for another summer session, as Olson had bidden me to, and showed him my journal. There followed a few treasured days when I was the Victor of that season's workshop, then reduced to six students. The first week of the seminar, Olson towered over us, glowering through his thick spectacles, his finger poised on a stark, reductive line of my journals. It had to do with my father: "I pointed westward, towards his grave."

"*Sí, sí,* girl! That's *space!*" Big Charles triumphed. "*Sí,* you've got it, kid!"

But I didn't remain in favor long. For I'd brought Olson some other texts to read: three very autobiographical stories about my childhood which had followed his dictate to "Concentrate on what you know about, Write from the Center." Clearly inspired by my obedience to Big O., they had won me the annual Creative Writing Award given to a graduating senior at Barnard. Five hundred dollars, a tidy sum for those years, and all the ego trips such minihonors bring. But Olson didn't give a damn about jurors from fancy New York publishing houses doling out prizes at a Seven Sisters school. He was pioneering a counterculture, and such details made him all the more hostile. Once more he raged at me during a tutorial, shouting: "You're still writing conservative junk! If you want to be a writer keep it to a journal . . ." The giant walrus rising from his chair, six feet seven of him towering. "AND ABOVE ALL DON'T TRY TO PUBLISH ANYTHING FOR TEN YEARS!" More censorship into silence, this time, perhaps, for the best.

I remained, as ever, an obedient daughter. I again followed Big Charles's advice. I kept my journal in New Orleans while following a jazz clarinetist on the rounds of Bourbon Street; in the dawns of New York when I relished being the only woman on the overnight shift at United Press, wrote "World-in-Briefs" about Joseph McCarthy's purges, drank martinis with my colleagues at 8:00 A.M. in sleazy bars under the Third Avenue El. I remained loyal to it throughout a myriad of other transient aspirations that all protected me from the fear of Becoming a Writer—flirting with the notion of entering Harvard's architectural school, or going to Union Theological Seminary for a degree in divinity. I persevered with the journal throughout my most misguided phase, when I earned my living in Paris as a fashion reporter, and dallied with a succession of consummate French narcissists to whom I eventually gave their literary due. I continued to write it after my return to the United

States and my marriage, when I realized one of my earliest dreams and spent five years as a painter of meticulous landscapes and still lifes. For my Black Mountain guru had offered me an important metaphor: journal keeping is comparable to the process of sharpening a pencil; our emotions, and the power of their expressions, are kept at maximum intensity by the daily routine of being inserted into the journal's sharpening edge.

By 1962 I had two children. I lived in deep country and in relative solitude, encompassed by domestic duties. The journal was becoming increasingly voluminous, angry, introspective. The nomadic tomboy, finally denied flight and forced to turn inward, was beginning to explode. One winter day I felt an immense void, great powerlessness, the deepest loneliness I'd ever known. I wept for some hours, took out a notebook, started rewriting one of the stories that had won me my college award. It was the one about my governess. It was published shortly afterward in *The New Yorker*, precisely one year past the deadline Charles Olson had set me. Twelve years and two books of nonfiction later, it was to become the first chapter of my first novel, *Lovers and Tyrants*. The process of finishing that book entailed a solid and delicate psychoanalysis which forced me to accept my father's death. Epiphany achieved, I was able to write the novels's last three chapters—my first serious attempt at fiction—in a mere six months.

I may have had to bury the first Censoring Father to set my tongue free. I may have had to go to Black Mountain to bury many grandfathers, many mothers. I may have had to abide by Censor Two, Charles Olson, to let my tongue speak with any measure of integrity.

"A frontier society sometimes raucous and raw," so Martin Duberman would describe it in his fine book, *Black Mountain: An Experiment in Community*, ". . . bold in its refusal to assume any reality it hadn't tested, and therefore bold in inventing forms, both in life styles and in art."

Charles Olson attempted to keep Black Mountain alive during the last five years of its existence through the sheer force of his personality, with total disdain for all administrative detail. He was a tortured man who had talked like a puritan about "clean writing" being solely produced by "clean experience," and left his wife and baby to marry a student whom he had gotten with child. It was the way he had treated many women throughout his life, and I suspect he had too much integrity not to feel his guilt, which he allayed by bouts of severe alcoholism after Black Mountain's demise. By the time I wrote him to thank him for inspiring my first published texts, in the mid-sixties, he was too far gone to answer. Charles Olson died at fifty-nine, a great talent which may never have found its true center.

His leavening influence on American literature can still be felt by reading through back issues of *The Black Mountain Review*, founded by Olson and Robert Creeley with the intent of loosening the grip of the New Criticism. It provided more fascinating reading, for my money, than *Partisan Review*, *New Directions*, or any other classy periodical of the 1950s. In its last number, dated 1957, one finds Allen Ginsberg's "America," Kerouac's "From October in the Railroad Earth," poems by Gary Snyder and Michael McLure, a section of William Burroughs' then unpublished *Naked Lunch* and part of Hubert Selby, Jr.'s, also unpublished *Last Exit to Brooklyn*.

Notwithstanding Olson's demanding, oppressive presence, the more gifted writers of the community he nurtured were able to avoid all sectarianism. Of the ten poets since categorized as "The Black Mountain School" (a term originally coined by an outsider, Donald Allen, in his 1960 anthology, *The New American Poetry*) only six had some connection with the college. Others had simply published in the *Review*. And the vast range of stylistic differences among the writers indebted to him—be it Joel Oppenheimer's domestic lyricism, Jonathan Williams's pungent sparseness, Fielding Dawson's Joycean memoirs, or my own discursive prose—makes the very term "school" ridiculous. Olson himself had clearly spelled out the terms of Black Mountain's adamant individualism: The writer "is not free to be a part of, or to be any, sect . . . the poet can not afford to traffick in any other sign than his own, his self, the man or woman he is."

Few communities of its modest size—it seldom exceeded 120 in any given year—were ever nurtured within two decades by so distinguished a group. In addition to the ones already mentioned: Edward Dahlberg, Buckminster Fuller, Paul Goodman, Robert

Creeley, Aaron Siskind, Stan Van Der Beek, Jasper Johns, Robert Rauschenberg, Cy Twombly, Kenneth Noland, Willem de Kooning, Arthur Penn, Alfred Kazin, Robert Duncan, Walter Gropius, Stefan Wolpe, Franz Kline, among many others. But this proliferation of stars led Black Mountain to a very incongruous self-image: While trying to remain the City on the Hill, it saw itself both as a frontier and as a frontier salon. There were also the contradictions of its last rector: Olson's Black Mountain was obsessed by its unique and redemptive Americanism and by a totally opposite nineteenth-century romantic vision of the artist as pristine prophet—Olson's favorite dictum was "Only the artist is on time." How to reconcile this narcissistic sacralization of art with a community dedicated, in good part, to abolishing all traditional barriers between art and life? "Write as you breathe," Olson always taught. "I want to erase *all* differences between art and life," Cage said. "Rauschenberg just wants to fill in the gaps between the two, which strikes me as a little too Roman Catholic."

Like Brook Farm, Oneida, and most other Utopias ballasted by a belief in their redemptive purity, Black Mountain would eventually founder on reality's edge. By 1955 the few dedicated faculty members who had remained had not drawn salaries for a year, and many had used up their personal savings. Olson's attempts at economic revival were of a tragicomic nature. He tried to get approval from the state to enroll Korean War vets, and the college's remaining six students rushed from class to class, changing disguises every few minutes, to convince Veterans Administration inspectors that the community was thriving. A few months later, Black Mountain decided that despite its "principles" it would accept the mentally retarded son of a wealthy Southerner who had suggested that he might put some money into the community. The father was to fly his private plane over the college and dip its wings in a certain way to make it known that he had decided to offer a bequest. For a few days members of the saving remnant spent their time wandering about the fields, staring at the sky and waiting for the sound of a plane which never came. One can think of few gifted men put to such an absurd task.

I don't fully understand Olson's magnum opus, *The Maximus Poems*, but I believe he has an important, underestimated place in American letters. He left many fascinating essays ("Projective Verse," "Human Universe") and a remarkable book on Melville, *Call Me Ishmael*, a classic of engaged, iconoclastic criticism comparable to William Carlos Williams's *In the American Grain*. His legacy went beyond published texts. I do not adulate Olson or Black Mountain the way most of its members have, feeling ambivalent about the sham and the magnificence of the man, the dangers and the vision of the place. But I thank him every week of my life for his prophetic emphasis on the valor of subjectivity and candor, of disobedience against form and state; and also for that fatherly rigor which eventually enabled me to write at all.

Decades later, as a woman nurtured by twenty years of feminism, memories of Black Mountain and Charles Olson still make me worry about the constant temptation, and great hazards, of being dutiful daughters. And they lead me to muse on these bittersweet paradoxes: how certain male mentors can force us to acknowledge our femaleness; how some male oppressors, by teaching us to rebel, may eventually become our liberators.

On Women's Rites

O N the morning of May 1, 1949, I was said to be the only member of the Bryn Mawr freshman class who refused to dance around the Maypole. I had not overslept, quite the contrary. I had been up since 5:00 A.M. in a state of indignation, staring at the preparations for May Day with the disdain of an agnostic British colonel observing, in New Delhi, some archaic ceremonial of the Indian religion. Surrounded by nostalgically preserved Henry Wallace-for-President buttons, I paced my room at the Pembroke West dorm muttering Wordsworth's line about "a Pagan suckled in a creed outworn." I felt proud of being an emancipated woman, some kind of Marxist, a Freudian, and thus a predestined anti-Maypoler. Having read *The Future of an Illusion* (just once) with enthusiasm unbounded, I then looked upon any ritual that savored even faintly of myth or liturgy as a vestige of humanity's childhood which must be instantly dismantled to speed the progress of mankind. I may have been excessive in the virulence of my disapproval, but I was hardly an anomaly. For I belonged to that last generation which could still believe blindly in the Enlightenment myth that salvation lies in increased rationalization and secularization, and in the improvement of scientific method.

There's another, more subtle way in which I'd been indoctrinated against the Bryn Mawr Maypole by the ethos of the past two centuries. The efficient propaganda machine of the male ruling class had brainwashed me into looking upon all exclusively female rites as trivial, petty, faintly comic. Quite as deplorable as the Maypole were baby showers, garden clubs, pie-baking contests, the sight of women knitting together in a college lounge, and numerous other civilities replete with symbols of nurturing which effect deeper bonding among women. In fact, what frightens me most about the adolescent I describe in 1949 is the extent to which she respected and envied most *male* cults of bonding, short of football, the hunt, or the military life; the way she reverently participated, whenever allowed, in such male rites as poker games, poolrooms, backgammon tournaments at the Harvard Club, Saturday-night drinking fests. Suffice it to say that if I were to encounter today that young woman who refused to celebrate the resurrected spring in May of 1949, I'd look upon her as a hopelessly outdated relic of early twentieth-century materialism, a kind of mastodon. For the past decades have made it painfully clear that we've been secularized and deritualized beyond forbearance, that the Enlightenment's promise of salvation through technology has radically failed, that in the great debate between Freud and Jung concerning the transience of permanence of religious ritual, Jung's view has been the prophetic one: Our expressions of joy, sorrow, hope, and particularly our need to honor some form of transcendence will always seek ritual channels if our psychic balance is to survive. And it may be more important than ever in the 1980s to stress the historic role women have played as guardians of the many rituals for which we're now so famished, and to confront the problems we may face if we wish to *remain* the guardians of these traditions.

So there stood the Maypole, garlanded with flowers and bright-hued ribbons, surrounded by dancing, singing maidens, an archaic and beautiful sight. . . . The ritual bothered me then for most of the reasons I honor it in the 1980s. I see it now as a profoundly female ceremony with rather sacred overtones. It is a celebration of the regenerative forces of nature, a vestige of the tree worship that has thrived in every corner of the globe since the beginning of ritual consciousness. Throughout the Mediterranean culture which was the matrix of our own, the tree was a prevalent embodiment of the Mother Goddess; more exultantly than any other object in nature, it has symbolized for millennia the glory of the resurrected year.

And according to Sir James Frazer, who still remains uncontested on this point, Bryn Mawr's tenaciously preserved Maypole ritual seems to descend directly from this venerable cult of the tree as symbol of immortality and rebirth.

To keep such a primeval tradition alive throughout those materialistic decades, when skeptics such as I saw it as an archaic eccentricity, has been a prophetic gesture. By the end of the Vietnam years, the massive exodus of our youth to Oriental sects, our renewed fascination for the mythic and the occult evidenced our nostalgia for some blessed past in which our lives were still structured by the authority of ritual observance. However sympathetic we may be with such archaic longings, we must remain wary of their excesses. Most cultural regressions to past forms tend to bastardization and barbarism. A craving for unduly authoritarian modes of religion can lead to the shabby travesties of the Reverend Sun Myung Moon, or to the tragedy of Jonestown, Guyana.

There might be only one domain of experience in which our renewed thirst for authority and tradition can find a genuine expression. And that is on the tribal level, in those ritual observances of the home and the community which have to do with the secular and sacred core of human affections: with our need to civilize the young, tend to the ill, the aged, and the dying, to maintain strong family ties, to preserve the religious rituals of our own native traditions. It's important to stress that many of these rites customarily have been performed and preserved by women. For until very recently, the human race has been traditionally divided into the opposite models of Penelope and Ulysses, or, more subtly, of Antigone and Creon. Woman as tender of the hearth, custodian of most ethnic rituals and religious customs, safeguarder of tribal memory versus man the explorer, innovator, technocrat, who in his nomadic obsession for power and control tends to neglect many time-honored traditions. This division between cultic woman and secular man is poignantly expressed in a letter written by Cicero to his wife in the year 58 b.c. "My dear, I truly desire to see you as soon as possible, and to die in your arms, since neither the gods whom you have piously worshiped nor the men whom I have always served have shown us any thanks."

Women's historic role as guardian of rituals has been as exalted by some as it's been condemned by others. Henry Adams, for instance, sees woman's cultic nature as the very glue of civilization, a felicitously conservative power which "has preserved the customs of civility, supplied the intelligence, and dictated the taste." Freud, on the other hand, sees it as a perniciously reactionary force which tends to curb the progress of mankind. And popular folklore divides the sexes into woman the rememberer and man the forgetter, as evidenced by the archetypal wife who weeps as her husband comes home from the office: "Today is my birthday," or, "You forgot our anniversary for the third year in a row." Yet all these views overlook the following issue: What is the particular effect of ritual on *women's* lives? I sense that our so-called conservative guardianship of tribal memory can be a paradoxically radical and liberating force, and that our fidelity to ancient observances has often been an effective way of achieving autonomy from male society. It's in this context that I think of the more ritualistic women in legend and history, beginning inevitably with Antigone.

Antigone commits civil disobedience against her uncle Creon, king of Thebes, by giving her brother the burial rites that are a central feature of the Greek religion, rites denied him by the king because he has sinned against the state. The essence of tragedy is to oppose two different but equal levels of justice; Creon is not necessarily a tyrant, he is simply an efficient bureaucrat, *le politicien moyen sensuel.* One of the most striking aspects of this play is the manner in which Antigone totally transcends the sex roles traditional to her society. She is profoundly female in her fanatic guardianship of religious rites. Yet, she has rejected the warning of her sister, Ismene, that women were not born to contest any man-made laws; she is very masculine in her disobedience of male authority. And Antigone's androgynous behavior throws Creon into a state of confusion. Although Creon keeps accusing Antigone and her followers of excessive femaleness for upholding the sanctity of religious rites ("Abominable spirits, woman-led!"), he simultaneously attacks Antigone for her repugnantly masculine behavior. And in the latter part of the play, he keeps referring to her in the male gender. Creon's confusion is understandable, for Antigone indeed fuses the male and female principles as few heroines ever have. After acting out a virile role by her defiance of male authority, she reverts to the most traditional female instincts as she is taken to her death, lamenting, "He has taken me away before my nuptials, having never known married joy or tender motherhood." Antigone typifies a quality very precious to contemporary women, a spiritual androgyny that might enable us to contend in a man's world while fully retaining our female instincts.

There is another kind of woman who has preserved her autonomy and power through rigid observance of ritual tradition—the Roman Catholic nun. While attacking the misogyny of medieval times, most feminist historians are overlooking the liberating power of one of its central institutions—the monastic enclosure. Even though she might have to pay fealty in times of crisis to a male hierarchy of bishops, the nun's only vow of obedience is to the superior of her women's order, and until the twentieth century, monastic communities created one of the greatest measures of autonomy ever offered to us. Here were women who chose celibacy rather than enter into prearranged marriages that would enslave them to the cycle of childbearing, who founded colonies in which the hierarchies of sexual dominance were quite overturned. Nuns are women who say, not unlike Antigone, my ultimate allegiance is to a transcendent immutable order that is superior to the fluctuating laws of any secular male state. They are women who have gained and retained their power base by upholding the more ancient traditional modes, and who have often served as the most prophetic critics of their male peers. It was Catherine of Siena and Saint Bridget of Sweden who first told the pope to get out of Avignon and back to Rome where he traditionally belonged. It was Teresa of Ávila who helped reform monastic life by resurrecting the finest elements of the Carmelite tradition, and who became the spiritual mentor of Saint John of the Cross.

"The proper study of mankind is woman." Words not written by Kate Millett or Germaine Greer, but by Henry Adams in the 1880s. Surveying the decline in quality of life enjoyed by women in the West, it is clear that it decreased in proportion to the decrease of meaningful rituals in their lives. The quality of life enjoyed by the community at large degenerated simultaneously. And its most accelerated rate of decline is traceable to late nineteenth- and early twentieth-century Protestant America.

What *was* left to us at the turn of the century? Not only were we deprived of the elaborate ritual life of the Roman matron, who, while directing a veritable factory of domestic crafts, took part in a number of sacred rites solely reserved for women; we didn't begin to have the financial independence offered by law to all classes of Roman women, nor the sexual freedom they enjoyed in the upper levels of their society. The Reformation had deprived us of the choice of celibacy offered by the Catholic nunnery. The Industrial Revolution had robbed us of much of the pride and power we enjoyed for centuries by helping to run small family-owned enterprises. Our intelligence was considerably less esteemed than that of women in many European cultures. Even in the American upper classes, the ritual of the literary salon—through which generations of French women played an immense role in refining the manners and literature of their nation—was made barely possible by the segregationist misogyny of the American Protestant ethos.

So we nursed and preserved the modest rituals left to us, our quilting bees, our sewing circles, our reading circles, our church fairs, activities often derided by our men, rites whose creativity we've only recently begun to appreciate as we emancipate ourselves, thanks to the Women's Movement, from the more aggressive models of male rituals.

What else did we go on to lose? The dehumanizing efficiency of science now makes it increasingly hard for us to experience the intimacy of childbirth, to preserve our ancient roles as comforters of the ill and the aged. Our isolation deepens with the decades in this immense continent; we're increasingly separated from kinsmen, siblings, parents. The rituals of the extended family are growing most infrequent.

The most grievous loss of all we endured after the 1950s was caused by the tyranny of the media, which deprived us of our most central and precious role as civilizers of the young, as educators of our own children. This is indeed the nadir of women's history, the idle and lonely housewife, surrounded by kitchen appliances, who increasingly resorts, as medical figures show, to Valium and alcohol and the equally drugging effects of daytime television to relieve her sense of powerlessness and isolation.

And so I offer the following conclusion, which might make

most Freudians and Marxists extremely uncomfortable: I believe that the Women's Movement that surfaced in America shortly after mid-century was in some part caused by the fact that women's lives had been more severely deritualized—and therefore made more meaningless—than at any other time in human history.

But what is significant ritual about? And how might we salvage the few important rites and rituals left to us at a time when our society is so famished for them?

In its deepest, most spiritual sense, ritual is a sequence of gestures that repeats a primordial act, such as the Christian rite of communion which symbolizes our brotherhood and sisterhood in sharing the body of the Godhead, or the rite of Passover which symbolizes the miraculous survival of the Jewish people. On a more secular level, significant rituals are also those that fulfill our need to infuse a family or a community with greater harmony and love.

In either case, a ritual is a rigidly structured sequence of actions that brings us a heightened sense of our own identity and meaningfulness. And many traditional rites are presently threatened because their historic guardians—women—are leaving home by the millions finally to pursue the self-fulfillment they deserve. For even in those periods when the female principle was at its most dominant—when the colonizing of Greece was pursued according to the advice of female oracles, and the extinction of the Vestal Virgin's fire would spell doom for the Roman state—even then, there was a crucial freedom denied us: We were never allowed to be the wanderers, the explorers, the inventors we might have wished to be; we preserved the rituals of the tribe from the enclaves of our homes. Now, even this last obstacle is being overcome.

I'll describe our present situation as the Odysseizing of women, the Penelopizing of men. Many women will be working the night shift at the hospital, or pleading a case in court at 10:00 P.M.; many of us will face the painful choice of accepting a job in California while the persons we love prefer to keep theirs in Chicago. And if there are children from such a union, who will be there, for instance, to preserve that most basic unit of the ritual life which is the family meal?

Perhaps my French origins make me focus unduly on this particular aspect of cultic behavior. Yet, I can't think of any institu-

tion more laden with civilizing force. The act of nutrition is not a
merely physiological event. It remains, in its more civilized form, a
way of communion. The family meal is a formality that cultivates
in us from earliest age a curb of natural greed, a capacity for sharing, generosity, thoughtfulness, a talent for civilized conversation.
It is a custom that can enrich our knowledge of our historic roots
by preparing food of our own ethnic tradition, that can enlarge our
love of literature by reading poetry at the beginning or end of meals.

Can our men be Penelopized enough to preserve such fundamental rituals as carefully as we have for millennia? Or are women
formidable enough to take on the double tasks of Odysseus and
Penelope? It is up to our sons and daughters to resolve the dilemma.

Several years ago I ran across a most pathetic example of our
renewed thirst for cult and ceremony. It seems that all over the nation communities of teenagers and young adults were gathering at
midnight on Saturdays to view a film called *The Rocky Horror Picture Show*. They chanted litanic responses to the sound track, they
held lit candles in their hands, and some of them were seeing the
film for the thirtieth, fortieth, time in a row. In their desperate
search for liturgy, they were resorting to the most mechanical elements of ritual—mnemonic repetitions of sounds and gestures no
more transcendent than disco dancing.

The Rocky Horror Picture Show has been one of the many
cultic fads that prove how easily rite and ritual can degenerate into
mere rote in a society deprived of genuine ceremonials. And I
suspect that such rote tends to be engaged in by persons whose
childhoods were both deprived of adequate liturgy and of the sacred time of the family meal. Neither are they the kind of Americans who have traditions as eloquently and courageously primordial
as the Maypole to look forward to, or to remember.

I stress the word "courageously" because I think that courage
is essential to anyone who wishes to preserve a quality of life—a
life graced with significant rituals—in the late twentieth century.
Particularly in the United States the cult of novelty accelerates at a
vertiginous pace, constantly seducing us into the vortex of historical,
cultural, and tribal amnesia. And I honor one of my alma maters,
Bryn Mawr, for having refused, more adamantly than any other college I can think of, to capitulate to the siren call of the so-called

new. Society at large once said it was fashionable to go coed? It adamantly maintained its historic role as an institution of women. A generation of bogy positivists such as mine took it to task for its archaic customs? Watch what happened: Through fidelity to its tradition as an all-women's college and to such rituals as the Maypole, Bryn Mawr emerged, two decades later, as one of our more prophetic communities. And also, ironically, as eminently fashionable. And so this is the message I send to the graduating classes of the 1980s: Carry on the immutable female traditionalism of this school into your own lives. Let Bryn Mawr continue to inspire you to say no to the caprices of transient fashion. And take heed of that great Jewish proverb which says, "Today's news wraps tomorrow's fish." By your fidelity to the historic female need to safeguard the past, you will wrap the tomorrow of tomorrow, you will preserve the quality of quality.

Commencement Address, Bryn Mawr College, 1980

WHEN MEMORY GOES:
The Rise and Fall of Klaus Barbie

When Memory Goes:
The Rise and Fall of Klaus Barbie

WHEN asked why she became a writer, Flannery O'Connor put it better than anyone else: "I write because I don't know what I think until I read what I say."

For many years, the same intent made me wish I could document some aspect of contemporary France, for my first homeland evoked strangely conflicting passions of adulation and hostility. Mixed feelings for that nation—love for the splendor of its landscape and its culture, rage at the arrogance and frequent callowness of its people—are probably shared by most Francophiles around the globe. But I had much more to unravel than those contradictions. I sensed that recording some aspect of France's World War II years would force me to tread on areas of my own past which I had not yet dared to enter. In sum, I needed to read what I wrote in order to know how I felt, yet I could not define the particular theme which might unlock the door to those still uncharted feelings.

For a decade I considered topics linked to my many abiding concerns: the fate of suppressed worker-priests, the history of French feminism, the corrupt and Gallic isolence of Jacques Lacan's psychoanalytic method. All were fascinating. None had that inexplicable thrill—akin to the abrupt nascence of a poem—which comes upon us when we are suddenly confronted by a theme genuinely arousing to our past and our conscience, and are ordered by some mysterious force to pursue it to the limit.

And so this book ends the way it began, by acknowledging the very subjective, irrational impulses that lead writers to tackle the poetry of facts, as well as the facts of fiction. By 1983 I had dallied with, and rejected, numerous French themes, and I was deep into my third novel. On a February day that year I was suddenly gripped by a story on *The New York Times*'s front page which concerned a World War II Gestapo chief called Klaus Barbie; he had been extradited the day before from Latin America to France to stand trial for his crimes against humanity, which included the deaths of several thousand Jewish civilians and French resisters. As with my first sight of Philip Berrigan pouring blood on draft files, I knew again those emotions of anger, elation, soldierly resolve, which tell us that it will be our fate, for the next months or years, to abandon whatever life or fiction we have enjoyed to document a certain man, a certain moment, a certain horror of our time.

Chronicling those aspects of history relevant to the Barbie case— the Vichy government's persecution of its own Jewry, the heroism of the tiny group of citizens who made up the Resistance, the hypocritical amnesia indulged in by the French nation to obliterate the truths of its collaboration with Nazism and of its deep complicity in the Holocaust— all this unleashed a multitude of childhood memories and emotions which I had suppressed for decades. I suddenly recalled, with unprecedented clarity, the insanely delusionary song we were still being taught in the spring of 1940, in the weeks preceding the entrance of German troops, "We're Going to Hang Our Laundry on the Siegfried Line"; the terrifying exodus my mother and I made from Paris, to the sound of German and Allied shelling, the day it was declared an open city; the deceits imposed on me for a year concerning my father's fate in the Resistance. And as I started reading what I was writing, I began to know more clearly how I felt—about my childhood, my first homeland, the grief of early loss.

Friends often ask: Is it not hard to interrupt a novel when you go off to a reporting task? It is indeed a painful severance, but the fictions get finished in due time; and for some of us, the urgency of the historical moment supersedes all else. It may well be Charles Olson, once more, who freed me to stand ever ready for such abrupt changes of form and pace. He readied me by destroying the uniquely American myth that fiction is more "creative" than other kinds of prose; by forcing me to look on every written page as pure "text" without worrying about what form or genre it might fall into; by demolishing those dainty, archaic barriers between art and life which have held certain literary acts to be more "artistic" than others. Olson planted these seeds into suitable terrain. For I have always had a streak of Quaker populism which makes me feel uncomfortable with the elitism of the word "artist." I simply strive to remain a craftsperson, an honest cabinetmaker of texts, and, hopefully, some kind of a witness to our time.

Or in Big O.'s own words, which I still see tacked up on a wall, in the same room in which I have worked for over twenty years: "There are only these two accuracies, these two habits, the habit of yrself . . . and the habit of the practice of yr trade, be it pots, words, paint, cloth, the making of any goods—let them be *fine*, and you shall have honor, by way of the dignity of yrself & yr practice." More than enough to aspire to in any one lifetime.

Warren, Connecticut
January 1987

I

Late in the afternoon of June 6, 1944, an SS officer knocked on the door of Simon and Rachelle Kadousche's apartment in a suburb of Lyons. The Kadousches were Jews of Moroccan origin. Simon Kadousche worked as a foreman in a chemical plant and led a quiet, devout life. He read aloud from Scripture most nights; his family rigorously observed the Sabbath.

Of the Kadousches' three children, only the oldest—Simone, thirteen—was at home on the evening of June 6. Her brother and sister, like many other youngsters under twelve, had been sent to the country during the heavy bombardment that preceded the Allies' landing in Normandy, which had occurred that very morning.

The three Kadousches were driven to Gestapo headquarters on place Bellecour and led to one of the interrogation rooms used by Hauptsturmführer Klaus Barbie, head of the Gestapo in Lyons. Within a half hour Barbie came into the room "with a sweet smile on his face," as Simone remembers him, carrying in his arms a gray cat. Simone was struck by how short he was for a German: five feet six or so, with brown hair and dark eyes. He wore an immaculate, dandyish gray business suit. He walked up to Simone and caressed her cheek, then turned to her mother and said, "How pretty she is!

Do you have any more children at home?" "I have a younger son
and daughter; they've been sent out to the country with the rest of
their school." "And where in the country are they?" Barbie asked.
"We don't know," Simone's mother answered.

Klaus Barbie then turned back to Simone. "And you, do you
know where your siblings are hiding?" He spoke fluent, slightly ac-
cented French, repeating the question several times. Simone repeated that she did not know, which was the truth—few of Lyons's
families knew where the schoolchildren were being sheltered that
week. After some minutes Barbie put his cat down on the table.
He had ceased to smile. He returned to Simone, whipped off the
net that held her thick, thigh-length red hair. He pushed her to the
floor, his hands wrapped about her mane of hair, and kicked her
several times in the groin. Simon Kadousche took a step forward
toward his daughter. Barbie pulled out a revolver. He yanked Simone to her feet, threw her down again, repeatedly questioning her
about her brother and sister, pummeling her stomach with his fist.
One detail remains particularly vivid to Simone: Barbie kept pol-
ishing his nails on the lapel of his jacket between blows, looking attentively at his fingernails before he struck her again. After an hour
or so he ceased his questioning. He picked up the cat and started
stroking it again, looking at the Kadousche family with quiet eyes.
"Think about it," he said softly. "If you don't want me to continue, you can tell me tomorrow where those children are."

The beatings were to go on for a week. Every night Barbie si-
lently took Simone back to her mother's cell in the Prison Montluc,
her body covered with bruises and open wounds, her hair plastered
with blood. "See how she looks? It's all your fault. If you tell me
where your two other children are, I'll release all of you; the whole
family will be safe."

After a week of Barbie's fruitless attempts to ferret out two
more Jewish children, Simone and her parents were shipped to
Drancy, the transit camp in a suburb of Paris from which Jews were
sent to concentration camps in Eastern Europe.

The Kadousches were among the seven thousand Jews of the
Lyons region deported at Klaus Barbie's orders in the last two years
of the German Occupation. Simone's mother was gassed a few

weeks after arriving in Auschwitz: She had picked a few cabbage leaves for fellow inmates suffering from scurvy. Simone survived the forced march of 300 miles from Auschwitz to Ravensbrück which began in January 1945, when the advance of Russian troops forced the Nazis to move their camps westward: Of the twenty-five thousand women who walked half-naked through the snow and dug holes in the ground at night to shelter themselves from the glacial wind, only two thousand lived. The rest died of dysentery or pneumonia, or were shot for not walking fast enough. Simone saw her father one last time during the exodus from Auschwitz. She glimpsed him in a line of prisoners marching a few hundred feet from her group. They waved to each other. One of the German guards told her to run over to her father and embrace him. As Simon Kadousche approached his daughter, the soldier forced him to kneel and executed him.

Simone Kadousche is one of several hundred French survivors of Auschwitz still alive today. At the time she was liberated by Russian troops in May 1945, she was fourteen and a half years old and weighed 40 pounds. She now weighs 140. She stands by me in front of Barbie's former offices on Lyons's place Bellecour, a soft-spoken, affectionate housewife with russet hair, showing me the scars left on her forehead from Barbie's beatings, the thick chilblains engraved on her hands during the forced march from Auschwitz. Simone Kadousche Lagrange lives in Grenoble now with her seven children and her husband, who fought for several years with the Maquis in the Vercors region. When she married him, at seventeen, she weighed only sixty-five pounds, and he weighed only ninety-two; and now, she says, laughing, they go to spas in the Auvergne together to lose weight.

After discovering that we were born within three weeks of each other on French soil and that we both lost a father in the war, Simone often holds my arm during our walks through Lyons. She continues to tell me of her odyssey through German camps, shows me the place on her scalp where Dr. Josef Mengele injected the chemicals that made her bald for some years, describes the way he sang arias from *La Traviata* as he injected petrol into her veins. She offers this data in the same affable, confidential tone in which she would advise me on the making of a perfect quenelle: "Don't forget the pinch of nutmeg . . ." Simone seems suffused with the awe, the miracle, of having survived at all. She is eager to share her memories of camp life with anyone willing to listen, she tours schools throughout France to speak of her days in Auschwitz. Sharing the facts of the Holocaust seems to be her principal therapy, her only coming to terms with the demonic, just as silence is a panacea for other survivors of the same terror. She frequently speaks words startling in their fortitude. "Above all don't pity me," she says. "I am all that I am because of what I've endured. Those who pity me—I want to slap them in the face."

As we stand by the Prison Saint-Joseph, she points to the wing of the jail where her former torturer is now held and tells me of the role she played in the capture of Klaus Barbie, who shortly after the war had fled to wealth and freedom in Latin America.

"It was Shrove Tuesday, 1972. I was in the kitchen, making crepes for the children. My husband called to me from the living room, where he was watching television. 'Come quickly,' he said, 'they're asking everyone in Lyons to identify this man, they think he's Klaus Barbie. People in Paris called the Klarsfelds have just given his picture to the press. . . .'

"I went to look. The face on the screen was his; those were the dark, almost gentle eyes."

After thirty years of protection by successive Bolivian dictatorships, Klaus Barbie was flown back to Lyons in February of 1983 to be tried for his crimes, which include the murders of some four thousand French citizens and the deportation of more than seven hundred Jews to death camps in Germany. He had already been tried twice in absentia by French courts in the decade succeeding World War II and twice sentenced to death. His numbered rank of importance on the list of German war criminals as codified by the Allies was 239. But there were several reasons why he was one of the three Nazis most wanted in Europe, along with Alois Brunner and Josef Mengele, and the one most eagerly sought in France: the notoriously sadistic means of torture he employed in the city known as the Capital of the Resistance; his particularly ferocious persecution of Jews, symbolized by his deportation to the gas chambers of Auschwitz of an entire orphanage of Jewish children aged three to thirteen; his role in the torture and death of Jean Moulin, the man appointed by de Gaulle to be the leader of the French Resistance.

It was the first capture of a major Nazi war criminal since Adolf Eichmann was apprehended in 1960. And this tour de force on the part of a French government beleaguered by economic and social problems thrust the Fifth Republic into a momentary elation. The inevitable media madness ensued. Reporters from French television, the BBC, and other networks descended upon any old resisters who might offer their memories of the "Butcher of Lyons"— many of them disabled Veterans, armless, legless, blind in one eye, ending their days on veterans' pensions in remote areas of the nation. "*Les camions de CBS a minuit . . . dans la Lozère . . . c'est impensable, je n'en peux plus!*" ("CBS vans at midnight . . . in the Lozère . . . it's incredible, I can't take anymore!") one of them growled to me on the phone.

Raunchier members of the Soldiers of the Night (former Resistance fighters) enjoyed elaborating on the methods used by Barbie to elicit information from his captives. Rather than delegate the task to his lieutenants, Barbie enjoyed whipping his victims himself with the riding crop he often carried. He stopped only when the prisoners lost consciousness, reviving them with kicks in the groin or by plunging them into tubs of water filled with ice cubes. Skin was seared off the soles of captives' feet with red-hot irons; acids were injected into their bladders when they refused to yield desired information. There were tales of Barbie kissing and fondling a bejeweled woman on his lap while he whipped his victims; reports of naked blondes being led into his interrogation rooms accompanied by German shepherd dogs trained for bestiality; of Barbie strolling to a piano in the middle of a torture session and playing "Parlez Moi d' Amour" on the piano with his bloodstained fingers, unleashing his vicious Alsatian dog, Wolf, to tear at the flesh of a captive resister.

The henchman's behavior was observed by the French press with the ardent attention that might be bestowed on a captured Martian, or a live dinosaur found lurking in the Amazon basin: Barbie refuses to take the daily walk allotted him. He turns down all offers of books and spends his days leafing through old German magazines left behind by a former inmate. On the Sunday after

his arrival he asks to have the rumpled gray suit he has worn since
he left La Paz spruced up for a meeting with the prosecuting attorneys. The community of women prisoners at Montluc, who are
in charge of laundering services for all of the prison's inmates and
staff, refuse to press Barbie's clothing. Their ranks are combed until one young detainee finally offers her services, asserting that
Barbie is "just another prisoner." A week after his arrival, when he
is moved out of Montluc, it becomes clear that the government has
jailed him there temporarily for purely symbolic reasons—it had
been the site of his principal atrocities. He is transferred across
town to the considerably more obscure Prison Saint-Joseph, where
he is meant to remain until his trial. He lodges there to this day
in a cell about ten feet square furnished with a sink and toilet;
a dozen jailers are assigned to watch him around the clock and
to "assure his security." In these present quarters, so penny-wise
French law rules, he is allowed to listen to the radio, provided that
he pays for the set himself.

     Klaus Barbie is even shorter than Simone Lagrange remem-
bers him—five foot five. He was born in 1913, near the city of Bonn,
into a Catholic family of the lower middle class. His father died of
wounds inflicted in World War I, a fact to which Barbie has attributed his hatred of the French. A talent for anti-Jewish activities
seemed to mark his World War II career from the start. In one
of the first posts he held outside Germany, as a lieutenant in occupied Holland, he participated in the arrest of some three hundred
Jews, who all died at Mauthausen. Shortly after German troops
swept into France's Free Zone, in November 1942, he was pro-
moted to captain's rank and sent to Lyons. He was only twenty-
nine. He became noted for recruiting aid in his hunt for Jews and
resisters, and for his melodramatic acts of vengeance. (The slaughtered bodies of Montluc inmates, for instance, were left in public
sight on Lyons's central thoroughfare in reprisal for the bombing of
Barbie's favorite café.) He was praised in a report by his superiors
as "an exemplary comrade, the soul of the Gestapo." Klaus Barbie
crammed his atrocities in Lyons into a span of twenty months. He
fled Lyons just before Allied forces liberated the city in August
1944, and the next reliable data we have on him show that he was

interned in 1947 by American forces in an interrogation camp at Oberursel, near Frankfurt, the seat of the American High Command.

The events that follow are part of the grotesque and anarchic activities undertaken by American intelligence units (without the knowledge of the State Department or the U.S. High Command) at the start of the Cold War. It seems that Barbie was released by his American jailers in exchange for espionage services, for by the spring of 1948 he had become one of numerous Nazis being used as anti-Soviet agents by our Counterintelligence Corps. A candid explanation of CIC policy from one of Barbie's former employers: "Germans were not our enemies anymore. . . . All our fears had been transferred to the Russians." According to a former CIC officer, Edward Dabringhaus, who claims to have been in charge of Barbie's security and salary when he was being kept in a safe house near Augsburg, the former Gestapo chief was paid $1,700 a month of our taxpayers' money for his work. And his former supervisor reports that this work was as mediocre as it was dishonest; Dabringhaus once caught Barbie studiously copying from a German newspaper an article that he was about to sell to the CIC as valuable information.

A period of three years ensued during which the French government repeatedly pressed the United States High Command to release Barbie for trial in France; but it could never even issue an official demand for his extradition because our intelligence refused to yield Barbie's address in Germany. A judge of the Paris military tribunal, in August 1948, confirmed in writing to one of his colleagues that American authorities were opposed to delivering Barbie to France "for reasons of the United States' national defense." But the higher echelons of our military authorities were comically out of touch. Several months earlier, American intelligence units had granted Barbie a temporary travel document, falsifying his place and date of birth, and provided him with an American army uniform to facilitate his escape. These actions were undertaken without the knowledge of the U.S. High Command or even of the CIC headquarters, which two years earlier had ordered its agents to "cut Barbie loose." According to the Justice Department, the officers in charge of Barbie's transfer were guilty of obstruction of justice, and are being spared punishment in the 1980s only because the statute of limitations has run out.

Barbie and his family were taken across the borders of Austria and Italy by relays of U.S. counterintelligence men and Catholic priests and taken to Genoa, where they boarded a ship to South America. A former CIC colonel who claims to have masterminded Barbie's escape has testified that hundreds of Nazis were smuggled out of Germany by the same route, and that "everyone who went through the 'Rat Line' was personally accompanied to the ship by a member of our organization." The Italian end of the Rat Line was operated by a Croatian priest in Rome who was paid for his services by the CIC, and whose record was as infamous as Barbie's: Father Krunoslav Draganovic was a leader of the ultra-Fascist Croatian Ustasa movement which during the war years had exterminated several hundred thousand Serbs of the Orthodox faith, aiming at a 100 percent Catholic state. Klaus Barbie-Altmann embarked for South America with a visa granted by the International Red Cross, with the probable intercession of individuals in the Vatican hierarchy. For according to a 1947 memorandum written by a member of the American embassy staff in Rome to Secretary of State George Marshall, the Holy See was "the principal organization implicated in the illegal passage" of former Nazis to the safe havens of Latin American dictatorships. The Holy See "particularly feared the effect of Communist activities in Latin America, and for this reason welcomed favorably requests of persons with Fascist pasts." (French euphemisms for the Rat Line were *"la route des monastères"* and *"la filière des couvents,"* the monastery route and the convent network.)

Thus, with the assistance of several venerable organizations, this much-wanted criminal went on to a lucrative career in Bolivia, allegedly dealing in sawmills, armament sales, and the cocaine trade. For some twenty years he managed to exchange his services for the protection of numerous short-lived Bolivian oligarchies, and in 1972 was even appointed security adviser to the secret police by that particular year's dictator, General Hugo Banzer Suárez.

It was not until 1972, after a Parisian couple named Beate and Serge Klarsfeld had unmasked him, that Barbie began to reveal publicly his gift for lying, and his caddish, swaggering unrepentance. "I am an SS. It's like a superman chosen by Hitler," he said in one of the press interviews he enjoyed giving in Latin America. "I am prouder of what I've done than I am of Willy Brandt, who committed treason to Germany during the war in a Norwegian uniform." Barbie particularly enjoyed flaunting his extensive travels, which included several trips to the United States, Portugal, France, and Spain, where he had sent his younger child, Klaus, Jr., to university. Although at first he denied ever having heard of Jean Moulin, he later boasted of the monumental catch he made in arresting the Resistance's greatest hero. He even spun a pretty tale about taking flowers to Moulin's grave in Paris. "Had Jean Moulin lived, he'd have become president of France instead of de Gaulle. I changed the course of history by arresting Moulin."

Once his true identity was revealed, this executioner's fate was left to the vagaries of Latin American politics. He was to enjoy eleven more years of freedom. The agent of his doom was Hernan Siles Zuazo, the first Bolivian president in some decades who seemed to desire an appearance of liberalism. Zuazo took power in November 1982. President François Mitterrand's entourage, which is notably more dedicated to the memory of the Resistance than was Pompidou's or Giscard d'Estaing's, sprang into legal action in a matter of days. Barbie was arrested in La Paz in January of 1983 for alleged nonpayment of debts and expelled two days later on the grounds that his Bolivian citizenship was invalid, since it had been obtained under a false name. He was sent to France following an official announcement that France was the only European nation willing to accept him.

The credit for returning Klaus Barbie to Lyons, and to justice, is not attributable to the valor of either government. It is due solely to two extraordinary residents of Paris, Serge and Beate Klarsfeld, who have made it their life's vocation to purge the world of Nazi war criminals.

Shortly after midnight on September 30, 1943, the Gestapo knocked on the door of the Klarsfelds, a Jewish family living in Nice.

The head of the family, Arno, was a prosperous Paris businessman in his thirties whose father had been an armaments manufacturer in Rumania. Like his Russian wife, Raïssa, he had moved to Paris in the late 1920s to study. They met in a café in the Latin Quarter, married, and had two children. Although Arno was not yet a French citizen at the onset of the war, he volunteered for the French army. A powerfully built man of considerable shrewdness and physical strength, he was captured and interned in Germany, but escaped from his stalag. After rejoining his family, which had fled the Occupied Zone in 1940 to settle in Nice, he enlisted in the Resistance.

Like many well-to-do Paris Jews who had the financial means to choose their place of exile, the Klarsfelds had enjoyed, in Nice, an impunity from persecution granted few Jews in Vichy France. When the Germans invaded France's Free Zone in November 1942, the Alpes-Maritimes, along with seven other southeastern districts, became the booty of Germany's Italian allies. The Italian high command, whose brand of Fascism was notably lenient regarding Jews, set out at once to block the numerous anti-Semitic measures passed by Pétain's cabinet (frequently without any prodding from the Germans) after the armistice of 1940.

The accreted anti-Semitic policies of the Vichy government reached their apogee in the summer of 1942 and were responsible for the often forgotten fact that some 90 percent of all Jews arrested in France during the war years were seized by French police. And when the Italian forces occupied a part of southern France, they began a policy of protection which enraged Vichy and Gestapo officials alike. Italian troops freed hundreds of Jews already rounded up for deportation by French prefects. Ordinances aimed at expelling foreign and stateless Jews from the Italian Zone were blocked with equal zeal. Carabinieri stationed in Nice mounted guard in front of the main synagogue, a haven for Jewish clandestine activity, and enabled Jews to issue their own identity cards. Their commander went so far as to threaten the arrest of any French policeman who interfered with his unit's benevolence.

The Jews' security thus had seemed assured in Nice until the sudden announcement, on September 8, 1943, that the Allies had signed a separate armistice with Italy. Three days later German forces arrived. And in revenge against Italian policies, the Gestapo, under the leadership of Alois Brunner, began a zealous application of the Final Solution, which, in the course of a few months, would take many thousands of Jews to concentration camps in Eastern Europe.

It was the sudden loss of Italian protection which the Klarsfeld family, like all Jews in southeastern France, had to face that September. Earlier that summer, a prescient fellow resister had persuaded the Klarsfelds to build a hiding place in their apartment in case there should be a German takeover; he helped them construct a false wall in the back of a hall closet. His apprehensions were accurate. Twelve days after the German troops' arrival, Raïssa Klarsfeld woke at midnight, saw her bedroom flooded with light, heard trucks roaring in the streets below. The family spent a few minutes straightening their beds and putting away their clothes, then entered their hiding place. Serge Klarsfeld was eight years old at the time, his sister eleven.

The secret closet was separated by a thin wall from the apartment of a family of Alsatian Jews whom the Klarsfelds often visited. Serge Klarsfeld remembers hearing the Gestapo knocking on the neighbors' door, and their young daughter's cries of pain as the soldiers beat her with revolvers, demanding to know the whereabouts of her older brother, who was out of town. Serge also heard the girl's father shouting futile words whose irony would still haunt him many decades later: "*Au secours*, help, French police! We are French citizens! *Au secours!*"

Serge then heard his father whispering to his wife, "I'm strong enough to survive another camp." And despite his wife's pleas Arno Klarsfeld went out to meet the SS. His family was saved by his sacrifice. After being told that his wife and children were in the country, the soldiers made a casual search which left the secret closet untouched, and took Arno Klarsfeld away. He died at Auschwitz after still another impetuous show of courage—striking down a *kapo* who had slapped him in the face. In reprisal he was sent to the coal mines, where he lasted barely six months.

Forty years later, Serge Klarsfeld still has recurrent dreams that his father returns.

Serge Klarsfeld's life has been shaped by his need to avenge his heroic Jewish father. The life of his wife Beate, a German and a Christian, has been forged by her need to punish hers.

□

In the spring of 1945, until Adolf Hitler committed suicide and German forces capitulated to the Allies, little Beate Kunzel was in grade school, still reciting poems in praise of the führer. Her father was a civil service clerk who had obediently done war service in the Wehrmacht. Beate described her family as dour, taciturn Berliners who broke their silence only when the father drank and the mother grumbled her remonstrances. Beate left for Paris at the age of twenty-one to escape parental oppression. She went on to be oppressed by a series of French families for whom she worked as an au pair girl, cleaning and cooking, sleeping in filthy attics, fired once for watching television and another time for not responding to an employer's sexual advances.

Beate met Serge Klarsfeld in 1960 on a métro platform. He had graduated from the Ecole des Sciences Politiques and completed a master's degree at the Sorbonne. They were married three years later after a courtship that involved an arduous process of education. The militant young Zionist assigned the innocent German girl to read the history of World War II. He forced her to accept the facts of the Holocaust, which were still unknown to the great majority of her compatriots. Serge proved to be a gifted teacher. A few years after their marriage, Beate abandoned the serene domestic life she had dreamed of as a proper German girl. She devoted herself to "restoring my country's honor," to keeping alive the memory of the Holocaust, to forcing to justice those who had a role in perpetrating it. Her career can be compared (her husband's metaphor) to Willy Brandt's symbolic gesture of kneeling before Warsaw's Jewish ghetto.

Two decades later, a few weeks after the Klarsfelds' perseverance has succeeded in returning Klaus Barbie to Lyons, I visit them in their apartment at the porte de Saint-Cloud. Every surface in these three rooms is varnished and polished to a gleam, all is dollhouse tidiness and gemütlichkeit. The noted Nazi hunter Beate Klarsfeld is a delicate, very pretty woman with short red hair and the reclusive manner of a former nun or a timid hausfrau. She seldom initiates a conversation except to inquire, with genuine curiosity, about some detail of my domestic life: What

careers are my children pursuing? What is my family's favorite dinner fare? Shreds of her biography flood my mind as I marvel at her
placid, housewifely smile. In the past twelve years she has confronted police in Damascus while protesting Syria's refusal to publish lists of Israeli war prisoners; she has been detained by police
in Morocco, and then expelled, for distributing leaflets in front of
the Arab League's summit conference; arrested in Warsaw and in
Prague for leading demonstrations against those governments' anti-
Semitic policies; held by police in Bolivia for protesting that government's protection of Klaus Barbie; jailed for five weeks in Co-
logne for civil disobedience while lobbying for the trial in German
courts of three former Nazi police chiefs (Kurt Lischka, Herbert
Hagen, Ernst Heinrichsohn) who had been responsible for the
deportation of some seventy-five thousand Jews from France to
Auschwitz. (She was successful. They were convicted, and received
sentences ranging from six to twelve years.)

Today Beate is posing for a photographer with particular pleasure because there is a new puppy in the household (a beloved former pet, she elaborates, died a few months ago at the age of sixteen) and this will be the first family photograph to include the
puppy. Its name is Scott. It is being held by the Klarsfelds' eighteen-year-old son, Arno, who had his bar mitzvah in a kibbutz on
the Golan Heights and has the swarthy handsomeness of an Israeli
movie star. "Be a good cat," Beate says as her ten-year-old daughter, Lida, tries to keep her red tabby from clawing the puppy.
"There's a good dog." She prattles proudly about her new apartment. This is the first flat in some years in which she and Serge
have a bedroom of their own. In the last one they slept on a
folding bed in the living room in order to give their children more
privacy.

When her son Arno was only three years old, in 1968, Beate
went to a meeting of the Christian Democratic party in West
Berlin, and before a large crowd of fellow Germans—government
notables, journalists, several hundred armed police—she slapped
Chancellor Kurt Georg Kiesinger in the face. Kiesinger, during his
difficult campaign for the chancellorship, had pleaded that he was
yet another passive, suffering German who had disagreed with Nazi
doctrine. By delving into the East German state archives in Pots-

dam, Beate discovered that he had been the deputy director of the Third Reich's radio propaganda for foreign countries. Posing as a reporter, scribbling in a notebook, she managed to get to the podium where Kiesinger was about to make a speech. "Nazi, Nazi!" she screamed as she gave him the slap. She went on trial, and was sentenced to one year in prison. She appealed the verdict and received a four-month suspended sentence. She was granted amnesty by Willy Brandt, who succeeded Kiesinger to the chancellorship a few months after Beate's performance. The decision to "publicly slap the generation of our fathers," as she puts it, was the turning point of her life.

After marrying Beate, Serge worked as an executive of the French National Radio, an officer of Continental Grains, and a volunteer in the Israeli army. At the age of thirty-seven he returned to law school for a year and passed his bar exam. Since then he has researched numerous law cases dealing with German war criminals, served several short stints in jail for his role in anti-Nazi demonstrations, and written some of the most exhaustive books and articles available on the persecution of French and Belgian Jews. He is now in his late forties, a plump man of average height given to wearing worn sport jackets and round dark glasses. He walks very fast, leaning forward, head down, frowning. He reminded me, at first sight, of those curt-mannered citizens one sees in the streets of Tel Aviv, bustling through crowds with no elaborate attempt at courtesy. Upon acquaintance one is confronted by his eloquence, his considerable literary and political education. There emerges the interesting hybrid of Zionist activist and razor-witted French intellectual, and a compassion for the enemy rare among militants.

"I had a dream about Barbie last night," Serge said to me once as we were seated in his office on the rue de La Boétie. "I was careful to keep my distance. We weren't face-to-face in the dream, we were talking to each other on the phone. Look, I told him, we mightn't be bothering you this way if you'd expressed your regrets, asked your victims' forgiveness . . . in short I was telling him all that he could have done to avoid his plight. You see, I have a conscience about having him incarcerated; I reproach myself a bit. I have a surge of pity for all men who're in prison. My father died in prison; I've been to jail several times, I know myself how dreadful it is. There are a lot of people out there who want to kill Barbie, and if there were a crowd outside his cell beating on his door, I might be the first to protect him. . . ."

These Klarsfelds are not an easy couple to decipher. The angry son of an Auschwitz victim, the German soldier's daughter whom he's educated to carry out his revenge. She has radicalized him in turn, and she is many women wrapped in one: tender and dedicated wife and mother, virtuoso of civil disobedience who slaps a head of state, battle-happy amazon who travels about the world unmasking war criminals. . . . The Klarsfelds are not given to introspection; they give few clues. I once asked her: "Have the victims of your father's generation—Jews—become the hero-martyrs with whom you identify, whose suffering you wish to share?"

"I suppose so," she said softly. And added: "Wherever Jews are persecuted, it is our German duty to intervene on their side."

Until the Klarsfelds began to track down Klaus Barbie, he had been living the life of a prosperous Bolivian businessman. Shortly before leaving Europe in 1948, he had acquired a Bolivian passport, issued to him by American authorities, under the name Klaus Altmann. The very choice of the name Altmann illustrates Barbie's savage brand of psychological sadism. For among the several hundred Jews whom Barbie dispatched to death camps during his SS stint in Holland there was a distinguished scholar called Adolf Altmann, formerly the chief rabbi of Barbie's hometown of Trier. One can only see this as a deliberate choice, the executioner toying with the identity of his victim, sarcastically defying the powers that had begun to hound him.

Unlike the reclusive, melancholy Adolf Eichmann, who survived in the suburbs of Buenos Aires in a house without light or running water, supporting himself as a rabbit keeper and part-time salesman, Barbie was a high liver. He was flourishing in La Paz as a citizen noted for his courtesy and his convivial, punctual habits. He was an accomplished pianist and frequented fancy restaurants and cafés. He had managed to survive some twelve coups d'état by rendering his services to Bolivian dictatorships of varying degrees of violence. It is most probable that he was linked to a secret terrorist group known as the Fiancés of Death, which has been responsible for political assassinations and kidnappings on several continents, notably the 1980 bombing of a train station in Bologna, Italy, in which eighty-four people were killed. For several years this lethal band of paramilitary thugs had a monopoly on Bolivia's flourishing cocaine trade and helped the Bolivian dictatorship to suppress all dissent by intimidation and murder. The star of the group, Pierluigi Pagliai, a particular buddy of Barbie's who was seen drinking with Barbie a few weeks before the Bologna bombing, would regularly appear for torture sessions of Bolivian dissidents wearing ballet tights, stripped to the waist, his torso oiled. He once killed two Bolivian peasants during a practical demonstration at one of his public seminars on "countersubversive techniques."

It was Barbie's good fortune that the president of Bolivia in 1972 was Colonel Hugo Banzer Suárez, who rose to power through a series of coups financed in part by Bolivia's German colony. For that was the year Beate Klarsfeld arrived in Latin America with her winsome smile, her impeccable matronly clothes, and a good quantity of irrefutable evidence concerning Klaus Altmann's true identity.

The Klarsfelds' decision to pursue Barbie stemmed from their outrage at the fact that a German prosecutor, in the summer of 1971, had declared invalid the suit filed against Barbie a decade previously by German Jews, and closed the case. The charges had been dismissed because there was no proof of genocidal intent; in other words, the Gestapo chief might not have known what fate awaited his victims when they were deported to the East. The prosecutor's decision had created a dangerous precedent on which numerous other former Nazis might seek impunity. The Klarsfelds sensed that if they interviewed enough Jewish survivors of the Lyons region who had had personal dealings with Barbie, his criminal foreknowledge could be brought to light.

Beate interviewed hundreds of such survivors and found one who provided proof. He had been a director of a Jewish agency in Lyons during the Occupation, and he had heard Barbie say the following words about a group of his victims: "Deported or shot, there's no difference." The witness joyfully signed an affidavit legalizing his testimony, and Beate took this document to a German public prosecutor. He was impressed enough by the evidence, and by its bearer, to reopen the Barbie case. The greatest treasures in his file on Barbie, which the Klarsfelds were now free to work with, were two photographs. One of them showed Klaus Barbie in 1943 in his SS uniform. Another showed a Bolivian businessman named Klaus Altmann, who looked strikingly like Barbie, attending a board meeting in La Paz in 1968. Within a few weeks, a study of the photographs undertaken by French police experts had attested that Altmann and Barbie were one and the same man.

It is interesting to note the indefatigable pace and passion with which Beate now pursued her prey:

The photographs, and the new evidence, are published throughout Europe. Within a few days a Jewish lawyer from the Lyons area has raised the funds to buy Beate a plane ticket to Peru, where Barbie had gone on an extended business trip. Upon arriving in Lima, Beate sits up until two A.M. with reporters, showing them the numerous proofs of Barbie-Altmann's identity. Front-page headlines on Peru's papers the next afternoon: GERMAN NAZI-HUNTER PROVES ALTMANN IS BARBIE.

She spends the afternoon with the French ambassador, a former deportee who embraces her and requests the Peruvian government to stop Barbie from crossing its borders until the French goverment makes an official demand for his extradition. But the tight alliance between former Nazis and Latin American oligarchies prevails. The Peruvian policemen who accompanied Barbie to the frontier have already delivered him into the benevolent custody of the Bolivian police.

The following morning Beate takes a plane and follows Barbie to La Paz, where she repeats her process of education with the local press. But she fails to obtain an appointment with the Bolivian president, Colonel Banzer Suárez, who throughout her stay shelters his friend Barbie-Altmann in a comfortable jail cell, holding him in protective custody for alleged nonpayment of debts. Several days after her arrival Bolivian authorities order Beate to leave the country and return to Paris.

But a mere eight days have passed, and Klaus Barbie's whereabouts and identity have been disclosed to the world. The week of Beate's return, film footage of Barbie is shown on French television. Several of his former victims identify him. Beate tries to persuade one of them, Simone Lagrange, to accompany her on another trip to La Paz, but Simone demurs. Beate flies back to La Paz a fortnight later in the company of Madame Halaunbrenner, an elderly survivor of Auschwitz, three of whose children and husband were executed on Barbie's orders.

As Beate arrives in La Paz, she hears that President Pompidou has made an official request for Barbie-Altmann's extradition. She holds a press conference against the government's orders, is arrested and taken into custody for two days at police headquarters. Shortly after her release, she goes to shop for chains and padlocks with which to stage her next protest. Beate and the aging Madame Halaunbrenner clamp the chains and padlocks around their waists and wrists and sit down on a bench on La Paz's busiest thoroughfare, in front of the building which houses Barbie-Altmann's offices. The placards they hold up to all viewers read, IN THE NAME OF THE MILLIONS OF NAZI VICTIMS, LET BARBIE-ALTMANN BE EXTRADITED.

Eleven years later Klaus Barbie would sit on a plane bound for Lyons, slumped in his seat, head bowed. "Vae victis," he would murmur after being read his arrest warrant: "Woe to the vanquished."

Beate sleeps as soundly as a child, even at an altitude of twelve thousand feet, and unlike Serge she never dreams.

I once asked her what hobbies or avocations she pursued to relax from her formidable schedule. "None," she answered with a gentle smile. "My only relaxation is to be home surrounded by the family mayhem. Children arguing, dog and cat scuffling about me while I cook and iron—that's my paradise."

In the summer Beate takes a week's vacation in Israel, where she has become such a heroine that free rooms are at her disposal in several hotels and all kibbutzim. There she likes to lie by a pool reading detective stories.

I also asked the Klarsfelds about fear. Had they not been afraid during their confrontations and arrests in such countries as

Syria, Morocco, Bolivia, where foreigners frequently disappear without leaving a trace?

"If you concentrate hard enough on the action, all apprehension disappears," Beate answered. "I only have childlike, elemental fears. I'm afraid of the dark. I'm more afraid of going into a cellar at night than of being arrested by Syrian police."

When asked about fear Serge Klarsfeld shrugged his shoulders, gave a disdainful pout.

"The kind of people we confront are not used to such direct actions, they're not used to the passionate opinions of those who fight for the memory of the past. . . . Look, I'll give you an example of how true conviction works. By 1976 Germany's neo-Nazi party had regained such strength that it was allowed to hold its meetings right in downtown Munich; its newspaper had a circulation of a hundred thousand and was publishing stories about how only two thousand Jews were killed in the Holocaust and most of them were victims of Allied bombings. I said to Beate, this is intolerable. Here are these guys about to meet right in the Burgerbraukellar, where Hitler made his first putsch. This is intolerable, I must create an incident. We pondered it and figured out a tactic. I decided that I'd become the first Jew since the war to be publicly beaten up by the Nazis. So I went to a beer hall, right into the Deutsche Volks-Union's meeting. I tell you, it's very entertaining, very exalting to go to a neo-Nazi meeting. I'd rather scuffle with Nazis or Iranian mullahs anytime than go to conferences, I detest conferences. . . . Anyhow, I went in and greeted them with a beautiful smile and said, 'Here I am, a Jew.' They started beating me up, of course. A lot of reporters came, and they took numerous photographs of the public beating. Note the following detail: I didn't come out with one black-and-blue mark on my body. And I bruise easily; I'm even full of blacks and blues after a mock fight with my little daughter . . . but every inch of me was so relaxed at that Nazi meeting that I didn't carry a bruise. This is just one example of how you create an incident and turn a situation of weakness—being beaten—into one of strength."

Whether Beate chains herself to a bench in La Paz or Serge tussles at Fascist meetings, the notion of "creating incidents" is central to the Klarsfelds' tactics of Nazi hunting. They feel uneasy about being compared to Simon Wiesenthal, for unlike Wiesenthal, they combine documentation with frequent, risky confrontations. Yet their way of creating incidents is distinctly different from the Gandhian tradition of civil disobedience that influenced Martin Luther King or the Berrigans, for it is strictly pragmatic, quite devoid of any religious notion of "witnessing." "There's no noble ideological influence whatsoever in our way of civil disobedience," Serge comments. "My only inspiration comes from the American films I loved as a kid, the Robin Hood or *High Noon* type of movie, which shows a loner upholding justice against an indifferent majority."

The Klarsfelds also confront an often indifferent majority through their publications on the Holocaust. Their most monumental achievement to date is a seven-hundred-page book, the size of a New York City telephone directory, which recounts the fate of every Jewish man, woman, and child sent to German camps from France during the Occupation. It is entitled *Memorial to the Jews Deported from France.* It reproduces, in chronological order, the passenger lists of the eighty convoys on which the victims were transported, from the first trainload on March 27, 1942, to the last one on August 11, 1944, which left Lyons for Auschwitz under Barbie's orders two weeks before the liberation of Paris. This grim and pious monument to the martyrdom of some 80,000 human beings, many of whose fates had remained unknown, also contains many eyewitness accounts of the arrests made by French police which preceded each departure. It chronicles, among others, the Vélodrome d'Hiver roundup in the summer of 1942, when some thirteen thousand Jews were packed for many days into one sports stadium, detained by Parisian cops in conditions so atrocious that many of the captives did not live to see the cattle cars for which they were destined.

From Serge Klarsfeld's introduction to the American edition of *Memorial:* "As the son of a deportee assassinated at Auschwitz, and having been miraculously spared the fate of the ramp at Birkenau, I imposed upon myself some years ago the task of putting an end to the impunity enjoyed by Nazi criminals who deported Jews from France. My partner in this work is my wife,

Beate, a non-Jewish German. It is an ongoing mission which we are accomplishing step by step, in spite of the powerful forces opposed to the cause we are defeating."

In 1979 the Klarsfelds' car was destroyed by a time bomb which set off a large fire in the underground garage servicing their apartment building. Not long after Barbie was exposed in Bolivia, Serge received a package which he correctly suspected should be taken to a police station for immediate inspection. It contained enough explosive to kill anyone within a radius of a hundred feet. Threatening letters from right-wing neo-Nazi and left-wing anti-Zionist sources come often; so do morbid phone calls, which Serge sometimes answers by quoting long passages from *Mein Kampf* in German, deterring the callers, he believes, from ever phoning again.

The Klarsfelds remain undaunted by fear. But there are many days when one senses that Beate has overestimated her strength and her capacity for solitude. This woman of latent rage and mysterious courage, whom young Jews reverently approach in the streets of Paris for an autograph, remains an intensely domestic, private person. And she is often plagued by her nostalgia for a more serene pace of life. There are evenings when she buries her chin in one hand and lapses into long silences. Such was her mood on a spring night when I dined with the Klarsfelds in New York City, at the Plaza Hotel. They had flown to Washington from Paris the previous Saturday, their trip paid by the Larry King television show, on which they were very amused to appear right before Mr. T. On Sunday they had worked all day with an official of the Justice Department who has studied the links between Klaus Barbie and the CIC. They were to fly back to Paris on Tuesday, after only three days in the United States, because, as Beate said, "the children, the dog, the cat have to be taken care of."

Serge was voluble throughout the evening. He talked about his childhood. I was amazed to hear that he considered it immensely happy. Although his family had lived in a state of extreme penury in the years after his father's death, moving several times to seek new shelter, he deeply loved his mother and his sister; he loved all the different schools he'd been to; he enjoyed the Catholic prayers he was taught by the priests who gave him a year's shelter in the Haute-Loire; he considered it a blessed childhood. He had, after all, survived. (I thought back to Simone Lagrange's "Don't you dare pity me.")

Serge talked about his favorite relaxation—visiting churches and museums throughout Europe. If he had to choose another vocation, he would be a museum guard at the Künsthistorische Museum in Vienna so that he could contemplate all its Breughels at leisure.

He talked about his love for Israel, his love for France, his complex double identity as Jew and Frenchman. "When I'm in Paris I'm a million times happier than when I'm in Tel Aviv, yet Tel Aviv is a psychic *chez moi* to which I'm profoundly attached. Many of us live with these difficult contradictions. . . ."

Beate sat staring at the tablecloth, fiddling with a bottle of aspirin. Serge stopped talking and looked attentively at an imposing woman in her seventies who had just entered the restaurant.

"*Regardes!*" he said excitedly to his wife. "There's Ginger Rogers, right across the room!"

"*Incroyable!*" Beate exclaimed, looking very cheerful again. "Wait until we tell the children!"

Serge Klarsfeld took his wife's hand. "I've always had an impeccable sense of history," he said. "Forty years from now we'll come back to this room, and everyone will turn to look at you and say, 'There's Beate Klarsfeld.'"

Of the 75,000 Jews deported from France during the Occupation, only 2,500 returned. Simone Lagrange is one of the few still alive today.

I keep remembering that day in Lyons when she stood by me in front of the prison in which Klaus Barbie is held.

She continues to describe the kingdom of death to which Barbie sent her. She speaks of Dr. Mengele meeting the train convoys at the ramp of Birkenau, selecting with a wave of his conductor's baton the children, the ill, and the aged destined for the gas chambers. Mengele merrily playing ball one morning with two young children he had reserved for his experiments. Then suddenly, at noon, ordering Simone and other women working in a nearby field to dig a ditch, calling the SS to shoot the children, commanding Simone's group to bury them in the freshly dug grave, offering them an extra ration of bread in reward.

One of the three Nazis most wanted in the West in the past decades, Mengele, a millionaire by inheritance, was living luxuriously in Brazil until his recent death. Alois Brunner, Eichmann's most efficient deputy, single-handedly responsible for the deportation of about a hundred thousand Jews, was tracked down by Serge Klarsfeld in Syria, where he has lived under the pseudonym of Dr. Georg Fischer. And Klaus Barbie has been brought to justice by avenging angels who have elected to stand above history and expunge some of the evils left unpurged by the governments of men.

There is a final solution to the problem of German war criminals—biological age. Klaus Barbie's might be the last of the important Nazi war trials. Simon Wiesenthal and Serge and Beate Klarsfeld are the last of the Nazi hunters.

The elation with which France initially greeted Barbie's return has given way to an increasing mood of misgiving, self-doubt, and feigned indifference. The French have become divided over the symbolic value of his trial and the pragmatic value of this aged man's incarceration. There are even Jewish survivors of Auschwitz, like the valiant Simone Veil, who are wary of the Barbie trial because it might further divide an already troubled nation, and who fear that the media will blur the major issues. There are former resisters with leftist leanings who are concerned that Barbie, by testifying to the numerous traitors in their ranks and the bitterness of the Resistance's inner divisions, might impugn the only honor left to France in the darkest years of its history. There are also those who fear that the trial will create a mood of undue contrition about Vichy collaboration, which, they still argue, shielded France from Nazi excesses and saved many lives. This national unease is being cloaked by such phrases as "It's too late, it's like putting Verdun onstage." And by that familiar French aphorism *"Il ne faut pas remuer la boue"*: "One mustn't stir up the mud."

Santayana once wrote that those who cannot remember the past are condemned to repeat it. In France it is the generation under forty, whose propensity to theories of communal guilt is sometimes excessive, that is most willing to heed that warning, and is most enthusiastically in favor of the Barbie trial. A generation with less sorrow to remember, nothing to fear, everything to learn.

"I want to see the maximum amount of mud being stirred," says the philosopher Bernard-Henri Lévy. "French mud has never been stirred enough, France is a country which is dying and drowning in mud left unstirred; the French people must learn, all the more so if they don't *want* to learn, they must hear, all the more so if they don't *want* to hear, that the Jews who were led to gas chambers took their first steps to them between rows of French cops who came knocking on their doors at dawn in the rue des Rosiers, the rue du Sentier, in 1942."

II

A windy night in Provence, shortly after midnight on January 1, 1942. A two-engine British plane circles over a moonlit field fifteen miles south of Avignon. Inside the aircraft, three Frenchmen in parachuting gear sit at action stations by the open trapdoor; they see a light in the cockpit turn from red to green.

At the shout of *Go!* each man leaps into the night. The parachutes open quickly. But the mistral is blowing hard, the partisans are swept away from the designated dropping zone and land a few miles from one another. It is imperative to regroup before dawn. So they rapidly search the countryside, whistling the first phrase of an old French folk song which they've chosen as a code: "There's a nest in the pear tree, I hear the magpie singing . . ." By five A.M. they are reunited; they bury their parachutes and start walking.

Thus begins one of France's most beloved heroic tales. The leader of the mission, the first to bail out of the plane, was a former official of the Third Republic named Jean Moulin, alias Max, Rex, Marchand, Mercier, Martel. He carried on him a small matchbox with a false bottom on which he had pasted a microfilm of his credentials. These had been signed in London the week before by Charles de Gaulle and read as follows: "I designate Monsieur Jean Moulin, prefect, as my representative and delegate to the French National Committee for the Unoccupied Zone of the nation. Monsieur Moulin's mission is to bring about a unification in this zone of all elements resisting the enemy and its collaborators."

Jean Moulin is now buried in the Pantheon in Paris, the sixtieth Frenchman since Mirabeau to be interred in the site reserved for his nation's greatest men. His heroic achievement was to turn resistant Frenchmen into a French Resistance, to weave dozens of anarchic, dissenting factions into the only redeeming honor of his nation's wartime years and rally it behind de Gaulle. His martyrdom came at the hands of Klaus Barbie, the Gestapo chief of Lyons. When the French government returned Barbie to justice in the city where he had tortured Moulin to death, it was exclusively motivated by the memory of the man whose valor and endurance have become legend.

Born in 1899 in Béziers, in Southwestern France, Jean Moulin wished above all to be an artist, and that repressed second self may have fostered his secretive nature, his gift for the clandestine, which would be essential to his wartime mission. From the age of six he showed a precocious talent for drawing and painting, and by fourteen he was publishing drawings in newspapers under the pseudonym Romanin, the name of a ruined castle near his home which he loved to visit. But Jean's father, a professor of history in Béziers, the first intellectual in a long line of artisans, fervently wanted his son to enter the civil service. And so Moulin's artistic calling was aborted by a parent whom he loved passionately and to whom he showed an obedience that seems, these days, excessive. Bowing to his father's will, Jean Moulin finished law school, passed his civil service exams, and became at twenty-six France's youngest subprefect, roughly the equivalent of a lieutenant governor in the United States.

"Romanin" continued to publish drawings during his rise in the prefectual system, serving in Savoie and Somme. While posted in Savoie, he married a young singer who chafed at the provincial life his career confined her to, and they divorced after eighteen months. During the 1930s Moulin made etchings for an edition of Tristan Corbière's poems and collected paintings by artists who would have been considered hazardously modern by his colleagues in government service—Severini, Chirico, Rouault.

The paradox of a hero whose fame was achieved in anonymity: forty years after Moulin's death there are few clear recollections of him. The few survivors who knew him well recall him as a man "of immensely magnetic presence . . . with a warm and penetrating gaze, laughing eyes, a sunny, lilting voice, a playful wit, and exquisite old-fashioned courtesy."

The few photographs of Moulin taken after 1940 show a short, slender man wearing a British-style trench coat and a fedora, his neck swathed in all seasons in a scarf. The scarf was there to hide a scar which dated from his first act of resistance.

It was June 17, 1940, three days after German forces had swept through northern France, a few hours after Marshal Pétain's trembling voice had announced on French radio the capitulation and the armistice. Moulin was living in Chartres, heading one of France's most populous departments, Eure-et-Loir. When he received news that a woman in his district had been shot to death by members of the Wehrmacht for protesting their occupation of her house, he called German headquarters and asked that action be taken against the soldiers. Shortly afterward two German officers arrived at Moulin's office; in order to mask the crime, they ordered Moulin to sign a document stating that French Senegalese riflemen had massacred several women in a nearby village. Indignant, the prefect refused to sign, and after seven hours of beatings he was taken to jail.

Moulin seemed to fear greatly, in those days, the effects of torture. The floor of his cell was littered with windowpanes shattered by a recent bombing. Choosing to risk death rather than dishonor any French soldiers, he picked up a piece of glass and gashed his throat. Members of the Gestapo opened his cell door a few hours later and found him lying on the floor in a pool of blood. Fearful of creating a military scandal and a French hero in the first days of the Occupation, they rushed Moulin to a doctor, who bandaged his wound in time to save him. "I never knew it would be so easy," Moulin wrote his mother that week, "to do one's duty."

Jean Moulin arrived in London in the autumn of 1941 with few credentials to present to de Gaulle beyond his former prefect's card, which he had cut into eight pieces and dispersed in his alarm clock and the handle of his suitcase. He had been dismissed from government service the previous year on the grounds that his penchant for Leon Blum's Socialist government had made him, in Vichy parlance, "a prisoner of the ancien régime." After his dismissal he had traveled extensively throughout France, making contacts with the diverse Resistance networks being formed in the Unoccupied Zone. He remained, until the Liberation, the only one of France's ninety prefects to offer his services to the Free French.

De Gaulle later described Moulin in his memoirs as "a man of shrewdness and faith, doubting nothing and defiant of all." During his very first meeting with Moulin, de Gaulle decided to appoint him as his personal delegate in France. There was an amazingly instant accord between these men of radically opposed ideologies— Catholic conservative and left-leaning atheist. Yet both, throughout their careers, had eschewed party affiliations; both had been untainted by those capricious conversions which had marked many French leaders of the 1930s. (Pierre Laval, head of the Vichy government under Pétain, was a member of the Socialist party through 1931. The ultra-right-wing Jacques Doriot, who castigated Laval for not adhering closely enough to the Nazi model, had been one of the leaders of the French Communist party until 1934.) However different their ideologies, de Gaulle and Moulin had followed them unswervingly.

The theory that Moulin propounded to de Gaulle concerning the Resistance perfectly suited the general's mystical ideal of the nation as person, spouse, *Notre Dame la France*. The Resistance, in Moulin's view, must achieve a seamless identity and transcend all political beliefs. Every resistant faction in France, whether composed of Catholic royalist or Communists, must be united into one tightly knit liberation movement. No other ideal could have bonded de Gaulle most closely to Moulin than this mystique of unification.

One must also remember de Gaulle's loneliness. His natural inclination to solitude, which he called "the wretched state of superior beings," was magnified by the stubborn aloofness of the Allied chiefs and by France's massive support of the Vichy regime. De Gaulle's virtual ignorance of the Resistance was remedied by the information Moulin had gleaned on his travels, and his instinctual trust was buttressed by Moulin's twenty years in civil service. The solitary general, obsessed with the idea that he incarnated France's destiny, must have seen in Moulin the ideal man through whom he could create a bond with his estranged flock.

And so Jean Moulin was parachuted into France at the dawn of 1942, into that grim, adventurous romance of the Resistance which mesmerizes the French to this day. Into the coded language of clandestinity, the timing of parachute missions to the cycles of the moon ("in the January moon, the August moon,") the chameleonic pseudonyms of leaders and maneuvers (agents Buisson, Renard, Aiglon, operations Biting, Acrobat). Into backwoods maquis ringing with the rebellious lyrics of the "Chant des Partisans": *"Ami, entends-tu les cris sourds d'un pays qu'on enchaîne . . ."* ("Friend, do you hear the muffled cries of a country enslaved . . ."). Into that courageous mayhem in which Trotskyist Jewish intellectuals elbowed and bickered with archconservative Catholic career officers, anarcho-syndicalists preaching total revolution, triggerhappy Communists eager to shoot (at the risk of severe German reprisals) every Nazi soldier they saw, and quasi royalists of my own father's ilk who had taken refuge from the moral rout of the 1930s in a predilection for anti-Semitism, medieval heraldry, and ultraright groups such as the Croix-de-Feu. It was this helter-skelter band, resembling both the First Crusade and the Paris Commune, ridden with more inner hatreds than its survivors tend to admit, that Moulin persuaded to rally behind de Gaulle's leadership and that he managed to unite into a movement which ultimately gave the Fourth Republic its only legitimacy.

Moulin's mission, the following year, kept him in constant contact with the Resistance in Lyons. The second-largest city of the Unoccupied Zone and a hub of the nation's railroad system, Lyons was in a strategic position for sabotage activity. It was also a major printing center, and French dissenters flocked there to publish their three principal press organs. Lyons's importance led the Third Reich to establish a Gestapo there second only to that in Paris, and to head it with one of its most brutally efficient young officers, Klaus Barbie. Barbie was assigned to Lyons in late November of 1942, shortly after German troops had swept into France's

Free Zone. In addition to his zeal for persecuting Jews, he was singled out by his colleagues for his gift for "turning" men, creating double agents and informers within the ranks of the Resistance: in his last post, in Savoie, he had recruited a network of more than a hundred French informers in the span of a few weeks.

During the eighteen months of his mission, Moulin's true identity as de Gaulle's delegate was revealed to only a handful of Resistance leaders. He was known to most of his fellow partisans as Max or Rex: to the Lyonnais as Marchand; to citizens of other regions as M. Martel, decorator and art dealer. For he had devised an ingenious cover to legitimize his extensive travels—an art gallery in Nice. He called it Galerie Romanin, after the name he'd once used on his drawings, and he exhibited there Chiricos and Utrillos from his private collection. He retained his artist's temperament and his innate gallantry in his life as a secret agent. He drew still lifes on tabletops while planning strategies with his colleagues. He carried a copy of Montaigne's essays throughout his travels underground. And many families that sheltered him on his clandestine trips received roses in gratitude for their hospitality.

In February 1943 Moulin made another trip to London, where he was inducted by de Gaulle into the Compagnons de la Liberation, an honor awarded by the general to "those who had performed in an exceptional manner in the task of liberating France and her Empire." "While de Gaulle gave him the accolade," André Malraux later wrote, "a tear heavy with pride, gratitude, and savage willpower ran down the pale cheek of our comrade Moulin. When he raised his head, we could still see, across his throat, traces of the wound he had inflicted on himself in 1940 rather than cede to the enemy's tortures."

He was parachuted again onto French soil in the April moon of 1943, his powers increased. His leadership, which previously had been restricted to France's southern zone, now extended over the entire nation.

"Gentlemen, there is always France," Moulin would say in the course of the bitter arguments that plagued the meetings he attended throughout the country.

There was perpetual dissent over de Gaulle's orders, relayed by Moulin, to refrain from paramilitary activity, apart from sabotage on objectives of strategic importance, until the Allied invasion. Furthermore, the conservative half of the underground accused Moulin of playing into the Communists' hands by including members of the Party in the Conseil National de la Resistance, the governing body appointed by Moulin, which held its first meeting in the spring of 1943. And there were hate-ridden personal rivalries on the part of several leaders who felt more deserving than Moulin of the leadership granted him by de Gaulle. These are only a fraction of the dissensions that plagued the Resistance and helped to hasten Moulin's death at Klaus Barbie's hands.

On June 12, 1943, Moulin received news of the Gestapo's most important capture to date. General Delestraint, chief of the Resistance's Secret Army and Moulin's second-in-command, had been arrested three days earlier at a metro stop in Paris with the aid of a former resister who had been "turned" by Barbie. For a month Moulin had felt the Gestapo chief's net tightening around him. "I am now hunted by both Vichy and the Gestapo," he wrote from Lyons to London in early May. "My task has become increasingly delicate, difficulties are multiplying daily." During the first half of June he began to center his operations in Paris in order to escape Barbie's zeal. But he felt obliged to attend a strategy session he had scheduled for June 21 in a suburb of Lyons to restructure the leadership of the Secret Army. Notwithstanding the apprehensions, the meeting took place in a doctor's office in Caluire, some five miles from Lyons. Shortly after the eight men arrived, several Gestapo cars pulled up to the door. The familiar shout: *"Police allemande!"* Barbie led the arrest himself, tearing a leg off a table and using it to pummel the shoulders and backs of his captives. Moulin, who was carrying important coded documents rolled into tiny pellets, managed to swallow them before the Gestapo seized him.

The weeks of Moulin's martyrdom and death remain as obscure as the treason that led to his capture. Because of the complex system of anonymity evolved by the Resistance, Moulin's identity as de Gaulle's delegate would not be known by the Gestapo for another few days. One of the other captives presumably disclosed his identity under torture. Once it was revealed, Barbie and his men seem to have employed the most brutal tactics in their repertory to wrest the central secrets of France's liberation movement. A resister who had been in Montluc since early May, the future minister Christian Pineau, has offered one of the last eyewitness accounts of Moulin's physical state.

Pineau, who had been appointed prison barber, was led to a cell where a man was laid out on a wooden plank, unconscious, his eyes "sunken as if they'd been pushed into his skull," his features hideously disfigured. Pineau recognized him as his fellow resister "Max." He was ordered to shave the victim's face. "After they brought me soap and water, I start shaving him, trying not to bruise the swollen parts of his face. . . . Suddenly Max opens his eyes, looks at me. 'Drink,' he whispers. I turn to the soldier. '*Ein wenig Wasser.*' I lean over Max, murmur a few words of comfort. He speaks five or six words in English, which are incomprehensible because of his broken voice, then loses consciousness again. . . ."

The exact date and place of Moulin's death will never be known. Within a week of his arrest, orders were issued to transfer him to the Gestapo's Paris headquarters at 84, avenue Foch. The Gestapo seems to have been extremely embarrassed by the excesses of Barbie's brutality. The leader of the French Resistance was dying without having yielded a shred of information. An eyewitness has described Barbie arriving at the Paris headquarters, "clicking his heels excessively." "I hope for your sake this man recovers," one of his Gestapo superiors said. Soon after reaching Paris, Moulin was transferred to the private villa of a high-ranking Nazi official in Neuilly, where the best doctors the Germans could find tried to revive him so that he could be questioned again. A resister who was being held captive in the same house later reported that he saw a near corpse lying on a couch in a state of coma, the head swathed in bandages, and that it may have been Jean Moulin. A few days later orders came from Berlin to have de Gaulle's delegate sent to a hospital in Germany. This may have been just another way for the Gestapo to save face. Moulin may have been dead before leaving Paris. Or he may have died on the train. Using a euphemism common in concentration camps, a German doctor filed a report in the city of Metz stating that the captive "probably died of heart failure" during the trip.

German authorities returned his corpse to Paris, and eighteen days after his arrest Moulin was incinerated at Père Lachaise Cemetery. These shreds of a martyr seem to have been shuttled from city to city by the Gestapo to delay reprimands from Himmler's headquarters. For the one certain thing about Moulin's death is that he endured the limits of human pain without yielding a single secret of the Resistance.

In 1964, when his ashes were transferred to the Pantheon, André Malraux pronounced the funeral oration: "Over twenty years ago Jean Moulin was parachuted onto the earth of Provence and became the leader of a people of the night . . ."

III

Every few years in June, a commemoration known as *La Journée Nationale Jean Moulin* is held in Paris and several other cities. This being France, there is much talk: panels and symposiums on Jean Moulin, and reverent speeches about his martyrdom at the hands of Klaus Barbie. The French could go on for decades listening to tales of Moulin's heroism, which they dearly wish were a reflection of their own communal valor. But there is a disturbing paradox at the heart of the Barbie case: It concerns the discrepancy between the simplistic joy ignited at first by the French government's capture of Moulin's torturer and the subsequent somber assessment of Barbie's extradition. Since French law imposes a twenty-year statute of limitations on war crimes, the Barbie dossier cannot focus exclusively on Moulin's martyrdom and other aspects of the glorious Resistance. It mostly deals with "crimes against humanity," against innocent, unarmed civilians, and, stresses Barbie's role in the deportation of some 780 Jews to the concentration camps of Auschwitz and Ravensbruck. By emphasizing the henchman's crimes against Jews, the Barbie case focuses on that area of history about which the French nation feels most uneasy: its own participation in the carrying out of the Final Solution. This is a historic fact which the French have only recently begun to accept, with varying degrees of grace, after four decades of flagrant self-deception.

In 1952 and again in 1954, during his lucrative refuge in Latin America, Klaus Barbie was tried by French courts, found guilty, and sentenced to death in absentia for war crimes committed in France. Klaus Barbie's first two trials, which dealt only minimally with his persecution of Jews, were conducted by a government still feeding on myths imposed by de Gaulle after the liberation of his pitifully divided country: the myth of a nation whose eminence as a great power must immediately be reestablished politically, economically, and morally; the fairy tale of a France "dedicated to an exalted and exceptional destiny," whose occasional flaws, in the general's words, "must never be attributed to the acts of Frenchmen."

Barbie's present trial is being brought to court by a generation of Jewish activists, led by Serge Klarsfeld, who are determined to keep alive the memory of the Holocaust and to emphasize Vichy France's participation in it.

If the most powerful symbol of Barbie's earlier trials was the martyrdom of Jean Moulin, the preeminent symbol of his final trial has been the martyrdom of forty-one Jewish orphans, aged three to thirteen, who were deported at Barbie's orders to the gas ovens of Auschwitz. Thirty relatives of these children are among the groups and individuals who became plaintiffs in the Barbie trial.

The Klaus Barbie case is the first to scrutinize explicitly the conduct of Nazis and their French accomplices toward French Jewry. It should not be seen as an isolated event but as part of a vast process which is demythologizing the nature of French conduct during the Occupation. Pétain's "shield" theory, which held that Vichy collaborationist policies were enforced by German authorities and engaged in to save French lives, is finally waning. It is being replaced by the quite opposite view of France as one of Germany's most docile provinces, a country whose collaborationist zeal was equaled only in occupied nations that had already been allied to Germany before the war, like Hungary and Rumania.

As the French and the rest of the world are learning four decades later, the basic facts concerning the Vichy regime's persecution of Jews are the following:

The government of Marshal Pétain and Pierre Laval began to pass anti-Semitic laws a few weeks after the armistice of June 1940. It did this without the least prodding from German authorities, who had far more urgent concerns that year than restricting the civil rights of French Jewry. The Vichy government autonomously deprived six thousand foreign-born Jews of their French nationality (July 22, 1940); passed a series of laws which purged Jews from all professions in which they could influence public opinion—teaching, journalism, medicine, law (August 16, September 10, and October 3, 1940); paved the way for the mass arrests of the next three years by forcing all Jews in France to register (October 3, 1940); passed a law authorizing police prefects to arrest foreign Jews, in both the Occupied Zone and the Free Zone, and intern them in camps (October 4, 1940).

In the summer of 1942, a few months after the Wannsee Conference had defined the terms of the Final Solution, it was at the instigation of a French police chief, Jean Leguay, that seven thousand foreign Jews were deported to German camps from France's Free Zone—an ignominious precedent for a territory not occupied by the Nazi enemy. As for the infamous Vélodrome d'Hiver roundup of July 1942, which was given the cynical euphemism *Vent Printanier* (Spring Wind), it led, in the course of a few days, to the deportation of some thirteen thousand Jews, conducted by four thousand French *flics* (cops) without any significant help from the Nazi police.

Late in 1942, when public opinion began to turn strongly against the Vichy government's Holocaustal policies, the French police force showed increasing reluctance in masterminding the arrest of Jews. But some thirty thousand more Jews would be deported from France by the Germans with the help of the Fascist-leaning French militia. One of the deans of French historians, François Furet, has emphasized that aside from Jean Moulin, he does not know of one prefect, or one member of the police force, who resigned in protest against the Pétain regime's racist measures.

If this perspective still seems novel, it is in part because French government archives relating to the Occupation years remained closed to scholars until a decade ago. The extraordinary network of taboos that forbade any scrutiny of the Vichy regime's conduct was also evidenced in the last decade by four *causes célèbres*: Alain Resnais' film *Night and Fog* and Marcel Ophüls' film *The Sorrow and the Pity*; an interview in the magazine *L'Express* with one of Vichy's most rabidly anti-Semitic henchmen; and the indictment in 1979 of the second-ranking police chief in the Vichy regime.

The original print of Alain Resnais's documentary film *Night and Fog*, released in 1955, included a shot of a French policeman, recognizable by his high, round kepi hat, conducting the arrest of Jews during the Occupation. The government board of censors forbade the film all public showing until the kepi was deleted from the print. As for *The Sorrow and the Pity*, it was the first major public document to overturn the Gaullist myth of a wartime France that was massively supportive of the Resistance. It intimated that Pétainism was not an aberrant phenomenon but the resurgence of a reactionary xenophobia often dormant but always present in French culture since the days of the Dreyfus affair. For Ophuls chronicled the existence of an absolutely native, home-grown Fascism: the epidemic of anti-Semitism in newspaper headlines, the Hitler-style mustaches that sprouted on the faces of Vichy officials, the sinisterly hearty paramilitary youth groups in which French students were taught to sing and goose-step like their Nazi occupiers.

The very week of its release in 1972, the French government-controlled television network banned this memorable film. "Myths," according to the Gaullist minister who gave the censure its official explanation, "are important in the life of a people. Certain myths must not be destroyed."

Six years later, another bitter controversy over the wisdom of resurrecting "the darkest years" occurred when *L'Express* published an interview with Louis Darquier de Pellepoix, the militant anti-Semite who had served under Laval as Vichy Commissioner General for Jewish Affairs.

Louis Darquier (the aristocratic surname was a fabrication) was a failed businessman and journalist who had caused a near riot in the Paris Municipal Council in 1938 by giving a speech on the *youpinisation* (kikeification) of France under the regime of Léon

Blum. He had described, in print, a leader of France's Jewish community as "a circumcised little pig, an excrement of the ghetto." Darquier had also been arrested three times before the war for picking fights with Jews in public places. It was this distinguished citizen, addressed by Pétain as "Mr. Executioner," who, along with the police chiefs René Bousquet and Jean Leguay, was most responsible for attempting to make his country *Judenrein*.

Darquier fled to Spain during the mayhem of the Liberation, thus escaping the military tribunals that sentenced some of the more militant collaborators. Since none of the succeeding French governments had bothered to extradite him and bring him to trial, he was peacefully supporting himself in Estremadura by giving French lessons when a reporter from *L'Express* went to interview him in 1978. A few excerpts:

L'Express: "One million dead at Auschwitz. Innumerable children among them. All gassed."

Darquier: "No, no, that's the satanic Jewish propaganda again. . . . Jews are ready to do anything to be talked about, make themselves interesting, excite pity. I'll tell you precisely what happened at Auschwitz. There was some gassing done there. But they only gassed lice."

The reporter shows Darquier a photograph of corpses being taken out of gas chambers. Darquier turns his head away and says, "No, I don't even want to see them. They're trumped up photos. . . . I know that after the war Jews fabricated falsities by the millions, intoxicated the earth with these falsities."

During the months that followed, *L'Express* received thousands of letters in reaction to the Darquier interview. It had been published shortly after a public opinion poll of French schoolchildren had been taken concerning their awareness of World War II. So few of them knew the basic facts that the poll was summed up in the press with the headline "Hitler? Never heard of him." Many readers thanked *L'Express* and its director Jean-François Revel for keeping memory alive and offering protection against "the Nazi seed, always ready for germination."

But the letters in praise of the interview were equaled by letters of protest. Bearers of bad news in ancient times were often executed; reporters of past horrors seem somehow tainted with the evil they record for us. Much of the protest against the Darquier interview came from citizens of clearly liberal views, some of them former resisters and survivors of concentration camps, who accused the magazine of "resuscitating a painful past whose wounds are just healing," "reawakening nightmares that we thought forever buried in memory," and even "providing a forum for anti-Semitic ideas."

In November 1978, barely two weeks after the Darquier interview appeared, Serge Klarsfeld accused two extremely prominent French businessmen, Jean Leguay and René Bousquet, of persecuting Jews during their tenure as Vichy's two principal police chiefs. These two men had masterminded the arrest and deportation of some forty thousand human beings; and if the martyrdom of young innocents is any index of criminality, their records were considerably more heinous than Darquier's. According to Klarsfeld, it was Leguay who had decided that the four thousand children interned during the Vélodrome d'Hiver roundup should be separated from their parents and sent in separate cattle cars to Auschwitz (even Darquier had argued that the children should be detained in France). It was Bousquet who had ordered that all foreign Jews arrested in the Free Zone should be accompanied to the camps by their children (until then parents had had the option of leaving their offspring behind in French settlements).

The extravagant pardon given both men at the time of the Liberation exemplifies the reverence with which early Gaullist regimes, with crass indifference to the fate of French Jewry, whitewashed the records of French police chiefs in their attempts to unify and glorify the nation. Anticipating an Allied victory, both Leguay and Bousquet had resigned their posts in the police force on December 31, 1943. Leguay had then returned to his prewar vocation in the prefectural corps, and though he was relieved of his official duties upon the liberation of Paris, he was sent on a business mission to the United States in 1945 by a Socialist member of de Gaulle's first cabinet, Robert Lacoste, secretary general for industrial production.

Ironically, Leguay's subsequently lucrative business career centered on the cosmetics trade. By the 1960s he had become a millionaire through his reported associations with the Nina Ricci,

Jacqueline Cochran, and Richard Hudnut companies, and had reached the apogee of his prosperity as a director of the Warner-Lambert pharmaceutical firm. Leguay would be the first Frenchman in history to be tried on charges of crimes against humanity.

Bousquet was absolved in an equally magnanimous fashion. In June 1944 he agreed to be "deported" to Germany with his wife and child. They were transported in the private car of Bousquet's friend Karl Oberg, head of the German police in France, and lodged in a pleasant lakeside villa in Tegernsee. After the German surrender Bousquet was returned to France and in 1949 was sentenced to five years of "national indignity," the legal parlance for loss of certain civil rights. But the sentence was immediately annulled because of his "services to the Resistance" during the Occupation. (Bousquet had warned some Maquisards of impending arrests, which clearly exonerated him, in the eyes of postwar regimes, of crimes against tens of thousands of Jewish innocents.) Like Leguay, Bousquet went on to a millionaire's career in business and banking, and in the 1970s was serving on the boards of directors of some eight prominent firms, notably the Banque de l'Indochine and the Union des Transports Aeriens, from which he resigned in 1978 under the pressure of Klarsfeld's exposure.

The Bousquet-Leguay affair confronted the French with the same kinds of truths the trial has finally brought to light—the fact that Vichyism is not a past nightmare to be forgotten but a scandal still very much alive; that the Vichy bureaucracy slid into the Fourth Republic with considerably less purging than the nation had been aware of. And since the moral stakes of these inculpations were higher than those exposed in Ophuls' film or Darquier's interview, the public discussions that followed the Bousquet-Leguay scandal were couched in even fancier French rhetoric. An editorial in Le Monde once argued that such periodic returns to the shame of the national past "subverted the ancestral instinct of the human species to suppress its guilt" and attacked "principles of amnesty" central to France's civilization. To which proponents of Leguay's indictment had a timely reply: That same year (1978) the three German police chiefs most responsible for the persecution of French Jews, Kurt Lischka, Herbert Hagen, and Ernst Heinrichsohn, were being tried in German courts for their roles in the deportation of

Jews from France. How curious that France did not seem psychologically capable of bringing Pétainism to trial when Germany was completing its trial of Nazism! (All three Germans received sentences ranging from six to twelve years.)

These themes are central to any discussion concerning the wisdom of reviving national shame by bringing Barbie to justice. Among members of the older generation there is a considerable fear of rekindling painful guilt, and a characteristically French fear of introspection which often outweighs any political ideology. There seem to be as many reactions to the possibility of a Barbie trial as there are French citizens.

"I do not feel joyful at the prospect of this trial," says Simone Veil, survivor of Auschwitz, former minister of health, who has served as president of the European Parliament's Judiciary Committee. "The French nation was originally made to look forward to a trial concerning the arrest and martyrdom of Jean Moulin. But Barbie cannot be tried anymore on charges of torturing Moulin. He will be tried for his crimes against Jews, and the French will have the impression of having been tricked. They'll say, 'Once again we're hearing only about the Jews.' "

"I was elated by the news of Barbie's return," says Jacques Chaban-Delmas, the former Gaullist minister who has also served as mayor of Bordeaux. "I was overjoyed to see an end to the scandal of his impunity."

"I'm against this trial," says Pierre Emmanuel, poet and former resister. "It'll be a parade of ghosts and aging war veterans; I don't believe that it can bring to light any historical truth."

"I welcome this trial for metaphysical reasons," says Marcel Ophuls. "We must retain a sense of history as a continuous unbroken spectrum, which makes life spiritually and aesthetically richer."

"The Barbie trial is more timely than ever," says Father Bernard Dupuy, Dominican scholar and a specialist on Judaic history. "For it's taken us forty years to realize that it's Auschwitz—not Hiroshima—which has posed the central moral dilemma of our century."

"We have a French expression which goes, 'Don't unpack the

shit,' " says Michel Braudeau, a novelist, editor, and critic for *Le Monde*. "Well, I want this trial to unpack all the shit about my country. I want to know the total truth, no matter how bad it is."

"A Barbie trial runs the danger of awakening memories not yet accepted by the nation's collective subconscious," says Jean Daniel, director of the left-leaning magazine *Le Nouvel Observateur*.

The "collective subconscious" is very much at issue, for the French seem to have a considerable capacity for historical amnesia. During my last stay in Paris, I drove to Drancy, the suburb from which some seventy-five thousand Jews were shipped in cattle cars to German camps between 1942 and 1944. The complex of cement-block buildings in which the captives were detained and in which hundreds died from the atrocious conditions imposed on them by French police has been remodeled into what it was before the war, a low-cost housing settlement. Although an immense memorial sculpture now stands at its entrance, some senior citizens whom I stopped for directions two blocks away looked puzzled at my mention of a former camp. "Camp de Drancy? What camp?" "You're telling me Jews used to be locked up here?" one elderly man exclaimed. "Don't bother me with any such crap about the past!"

Walking through the housing complex, I talked to an amiable resident in her seventies with two small white poodles who knew all about its history. Her husband, a retired postman, used to pass mail secretly to the camp's inmates. ("One does what one can for people.") But it didn't bother her at all to be living in Drancy in the 1980s. "We couldn't have done it right after the war, but it's all so far away now, we never think about it."

I also asked two thirteen-year-old girls who lived in the building whether they knew of its former function. "We've heard there were Jews here," one said, looking vague. But notwithstanding the presence of the memorial sculpture, they didn't know whether it had been a resort, a clinic, or a hotel.

Simone Veil tells an interesting story about the way French textbooks deemphasize the Holocaust. Her young son came home from school one day and said, "Maman, thank goodness we're not Protestants, or else we would have been killed at the Massacre of Saint Bartholomew."

□

"Time effaces time," as Chateaubriand put it. Can one deplore or judge the psychic defenses of a community if one hasn't shared its pain? It's with a curiosity verging on morbidness that I recollect details of my own childhood in wartime Europe: Marshal Pétain's trembling voice on French radio and his senile dicta: *"Labourage et paturage sont les deux mamelles de la France"* ("Labor and farming are the lifeblood of France"). The winter months during which there was little to eat beyond potatoes. The heroic guile and humiliating persistence with which my mother kept returning to the *Kommandantur* in Tours to obtain our *Ausweis* for the Free Zone. How vividly would I want to remember those painful years if I had stayed in France for the duration of the war instead of a mere sixteen months? Would I wish to have the sorrow and the pity of that past dredged up in the trial of a Nazi henchman? I do not know and cannot judge, for I too have indulged much in self-induced amnesia.

My father, Bertrand du Plessix, died on the side of the Free French during the first fortnight of its existence, and I never bothered to find out the precise date and circumstances of his death until several decades later. I knew only that sometime in late June 1940 he had organized one of the first convoys of French planes to leave North Africa for London; that he was shot down by pro-Nazi artillery stationed on the Spanish coast as he tried to land on Gibraltar; and that he was one of the first four Frenchmen to be named a Compagnon de la Libération, a member of that venerable group founded by de Gaulle into which Jean Moulin was inducted in 1943. The news of his death was broken to me a year later, when I was ten. And it was proffered in a rather awkward fashion, by a young woman a decade older than I who had taken it into her hands, unsolicited, to give me the harsh truth. I had come to look on her as a close friend, but I began to shun her soon afterward for reasons I was able to figure out only in the past few years—ancient Greek custom, ostracize and banish the bearer of bad news.

Apart from my aunt Simone and uncle André Monestier, whom I continued to look on as a second family, I cautiously avoided, for thirty years, any person or situation that would inform me about my father's life or death. At the age of forty, when I suddenly became ravenous for every shred of biography available on this heroic and ill-fated man, the last of his close friends was dying. I had arrived at my sources a few years too late.

One group in Paris could still give me information about my father, the Compagnons de la Libération, which describes itself as "an exalted chivalric order, tied forever to those exalting hours which rid our soil of its invader and reestablished the legitimacy of our free institutions." Mailings from the Compagnons' headquarters, La Chancellerie de l'Ordre de la Libération, which is most solicitous of its members' offspring, had come to me regularly for over thirty years. (Until the age of twenty-one I was even considered a ward of the state, and could have traveled at reduced fare on all public transportation in France or its colonies.) But I had seldom opened the Compagnons' missives, which seemed devoted mostly to obituaries of its aging members. As I entered the Chancellerie for the first time in the 1980s, during my research on Moulin and the Barbie case, I was immediately confronted with my father's name, inscribed in gold on a huge marble plaque a few feet away from Jean Moulin's name. I was filled with surprise that I had never attempted to come here before, and I peacefully accepted the fact that this visit, originally undertaken for professional reasons (surely *these* survivors must have strong emotions about the Barbie trial), might bring me some details about my father's death which I had not yet faced. The trial of Klaus Barbie was forcing even me to remember.

The Chancellerie de l'Ordre de la Libération, now a state museum, is lodged in a palatial eighteenth-century building on the boulevard de Latour Maubourg, near the Invalides. It often contains exhibits dedicated to de Gaulle's memory—his pens, inkwells, army hats—and is so obsessively dedicated to the glory of the Resistance that even the metal handles on the huge glass doors are in the shape of the cross of Lorraine. After a flurry of excitement on the part of two aging veterans serving as museum guards that morning (*"Fille de Compagnon! Fille de Compagnon!"*), I was ushered into the offices of the chancelier with a rapidity perhaps unique in the stately proceedings of the order. General Jean Simon is a tall, silvery, hawklike career officer with an eerily fixed stare acquired, I was to learn, in the thick of action—one of his eyes had been shot out by a Vichyite in Syria in 1942, and the blue orb fastened on me was made of glass.

So, very well, we sat down among a panoply of decorations, army portraits, flags, banners, more crosses of Lorraine. I had come to ask him his opinion of the Barbie trial, but he wished instantly to launch into a matter that interested him much more. He had long been fascinated by my father's dossier, and he let loose a cascade of words. "I saw him being shot down, I actually saw it! We were moored at Gibraltar, Pierre Messmer and I, waiting for petrol to join de Gaulle in London. . . . It was the thirtieth of June, we'd been stranded there for a good many days, we had nothing to do, we were very bored. Our chief distraction was to look at British or French planes trying to land on Gibraltar; every time a new plane came we'd ask each other how is *this* one going to get out of his mess. . . . Gibraltar is one of the world's most difficult landing strips, the Spanish were often firing . . ."

He stood up and drew me a grade-school picture of the Gibraltar airport. "Here's the Mediterranean. Here's North Africa. Here's the coast of Spain. And there, just in the center, is this wretched little landing strip . . ."

He sat down again, proud of his artwork. "*Alors on s'embêtait beaucoup*, there was nothing to do but see those poor pilots trying to land, and one afternoon we saw four planes trying to land in succession, a very dramatic sight. The first three made it, and then along came your father's. We heard shots from the Spanish coast, and then we saw nothing but a large, splendid spray of water rising skyward, and there, madame, was your father's plane . . ."

The cenotaph. The pain of history, flung in my face.

The general sat back at his enormous desk, a stern life-size portrait of de Gaulle in uniform hanging above him, and stared at me contentedly. The man with whom he'd witnessed my father's death, Pierre Messmer, had later become prime minister of France, and the general wished to enumerate every other compagnon who had served as prime minister, minister, or deputy since the Liberation. The inventory was long, and only at the very end of the visit did I manage to ask his opinion of the Barbie trial. He looked at me with a haughty air worthy of le Grand Charles. "Oh, we don't meddle with that kind of piddling event. We strive to maintain our distance above all politics. We stand aloof from such stuff, we are a chivalric order, akin to the Crusaders of the Middle Ages."

So those were *his* priorities. We parted on most cordial terms. He asked me to lunch with him the very next time I came to Paris. He presented me with the *Livre d'Or de la Libération*, a massive gilt-edged volume weighing about twenty pounds, which lists, in chronological order of induction, each of the 1,053 members of de Gaulle's order of chivalry. I did not look at it until later in the day, when I returned to my Paris lodgings. My father's name is listed on the first page, along with those of the three officers who were in the plane with him. Below the names is the following tribute, couched in the vibrant Gaullist bombast used forty years ago to heal the nation's wounds:

> Yes, this was the first blood to be shed at the General's appeal. The years will pass, and tears will ceaselessly break upon the rock of time. . . . But the night of May 8, 1945, will finally arrive. At dusk that day, de Gaulle will tell the world:
> "The war has been won . . . not one sacrifice, not one tear, will therefore have been lost."
> In that hour, France's first four Compagnons became immortalized in the nation's mourning.

I had finally learned the precise day, the circumstances, the names of the companions, perhaps all there was left to learn. I cried violently for a few minutes, then felt purged, cleansed, becalmed. I pulled myself together and went on to dinner with my aunt and uncle Monestier, who offered me their opinions of the Barbie trial before I'd even had a chance to ask for them.

"Another of Mitterrand's faux pas," my uncle vociferated. "When will that wretched boy ever come to his senses! Dividing the nation, rekindling ancient hatreds . . . why not do something truly *positive* for the country, like bringing the marshal's ashes back to the Pantheon where they belong. . . ."

"Barbie to the Gulag!" my aunt shouted over the dinner table. "Hand him over to the Soviets—our French jails are much too fine for him. Only those Communist bastards could give him his proper due!"

A few days later I lunched with their equally valiant and conservative son-in-law, former resister Jean de Laromiguière, who came out of Dachau weighing seventy pounds and has never regained his health.

"Klaus Barbie? I'll tell you what the government should do with him. Spare him the trial, the Communists will take it over for their propaganda . . . the government should just tattoo him on the forehead with the words 'I am Klaus Barbie,' open the doors of Montluc jail, and let him get out of his own shit."

So much for the suppression of pain, the high-mindedness of a chivalric order, and all manner of Cartesian rationality.

One segment of public opinion in France has held that it is decades too late to bring Barbie to justice, that there is no political or moral value in putting on trial an aging war criminal at the risk of causing the nation further discomfort. But I agree with those who argue that justice can never remain quiescent before crimes as massive, unatoned, unexpiated as Barbie's; that his trial, which must focus on his contribution to the Final Solution, might have been more timely than ever. For it could help to curb a perilous new tendency to minimize the importance of the Holocaust and deny its uniqueness. This inclination to relativize the slaughter of six million humans is presently shared by an unsavory alliance of the neo-Nazi Right, the Solzhenitsynian Right, the Marxist anti-Zionist old Left, the newer pro-Palestinian Left, and a multipartisan brand of anti-Semitism in part caused by the intransigence of Israeli government policies. It is neatly and atrociously summed up in graffiti I recently saw on the walls of East Berlin, which list the sites of four twentieth-century tragedies, implying that they are of an equal order of atrocity: "Dresden, Hiroshima, Auschwitz, Shatila."

In the past year few aspects of the Barbie trial have been more controversial than the inflammatory tactics of Barbie's enigmatic lawyer, Jacques Vergès. A member of the French Communist party after World War II, he has expressed extreme left-wing views since the beginning of his career at the bar. He took Algerian citizenship in the early 1960s. His more notorious clients have included members of the Baader-Meinhof gang, associates of the terrorist Carlos, and members of the FLN, one of whom he married.

He left France in 1970 and vanished for eight years, during which time he is reported to have trained Palestinian guerrillas in Lebanon. A decade after his return to Paris, in the winter months of 1986 and 1987, Vergès served as chief defense counsel for the Lebanese terrorist Georges Ibrahim Abdallah.

An outspoken critic of Western democratic institutions, Vergès specializes in a courtroom strategy known as "defense by rupture," in which the accused challenges the entire "system" that has placed him on trial and refuses to accept its legal procedures. Within the framework of this strategy, it is possible for the defense to defy all statutes of limitations on war crimes, reopen the Jean Moulin case, and argue that traitors within the Resistance, rather than Barbie, were responsible for Moulin's arrest and death. Thus the Barbie case presents the monstrous spectacle of a lawyer long associated with anti-Zionist groups defending the Fascist murderer of hundreds of Jews in order to broadcast his own far left doctrines, and to destroy whatever wartime honor France ever had. Venom calls forth venom, as it has throughout Klaus Barbie's career.

Notwithstanding its risks, the bringing to justice of Klaus Barbie may still help to remind the world that the genocide practiced by Nazis was uniquely imbued with absolute evil because it was not motivated by political or military expediency. It belongs to a quite different ethical and ontological order. For the dead of Auschwitz and Treblinka were systematically slaughtered not for what they personally did, or said, or owned, but because of what they *were*. The gassing of six thousand Jewish children under twelve deported from France, hundreds of whom were doomed by Barbie, incarnates both the specific horrors of the Nazi regime and the general mystery of human suffering.

However many French citizens Barbie denounces as his accomplices, whatever new disparagements he casts on the conduct of the Vichy regime, one would hope that his trial will help the French nation to strike a new balance between pride and contrition, between the denial of culpability it engaged in for three decades and those flagellatory self-accusations (newly in vogue among a faction of the citizenry too young to remember the Occupation) which lead to theories of a guilt communally shared by a nation of latent Pétainists. When everyone is responsible no one is responsible, and the threat of totalitarianism is made all the more present by such a negation of accountability. A careful analysis of the self-interest and lust for power motivating cynics like Pétain and Laval, of the pressures brought to bear on them by xenophobic groups seeking revenge for decades of France's liberalism and hospitality to foreigners, is more edifying than any visceral contrition. And a more realistic, if grimmer, vision of the Vichy regime's culpability should lead us to honor all the more the tens of thousands of heroic French citizens who saved the lives of a great many Jews and partisans during the years of the Occupation. For one such act of courage I offer the testimony of Raymond Aubrac, a Jew and a resister who was one of the chiefs of the Secret Army in southern France.

Aubrac was arrested alongside Jean Moulin at the meeting in Caluire and underwent extensive torture at Barbie's hands. A week later he was freed by his wife and a band of friends in one of the most spectacular rescue operations of the Resistance. After his escape he became one of the partisans most zealously hunted by Barbie and the entire Gestapo. He went into hiding with his wife among the Maquis in the Jura Mountains, waiting for the day when a British plane would take them to safety in London. Raymond Aubrac told me about the valor of the French community that saved their lives:

"When a plane finally landed in our hills to take us to England, it had rained heavily all day, and the plane was immediately mired in mud, its wheels embedded two feet deep—no way we could dig it out for takeoff. We'd waited three months to be rescued. An entire German regiment had just been stationed twenty miles away. And there was our nineteen-year-old pilot, looking at his wristwatch and saying, 'It's midnight. In two hours we'll have to destroy the plane. London will try to send another one next month. I'd better figure out the quickest way to walk to Spain.' So my wife and I went to the nearby village and woke everyone up and made a public appeal, saying you've got to help us get this English plane out of its mess. Well, the entire village arrived, with horses, carts, wooden boards—even the cops came and blockaded the roads to make sure that no one would disturb us. One hundred and fifty men and women of that village risked their lives by helping us to dig out that plane, and by one-thirty A.M. we were off to London. There were a lot of bastards in France, a great number of bastards motivated by personal gain, yet there was also a majority of citizens who brought aid and protection when it was needed. For that is the deep instinct of the French people, and that's why I'm still here today to tell the story. It needs to be told."